***Very highly recommended
**Recommended
*Interesting

LEGEND

★★★ Very highly recommended
★★ Recommended
★ Interesting
See if possible

THE EMPIRE STATE BUILDING
CITICORP
ST THOMAS
IBM BUILDING

95 Interstate Highway
1 U.S. Highway
24 State Highway

Urban Street System

General maps

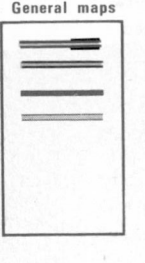

Detailed maps

Divided highway, Elevated highway
Divided scenic highway
Main crosstown street
Other crosstown street
Sightseeing route and recommended direction
Tree-lined street
No entry or street closed to traffic
Steps

Traffic-slowing Structures

Underpass
Overpass or bridge
Interchange or junction
Railroad
Elevated rapid transit
Tunnel

Miscellaneous Symbols

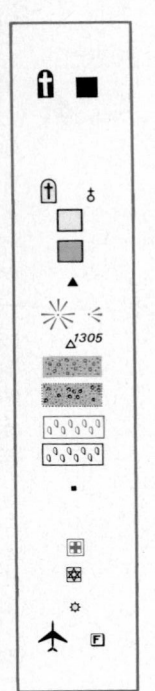

Start of sightseeing tour
Church or building described
Church or building described in a different walk
Church or building mentioned
Church, chapel (landmark)
Building (landmark)
University
Isolated point of interest
Panoramic view ; partial view
Alt in feet
Park
Park described
Cemetery
Cemetery described
Monument or statue
Fountain
Hospital
Synagogue
Factory
Airport — Ferry (automobiles and passengers)

AZ **B** Reference letters locating points of interest

Visiting New York City

Pressed for time? Then you will find the suggested two and four day programs (pp 18-21) for visiting New York, especially helpful.

If you have more time consult the map of the walks and main sights (pp 9-12) and use the descriptive texts of the guide (pp 35 to 166) to plan your own visit.

4

PRACTICAL INFORMATION

WHEN TO VISIT NEW YORK

The Seasons. – The best season to visit New York is certainly the **fall**. Between late September and early November, nature explodes in a blaze of color. Warm temperatures, the clear transparency of the air and the brilliant colors of the trees, especially the reds and oranges of the maples, are typical of this favored season. In the **summer,** temperatures may rise into the 90's, however, practically all buildings and many buses and subway cars are air-conditioned. Although quite cold in **winter** (often around 32°F), New York's climate is fairly dry and brisk. The sky is usually a clear bright blue, which may suddenly be covered over with clouds bearing a rain or snowstorm, snarling traffic temporarily. **Spring** is a brief and for the most part unpredictable season.

HOW TO GET AROUND NEW YORK

On Foot

In the center of town, where traffic moves slowly at rush hours and "No Parking" signs abound, the best way to get around is on foot. A pleasant pastime during the day, walking by oneself is less safe at night in certain areas and reasonable precautions should be taken. *In general, it is advisable to avoid the parks after nightfall.*

By Car

It is fairly easy to get around by car, but not to park. Traffic moves smoothly except during the morning and afternoon rush hours.

Renting a Car. – It is very easy to rent a car in New York if you hold one of the major credit cards. Compact model rentals are $75 to $80 a day or $300 to $330 weekly with 100 free miles per day and 35¢ each additional mile. A chauffeur-driven limousine costs about $45 an hour up or $1.35 per mile, plus tips.

Taxis. – Yellow medallion taxis are the only vehicles authorized by law to pick up street hail. They are identifiable by their color, yellow, and rooflights displaying their medallion number. There are very few taxi stands, but taxis abound in Manhattan and hailing one is quite easy except at rush hours and on rainy days.

A cab ride costs $ 1.50 for the first 1/8 mile and 25¢ for each additional 1/5 mile. An additional 20¢ is charged for each 60 second waiting period as well as 50¢ is added to the total meter fare on trips taken between 8 PM and 6 AM.

A recommended tip is 15 % of the total fare shown on the meter at the end of the trip.

MASS TRANSPORTATION

Consult separate fold-out map of the bus and subway routes.

Buses

There are more than 200 local bus routes in the city over which some 3 642 buses operate. The bus system is a supplement to the subway system. In Manhattan, buses run north and south (uptown and downtown) on most avenues and east and west (crosstown) on principal crosstown streets. The route number and destination are indicated on the front of each bus. Buses stop frequently, about every two blocks. Passengers board the front of the bus and deposit $1.15 in coins *(exact fare required)* or a subway token. Most lines run all night with reduced service after midnight.

The Subway

The subway system is the most popular means of transportation in New York and certainly the most practical for traveling long distances and for avoiding congested street traffic. Comfort has increased with the introduction of a new type of subway car which is larger, quieter and air-conditioned.

Originally, some of the tracks were elevated (hence the nickname, "the El"). Now they are underground, except on some lines outside central Manhattan.

Some 3.6 million passengers daily ride over 230 miles of track. The subway system never closes. All stations are serviced 24 hours a day; however, not all routes operate at all times. On our map, which shows only the subway system in Manhattan, we have indicated in **red** the lines which have part-time service. *An official map can be obtained free of charge at the Information Booth in the Port Authority Bus Terminal, Grand Central Station or at the change booth at any subway station; or by sending a stamped self-addressed envelope to: New York City Transit Authority, 370 Jay Street, Box "M", Brooklyn, New York 11201 (specify the map you are requesting).*

A subway token may be purchased at any change booth and costs $1.00 for a ride. You must deposit a token in the turnstile.

Stations. – There are 463 stations in all. Many stations have signs above the platform that indicate what trains stop there. Some stations, especially the small local stops, have separate entrances for the uptown and downtown trains. *Be sure to read the sign carefully before entering.*

Trains. – There are express trains which stop only at the most important stations and local trains, which make all stops. Before boarding, check the letter or number (i.e. the line) and the destination which appear on the front of the train and the sides of each car. *Trains for several different points often use the same track.*

Changing Trains. – Any possibility of transfer is indicated on our map. The same station may have different names on different lines or different lines may have different stations with similar names.

TO AND FROM THE AIRPORTS

The major New York airports are John F. Kennedy Airport, La Guardia Airport and Newark Airport (New Jersey).

Express Bus Service. – Carey Transportation, Inc. provides service between JFK and La Guardia airports and midtown Manhattan.

Carey bus service to each airport departs from the Port Authority Bus Terminal *(at 8th Avenue and 42nd Street)* and stops at the corner of East 42nd Street and Park Avenue *(125 Park Avenue, opposite Grand Central Terminal)* before proceeding to the airports. *From Park Avenue to JFK: buses depart every 20 min 5 AM to 1 AM (fare: $8.00); to La Guardia: buses depart every 20 min 6 AM to 1 AM (fare: $6.00).*

Carey also provides service between JFK and La Guardia *(fare: $7.00). Information ☏ (718) 632-0500.*

Express buses to Newark Airport *(time: 30 min)* operate from the Port Authority Bus Terminal: *every 10 to 20 min, 24 hours a day, seven day a week. Fare: $7.00 one way. Look for signs: "Airport Bus Center». Information ☏ (201) 460-8444.*

Gray Line Air Shuttle. – A share-ride service between New York airports and mid-town hotels is offered by Gray Line Air Shuttle. Arrangements for pick-ups can be made at the ground transportation desk in the baggage claim area where courtesy phones for the service are available. Hotel pick-up can be arranged through hotel transportation desks or by phone ☏ *(800) 451-0455.*
The shuttle operates from 8 AM to midnight, seven days a week. Fares are $13.00 for JFK, $10.00 for La Guardia and $15.00 for Newark.

Chauffeur-driven Cars. – Carey Limousine operates chauffeur-driven sedans at a fixed rate between midtown Manhattan and JFK Airport $55 plus tolls and tips; La Guardia Airport $45 plus tolls and tips ☏ *toll free (800) 336-4646.*

STAYING IN NEW YORK

This section includes practical information intended to facilitate your stay in New York. *Consult fold-out map of Useful Addresses pp 5-8.*

HOTELS

Most hotels in New York City are concentrated in Manhattan, however, clusters of hotels and motels will also be found near the major airports.

In Manhattan the largest number of hotels will be found in the midtown area. The most luxurious are located on, or a short distance from Fifth, Park and Madison Avenues, while other more moderately priced hotels will be found in the theater district. Visitors who favor a less bustling atmosphere may prefer the Murray Hill or Gramercy Park areas or Central Park South, facing the park.

Manhattan hostelleries include the ultramodern hotel chains with their extensive convention facilities, such as the Marriott Marquis, the New York Hilton and the Sheraton Centre; as well as the more intimate, continental-type hotels sought out for their elegance and old-world charm: the Pierre, the St Regis, the Plaza, the Sherry-Netherland. Attractive newcomers, among which are the Grand Hyatt, Helmsley Palace, Parker Meridien and Vista International, combine a wide range of modern amenities with refined decor. In addition, the visitor will find a good selection of modest hotels scattered throughout the East and West Sides.

Reasonably priced lodging is also available at Bed and Breakfast (B&B) establishments: private homes, apartments, town houses, studio lofts in the city. Contact Urban Ventures, Inc., P. O. Box 426, New York, N. Y. 10024, ☏ 594-5650.

Low-cost accommodations can be provided to students and travellers by the New York Student Center located at the William Sloane House (YMCA) 356 West 34th Street, between 8th and 9th Avenues; 760-5850.

Further information can be obtained from the New York Convention and Visitors Bureau 397-8222 *(p 15).*

USEFUL ADDRESSES

Unless otherwise indicated all telephone numbers listed have the area code 212.

Airports, Heliports, Airline and Ship Terminals. – *For their location and main routes of access, see p 23. To get to and from the airports see above. For detailed information on flights contact the airline concerned (see map pp 5-8).*

For airport facility information: (718) 656-4520.

Kennedy International Airport: Jamaica, Queens, New York.

La Guardia Airport: Flushing, Queens, New York.

Newark Airport: Newark, New Jersey.

34th Street East Heliport: 34th Street at East River; 889-0986.

New York Helicopter: (800) 645-3494.

Island Helicopter: 683-4575.

Pan Am Metroport: 60th Street at York Avenue; 880-6234.

Port Authority Downtown Heliport: Pier 6 at East River; 248-7240.

Passenger Ship Terminal: 711 12th Avenue at 52nd Street; 466-7974.

Manhattan Air Terminal: 100 East 42nd Street; 986-0888. Ticket Offices for major American-based airlines located here.

American	431-1132	Northwest	736-1220	TWA	290-2121
Delta	239-0700	Pan American	687-2600	United	800-241-6522
Eastern	986-5000	Trump	800-247-8786	US Air	736-3700

Ferry and Boat Terminals. — Circle Line Statue of Liberty Ferry: Battery Park, South Ferry; 269-5755.

Staten Island Ferry: Whitehall Ferry Terminal; 806-6940.

Circle Line Sightseeing Cruise Around Manhattan (3 hours): Pier 83, West 43rd Street; 563-3200.

Information Bureaus. – New York Convention and Visitors Bureau: 2 Columbus Circle; 397-8222.
Open Monday to Friday 9 AM to 6 PM; closed Saturdays, Sundays and holidays.

Places of Worship. – A list is posted in most hotel lobbies. It gives their addresses and hours of services.

Among them, we have chosen the best known.

Roman Catholic Churches: St Patrick's Cathedral, Fifth Avenue at 51st Street; 753-2261.
Notre-Dame, Morningside Drive at 114th Street; 866-1500.
St Ignatius Loyola, 980 Park Avenue at 84th Street; 288-3588.
St Paul of the Apostle, 60th Street and Columbus Avenue; 265-3209.
St Vincent-Ferrer, Lexington Avenue at 66th Street; 744-2080.
St Vincent de Paul, 120 West 24th Street; 243-4727.

Greek Orthodox Church: St Nicholas, 155 Cedar Street; 227-0773.

Baptist Church: Calvary Baptist, 123 West 57th Street; 975-0170.

Episcopal Churches: Cathedral Church of St John the Divine, Amsterdam Avenue at 112th Street; 316-7540.
St Bartholomew's, Park Avenue at 51st Street; 751-1616.
St Thomas, Fifth Avenue at West 53rd Street; 757-7013.
Trinity, Broadway at Wall Street; 602-0800.

Lutheran Churches: Gustavus Adolphus, 155 East 22nd Street; 674-0739.
Holy Trinity, Central Park West at 65th Street; 877-6815
St Peter's Church, 619 Lexington Avenue (Citicorp); 935-2200.

Methodist Churches: Christ Church United Methodist, 520 Park Avenue; 838-3036.
John Street, 44 John Street; 269-0014.

Presbyterian Churches: Fifth Avenue, at 55th Street; 247-0490.
Rutgers, 236 West 73rd Street; 877-8227.

Synagogues: Temple Emanu-El, Fifth Avenue at 65th Street; 744-1400.
Congregation B'Nai Jeshurun, 257 West 88th Street; 787-7600.
Central Synagogue, 123 East 55th Street; 838-5122.
Spanish and Portuguese Synagogue (Congregation Shearith Israel), 8 West 70th Street, 873-0300.

Miscellaneous Information

U.S. General Post Office: Eighth Avenue at 33rd Street; 967-8588.
Foreign Newspapers: Hotalings, 142 West 42nd Street; 840-1868.
Baby Sitters: Baby Sitters Guild; 682-0227.
Part-time Child Care; 757-7900.
Lost and Found: taxi, 221 West 41st Street; 869-4513;
subway or bus, Eighth Avenue at 34th street; (718) 625-6200.
Weather forecast: 976-1212.
Exact time: 976-1616.
New York County Medical Society: 399-9040.
Transit Authority Travel Information: (718) 330-1234 *(24-hour a day service).*
Emergency — Fire; Police; Ambulance: 911.

For recorded information on current events and activities in the city: music, dance, street fairs, festivals, etc...
Telephone Parks and Recreation Information: 360-1333.

ENTERTAINMENT IN NEW YORK

For New Yorkers and out-of-towners in search of entertainment, New York, and in particular Broadway, exerts a special magnetism and glamour.

There is so much to do that the tourist could no doubt spend every evening out at a different spot for several months. Since such hardy souls are rare, we shall merely sketch briefly some general information on the great variety of cultural and sports events in New York.

For details you should consult a newspaper, or the weekly New Yorker *or* New York *magazines.*

In many museums, libraries and other institutions, there are musical evenings, lectures or film shows. In addition each borough has a cultural center of its own.

Opera, Concerts and Ballet. – A temple of the vocal art, the Metropolitan Opera moved in 1966 to Lincoln Center *(p 93).*

The **opera** season is extremely popular, due to the quality of the troupe as well as the star performers. *The season lasts from mid-September to early May.* There are many regular subscribers, and tickets may be difficult to obtain.

At the New York State Theater, also in Lincoln Center, the New York City Opera Company gives excellent performances. Tickets are relatively moderately priced and easier to obtain than seats at the Met.

The most famous **concert halls,** presenting internationally known artists and orchestras, are Carnegie Hall *(154 West 57th Street) (p 141)* and Avery Fisher Hall at Lincoln Center *(p 93).*

Ballet can be seen at the New York State Theater (facing Avery Fisher Hall) where the New York City Ballet performs. The Metropolitan Opera and City Center are host to other major dance companies, and the American Ballet Theatre appears at the Metropolitan Opera House at the close of the opera season *(see above).*

Legitimate Theaters. – The Broadway theater district in the Times Square area *(p 123)* has the greatest concentration of legitimate theaters in the world, presenting musicals, dramas and comedies. Hit plays are often sold out for months in advance. Tickets are available at the box office, by mail order, through ticket agents, many of whom have desks at the major hotels, and by telephone through Ticketron *(947-5850)*: major credit cards are accepted, a service charge of $3.00 to $3.75 per ticket is charged.

"**Off-Broadway**" theater, centered in Greenwich Village, the Lower and Upper East Side and the West Side, presents new and experimental plays and revivals of the classics in smaller playhouses (between 100-299 seats).

"**Off-Off Broadway**" theater offers a wide spectrum of theatrical material from avant-garde to classical revivals with an experimental approach. Presented usually in small intimate houses (under 100 seats) located throughout the city, Off-Off-Broadway theaters include play readings, workshops and full-scale productions, and frequently provide the audience with a more personalized experience than do more formal theater settings. *For information on current events ☏ 587-1111 or consult the weekly newspaper The Village Voice or the New York Times Sunday Going Out Guide.*

In the summer, **open-air theater** is quite popular: Shakespeare played in the evenings in Central Park draws so many enthusiasts that one often has to line up several hours in advance. *Tickets (free of charge) may be obtained starting at 6:15 PM the evening of the performance at the Delacorte Theater at 81st Street and Central Park West.*

Movie Theaters. – Many first-run movie houses are now located on the upper East Side. Most of these have continuous shows from noon to midnight. A great variety of films are shown in the Times Square area.

Some movie houses midtown and in Greenwich Village specialize in revivals.

Art and experimental films and special film series are programmed by the Film Society of Lincoln Center, the Museum of Modern Art and the Whitney Museum.

"New York by Night". – In New York you will find everything from the students' dive in Greenwich Village, with whimsical or macabre decoration, through supper clubs to nightclubs with elaborate floor shows. Many of the latter are in large hotels.

Clubs, both formal and informal, cabarets and piano bars offer disco, rock, jazz, western and Latin music and other entertainment. *It is wise to reserve in the elegant establishments.*

Sports. – The two most popular sports are football and baseball. Basketball, boxing and ice hockey are also avidly followed.

The football season lasts from September to December; baseball is played from April to October. Many games are played at night to avoid the heat, at Yankee Stadium *(p 145)* or Shea Stadium *(advance booking recommended)*. Giants Stadium, part of the Meadowlands complex in New Jersey, is the home of the Giants and the Jets football teams.

Madison Square Garden *(p 125)* is the center of high quality sporting events: the famous horse show, rodeos, ice hockey, basketball and boxing in particular.

There is horse racing almost all year round: thoroughbred racing at Aqueduct and Belmont Race Tracks, and harness racing at Yonkers Raceway; at the Meadowlands Racetrack, East Rutherford, New Jersey there is both thoroughbred and harness racing.

Sports Centers

Name	Location	Tel.	Activities
Madison Square Garden	Seventh Ave. and 32nd Street above Penn Station, NYC	(212) 563-8300	Basketball, hockey, tennis, track and field sports, games, ice shows, boxing, circus, concerts, wrestling
Meadowlands Brendan Byrne Arena, Racetrack and Giants Stadium	East Rutherford, N.J.	(201) 935-8500 935-8222	Basketball, soccer, family shows, concerts, wrestling, field and track; harness and thoroughbred racing; football
Aqueduct Race Track	Rockaway Blvd, Ozone Park, Queens	(718) 641-4700	Thoroughbred racing
Belmont Park	Hempstead Ave, Elmont, L.I.	(718) 641-4700	Thoroughbred racing
Shea Stadium	Flushing Meadow, Flushing, Queens	(718) 507-8499	Baseball
USTA National Tennis Center	Flushing Meadow Park, Flushing, Queens	(718) 271-5100	Public tennis courts, U.S. Open Tennis Championships
West Side Tennis Club	1 Tennis Place, Forest Hills, Queens	(718) 268-2300	Tennis tournaments, musical events
Yankee Stadium	River Avenue at East 161st Street, Bronx	(212) 293-6000	Baseball
Yonkers Raceway	Central and Yonkers Avenues, Yonkers	(914) 968-4200	Harness racing

Telephone area codes for New York City:
The Bronx and Manhattan - (212)
Brooklyn, Queens and Staten Island - (718).

BOOKS TO READ

Picture Books

Old New York in Early Photographs by Mary Black *(Dover Publications, Inc., New York, 1973).*

New York Then and Now by Edward B. Watson and Edmund V. Gillon, Jr. *(Dover Publications, Inc., New York, 1976).*

New York in the Thirties by Bernice Abbott *(Dover Publications, Inc. New York, 1973).*

History and Architecture

New York, A Pictorial History by Marshall B. Davidson *(Charles Scribners Sons, New York, 1981).*

Beyond the Melting Pot by Nathan Glazer and Daniel Patrick Moynihan *(M.I.T. Press, Cambridge, Mass., 1970).*

The AIA Guide to New York City by Norval White and Elliot Willensky *(MacMillan Company, New York, 1988).*

The City Observed: New York by Paul Goldberger *(Vintage Books, a division of Random House, New York, 1979).*

Colonial New York, A History by Michael Kammen *(KTO Press Millwood, New York, 1987).*

Manhattan Architecture by Donald M. Reynolds *(Prentice Hall, New York, 1988).*

Literature: *See New York and Literature p 33.*

A NEW YORK CITY CALENDAR

Listed below are a few of the most popular events held annually. For up-to-date recorded information on park events and special events in the city ☏ 360-1333.

Date	Event	Location
January	Winter Antiques Show	7 th Regiment Armory/
	Chinese New Year *(first full moon after January 19)*	Chinatown
February	Westminster Kennel Club Dog Show/	Madison Square Garden
	Empire State Building Run-Up	Empire State Building
March	**17:** St Patrick's Day Parade	Fifth Avenue
	Ringling Bros., and Barnum & Bailey Circus *(late March through April)*	Madison Square Garden
April	**Easter Sunday:** Easter Parade	Fifth Avenue
	Greater New York Orchid Show	New York Botanical Gardens, Bronx
	Easter Extravaganza	Radio City Music Hall
May	Ninth Avenue International Food Festival	Ninth Avenue (37th - 57th Streets)
	Washington Square Outdoor Art Show *(in September also)*	Washington Square
	Sakuri Matsuri (Cherry Blossom Festival)	Brooklyn Botanic Garden
	You Gotta Have Park	Central Park, Prospect Park
June	**Museum Mile** *(second Tuesday in June 10 cultural institutions on Fifth Avenue are open free 6 to 9PM)*	Fifth Avenue (82nd - 106th Streets)
	Metropolitan Opera *(free concerts through early August)*	Parks throughout the city
	"Summerpier" concerts *(Saturday nights through August)*	South Street Seaport
	Shakespeare in Central Park *(p. 16)*	Delacorte Theater
	Jazz Festival *(10 days ending July 4)*	Location varies ☏ 787-2020
July	**4:** Macy's Fireworks	Best viewing East River
	Harbor Festival (parade, races, concerts, street fair)	Lower Manhattan
	NY Philharmonic Park Concerts *(free, through August)*	All five boroughs
August	Lincoln Center Out-of-Doors Festival	Lincoln Center
	U. S. Open Tennis Championships *(through early September)*	USTA National Tennis Center, Flushing Meadow, Queens
September	Feast of San Gennaro	"Little Italy" (Mulberry Street)
	Mayor's Cup Schooner Race	South Street Seaport
	New York Film Festival *(late September-early October)*	Lincoln Center
October	Columbus Day Parade	Fifth Avenue
	Halloween Parade	Greenwich Village
November	Virginia Slims Tennis Tournament	Madison Square Garden
	New York City Marathon	Start: Verrazano-Narrows Bridge Finish: Central Park (67th Street)
	Macy's Thanksgiving Day Parade	Central Park West to Broadway, Herald Square
	"The Christmas Spectacular"	Radio City Music Hall
December	Christmas Tree Lighting	Rockefeller Center
	Fifth Avenue holiday store windows *(early December to the first week in January)*	Fifth Avenue (34th - 57th Streets)
	New Year's Eve Countdown	Times Square

SUGGESTED PROGRAMS FOR A SHORT VISIT

You will find in the pages of this guide all necessary historical and practical information on museums and monuments, as well as maps to direct you during your visit.

Guided Tours. – The Museum of the City of New York *(℡ 534-1672, April through November)* and the Municipal Art Society *(℡ 935-3960)* operate programs of two to three hour walking tours of New York's most fascinating neighborhoods and historic sites. For schedules of these and other guided tours consult a newspaper or *New York Magazine.*

Sightseeing by Helicopter. – Helicopter tours available *(9 AM to 9 PM - 6 PM January through March)* every day year round at Island Helicopters, 34th Street East Heliport, 34th Street at East River: *for further information ℡ 683-4575.*

PROGRAM FOR TWO DAYS

First Day *(Itinerary in black)*	**Getting acquainted with New York**
Morning	**Gray Line Grand Tour** (Tour no 3) ★★★ *Tour (time: 4 1/2 hours), departure 9 AM from terminal 900 Eighth Avenue at 53rd Street; $22.00, children $14.85. Information ℡ 397-2600.*
Lunch	In midtown at one of the ethnic restaurants on the West Side.
Afternoon	**Circle Line Boat Tour** ★★★ *From pier 83, West 43rd Street. Frequent sailings (tour time: 3 hours) mid-March to late November; $15.00, children $7.50. Information ℡ 563-3200.* or Sightseeing by helicopter *(see above).*
Evening	**Broadway Theater District** ★★ for dinner and a show or **Lincoln Center** ★★★ for dinner and a concert, an opera or a ballet *(ticket information pp 15-16 and p 76).*

Second Day *(Itinerary in brown)*	**From Rockefeller Center to SoHo**
Morning	**Rockefeller Center** ★★★ *(p 35)* **(Museum of Modern Art** ★★★**)** **Empire State Building Observatory** ★★★ *(p 43)* **Financial District** ★★★ *(p 83)*
Lunch	In Lower Manhattan.
Afternoon	*From Battery Park, South Ferry take the Circle Line Ferry* **Statue of Liberty** ★★★ *(p 90)* **Battery Park** ★★ *(p 110)* and **Water Street** ★ *(p 112)*
Dinner and Evening	**SoHo** ★★ *(p 105)*

For an extra day see p 20

MANHATTAN

Some of its museums or exhibits by subject *(for page number see index)*

Art:

American: American Wing at Metropolitan Museum of Art, National Academy of Design, Whitney Museum of American Art

Decorative, Crafts: American Craft Museum, Cooper-Hewitt Museum, The Smithsonian Institution's National Museum of Design

European: Frick Collection

Modern: Guggenheim Museum, Museum of Modern Art, The New Museum

Oriental: Asia House, Hagop Kevorkian Center for Near Eastern Studies (NYU), Japan House

Books: New York Public Library, Pierpont Morgan Library

Ethnic:

American Indian: Museum of the American Indian

Black: Schomburg Center for Research in Black Culture, The Studio Museum in Harlem

Hispanic: El Museo del Barrio, Hispanic Society of America

Jewish: The Jewish Museum

On New York City: Federal Hall National Memorial, Fraunces Tavern, Museum of the City of New York, The New-York Historical Society

Immigration: American Museum of Immigration

Maritime: South Street Seaport

Media: Museum of Broadcasting, NBC Studios

Personalities: Grant's Tomb, Theodore Roosevelt Birthplace

Photography: International Center of Photography, Museum of Holography

Science: American Museum of Natural History, Hayden Planetarium

PROGRAM
FOR TWO DAYS

Each day's program is shown in a different color

1ST.DAY Start of the itinerary

G. WASHINGTON BRIDGE ★★

★ COLUMBIA UNIVERSITY

ST JOHN THE DIVINE ★★

THE BRONX

HARLEM RIVER

N E W J E R S E Y

RIVER

CENTRAL PARK ★

1ST. DAY

LINCOLN CENTER ★★★

METROPOLITAN MUSEUM OF ART ★★★

MANHATTAN

QUEENS

2ND DAY

★★★ GRAY LINE 53rd St.

ROCKEFELLER CENTER ★★★

★★★ CIRCLE LINE Pier 83

★★ BROADWAY THEATER DISTRICT

FIFTH AVE. ★★★

HUDSON

★★★ EMPIRE STATE BUILDING

UN HEADQUARTERS ★★★

MADISON SQUARE

Heliport

NORTH RIVER

★★ GREENWICH VILLAGE

EAST RIVER

★★ SOHO

CHINATOWN ★★

CITY HALL ★★

B R O O K L Y N

FINANCIAL DISTRICT ★★★

WATER STREET ★

BROOKLYN BRIDGE ★★

BATTERY PARK ★★

STATUE OF LIBERTY ★★★

If You Are Traveling By Air

*For location of facilities refer to
page 23: the map of "FEEDER ROADS AND THROUGH ROADS"*

Name	Location	Telephone	Distance to midtown
Airports			
Kennedy International Airport.	Jamaica, Queens, New York . . .	(718) 656-4520	15 miles
La Guardia Airport	Flushing, Queens, New York . . .	(718) 656-6520	8 miles
Newark Airport	Newark, New Jersey	(718) 656-4520	16 miles
Heliports			
Pan Am Metroport	60th Street at York Avenue.	(212) 880-6234	
Port Authority Downtown Heliport	Pier 6 at East River	(212) 248-7240	
34th Street East Heliport	34th Street at East River	(212) 889-0986	
Airline Terminal			
Manhattan Air Terminal	100 East 42nd Street	(212) 986-0888	

19

First Day
(Itinerary in black)

From Rockefeller Center to Broadway

Morning	Rockefeller Center★★★ *(p 35)* (Museum of Modern Art★★★)
Lunch	In midtown at one of the ethnic restaurants on the West Side.
Afternoon	Circle Line Boat Tour★★★ *(p 18)* or Sightseeing by helicopter *(p 18)*
Evening	Broadway Theater District★★ for dinner and a show *(ticket information pp 15-16 and p 76)*.

Second Day
(Itinerary in brown)

From the Empire State Building to Lincoln Center

Note: *If you are pressed for time concentrate only on the museums' departments which have three stars.*

Morning	Empire State Building Observatory★★★ *(p 43)* Stroll along Fifth Avenue★★★ *(p 42)* (Grand Army Plaza★★) Central Park★ *(p 127)*
Lunch	Near Central Park.
Afternoon	Metropolitan Museum of Art★★★ *(p 52)* or Guggenheim Museum★★ *(p 114)*
Evening	Lincoln Center★★★ for dinner and a concert, an opera or a ballet *(ticket information pp 15-16 and p 76)*.

Third Day
(Itinerary in blue)

From the Statue of Liberty to SoHo

Morning	*From Battery Park, South Ferry take the Circle Line Ferry* Statue of Liberty★★★ *(p 90)*
Lunch	Lower or midtown Manhattan.
Afternoon	Financial District★★★ *(p 83)* (World Trade Center★★, Wall Street★★) City Hall★★ *(p 107)*, Chinatown★★ *(p 104)*
Dinner and Evening	SoHo★★ *(p 105)*

Fourth Day
(Itinerary in green)

The United Nations Headquarters, The Cloisters, Park Avenue

Morning	United Nations Headquarters★★★ *(p 77)* Walk along East 42nd Street★★★ *(p 80)* (Chrysler Building★★★, Grand Hyatt Hotel★, Grand Central Terminal★★)
Lunch	In midtown.
Afternoon	Take a bus or subway: consult fold-out map. The Cloisters★★★ *(p 97)*, Fort Tryon Park★★ *(p 101)* Park Avenue★★★ *(p 74)* (Seagram Building★, Park Avenue Plaza★★, Citicorp★★)
Evening	Dine in one of the elegant hotels or supper clubs near Park Avenue.

FINAL DAY

If you have an extra day, visit the highlights of one of the other boroughs. A selection of their main sights is briefly described at the end of the guide: The **Bronx** *(pp 143-146)*, **Brooklyn** *(pp 147-153)*, **Queens** *(pp 154-156)*, and **Staten Island** *(pp 157-158)*.

THE OTHER BOROUGHS AND BEYOND THE CITY LIMITS

Some of their museums and exhibits by subject *(for page number see index)*

Art:
American: Art Museum (Long Island); Parrish Art Museum (Long Island)

Botany: Bayard Cutting Arboretum (Long Island); Brooklyn Botanic Garden; The New York Botanical Garden (Bronx); Planting Fields (Long Island)

History:
On the Bronx: Valentine-Varian House (Bronx)
On Brooklyn: Brooklyn Historical Society (Brooklyn)
On Queens: Kingsland House (Queens)
On Staten Island: Staten Island Institute of Arts and Sciences (Staten Island)

Maritime: Suffolk County Whaling Museum (Long Island); The Whaling Museum (Long Island)

Media: American Museum of the Moving Image (Queens)

Personalities: Home of Franklin D. Roosevelt National Historic Site (Hudson River Valley); Eleanor Roosevelt National Historic Site (Hudson River Valley); Poe Cottage (Bronx); Sagamore Hill National Historic Site (Long Island); Sunnyside (Hudson River Valley)

Restoration Villages: Old Bethpage Restoration Village (Long Island); Richmondtown Restoration Village (Staten Island)

Zoology: The Bronx Zoo; The Staten Island Zoo (Staten Island); The New York Aquarium (Brooklyn)

PROGRAM
FOR FOUR DAYS

Each day's program is shown in a different color

1ST. DAY   Start of the itinerary

THE CLOISTERS ★★★
FORT TRYON PARK ★★

G. WASHINGTON BRIDGE ★★

THE BRONX

NEW JERSEY

HUDSON RIVER

HARLEM RIVER

MANHATTAN

CENTRAL PARK ★

GUGGENHEIM MUSEUM ★★

METROPOLITAN MUSEUM OF ART ★★★

LINCOLN CENTER ★★★

1ST. DAY

ROCKEFELLER CENTER ★★★

GRAND ARMY PLAZA ★★

★★★ CIRCLE LINE Pier 83

42nd St.

★★ BROADWAY THEATER DISTRICT

QUEENS

FIFTH AVE. ★★★

PARK AVE. ★★★

2ND DAY

EMPIRE STATE BUILDING ★★★

42nd ST ★★★

UN HEADQUARTERS ★★★

4TH DAY

Heliport

EAST RIVER

NORTH RIVER

SOHO ★★

CITY HALL ★★   CHINATOWN ★★

FINANCIAL DISTRICT ★★★

BROOKLYN

3RD DAY

BATTERY PARK ★★

BROOKLYN BRIDGE ★★

STATUE OF LIBERTY ★★★

NEW YORK: A BRIEF SKETCH

THE CITY AND THE STATE OF NEW YORK

A magnet for much of the northeastern United States, the city of New York is a world unto itself because of its size, the density and diversity of its population, its dynamic economic activity and its vibrant cultural life.

Location. – On the east coast of the United States, New York is bathed by the Atlantic Ocean; the nearby Labrador current chills its waters, but not the summer temperatures in the city. The location of the Port of New York is unique *(p 28);* the Hudson River and the East River (in fact an estuary, like the Harlem River) are two relatively protected waterways, ideal for ocean-going vessels.

New York Bay is also protected by two islands to the south. The Narrows lead out to the open sea from one of the largest and safest bays in the world.

New York City is located at 40° north latitude and 74° west longitude. Its height above sea level varies from 5ft (Battery Park) to 400ft (Washington Heights). The climate is of the continental type *(see details on the seasons p 13),* with predominating westerly winds, although there is frequently a refreshing sea breeze.

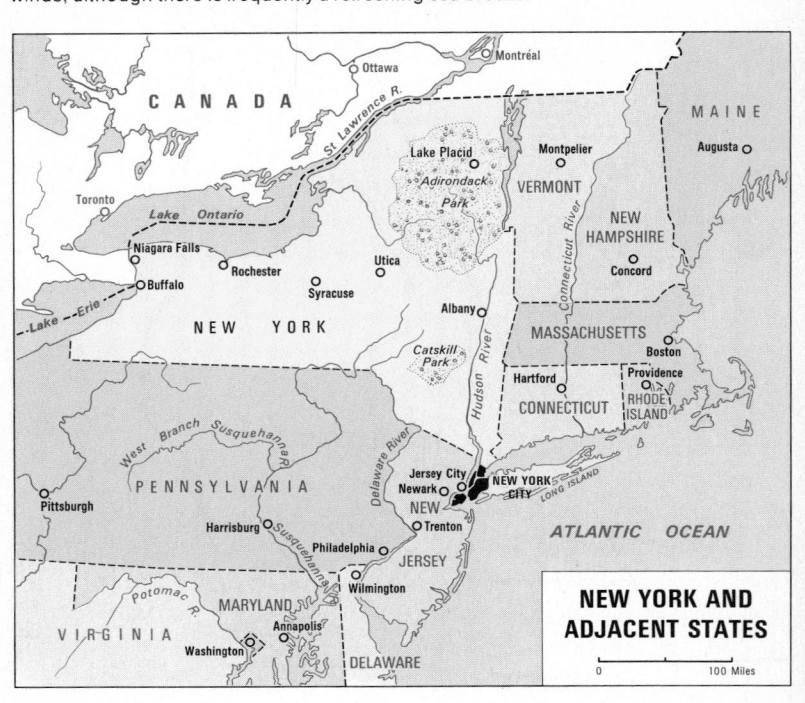

NEW YORK AND ADJACENT STATES

0   100 Miles

Size and Population. – The total area of the five boroughs *(see below)* which makes up New York City is about 300sq miles; the longest distance between its boundaries, from the northeast to the southwest, is about 35 miles.

The total population of New York City is 7 352 700 inhabitants, of whom approximately 20% are Manhattanites. If we add the daily commuters, it raises the total to about 8 000 000. Few cities in the world can rival these imposing figures. The population is of various origins, a result of successive waves of immigration *(p 26).*

The Five Boroughs. – New York City, limited to the borough of Manhattan until 1898, has since then incorporated the other four boroughs; their boundaries are the same as the counties which previously existed: **Manhattan** (New York County), **Brooklyn** (Kings County), **Queens, The Bronx** and **Staten Island** (Richmond County). These counties correspond to the original colonial administrative divisions: the names of the counties still persist to designate judicial districts.

The Bronx is the only borough which is a part of the continent, for Manhattan and Richmond are islands, and Brooklyn and Queens are on the western end of Long Island. As geographers have pointed out, New York is, indeed, an archipelago, a city on the water.

The five boroughs are not developed to the same extent. A few open spaces exist on the fringes of Brooklyn and Queens; and Staten Island, despite the construction of many new dwellings in the 1970s and 1980s, is still somewhat countrified.

	Manhattan	The Bronx	Queens	Brooklyn	Staten Island
Surface in square miles	22.7	41.2	108	70.3	57.5
Population 1988	1 509 900	1 223 400	1 925 100	2 314 300	380 000

The New York Metropolitan Area. – This is the name of the economic entity of 22 counties and planning regions around New York City.

Seven of these counties are in New York State, nine in New Jersey and six in Connecticut *(see map p 22)*.

The region extends over 7 000sq miles and includes about 18 441 900 inhabitants.

In addition to the city of New York itself, the area includes Newark (315 200) and ten other cities of over 100 000 in population.

Among the organizations responsible for the operation and expansion of transportation facilities in the Metropolitan Area are the Port Authority of New York and New Jersey, which plans for the 17-county area in New York State and New Jersey; and the Triborough Bridge and Tunnel Authority *(see details on these two bodies p 29)*.

The State of New York. – The city gave its name to the state, the 11th of the original 13 states of the Union, which by virtue of its economic expansion and political influence became known as the "Empire State," as Washington had foreseen.

New York State extending from east of the Hudson to the Great Lakes and Niagara Falls, borders Canada on the north. The state is divided into counties and its capital is Albany (New York City was the capital from 1784-97).

The flag of New York City, with its blue, white and orange vertical stripes, was inspired by the flag of the Netherlands in the 17C.

FEEDER ROADS AND THROUGH ROADS

The map below shows the main roads leading into the city, as well as through roads which cross or bypass it; also included are the bridges, tunnels, railroad, bus and ship terminals, airports, airline terminals and heliports most used by visitors.

For toll rates of toll tunnels and bridges see p 126.

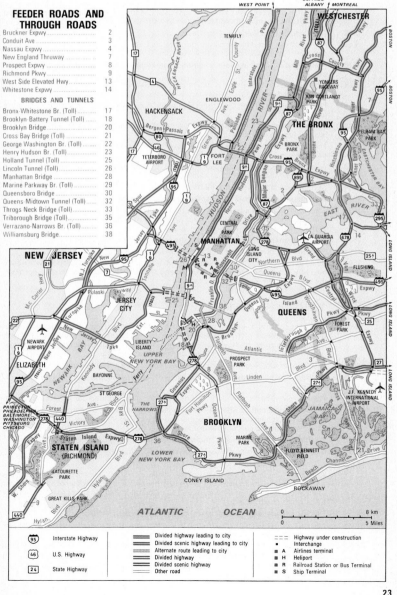

95	Interstate Highway		Divided highway leading to city
46	U.S. Highway		Divided scenic highway leading to city
24	State Highway		Alternate route leading to city
			Divided highway
			Divided scenic highway
			Other road
		===	Highway under construction
		■	Interchange
		A	Airlines terminal
		H	Heliport
		R	Railroad Station or Bus Terminal
		S	Ship Terminal

NEW YORK

IN THE PAST

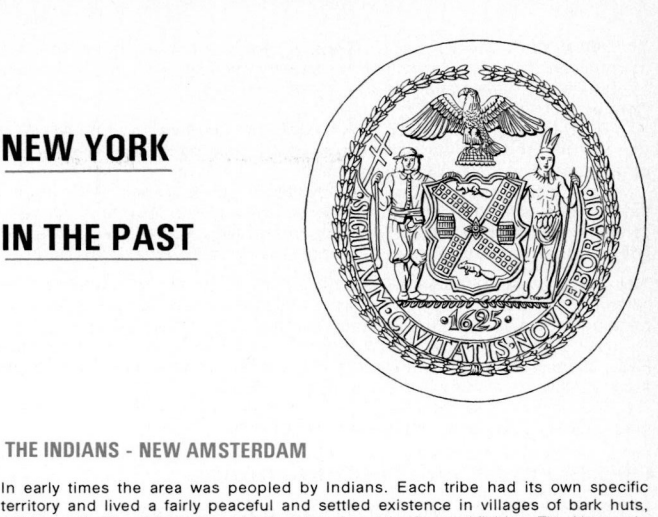

THE INDIANS - NEW AMSTERDAM

In early times the area was peopled by Indians. Each tribe had its own specific territory and lived a fairly peaceful and settled existence in villages of bark huts, gaining a livelihood from crop planting, hunting, trapping and fishing. The Algonquin tribe was the most numerous in the New York area.

1524 The first European explorer enters the bay. **Giovanni da Verrazano,** an Italian in the service of the French king, Francis I, discovers the island of Manhattan *(p 110).*

1609 **Henry Hudson** sails up the river which bears his name, in his ship the *Half Moon,* while on a voyage for the Dutch East India Company.

1613 The Dutch explorer cum trader, Adriaen Block, is forced to winter on the island when his boat, *The Tiger,* burns off Manhattan *(p 130).*

1614 The name New Netherland is first used.

1619 Arrival of the first African slaves on American soil in Jamestown and in the early settlement which later became New York City.

1624 A shipload of Dutch settlers, including some Walloons, arrive and settle in various places throughout the province.

1625 First permanent settlement is established on Manhattan. The trading post is named **Nieuw Amsterdam.**

1626 **Peter Minuit** of the Dutch West India Company buys Manhattan from the Indians for the equivalent of $24.

1628 With the arrival of a regular minister, a member of the Reformed Dutch Church, the island's first church is established.

1639 The Dane, Johannes Bronck, settles beyond the Harlem River in the area now known as the Bronx.

1642 A settlement is made at Maspeth (Queens), but first permanent settlement in Queens is not established until 1643, at Flushing.

1644 Some slaves are given partial freedom.

1647 **Peter Stuyvesant** becomes Director General of the community *(p 131).*

1653 The settlement of Nieuw Amsterdam (New Amsterdam) is recognized as a town and receives a charter. Stuyvesant has a protective wall built on the present location of Wall Street.

1654 First permanent Jewish settlement in the colonies established in New Amsterdam.

1661 First permanent settlement on Staten Island established at Oude Dorp.

1664 As a repercussion of the English and Dutch trading rivalries in Europe, the English take New Amsterdam without a struggle and rename it **New York** after the Duke of York, the brother of the English king, Charles II.

TOWARD INDEPENDENCE

1667 The Treaty of Breda, ending the second Anglo-Dutch war, confirms English control over the province of New Netherland, while the Dutch retain Surinam or Dutch Guiana. The town of New York passes under the English system of municipal government. English replaces Dutch as the official language.

1673 The Dutch retake New York without a fight and rename it New Orange.

1674 By the Treaty of Westminster the province of New Netherland becomes permanently English.

1686 The Dongan Charter, the second English charter, is granted carrying the city seal.

1689 A rebellion in England against the Catholic king, James II, the former Duke of York, causes him to abdicate and flee the country. Leisler's Rebellion in New York is a rising led by Jacob Leisler against English rule.

1725 The first New York newspaper, the *New-York Gazette,* is founded by **William Bradford.**

1729 Beaver Street is the site of New York's first synagogue.

1732 The first theater opens in the vicinity of Maiden Lane.

1733-34 **John Peter Zenger** starts the *New-York Weekly Journal,* in which he attacks the governor. A year later some of the offending works are publicly burned in the street and Zenger is imprisoned for slander. The acquittal of Zenger marks the beginning of a free press *(p 83).*

1754 The first college, **King's College** now Columbia University *(p 116)* opens.

1763 The Treaty of Paris marks the end of the French and Indian War or Seven Years' War and confirms English control on the North American continent.

1765 Meeting of the Stamp Act Congress in New York, where representatives from nine colonies denounce the English colonial policy of taxation without representation.

1766 Repeal of the Stamp Act. A statue is erected to **William Pitt,** the British statesman who did most to obtain the repeal.

1767	**The Townshend Acts,** named after the British Chancellor of the Exchequer, a series of four acts which increased taxation and threatened the already established traditions of colonial self-government. The repeal three years later coincided with the Boston Massacre.
1775-83	The War of Independence, also known as the **American Revolution.**
1776	**Declaration of Independence** *(p 108)* sets off the American Revolution. The British take control of Long Island after the Battle of Long Island and General Washington safely withdraws his forces to Manhattan. From his headquarters at the Morris-Jumel Mansion *(p 133)* he masterminds his victory at the Battle of Harlem Heights *(p 115)*. The Americans temporarily drive back the British in the Bronx (Westchester County) in October, but on November 17, Fort Washington in northern Manhattan falls and the British occupy all of the present New York City until 1783.
1783	**The Treaty of Paris** (September 3) ends the U.S. War of Independence and England recognizes the independence of the 13 colonies. The last British troops evacuate New York and Washington returns to the city in triumph before bidding farewell to his troops at Fraunces Tavern on December 4 *(p 87)*.

NEW YORK AND THE UNION

1784	New York City becomes the capital of New York State and a year later is named U.S. capital under the Articles of Confederation.
1787	The Congress, sitting in New York City, enacts the Northwest Ordinance.
1789	The **Constitution** of the United States is ratified. **Washington,** elected first President, takes the oath of office at Federal Hall *(see illustration and p 89)* in New York City, the first capital under the Constitution.
1790	First official census of the population of Manhattan: 33 000. Federal capital moves to Philadelphia.
1792	Founding of the forerunner to the New York Exchange by the buttonwood tree *(p 89)* on Wall Street.
1797	Albany becomes the permanent capital of New York State.
1807	**Robert Fulton** launches his steamboat, the *Clermont,* on the Hudson. The first demonstration had been made on the Collect Pond by John Fitch in 1796.
1812	The United States declares war on Britain and the port of New York suffers from the ensuing blockade. Present City Hall opens *(p 107)*.
1814	A peace treaty signed in Ghent ends the war.
1825	Opening of the **Erie Canal.** New York becomes the gateway to the Great Lakes and the West. Growing overseas trade makes New York a leading port.
1828	South Street becomes the center of New York's port activities.
1834	City of Brooklyn incorporated.
1835	The Great Fire destroys an extensive area in the business district.
1853	World's Fair at the Crystal Palace *(p 44)*.
1858	Central Park is begun and soon sections are open yet not officially completed until 1876.
1861	Start of the **Civil War** with New York one of the 23 Northern States.
1863	Draft Riots.
1865	End of the Civil War. Assassination of President **Abraham Lincoln** *(p 107)*.
1868	Opening of **the El,** first experimental elevated railway in Lower Manhattan.
1870	Economically New York is the wealthiest and most influential city in the nation.
1882	Electricity is offered for general use by Thomas Edison's plant in Lower Manhattan.
1883	Opening of **Brooklyn Bridge** *(p 109)*.
1886	Inauguration of the **Statue of Liberty** *(p 91)*.
1898	**Greater New York** is created comprising the five boroughs of Manhattan, Brooklyn, the Bronx, Queens and Staten Island. With a population of more than 3 million, New York is the world's largest city.

NEW YORK IN THE TWENTIETH CENTURY

1902	Completion of one of the first skyscrapers in New York, the **Flatiron Building** *(p 142)*.
1904	Opening of the first underground line of the subway.
1913	**Armory Show,** an international exhibition introducing modern art to America.
1929	Financial panic of October – the start of the Great Depression.
1931	The **Empire State Building** is completed after two years work *(p 43)*.
1939-40	World's Fair at Flushing Meadow attracts over 44 million visitors.
1945	**United Nations** charter is drafted.
1948	The John F. Kennedy Airport (formerly Idlewild) opens in Queens.
1952	The General Assembly of the United Nations meets for the first time in its new headquarters overlooking the East River *(p 77)*.
1964-65	World's Fair on the same site as the 1939-40 Fair.
1969	Ticker Tape Parade: New York gives a triumphal welcome to the crew of Apollo II, the first astronauts to land on the moon: Neil A. Armstrong, Jr., Edwin E. Aldrin, Jr., and Michael Collins.
1973	Opening of the World Trade Center in Manhattan.
1975-76	American Bicentennial celebrations (New York City: May 1975 - Nov. 1976).
1986	**Statue of Liberty Centennial** celebrations (New York City: July - Liberty Weekend '86)

NEW YORK'S POPULATION

New York has always been known for its cosmopolitanism. The diversity of the population can be traced to the successive waves of immigration which arrived through the major port of entry into the New World. New York has occasionally been described as "the largest Jewish city" or "the largest Irish town" or "the second largest Italian community" in the world, and the influx of Latin Americans and Asians since the mid-1960s has again changed its physiognomy. It is a tribute to the city that New Yorkers have come to share a common outlook and way of life, retaining their ethnic identity and the pride of their cultural heritage.

Population from 1626 to 1988:

Year	Number of inhabitants	Events
1626	200	The first boatload of settlers brought by the Dutch to Nieuw Amsterdam consists primarily of Protestants of French origin.
1656	1 000	The first immigrants are followed by English, Scots, Germans and Scandinavians.
1756	16 000	
1790	33 000	
1800	60 000	Half of New York's population is now of English origin.
1856	630 000	In the middle of the 19C, Germans and Irish arrive in large numbers.
1880	1 911 700	Beginning in 1880, Eastern Europeans and Southern Italians immigrate in great waves. This influx will continue until 1924.
1900	3 437 200	This figure includes the five boroughs for the first time.
1920	5 620 000	After World War I, Black migration grows, both from the South and from the West Indies.
1924		The immigration law limits foreign immigration.
1930	6 930 500	The rate of growth starts to decline.
1950	7 892 000	After World War II, a large Puerto Rican colony settles in New York.
1960	7 782 000	From 1950-60 New York loses more than 100 000 inhabitants. Many New Yorkers have left the city proper for the suburbs.
1970	7 896 000	Out-migration of New York's population from the city to the suburbs is an indication of the overall trend of cities in the northeast.
1976	7 454 000	
1986	7 262 700	New York's foreign-born population of 1.5 million persons reflects the great influx of immigrants from Asia, Latin America and the Caribbean since 1965.
1988	7 352 700	

A Population of Various Origins

In the 19C and at the beginning of the 20C, recent immigrants, referred to as "hyphenated citizens" (Irish-Americans, Italian-Americans, German-Americans, etc.), were often denied social status by the "aristocracy" of British and Dutch origin. However, the pyramid of New York society was unable to withstand the forces of change, and today these multi-cultural strands together with the more recent waves of immigrants, make up the very fabric of New York's population.

The Italians. – Large-scale immigration, mainly of laborers and peasants from Southern Italy and Sicily started only after 1870. Many returned to the old country with their first savings, but the largest majority brought their families to settle in America.

A great number of Italian immigrants started out in the building industry where they worked under the heavy hand of "padroni" (construction bosses), but over the years hard work and enterprise often combined to establish a small family business, especially in the restaurant, contracting and trucking trades.

After generations of economic and social rewards in the New World, Italian-Americans remain deeply attached to the traditions of their family and community life. The colorful atmosphere of their homeland is reflected in "Little Italy *(p 103)*."

Russians and Ukrainians. – The massive waves of pre-World War I emigration from the old Russian Empire were not made up of Russians, strangely enough, but mostly of representatives of various minority nationalities – Ukrainians, Poles, Jews, Lithuanians, and others.

At first on the bottom rungs of the American social and economic ladder, like most newly arrived immigrants they tended to congregate in the same neighborhoods as their countrymen. The 1917 Revolution brought only a trickle of so-called White Russians to New York as compared to the large numbers who emigrated to Paris and other European capitals. Many Ukrainians and Russians, however, were among the displaced persons who settled in New York in the wake of World War II.

The Jews. – Sephardic Jews, originally from Spain and Portugal, had come to New York in the 17C, mostly via Holland and Latin America. Today, however, the majority of the New York Jews are of Eastern and Central European descent. The Lower East Side was the first home for 1.5 million Jews who entered America between 1880 and 1910: a great number settled in Brooklyn communities. New York Jewry has actively participated in all economic and cultural endeavors, and the names of many Jewish individuals and institutions are woven into the history of New York.

The Blacks. – Although there were Blacks among the early inhabitants of New York, it was only in the 20C that Blacks migrated to the city in large numbers. Today, they total some 1 757 000 or roughly one-fourth of the New York population.

The Black community has richly contributed to the character of the city. It has produced distinguished writers, playwrights and performers, and the influence of Rhythm and Blues and Jazz is deeply felt on the American musical scene.

During recent decades many Blacks have availed themselves of the great educational and economic opportunities offered in New York, thus increasing their numbers in the professions as well as politics, government and private business. On January 1, 1990, David Dinkins became the first Black to serve as mayor of New York city.

Hispanics. – The rapid growth of the Puerto Rican population has brought their number from less than a thousand in 1910 to almost 900 000 in 1984. Members of the Puerto Rican Commonwealth are American citizens, and as such are free to travel between Puerto Rico and the continental United States without a visa or regard to quotas. Together with the latest newcomers from the south, Cubans, Dominicans, Colombians, Ecuadorians and other Latin Americans, the Hispanics now form about one-fifth of the city's population, numering 1 704 000 in 1987, and representing its largest foreign language group. The major concentration of the Puerto Rican population in the city is in the Bronx, but the heart of New York's Puerto Rican community is East Harlem, better known as *"El Barrio."* Parts of the Upper West Side, the Bronx, Brooklyn and Queens are also host to significant numbers of Latin Americans. Frequent visits to their home countries help maintain traditionally strong family ties. Mindful of their culture, Hispanics have emerged as a vital community, lending a distinctive Latin flavor to the life of the city.

Germans and Austrians. – This was probably the most rapidly assimilated group, although one of the largest. Composed of conservatives and liberals, craftsmen, laborers, businessmen and intellectuals, they no longer form a very unified group. Leaving behind them in most cases the language of the "old country," they still share a few national traditions. Germans arrived in great numbers during the 19C, particularly after the 1848-49 revolution in Germany had failed. They settled mostly around Tompkins Square from where they later moved further uptown. Some German atmosphere can still be found in Yorkville *(p 140).*

The Irish. – Irish immigration dates back to the 17C, but it was the outbreak of the Irish Potato Famine, in 1846, that touched off the mass exodus from Ireland. In 1890, one-fourth of all New Yorkers were Irish.

From the begining, the Irish were drawn to public affairs and actively participated in city government. Carrying on the religious tradition of their homeland, they have largely contributed to the influence of the Roman Catholic Church in the United States.

Still a quite homogeneous group, Irish-Americans are famous for their exuberant celebration of St Patrick's Day, March 17, to honor the patron saint of the "ould sod."

The Chinese. – Coming to America first after the Civil War, Chinese immigrants were mainly from Canton. The most recent newcomers, primarily from Hong Kong, Shanghai and Taiwan, have swelled their numbers to an estimated 360 000 with the greatest concentration in steadily expanding Chinatown *(p 104).* Many second-generation Chinese make their home in boroughs other than Manhattan, and particularly in Queens.

Others. – Among those from Eastern Europe, the Polish colony should be noted for the big Polish parade on Fifth Avenue *(see A New York City Calendar p 17).* A sizable Greek community lives in Astoria, Queens and a number of Armenians have settled in the Bronx. The liberalization of the immigration regulations has brought an influx of such diverse ethnic groups as Koreans, Indians, Vietnamese and Haitians, making New York City home to more than 100 different nationalities.

Terminals

Name and Telephone	Location	Services
Grand Central Terminal 532-4900	East 42nd St Vanderbilt to Lexington Avenues.	Metro-North, Harlem, Hudson and New Haven Commuter lines. AMTRAK long-distance trains. Grand Central is also a subway stop.
Pennsylvania (201) 460-8444 Station (718) 454-5477 582-6875	Seventh Avenue from 31st to 33rd Streets.	New Jersey Commuter lines. Long Island Railroad (L.I.R.R.) trains AMTRAK long-distance trains. Pennsylvania Station is also a subway stop.
Port Authority Bus Terminals Midtown . . . . . . 564-8484 Uptown 564-1114	Eighth and Ninth Avenues at 41st St. George Washington Bridge at 178th St and Broadway.	Suburban and long line service. Suburban and long line service.

If you are traveling by air . . . . *p 19*
Toll tunnels and bridges. . . . . *p 126*

NEW YORK'S ECONOMY

Since colonial times, shipping, banking and manufacturing have been the main-stays of the economy. Other sectors are the activities in the headquarters of most major American corporations, the garment industry, publishing and communications.

The Port. – The first ship berths were built in Lower Manhattan on the East River around Fulton Street. The piers originally were extensions of the city streets. As the city grew in the 18 and 19C, wharves and piers were developed along the Hudson River in Manhattan, on the East River in Brooklyn, and in Jersey City and Hoboken, New Jersey. Today, the port, with some 750 miles of shoreline, provides docking space for more than 250 large ships at one time with specialized facilities to handle any type of cargo. The Manhattan shoreline, ill-suited for modern cargo handling methods, is now being studied and developed for commercial, residential and recreational projects (East River Landing on the East Side, Battery Park City on the West Side) while containerization and other industrial projects are being concentrated on the shorelines of other sections of the harbor. Automated handling of cargo in large steel containers has been adopted by major shipping lines and freighters now use new specialized terminals in Brooklyn, Staten Island and New Jersey. The world's largest and busiest container terminal is operated by the Port Authority in Port Newark/Elizabeth, New Jersey.

Natural Advantages. – They can be listed as follows:
- a huge and safe harbor
- a protected anchorage area within the Upper Bay
- channels at least 45ft deep leading to many pier areas
- proximity to the open sea and freedom from ice
- a climate usually free of fog
- a relatively small (less than 5ft) difference between high and low tides.

Traffic. – In 1988, 57 208 492 long tons of cargo passed through the port.

Cargo tonnages are increasing for foreign trade and total port tonnages: in 1988 a total of 57 000 000 tons of cargo (estimated at $49.9 billion) passed through the port of New York and New Jersey. The principal export commodities are machinery, plastic materials, paper and waste products. The main imports are vehicles, steel ingots, alcoholic beverages, and food products such as vegetables, fish, bananas, coffee and vegetable oils.

THE TRAFFIC OF THE PORT OF NEW YORK

Passengers. – Some 199 356 passengers entered and left the port in 1988 using the **New York City Passenger Ship Terminal.** Opened in 1974, it consolidates all passenger ship operations for the port of New York. The piers, providing six berths, are located on the Hudson River between 48th and 52nd Streets. This efficient, modern terminal has three levels: the street level is for supplies, the second or passenger level has comfortable traveler and visitor lounges, the upper level is a roof-top car park providing spaces for 1 000 vehicles. To facilitate arrivals and departures cars have direct access to the passenger level by means of a ramp. The terminal, built at the request of the City of New York, cost $40 million.

The world's largest and most luxurious cruise ships regularly call at the port. They include the *Queen Elizabeth 2, Royal Viking Star, Cunard Princess, Galileo, Nordic Prince, Bermuda Star* and the *Amerikanis.*

Port Services. — The Conrail system and five terminal railroads link the port with the rest of the country. The network of tracks leads into vast storage yards on the New Jersey side, and the freight is then moved to the piers either on barges or car floats, or is carried by truck on the last step of the shoreside journey.

Every day, some 60 000 long and short haul trucks move through the port area. Over 100 steamship lines regularly call at the port.

The Port Authority. – One of the agencies involved in the administration of the harbor is the Port Authority of New York and New Jersey, founded in 1921 by a compact between these two states. It was given responsibility to plan, build and operate a variety of transportation facilities, and to promote and protect the commerce of the great port. The agency's area of jurisdiction covers 1 500sq miles, equivalent to the area within a 25-mile radius of the Statue of Liberty.

The Port Authority built and operates several waterfront terminal areas. In addition to the Passenger Ship Terminal, it runs general cargo piers in Brooklyn, as well as container ship terminals in Port Newark/Elizabeth, New Jersey, Staten Island and Brooklyn, New York.

The Port Authority is also responsible for six tunnels and bridges connecting New York City with New Jersey, the world's busiest bus terminal, the Port Authority Trans-Hudson (PATH) rail rapid transit system, two heliports and three airports *(p 19)*.

In Lower Manhattan, the Port Authority has built and operates the **World Trade Center.** The World Trade Center features two tower buildings each 110 stories tall *(p 83)*.

In addition, the **New York City Department of Ports and Terminals** leases the three city-owned marine terminals located in Manhattan, Brooklyn and Staten Island. Another organization also operating within New York City is the **Triborough Bridge and Tunnel Authority,** which has constructed bridges and tunnels to improve the flow of traffic within the city.

Commerce and Industry. – New York is a powerful financial center. Whoever visits Manhattan is struck by the number and appearance of banks revealing the self-assurance of an old well-established banking system.

As early as the end of the 18C, in fact, New York's economic life revolved around credit: the Bank of New York was founded in 1784, the Bank of the United States in 1791, and the Bank of the Manhattan Company in 1799. Today, New York banks have about 25 % of the international banking market. Crowded into the narrow streets of the Financial District, American banks and more than 200 different foreign banks are now a predominant feature of Park Avenue, Madison Avenue, Fifth Avenue and other busy thoroughfares as well.

New York is the seat of the famous New York Stock Exchange *(p 89)*, the American Stock Exchange, and major stock and commodity exchanges which trade in such products as gold, silver, oil, cotton, cocoa and coffee. With the attraction of its financial community, the city hosts more than 3 800 major American corporations, twice as many as second-ranking Chicago.

The shipping industry, which handles 15% of the country's maritime trade, has attracted to the city the leading marine insurance companies and stimulated the development of warehousing and transportation.

Highly Specialized Industries. – New York is not what one would envision as the typical industrial city. Traditionally skilled labor has played a significant role in New York's industrial development. From the 19C's clothing workshops has emerged the modern fashion industry *(see garment center p 125)*, a principal contributor to New York's economy; publishing, printing, food products and electrical equipment rank next. A number of medium and small-sized establishments are located in Brooklyn, Queens and the Bronx, but more than half the city's manufacturing is centered in Manhattan.

The Service Industries. – New York is also the leader in communications and in the service industry. Over 24 000 companies specialize in business services: advertising, management and consulting, public relations, commercial research computer services and equipment rental.

Excellent educational facilities make New York, with its more than 90 two and four year colleges and universities, an outstanding center for higher learning and scientific research.

With the location in the city of all national television networks, many American and foreign newspapers and two of the major news wire services, New York is the communication center of the nation.

Readily available contacts with major corporations, high-quality entertainment and first rate hotel accommodations have made New York an important convention center and tourist spot. The wide variety of offerings in the Big Apple have, in the past decade, been responsible for making tourism and the production of feature films two of New York's fastest growing industries.

To get around Manhattan
use the subway and bus map
folded into the guide.

ARCHITECTURE AND CITY PLANNING

From the wooden warehouse of the Dutch trader to the proud skyscraper of the great international corporation, New York's architecture has gone through many stages before achieving its current dominant position in the art of the industrial and atomic age. Through the work of the New York City Landmarks Preservation Commission, a city agency, almost 840 individual landmark buildings of architectural, cultural or historical significance and over 53 historic districts have been preserved.

Colonial Architecture. – This style flourished when the American provinces were still British colonies. At its height in the 18C, the colonial tradition persisted until well into the 19C. Colonial architecture is also often called **Georgian** because it was inspired by the style which prevailed in England under kings George (I-IV, 1714-1830). Frequently painted white, colonial buildings are usually constructed of wood or brick, and adorned with a portico or a colonnade. Steps lead up to the front door which sometimes is crowned by a fan window, and the building corners are often decorated with quoins (wooden blocks imitating stonework). Among the examples of colonial or Georgian architecture to be found in New York are Fraunces Tavern, the Morris-Jumel Mansion and St Paul's Chapel. More than 100 pre-1800 houses still exist throughout the city.

The "Revivals". – The 19C brought a multiplicity of styles reminiscent of the classic or medieval manner: "Greek Revival," or "Gothic Revival," for example.
 Greek Revival architecture, inspired by the monuments of ancient Greece, was more widespread for churches and public buildings than for private homes, at least in the city. Examples of this style which have survived include: the Federal Hall National Memorial, which reproduces the proportions of a Doric temple, Colonnade Row, and Grant's Tomb.
 With their Ionic porticoes, the houses of Washington Square reflect the popularity of the neo-Grecian style which flourished in the mid-19C.
 Less prevalent than Greek Revival, but well represented, **"Gothic Revival"** was exemplified in the first St Patrick's Cathedral *(p 131)* built early in the 19C by the French architect Mangin, and is evident today in the present St Patrick's Cathedral, Trinity Church and Grace Church.
 At the end of the 19 and the beginning of the 20C, New York architects cultivated the art of the Revival with enthusiastic eclecticism, recreating almost every imaginable European style for the magnates of industry and finance: feudal, Louis XII, Renaissance and Tudor competed in splendor. However, there was a distinct preference for the Italian Renaissance, the hands-down favorite of the most famous architects of the day, McKim, Mead and White, who designed the Morgan Library, the Villard Houses and the Vanderbilt Mansion.

Cast-Iron Architecture. – The use of cast-iron architecture was first introduced in America in 1848 by **James Bogardus** in Manhattan. Nowhere else did its development occur on such a large scale. Attractive cast-iron building fronts, prefabricated in numerous separate pieces then assembled at the building site, became a speedy and economical means of adorning a conventional brick and wooden structure, with a stylish Victorian facade. The vogue for cast-iron continued until the early 20C. New York City has, by far, the greatest concentration of cast-iron structures in the world; with the largest, most distinguished group being found in downtown Manhattan, and particularly SoHo.

The Brownstones. – These town houses were built primarily in the second half of the 19C with brownstone from Connecticut and New Jersey. Usually three or four storied, their steps are perpendicular to the facade, often forming geometrical patterns on streets where rows of brownstones have survived. Their cast and wrought iron banisters and railings are quite striking. Originally richly appointed family homes of the wealthy middle class, these town houses are now mostly divided into apartments and condominiums. Until recently there were still large numbers of brownstones in the midtown area, but now few remain except for those surviving in Harlem, the Murray Hill and Gramercy Park areas, Greenwich Village, Chelsea, the Upper West Side and several areas of Brooklyn (Park Slope, Cobble Hill, Brooklyn Heights, Boerum Hill, Fort Greene and Clinton Hill).

Yesterday's Skyscrapers. – At the beginning of the 20C, New York's population grew very rapidly *(p 26)*. The price of real estate rose accordingly, a fact which caused the promoters to build higher and higher. Earlier, architects had been limited by the weight of masonry, but the use of steel and subsequently reinforced concrete, enabled them to attain greater building heights. Then, with the introduction of caisson foundation, skeleton steel construction and fireproof protection for columns and beams, as well as the high-speed elevator, the way was open for the era of the "skyscraper."
 These techniques did not at first inspire a new architectural style. One of the first skyscrapers, the Flatiron Building *(p 142)* erected in 1902 on a steel framework, was decorated with pilasters and a wide cornice in Florentine Renaissance style. The Woolworth Building, on the other hand, which was finished in 1913, is a "Gothic cathedral of commerce," adorned with delicate stone lacework, gargoyles and a pinnacled tower. A number of edifices were inspired by the French classical period, with Versailles as a constant model, while still others were covered with ornate sculptures and colonnades, often freely adapted from Greek or Roman styles.
 Changes in design occurred following the **zoning law** of 1916 which regulated the height and volume of buildings in relation to the width of the streets, to ensure light and a sense of openness in the area. As a result skyscrapers were built in layers with successive setbacks. Some were so oddly shaped or so elaborately decorated they were referred to as "wedding cakes."
 Gradually, there was an evolution in style: skyscrapers tended to be more vertical, devoid of stylistic ornamentation, and gracefully proportioned in their soaring upward movement. The Chrysler Building, the Empire State Building and the RCA Building (in Rockefeller Center), all erected in the 30s, are among the finest examples of this period of architectural pioneering.

Today's Skyscrapers. – After an interruption due to World War II, skyscrapers once more sprouted in Manhattan, but built with different techniques and styles of construction.

In the following decades, steel and reinforced concrete gave way to aluminum and glass, a weight and time-saving combination. The conventional skyscraper normally has a maze of interior columns, but recently a new technique has been employed, in which the exterior walls consisting of closely spaced columns of steel, are used as load bearing walls, leaving a maximum of open column-free space. (The towers of the World Trade Center and One Liberty Plaza).

(From photo Éd. Sun, Paris.)

Park Avenue
View of the Helmsley Building and the Pan Am Building

Rising straight up without setbacks, the buildings are often set back from the street, leaving free space for gardens or plazas, sometimes graced with fountains. The **atrium**, an interior multistory courtyard with shops and eating places, is a feature of many buildings erected since the 1970s such as Citicorp, Park Avenue Plaza and Trump Tower.

Architects of great renown have designed some of New York's finest skyscrapers among them: Mies van der Rohe and Philip Johnson (Seagram Building); Gropius and Belluschi (Pan Am Building); and Eero Saarinen (CBS Building).

The main groups of skyscrapers are in the downtown and midtown area. The oldest are downtown, around Wall Street, but this area also takes pride in the Chase Manhattan Bank, the twin towers of the World Trade Center, and the riverview buildings of Battery Park City. New buildings are clustered in mid-Manhattan, particularly on Park Avenue, Fifth Avenue, the Avenue of the Americas, Third Avenue and Lexington Avenue.

Recent building activity, concentrated on the East Side between the 40s and 60s, has resulted in the addition of no less than two dozen high-rise office towers to the skyline, including the IBM Building and the headquarters of American Telephone and Telegraph.

City Development. – City development and redevelopment are planned, guided and carried out by a number of local public agencies. The New York City Planning Commission is the major policymaking body concerned with the city's future. Its functions include zoning regulation and overall land use planning. A number of operating agencies, including the Office of Economic Development, the Departments of Housing Preservation and Development, Transportation, Parks and Recreation, Human Resources, and Cultural Affairs, plan and execute major programs and projects. In addition, several other agencies, particularly the Public Development Corporation, the New York State Urban Development Corporation and the Port Authority of New York and New Jersey, undertake their own development projects in cooperation with the city.

The city has implemented major programs, including: innovations in zoning concepts through the creation of special districts such as the Union Square and Hunters Point Special Districts.

Creative zoning initiatives have included land use actions approving or designed to induce new development in the four boroughs of the city other than Manhattan; and the establishment of a Midtown Special District which, by reducing permitted building densities on the East Side and increasing those on the West Side, was intended to shift development from the East Side to the West and South. An important current project is the redevelopment of the West 42nd St area and the preservation of its many legitimate theaters.

PAINTING: The New York School

Prior to the 1930s it was necessary for American artists to travel abroad to study and observe the latest developments in experimental art. But as war fermented and the depression lingered in Europe, many foreign artists began to arrive in the United States. The best talents came, some to stay for a brief time, some to remain. This infusion of talent and ideas helped a great deal to shape an art that was truly American.

The establishment of the Museum of Modern Art, the Whitney Museum and the efforts of Peggy Guggenheim, the art lover and collector, sparked new currents and a sympathetic audience was eager to embrace the new forms of artistic expression.

A Precursor: Marcel Duchamp. – Early in this century most American painters were inspired by European masters. Some artists from the West Coast pioneered original forms but few others followed their example.

Marcel Duchamp, brother of the sculptor Raymond Duchamp-Villon and of the painter Jacques Villon, settled in New York in 1913. That same year he created a sensation by exhibiting at the Armory Show his *Nude Descending a Staircase* in which he expressed the results of his studies on the representation of movement. Along with Picabia, he laid the basis for "Dada" *(p 41)* and created his provocative ready-mades, which consist of simple, even ordinary objects, which the artist exhibits as works of art (having intervened only to give them names); thus *The Bicycle Wheel* and *A Fountain*, nothing more than a basin bought in a department store.

Action Painting. – The events of the 40s brought many painters fleeing wartime Europe to New York: Frenchmen such as Chagall, Léger and Masson, along with the German Max Ernst and the Dutch Mondrian, contributed to the new artistic atmosphere.

But it was only with Action Painting that the New York school came into its own. Action Painting is a form of abstract art where instinct plays the greatest role: the artist, in a sort of reverie, expresses himself with great brushstrokes.

Jackson Pollock (1912-56) was a master of Action Painting. He used to lay out the canvas, unstretched, on the bare floor and throw his pigments on it, sometimes mixing them with sand or crushed glass to form a sort of paste which he worked with sticks, trowels and knives. Along with Pollock there were Kline (1910-62), whose huge black and white compositions exude anxiety, and Rothko (1903-70), of Russian origin, whose vast compositions in subtle colors are compelling. Other artists in this group include Willem and Elaine de Kooning, Jack Tworkov, Adolph Gottlieb, Barnett Newman and William Baziotes.

Pop and Op Art. – Around 1960 a new trend appeared in New York art circles, which its adepts called Pop Art. The artists swung the pictorial imagery of art from the purely abstract back to recognizable subjects. But it was an all new imagery – comic strip characters, street signs, light bulbs, movie stars – popular imagery transformed, demanding a new approach to looking. **Rauschenberg** incorporated objects from real life into his paintings. Among his best-known contemporaries are Roy Lichtenstein, Ellsworth Kelly, Jasper Johns, Frank Stella, Claes Oldenburg and Andy Warhol.

By the mid-60s two new movements appeared on the scene: "Op" and "Minimal" art. Op Art seeks to reveal movement to the beholder. Inspired by the works of Delaunay and Duchamp, it is illustrated by the transformable paintings of Agam, the kinetic compositions of Vasarely, and the cybernetic constructions of Schöffer. Minimal art rejects all extraneous elements.

MODERN SCULPTURE IN MANHATTAN

Many visitors to New York have been welcomed by the town's most famous sculpture, Bartholdi's Statue of Liberty. Sculptures of various styles and periods are represented, but the city is particularly rich in 20C works.

Very often sculptures decorated the early religious and civic buildings: Jean-Jacques Caffieri (Major General Montgomery's tomb at St Paul's Chapel); Daniel Chester French and Augustus Saint-Gaudens (facade of the former U.S. Custom House); A. Stirling Calder (a statue of Washington on the north side of Washington Arch).

Parks, greens and squares were also decorated with commemorative statues: Giovanni da Verrazano, the Florentine navigator (Battery Park); Peter Stuyvesant, the Dutch Governor of New Amsterdam (Stuyvesant Square); equestrian statue of George Washington and a statue of Abraham Lincoln by Henry Kirke Brown (Union Square); Benjamin Franklin by Plassman (near Pace University), and statues of Washington and Lafayette by F.A. Bartholdi (Morningside Park).

Construction in New York during the 60s and 70s saw the introduction of plazas and mini parks as integral parts of the urban landscape. The installation of modern art works in many of these plazas gives every New Yorker the opportunity to appreciate and enjoy modern sculpture. Among the most striking examples of urban design are the great architectural ensembles such as the United Nations, Rockefeller Center, Lincoln Center, the World Trade Center and Battery Park City.

Rockefeller Center is adorned on the lower plaza by the gilded bronze statue of Prometheus stealing the sacred fire for mankind; and that well-known landmark by L. Lawrie, the monumental bronze statue *(illustration p 39)* of Atlas supporting the world, is in front of the International Building.

The United Nations is the setting of great international art works, among which are the statue of *Peace* in the gardens presented by Yugoslavia, and in the pool in front of the Secretariat Building a sculpture by Barbara Hepworth.

The Chase Manhattan Bank, famous for its art collection, has on its lower plaza a sunken Japanese stone garden by the sculptor Isamu Noguchi. A striking feature of the upper plaza is Jean Dubuffet's *Group of Four Trees*. This fiberglass construction painted black and white, rises to 42ft and weighs 25 tons. The work was commissioned by David Rockefeller to celebrate the bank's 25 years on Wall Street.

Lincoln Center is famous for the outstanding art objects displayed in the interior of the various buildings. Also noteworthy are Henry Moore's bronze *Reclining Figure* in the plaza pool and Alexander Calder's work *Le Guichet* on the plaza north.

The plaza of the World Trade Center has as a centerpiece a fountain and pool. At the center of the pool is the bronze sculpture by Fritz Koenig of Munich, representing a free form globe, which revolves almost unnoticeably

In Lower Manhattan the triangular vest-pocket park, Louise Nevelson Plaza, contains seven enormous black steel sculptures by Louise Nevelson.

The great centers are not alone to have architectural decoration, many individual buildings are enhanced by a sculptural work on the sidewalk or plaza: Yehiel Shemi's *Window Sculpture* (Jewish Museum); Ivan Chermayeff's No. 9 sign (9 W 57th Street), Robert Cook's bronze and Luis Sanguino's *Amor* (345 Park Avenue); Noguchi's cube (140 Broadway); Beverly Pepper's *Contrappunto* (777 Third Avenue); Yu Yu Yang's two part sculpture (plaza of 88 Pine Street); Lipchitz's bronze *Bellerophon Taming Pegasus* in front of the Law Building at Columbia University; and Louise Nevelson's environmental sculpture *Night Presence IV* (center island on Park Avenue at 92nd Street) and two-dimensional construction *Sky Gate-New York* (No 1 World Trade Center).

The various sculpture gardens in the city also provide a collection of works by different artists: the New School for Social Research at 66 West 12th Street between Fifth Avenue and Avenue of the Americas; the Whitney Museum of American Art, and the Museum of Modern Art where recent acquisitions include works by Scott Burton and Tony Smith.

NEW YORK AND LITERATURE

From Knickerbocker to the "New Yorker". – In the rich literary life of contemporary America, New York is no doubt the most vital force. Attracted by its intellectual climate and receptive public, publishing and printing have been leading industries in New York for over a century.

A distinguished literary tradition goes back to Washington Irving *(p 160)*, a native New Yorker, author of *A History of New York* (written in 1809 under the pen name of Diedrich Knickerbocker), an irreverent account of the city's first Dutch families which shows that the satirical strain embodied in today's *New Yorker* magazine has firm roots in New York soil.

Classics and Bohemians. – A galaxy of outstanding figures in American literature were associated with New York throughout the 19C, either because they lived here for some time *(see Greenwich Village p 102 and Brooklyn Heights p 147)* or because they chose New York as the setting for their work.

These include the poet and short story writer Edgar Allan Poe *(p 146)*; the author of *Moby Dick*, New York-born Herman Melville *(Bartleby, A Story of Wall Street)*, the poet and New York journalist Walt Whitman *(Mannahatta* and *Crossing Brooklyn Ferry)*, the New York-born novelists Edith Wharton *(The Age of Innocence)* and Henry James *(Washington Square)*, Stephen Crane, the author of *The Red Badge of Courage (New York City Sketches)* and Mark Twain, a correspondent for Western newspapers in his early days in New York.

In the first decades of the 20C, artistic and literary life in New York centered around Greenwich Village, so much so that it has been described as "the home of American arts and letters" during this period. The names of the poetess Edna St. Vincent Millay, the playwright Eugene O'Neill and the novelist Theodore Dreiser are remembered for their close associations with Greenwich Village.

"All Around the Town". – Further uptown, and somewhat later, a group of wits, writers and wags made the Hotel Algonquin their headquarters. Among these poker-playing "knights" of what became known as the "Round Table" *(p 124)* were the raconteur and drama critic Alexander Woollcott, the humorist Robert Benchley and the editor of the *New Yorker*, Harold Ross; Dorothy Parker, short-story writer and master of barbed witticism, and Franklin P. Adams ("F.P.A."), columnist and New York diarist, were also members of this group.

Carl van Vechten and Langston Hughes presided over the literary and artistic renaissance in the Harlem of the 20s.

The "Age of Jazz" which was also the age of the flapper, bathtub gin, the New York speakeasy and the "Lost Generation," saw the emergence of its prophet in F. Scott Fitzgerald *(The Great Gatsby)* and of a then left-oriented critic in John Dos Passos *(Manhattan Transfer U.S.A.)*.

Broadway had its chronicler in Damon Runyon, who was in some ways the successor of an earlier historian in *Bagdad-on-the-Subway*, O'Henry, the author of many short stories. Ring Lardner cast a critical eye on the *Big League* that was New York. John O'Hara *(Butterfield 8)*, James Thurber, and more recently, John Updike were among the *New Yorker* writers who made that magazine uniquely characteristic of New York. The essayist E.B. White *(Here is New York)* may be called a New Yorker's New Yorker. The novelist Norman Mailer who grew up in Brooklyn commanded attention and acquired fame with his novel *The Naked and the Dead* (1948).

"The Center of the Universe". – New York has always acted as a magnet, drawing unto itself the best the country had to offer.

Long before the term "brain drain" was coined, the migration of the brightest young talents from farms, small towns and other remote areas to the big city was already an established phenomenon.

One of the most brilliant success stories of this type was that of Thomas Wolfe *(Look Homeward, Angel, You Can't Go Home Again)*, the ebullient North Carolina writer who used to dash out of his Brooklyn room after protracted sessions of work to celebrate by pouring pitchers of beer over his head in a nearby saloon.

But New York has attracted writers not only from the United States. Among those who have come from abroad and who have written about New York are the Russian poet Vladimir Mayakovsky *(Brooklyn Bridge)*, the Spanish poet Federico Garcia-Lorca *(Poet in New York)*, the Irish playwright Brendan Behan *(Brendan Behan's New York)*, the French novelist Paul Morand *(New York)*, the English photographer and decorator Cecil Beaton *(Cecil Beaton's New York)* and the Russian poet, Andrei Voznesensky *(Airport in New York)*.

New York has stimulated the imagination of writers, foreign and American alike, because of the fascination exercised by this greatest and most exciting of all cities, "the center of the universe," as one of its mayors called it, constantly changing its skyline and even its population, full of contrasts and paradoxes: poverty amidst riches, cosmopolitanism befitting a world capital alongside strong neighborhood loyalties, local patriotism and ethnic pride, loneliness in spite of the crowds, toughness and cynicism mingling with sentimentality and soft-heartedness, essentially American but shaped by immigrants from a hundred lands.

These are some of the elements which make up the unique human adventure of New York, whose challenge to the creative imagination is as great as that of life itself.

"New York is a sort of anthology of urban civilization. The song that any city sings she sings. All that anybody can seek for that can be housed in steel and cement is here, and with it, never lost in all the city's drabness, respect for the striving, combative beauty-loving spirit of man."

R.L. Duffus.

MANHATTAN

Celebrated for its impressive and dramatic skyline, the island of Manhattan, the smallest of the five boroughs of New York City, is by far the one which is the most popular with the tourist. The island measures 13.4 miles long and is only 2.3 miles across at its widest point. Between 1950 and 1960 the move to the suburbs and the more residential boroughs of Queens and Staten Island caused a decline in the total population of Manhattan, but the number of inhabitants now seems to be fluctuating, due to new arrivals and in some places to a return of suburbanites from the outlying areas.

Manhattan, whose name is derived from an Algonquin word meaning "island of the hills," is the nerve center of the city. Broadway, the longest and best-known thoroughfare, winds its way from south to north, following an old Indian trail. From its southern tip, Manhattan grew northward in an irregular street pattern which still prevails in the oldest parts of town. Geometric regularity takes over beyond Union Square and the neat pattern of numbered streets and avenues crossing at right angles covers most of the rest of the island. Fifth Avenue marks the boundary between east and west for the numbered streets. The lower numbered streets are considered "downtown" while the higher numbered streets, beginning at Central Park, are considered "uptown".

Feverish activity and extraordinary feats in construction are typical of Manhattan. The tallest skyscrapers, the biggest banks, the largest and best stocked department stores, the greatest variety of restaurants, and the densest crowds in the world, tend to overwhelm the visitor.

Exploring the city, the walker will soon discover Manhattan's diversity: busy avenues bordered with luxurious shops, the more quiet side streets lined with town houses, and stretches of doorman-attended apartment houses with colorful canopies. Picturesque historic enclaves adjoin bustling commercial districts, and there are whole cities within the city: Greenwich Village, Chinatown, Harlem, affording fascinating cultural insights. As the visitor becomes familiar with New York, he will enjoy, too, the pleasing contrast between its canyons of concrete and glass, and the airy landscaped plazas and small park-like spaces adorned with sculptures and fountains.

New York also enjoys the cosmopolitan distinction of being a major center of the arts. The educational facilities within its boundaries and in the metropolitan area make the city an outstanding center for higher learning and scientific research.

For the visitor, the city presents a wide range of attractions: traveling here on business or pleasure, he is swept up in the exciting pace of the city. A sort of New Babylon, New York offers all types of amusements, heralded by the bright lights of Broadway or the tinsel of Greenwich Village. As a shopping center, Manhattan is a vast bazaar where you can buy absolutely anything you wish. There are the famous department stores such as Macy's and Bloomingdale's, as well as the boutiques and specialty shops for gifts, jewelry, cameras, etc.

And then there is Manhattan at night, a truly unforgettable sight. Viewed from the top of the World Trade Center, the observation deck of the Empire State Building, or the Brooklyn Heights esplanade across the river, the brilliant lights of the buildings, the glittering bridges strung like precious jewels above the waterways, the flashing neon signs, and the illuminated pattern of moving automobiles, form a spectacle which never ceases to dazzle the eye and excite the imagination.

View of Lower Manhattan.

Distance: about 1 mile – Time: 1 day (including guided tours and museum visits).

Located in the heart of midtown Manhattan, between Fifth and Seventh Avenues and 47th and 52nd Streets, Rockefeller Center is an imposing group of harmoniously designed skyscrapers, most of which were constructed before World War II. Vital, dignified and steeped in an air of festivity year round, the Center is a magnet that draws thousands of office workers and tourists daily.

The 19 buildings cover about 22 acres and house a working population of 65 000. Add to that the number of tourists who visit the Center each day and the result is a workday population of more than a quarter of a million persons. The various buildings are connected by a maze of underground passages, the Concourse, lined with shops and restaurants and providing access to the subway system.

Rockefeller Plaza, a private street running from north to south between 48th and 51st Streets, was constructed to provide access to the GE Building. The street is closed one day each year so that by law it does not become public property.

GE BUILDING	A
RADIO CITY MUSIC HALL	B
STEVENS TOWER	C
CELANESE BUILDING	D
McGRAW-HILL BUILDING	E
EXXON BUILDING	F
TIME & LIFE BUILDING	G
OLYMPIA & YORK BUILDING	H
EQUITABLE CENTER	J
PAINEWEBBER BUILDING	K
CBS BUILDING	L
SHERATON CENTRE	N
NEW YORK HILTON	P
BURLINGTON HOUSE	R
AMERICAN CRAFT MUSEUM	S
DONNELL LIBRARY CENTER	T
THE MUSEUM OF MODERN ART	V
INTERNATIONAL BUILDING	W

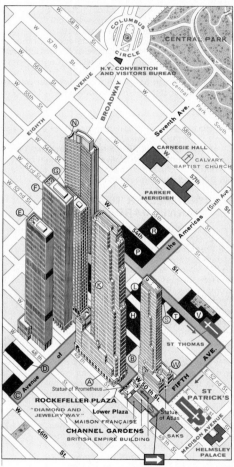

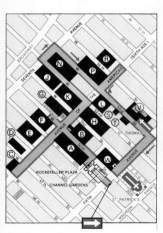

Fields and Meadows. – At the beginning of the 19C, the site now occupied by Rockefeller Center was part of the "Commons Lands," vacant or unpatented lands on Manhattan. **Dr. David Hosack,** a professor of botany, acquired 15 acres from the city for $5 000 to establish a public botanical garden which he called "Elgin Garden." Hosack soon found the upkeep of the gardens too expensive. So, in 1811, he decided to sell the land to the State of New York, which turned it over to Columbia University. The university then rented the land to farmers for $100 a year.

City Blocks and Brownstones. – By 1850, the present gridiron pattern of streets and avenues was laid out and the first buildings appeared on the site. The area soon developed into a fashionable residential district where splendid mansions stood side by side with more modest brownstones. A few of these residences, on 53rd Street, have survived to this day.

In the early 1900s the neighborhood began to decline. The area had become noisy especially after the construction of the Avenue of the Americas "El" (the elevated railway) in 1878 and the millionaires and the middle class moved away, leaving their fine homes to poorer tenants. Later, during the Prohibition era, this once elegant district became notorious as the "speakeasy belt."

John D. Rockefeller, Jr. – Son of the oil multimillionaire and father of the "Rockefeller Brothers," "John D. Jr." leased the land from Columbia University in 1928. With associates from the Metropolitan Opera, Rockefeller planned to erect a gigantic, new opera house on the site. The initial lease ran 24 years and was renewable until 2015, when the land and the building would revert to the university; but the crash of 1929 brought this project to an abrupt halt.

(From document, Museum of the City of New York.)

Rockefeller Center area early 19C.

Left during the Depression days with a long-term lease on this parcel of land and a sizable rent to pay, John D. decided to build a commercial center, a "city within a city." The core of the project, including what is now the GE Building, was completed in 1940. One of the architects in charge was Wallace K. Harrison, later one of those mainly responsible for the design of the United Nations Headquarters *(p 77)* and Lincoln Center for the Performing Arts *(p 93)*.

During the building of Rockefeller Center a practice was initiated which New Yorkers now take for granted. It is said that Rockefeller himself stopped by to observe the progress that had been made one day, and was asked to move on. The occasion gave rise to the use of the peephole, now a part of every construction site.

VISIT

We suggest the following itinerary for a brief visit to the main buildings of Rockefeller Center and the Avenue of the Americas.

Begin in front of Saks Fifth Avenue. From here you have a good view of the Channel Gardens, a promenade between the Maison Française on the left and the British Empire Building on the right, both topped by roof gardens. Beyond, the silhouette of the GE Building rises against the sky.

■ ROCKEFELLER PLAZA AND CHANNEL GARDENS★★

A relaxing spot, the "Channel Gardens" (so named because they separate the French and British buildings) contain a series of pools surrounded by flower beds, which are changed regularly in season, beginning with Easter Lilies on Good Friday. During World War II a model "Victory Garden" was cultivated here. The benches along the flower beds will be especially appreciated if you have been window-shopping. At Christmas time, spectacular lighting displays attract a crowd.

The Channel promenade leads down to the Lower Plaza, an open area below street level around which are flown the flags of the United Nations member countries. At the top of the steps leading to the Lower Plaza is a plaque citing "John D. Jr's" Credo. An outdoor café in summer, the Plaza, the showpiece of the Center, serves as a skating rink in winter.

On the other side of the Lower Plaza stands Paul Manship's bronze statue of Prometheus stealing the sacred fire for mankind. The statue, covered in gold leaf,

(From photo Rockefeller Center, Inc.)

Channel Gardens.

is flanked by two smaller figures (also by Manship) symbolizing mankind receiving the fire. Every December, a huge Christmas tree towers from 65 to 90ft above this setting. Visitors come to admire the colored lights, to observe the ice skaters in the rink below, and to hear occasional concerts of Christmas carols.

■ GE (General Electric) BUILDING★★

Seventy stories tall, the GE Building (formerly known as the RCA Building) soaring 850ft above street level, is the loftiest of the Center's towers, and is also the most harmonious architecturally. General Electric and National Broadcasting Company are headquartered in the building, making it a major communications center. The main entrance at 30 Rockefeller Plaza leads to the lobby, decorated with immense murals by the Spanish artist José Maria Sert, depicting man's progress. These murals are actually the second series executed for the building. The first set, designed by the fiery revolutionary Diego Rivera, were considered too radical by "John D. Jr."

On the 65th floor is the Rainbow Room, a well-known restaurant with impressive views of the Rockefeller Center area and the Manhattan skyline.

NBC Studios (National Broadcasting Company)★. – *Guided tours (time: 55 min) 9:30 AM to 4:30 PM; no tours Sundays (except during summer months), January 1, Labor Day, Thanksgiving Day and December 25. Tickets ($7.25) may be purchased in the lobby at the Tour desk. Tours leave from this point approximately every 15 minutes.*

Several floors of the GE Building are devoted to NBC television studios. During this tour, you will visit the sets of several radio and TV shows and find out what goes on behind the scenes of a broadcasting studio.

The Concourse★. – On the first level below the main floor an underground passage lined with attractive shops, restaurants and exhibits links all the buildings of Rockefeller Center.

■ RADIO CITY MUSIC HALL★★

A treasured New York landmark and the "showplace of the nation," Radio City Music Hall presents musical spectaculars live on its Great Stage. In addition, concerts by top performing artists are presented as part of the Music Hall's new entertainment format that began in 1979.

The Stage Show. – *A spring show, the «Easter Extravaganza», and "The Christmas Spectacular," which runs from mid-November to the first week in January, are the major stage productions featured annually.*

During the rest of the year there are concerts and special events featuring a wide range of artists. The renowned precision dance team, the Rockettes, perform in the spring and Christmas shows as well as other stage events. For show times and tickets ℡ 757-3100.

The Rockettes, founded in St. Louis, Missouri in 1925, have been a star attraction at the Music Hall since opening night December 27, 1932. Known originally as the Missouri Rockets, then as the Roxyettes when they were resident performers at New York's Roxy Theatre, the troupe was renamed the Rockettes in 1934, the name by which they have become famous throughout the world.

The Interior★★★ – *You may visit Radio City Music Hall by taking the Behind the Scenes Tour (time: 1 hour) which departs from the main lobby 10:15 AM to 4:45 PM (11 AM to 5 PM Sunday); hours vary during Christmas holiday season; $6.00. ℡ 632-4041.*

The luxurious Art Deco interior of Radio City Music Hall was completely restored in 1979, allowing guests, today, to marvel at the same architectural splendor that awed the public when the Music Hall first opened its bronze doors a half-century ago.

On entering the Grand Foyer your feet sink into the deep pile of the carpet, below the sweeping Grand Staircase.

In the foyer you will see chandeliers which are among the largest in the world sparkling overhead. Each weighs 2 tons – a ton of crystal and a ton of steel – and can be lowered for cleaning merely by pushing a button.

In the auditorium, the curved wall and ceiling design leads the eye toward the immense proscenium arch (60ft high), the most striking feature of the 5 882-seat theater. The stage, itself, a masterpiece of technical expertise, is equipped with complex machinery: three elevators, a three-section turntable, and an orchestra elevator. The musicians in the orchestra and the two electric organs (with pipes up to 32ft high) complete with their organists can be whisked away behind the walls or below the floor when necessary, without interrupting their playing.

An imposing series of tall office towers with spacious plazas lines the west side of the Avenue of the Americas. Walk south to the **Stevens Tower** at 1185 Avenue of the Americas, between 46th and 47th Streets. This 42-story office tower of black glass and white marble adjoins, in the rear plaza area, a building which incorporates a legitimate theater and a restaurant. Across 47th Street is the **Celanese Building,** a 45-story building similar in design to the other two additions to Rockefeller Center to the north.

■ McGRAW-HILL BUILDING

Set back from the street, this 51-story building constructed of flame finished granite and solar bronze glass, is surrounded by plazas.

The lower plaza in front of the building contains The Pool of the Planets, an exhibit demonstrating the relationship of the planets. The main element of the exhibit, a sleek 50ft steel sun triangle, points to the four seasonal positions of the sun at solar noon in New York during the solstices and equinoxes. This plaza leads to the lower concourse and the McGraw-Hill Bookstore.

In addition, the McGraw-Hill Park, along the western edge of the building, features a walk-through waterfall. It leads to a tree-shaded mall with an ornamental pool, hanging plants, umbrella-covered tables and chairs, and refreshment facilities. *(Summer concerts 12:30 to 1:30 PM several times each week.)*

■ EXXON BUILDING

This, the corporate home for Exxon Corporation, with a height of 750ft, and 53 stories, is the second tallest skyscraper in Rockefeller Center after the GE Building which it faces across the Avenue of the Americas. Rising from a landscaped plaza, piers of limestone alternate with windows and beams enframed in bronze-tinted aluminum. Inside, in the 2 1/2 story high spacious lobby with its giallo beige marble walls and striking reddish floor, note the tapestry reproduction of a theater curtain painted by Picasso and the abstract hanging sculpture *Moon and Stars*.

Situated behind the tower, a peaceful mini-park with flowers, trees, food stands and a cascading waterfall provides a welcome refuge from the busy streets and sidewalks.

■ TIME & LIFE BUILDING

Across from Radio City rises the smooth, glistening exterior of the building where *Time, Life, Money, People, Sports Illustrated,* and *Fortune* are published. Erected in 1960, the building was the first modern skyscraper constructed on the west side of the Avenue of the Americas.

You may admire the pure vertical lines of this 48-story building, 587ft in height, covered with limestone, aluminum and glass. On two sides of the building is the Americas Plaza, paved with a two-toned terrazzo pattern. The undulating design contrasts pleasantly with the rectangular pools and their fountains. The same type of serpentine design is found on the floor of the lobby. On the east side a large abstract mural by Fritz Glarner, a modern American painter, harmonizes with the stainless steel panels, alternately polished and dull, which cover the walls.

■ EQUITABLE TOWER★

The itinerary next takes us between the **Olympia & York Building** and the **Equitable Center.** The Equitable Center, a block-long complex named for the insurance company, has as its centerpiece Equitable Tower (1985), an elegant 54-story granite, limestone and glass structure designed by Edward Larrabee Barnes. In the Tower lobby *(entrance on 7th Ave)* is Thomas Hart Benton's expressive ten-part mural *America Today,* depicting life across the nation on the eve of the Great Depression. An atrium, dominated by the bold images of Roy Lichtenstein's 65ft-high *Mural With Blue Brushstroke* adjoins Equitable Tower on the west; the atrium houses galleries of the Whitney Museum of American Art *(open 11 AM to 6 PM - 7:30 PM Thursdays; Saturdays noon to 5 PM, closed Sundays and holidays).* On the east rises the **PaineWebber Building** (1961), with changing exhibitions on the lobby level *(open weekdays 8 AM to 6 PM).*

■ CBS BUILDING★

Beyond 52nd Street is the CBS Building designed by the architect Eero Saarinen. The framework of reinforced concrete is covered with dark Canadian granite.

Turn left on 52nd Street to have a good view of the south side of the Sheraton Centre, originally known as the Americana Hotel.

■ SHERATON CENTRE

The tapered silhouette of the Sheraton Centre, one of the largest hotels in the world, is particularly elegant seen from the south, where the line is slightly broken. Built almost entirely of glass over a stone framework, it was erected in 1962, and contains 1 828 rooms on 50 floors. Many conventions are held here. Off the lobby you will find a variety of shops.

■ THE NEW YORK HILTON AND TOWERS

Covered with steel and glass panels, this 46-story hotel employs 1 500 persons who speak a total of 30 languages. Completed in 1963, the building includes a 4-story base with service and reception facilities, and a high tower given over to the 2 034 guest rooms and suites, each designed to have a view of the New York skyline.

The interior is as modern as the architectural lines. On the main floor, next to the lobby, is The Promenade café with its tall glass walls looking out onto the Avenue of the Americas. On the upper floors are elegant suites for business meetings, some of which are decorated in French period styles, including two duplex penthouses.

Across 54th Street is **Burlington House** which, although it does not belong to Rockefeller Center, extends the row of tower buildings on the west side of the Avenue of the Americas. This brown tinted building, climbing to 50 stories, is surrounded by a plaza with a vest pocket park behind, and in front two pools with original fountains which when operating form attractive spheres of water.

Take 53rd Street, the site of several museums including the Museum of Modern Art *(see opposite).*

Museum of American Folk Art. – The museum of American Folk Art is currently involved in a building project at West 53rd Street. During this period, the museum is holding exhibitions at 2 Lincoln Square, Columbus Ave at 65th. *For information* ☏ *977-7170.*

American Craft Museum. *– 40 West 53rd Street. Open 10 AM to 5 PM (8 PM Tuesdays); closed Mondays and major holidays; $ 3.50.*

Located at street level in the E. F. Hutton building, the museum's space is enhanced by its major architectural feature, a 4-story atrium with a graceful oval staircase leading to the exhibit area. Through a program of changing theme shows, the American Craft Museum brings to the attention of the public the new directions and achievements of the contemporary craft movement. Exhibits cover a wide range of American and foreign crafts and touch on all media: ceramics, textiles, wood, glass, etc.

Returning to Fifth Avenue you will pass, across from the Museum of Modern Art, the **Donnell Library Center** at 20 West 53rd Street, one of three buildings which constitute the Central Library of the New York Public Library's Branch System. It provides such special services as the Central Children's Room containing 100 000 books for and about children; the Nathan Straus Young Adult Library, a special foreign language collection with books in more than 80 languages, and the Media Center with its large collection of films, videotapes, recordings and film and videotape viewing facilities.

Cross Fifth Avenue to the steps of St Patrick's Cathedral *(p 46)* to admire Lee Lawrie's monumental statue of Atlas supporting the world. For taking part in the war against Zeus (Jupiter), Atlas was condemned to uphold the sky for eternity. The figure of the giant stands in front of the International Building.

(From photo Samuel Chamberlain.)

Atlas.

■ INTERNATIONAL BUILDING

This 41-story building was originally intended to house consulates and other offices of foreign countries – thus its name. You should cross Fifth Avenue once more and enter the lobby inspired by ancient Greece, with its columns and walls of marble from the Greek island of Tinos. The ceiling is covered with very thin copper leaf. If all this copper were removed from the ceiling, it would weigh about a pound and, melted down, could be held in the palm of your hand.

A colorful limestone screen by Lee Lawrie depicting the red, yellow, black and white races adorns the south entrance.

There are many services on the Concourse level of the building: bookshops, retail stores and restaurants. A passport office is located on the mezzanine.

■ THE MUSEUM OF MODERN ART★★★

A pleasant place to relax or meet a friend, the Museum of Modern Art is a particularly refreshing haven during the hot summer days thanks to its delightful outdoor sculpture garden and its cafeteria. But above all it is the museum's masterworks of the visual arts that attract, along with an intellectual elite, a colorful range of visitors.

The Museum. – Founded in 1929 by seven private citizens, the Museum of Modern Art has since developed into an institution that is world famous for the comprehensive survey of modern art it offers.

The museum was, in its early days, housed in a few rooms of an office building. Its permanent home on 53rd Street was erected in 1939 after a number of donations, particularly the Lillie P. Bliss Bequest (235 works), had enriched the collections. The new building was designed by Philip Goodwin and Edward Durell Stone, and in 1964 two wings, the work of the architect Philip Johnson, were added.

More recently, in 1979, MOMA embarked on a large-scale program of renovation and construction which has more than doubled its gallery space and expanded its visitor services. The major feature of the project was the construction of a mixed-use building to include the new 6-story Museum West Wing, designed by Cesar Pelli. Another feature, a spacious Garden Hall with a 4-story wall of glass looking out onto the sculpture garden, allows sunlight to pour into the museum. The Garden Hall houses a system of escalators which provide visitors with easy access to the galleries on the floors above.

Rising on top of the West Wing is a 44-story residential tower, a private venture.

The Collections. – Although the first exhibit sponsored by the museum was intended to introduce the work of European Post-Impressionist painters, and featured artists such as Cézanne, Van Gogh, Seurat and Gauguin, the museum now embraces the entire range of the modern visual arts – not only painting and sculpture but also drawings, prints, architecture, industrial and graphic design, photography and film. As one of the first art museums to recognize the cinema as an art form, the museum is, in addition, a major preservation center for film. Its archive, the outstanding collection in the U.S., consists of films ranging from European, Third World and Hollywood, to films by American independent filmmakers. The Film Department has the use of the museum's two theaters and is capable of presenting 30 screenings a week.

The many trends in modern art since 1880 are illustrated by more than 100 000 works of art. These include 3 500 paintings and sculptures, over 3 000 design objects, 40 000 prints, 6 000 drawings, 6 000 design objects, architectural models and drawings and examples of graphic design, 20 000 photographs and 9 000 films. Obviously, only a fraction (about 30 %) of this great collection can be shown at any one time, so that the works on display are changed frequently: only the most representative are on permanent display.

The museum organizes significant temporary exhibits, drawing upon its own collections as well as outside loans. Many of these are then shown throughout the United States and abroad.

VISIT *Allow about 2 1/2 hours*

Open 11 AM to 6 PM (9 PM Thursdays); closed Wednesdays and December 25; $6.00, children under 16 accompanied by an adult free. Admission includes gallery talks and film screenings; request information and pick up a plan of the museum at the Information Desk. July and August concerts (free) are held in the Sculpture Garden Friday and Saturday evenings. The main entrance is at 11 West 53rd Street. The garden entrance is at 14 West 54th Street.

Ground Floor. – The bookstore, the information desk, the Garden Café (a public cafeteria), and large temporary exhibits will be found here. Galleries to the left of the Garden Hall display changing exhibitions; to the right is the Video Gallery. The lobby opens onto the **Abby Aldrich Rockefeller Sculpture Garden.**

Sculpture Garden. – The architect Philip Johnson designed the garden (1953), which has been renewed as part of the recent renovation program. The garden serves as a setting for the museum's sculptures, which are shown to best advantage outdoors: they can be studied from different angles, and their appearance changes with the natural light. Marble paved walks, reflecting pools, trees and terraces add to the charm.

Various schools are represented: romanticism by Rodin *(Monument to Balzac)*; classicism by Maillol *(The River)*; expressionism and abstraction by Henry Moore *(Family Group; Large Torso: Arch)* and Picasso's *She Goat:* her belly is made of a basket.

Upper Floors. – These floors house the museum's permanent collections: **Painting and Sculpture** (second and third floors), **Photography** (second floor), **Prints** and **Drawings** (third floor) and **Architecture and Design** (fourth floor). Historical continuity is clearly apparent in the installation of the galleries which is roughly chronological. The following description outlines the different schools and trends of modern art, and gives a general idea of the scope of the museum's collections.

Post Impressionism to Early Expressionism. – *Galleries 1, 2, 3.* At the turn of the century, the fluidity of the Impressionist palette gave way to clearly defined shapes. Post-Impressionists include such artists as the Pointillist Seurat, who uses dots or rectangles instead of the fluid palette of the Impressionists, as seen in his luminous landscapes *(Evening at Honfleur; Port-en-Bessin, Entrance to the Harbor).* Also included are the visionary Van Gogh *(The Starry Night, Hospital Corridor at St Rémy),* and that lucid observer of contemporary mores Toulouse-Lautrec *(La Goulue at the Moulin Rouge).*

The "Douanier" Rousseau was hailed as the greatest of naive painters *(The Dream),* pure in heart and dazzled by nature. Cézanne's firm, structural design and intense search for visual effects were to become a source of inspiration to the Cubists *(Still Life with Apples).*

The "Nabis" or Prophets, proclaim that "a painting is essentially a surface covered with colors arranged in a certain order." This idea is developed in the works of Gauguin *(Moon and Earth),* Vuillard *(Embroidering by the window)* and Bonnard *(The Breakfast Room).* De Chirico's *Nostalgia of the Infinite (gallery 18)* and Ensor's *Masks Confronting Death* are already expressionistic interpretations of these artists' tormented world.

Cubism. – *Galleries 4, 6, 7, 8.* Pioneers of this movement were Picasso and Braque, from 1907 to 1914, followed by Léger and Juan Gris from 1914 to 1921. Cubists try to interpret the sensation which the object creates rather than its physical image; they dissociate the elements of the objects and rearrange the fragments in new, often geometrical order; front and profile views may appear simultaneously. This conception opened a new era in art as seen in Picasso's *Les Demoiselles d'Avignon.*

Picasso's colorful, clownish *Three Musicians* contrasts with Léger's *Three Musicians,* a highly decorative but severe composition; it is interesting to compare too, the full rounded forms of Picasso's *Three Women* with the machine–like figures in Léger's *Three Women.* Braque's *Man with a Guitar* is outstanding for the economy of means used. Léger's *The City* evokes the dynamics of the modern city – a maze of pillars, cubes, cones and pipes.

Expressionists. – *Galleries 10, 11.* Anxiety and despair, but also compassion and social commentary, mark these painters who ask the observer to partake in their emotional experience. Rouault's haunting *Christ Mocked by Soldiers (Gallery 16)* is reminiscent of stained glass. The German School is represented by Nolde *(Christ Among the Children)* and by Kirchner in his boldly colored street scenes *(Street Berlin).* The style of the Austrian Kokoschka is shown in his powerful portraits and self-portraits. A masterwork by Lehmbruck is the sculpture *Kneeling Woman.*

Fauvism and Late Cubism. – The Fauvists delight in pure color, using a striking juxtaposition of colors to intensify their compositions. Champions of this early 20C movement were Matisse, Derain *(Bathers),* Vlaminck *(Autumn)* and Van Dongen.

Cubist fantasy appears in collages, the method introduces fragments of paper and cloth into painting, as in *The Breakfast* by Gris.

I and the Village reveals Chagall's poetic imagination.

De Stijl, Purism. – *Gallery 13.* The principles of De Stijl, advocating the purification of art, were laid down in a journal of the same name founded by a group of artists in Holland in 1917. Adopting a non-representational style, Van Doesburg and Mondrian *(Broadway Boogie Woogie)* moved toward complete abstraction which they achieved in their compositions reduced to horizontal and vertical lines in natural and neutral colors.

Monet: Water Lilies. – *Gallery 5.* Forms tend to dissolve in an extraordinary interplay of colors. Although Monet attempted to capture every nuance of the effect of light on the flowers floating on the water – admire the delicate shading of the hues – here he appears as a forerunner of abstract art.

Futurism. – *Gallery 12.* Italian futurism appeared on the art scene in 1909. The futurists stress movement in their visions of the dynamic forces of the machine age. Two followers of this movement are Boccioni *(The City Rises, Dynamism of a Soccer Player)* and Severini.

Matisse. – *Gallery 14.* Matisse, who started out as a Fauve, later moved toward the use of more subtle colors and simple figures set against flat surfaces. Among his early masterpieces are *The Blue Window, The Red Studio, Dance* and *The Piano Lesson.* The large decorative Matisse cutout *The Swimming Pool* is in gallery 28 and serves as an introduction to important works of the New York School and the Abstract Expressionists. Note, too, *Memory of Oceania (gallery 29)* one of the artist's last works.

Geometric Abstract Art - The Blue Rider. – *Gallery 15.* In the early 20C Delaunay *(Simultaneous Contrasts: Sun and Moon)* and some painters linked with "Der Blaue Reiter" (The Blue Rider) laid the foundations for Geometric Abstract Art. The followers of this movement reject realism, claiming that art should move by the effect of forms and color alone. Malevich, a member of the Russian Constructivist group, which also included Lissitzky and Rodchenko, created rigorously geometrical abstractions *(White on White-gallery 9).* Kandinsky *(No. 198, No. 199, No. 200, No. 201),* more spontaneous, abandoned himself in imaginative abstract color compositions; and Paul Klee created poetic fantasies in a world peopled by humans, animals and symbols *(Actor's Mask, Mask of Fear).*

Latin Americans. – Human suffering and social protest are the themes powerfully expressed by the Mexicans Siqueiros *(Echo of a Scream),* Tamayo *(Animals),* and Orozco *(Zapatistas).*

Primitives. – The Primitive painters Hirschfeld *(Girl in Mirror),* Pickett *(Manchester Valley)* and Seraphine *(Three in Paradise),* their inspiration independent of any particular movement, startle by their colorful figurative style.

Americans. – Powerful interpreters of the contemporary American scene are Hopper *(House by the Railroad),* Marin, Joseph Stella and Shahn. Note the popular *Christina's World (gallery 23)* by Andrew Wyeth.

Dada. – *(galleries 17, 18).* Disillusioned members of the 1914-18 war generation, the Dadaists denied all esthetic and moral value in art. Their works present parodies of reality and essentially aim to shock the public. Jean Arp in Zurich, Duchamp (The Passage from Virgin to Bride) and Picabia (M'Amenez'Y) in New York were exponents of "Dada," a movement which also attracted Schwitters and Max Ernst *(Two Children are Threatened by a Nightingale).*

Surrealism and its Affinities. – Dedicated to the projection of the subconscious and dreams, Surrealists tend to create fantasy objects with little reference to nature (Arp, *Enak's Tears (Terrestrial Forms);* Mirò, *(gallery 20)* The Hunter, Hirondelle/Amour), or they tend to paint realistic scenes set in hallucinating surroundings, such as Magritte *(The False Mirror),* Delvaux *(Phases of the Moon)* and Dali *(The Persistence of Memory-gallery 22).* Also drawn from the unconscious are the emotionally charged configurations by Gorky. An artist of great originality, the French Dubuffet *(Joe Bousquet in Bed-gallery 27),* uses childlike images as satirical commentary in his textured compositions.

Abstract Expressionism. – *Galleries 29, 30.* This art form emerged in the 1940s as an American, largely non-representational movement. Jackson Pollock, known for his "Action Painting" (Number 1), dripped paint on his canvases to form rhythmically intertwined lines. The structural arrangements by Kline and Motherwell are striking in their boldly dramatic style while Rothko uses subtle color changes to define geometric shapes. Tobey reveals a lyrical element in his art. Reinhardt's *Abstract Painting* is a square composed of nine smaller black squares of varying intensity. Unlike his peers, Willem de Kooning uses the human figure *(Woman, I)* in his tense and turbulent paintings.

Pop Art. – A descendent of "Dada," Pop Art advocates introducing into art the most ordinary objects of daily life: tin cans, cigarette butts, tires, photographs to create easily recognizable and often witty images. Notice the Warhol *(Gold Marilyn Monroe-gallery 32)* and Lichtenstein *(Girl with Ball-gallery 31).*

Sculpture. – Works of sculpture are displayed in the garden, in the Garden Hall, and in the galleries. The collection includes representative works of a number of artists such as Oldenburg, Rodin *(St John the Baptist),* Nadelman and Brancusi *(Bird in Space).* You may also see the abstract sculptures of Henry Moore, Duchamp-Villon and Calder, the haunting, elongated figures by Giacometti, and constructions created by Louise Nevelson.

Photography. – The collection covers the history of photography from its beginning in 1839, to the present. Master photographers Steichen, Weston, Stieglitz and others along with contemporary artists are represented.

Prints and Illustrated Books. – The Prints galleries present the art of printmaking from Degas and Van Gogh to the artists of today. Works by major artists such as Munch, Picasso and Johns are featured in special exhibitions illustrating the history of 20C prints.

Drawings. – The diverse collection of 20C drawings is particularly strong in its holdings of Dada, Surrealism, School of Paris, early Russian avant-garde, and historical and contemporary American drawings, with significant works by Ernst, Dubuffet and Klee.

Architecture and Design. – Drawings and building models by Mies van der Rohe, Le Corbusier, Frank Lloyd Wright *(Falling Water)* and others, trace the development of modern architecture. Examples of beautiful and innovative design of this century are illustrated in furniture, household appliances, tools, posters, etc. and an automobile and a helicopter; note on the fourth floor the helicopter designed by Arthur Young.

GREEN TOURIST GUIDES

Picturesque scenery, buildings
Attractive routes
Touring programmes
Plans pf towns and buildings.

Distance: 3 1/4 miles – Time: allow two days (including visits to museums).

■ DAY 1 – FROM THE EMPIRE STATE BUILDING TO GRAND ARMY PLAZA (59th STREET)

It can never become tiresome strolling on Fifth Avenue, one of New York's major shopping thoroughfares. The striking views of principal skyscrapers, the frequently changing shopwindow displays, and the elegance and beauty of chic New Yorkers contribute to make it one of the most fascinating walks in the city. *It is preferable to follow this itinerary on a weekday morning, as some of the buildings are closed on Saturdays and Sundays.*

A BIT OF HISTORY

Millionaires Galore. – Laid out gradually, beginning in 1824, Fifth Avenue was becoming a more fashionable residential section than Broadway by 1850. About 350 town houses were built there following the Civil War. Each cost at least $20 000, a small fortune at the time.

By 1880 the avenue was a busy and noisy thoroughfare, teeming with carriages and fine horse-drawn omnibuses. Scattered among the mansions were private clubs and brownstones, more modest but still extremely comfortable. On the corner of Fifth Avenue and 34th Street, A.T. Stewart, a partner in several department stores, built his fancy marble home. Across 34th Street was the huge brownstone of William Astor. His wife, "the beautiful Mrs Astor" – the former Caroline Schermerhorn – a descendant of an old Dutch family, presided over New York society. In the 1890s her nephew, William Waldorf Astor, replaced his palace next door by the Waldorf Hotel, an act of vengeance upon his aunt, from whom his wife had been unable to wrest the leadership of New York society. He then left to live

(From engraving, Museum of the City of New York.)

Fifth Avenue in 1900.

in England. Within less than a year, Mrs Astor had decided to move north to Fifth Avenue and 65th Street, and by 1897 her son, John Jacob Astor, had built the Astoria Hotel next to the Waldorf. They were operated together, despite the family tiff, to the benefit of both branches until 1929, when they made way for the Empire State Building. *(See p 74 for the "new" Waldorf Astoria.)* Further north, the Vanderbilt dynasty established itself around 50th Street – in pseudo-Gothic and simulated Renaissance splendor.

The Talk of the Town. – In the spring of 1883, the aristocracy of New York society was in a dither. William K. Vanderbilt, the grandson of the famed "Commodore" *(p 82)*, was planning a ball in his Renaissance palace. 18C French court costumes were required dress, and the dances to be performed would be of the same period. The richest young belles of New York, including Miss Astor, rehearsed tirelessly to perfect graceful curtsies and complicated steps.

However, when the invitations were sent out she was not included. Her mother, a descendant of an "old family," had snubbed the " nouveau riche" Mrs Vanderbilt by not including her in her circle of friends.

The story, nevertheless, has a happy ending. Mrs Astor sacrificed her pride on the altar of motherly-love, and at last invited Mrs Vanderbilt to her home. The precious invitation arrived in time and Miss Astor could cavort in her period gown, dancing the minuet and the gavotte to music by Rameau.

The Marriage Mart. – Later, other balls caused nearly as much excitement. In 1892, Mrs Astor launched the term "the 400" by sending exactly 400 invitations to a ball. Apparently she thought there were only 400 persons worth knowing in New York, but it was also true that her art gallery-ballroom could accommodate only that number in proper style. You can imagine the anguish of those who were not invited!

Fashionable balls at the Waldorf Astoria were often graced by young European aristocrats whose titles were more brilliant than their fortunes. The results were sometimes spectacular: in one year, 1895, Consuelo Vanderbilt married the Duke of Marlborough, Pauline Whitney the grandson of the Marquess of Anglesey, and Anna Gould the greatest dandy of them all: Boni de Castellane.

SOME BOOKSTORES ON FIFTH AVENUE

Barnes & Noble Book Store	600 *Fifth Avenue*
Doubleday Book Shops	673 *Fifth Avenue*
	724
Brentano's	597 *Fifth Avenue*

Empire State Building ★★★

Rising vertically with a grace, elegance and strength that have made it one of the finest and most breathtaking skyscrapers ever built, the Empire State Building has remained for over half a century the primary feature of the Manhattan skyline.

The building is a landmark visible for miles, the slender TV antenna atop its tower, shining at a height of 1 454ft (the building itself measures 1 250ft) above the city.

Named for New York, the "Empire State," its 102 stories make it the third tallest building in the nation after the Sears Roebuck building, Chicago and the twin towers of the World Trade Center (p 83).

The view from the top is so impressive that it deserves two visits: by day, to observe the layout of New York; and then again in the evening, to enjoy the spectacle of the city's lights.

The Construction. – Less than two years after the first excavations in October 1929, the building was opened in May 1931. Work progressed at a hectic pace; at times, the building rose more than a floor each day. There are only two stories of foundations, but 60 000 tons of steel beams (enough for a double-track railroad from New York to Baltimore) also support the tower. These were in place within three days of their production in Pittsburgh.

At first the public was apprehensive about the stability of the building, but it has proved to be sound.

Empire State and Eiffel Tower.

Specialists intended to use the last floor as a mooring platform for dirigibles, however, the project was abandoned after one trial which nearly resulted in a catastrophe. Seventy-three elevators serve the 102 floors, and 5 acres of windows are washed once a month.

It takes half an hour to walk down the 1 860 steps.

The 203ft television antenna installed in 1985 measures 10ft less than the antenna it replaced. It is a mere 22 stories high! A beacon light at the top of the antenna serves as a warning signal for aircraft. The top 30 stories of the building are illuminated from dusk to midnight. They are turned off on foggy and cloudy nights during the spring and fall migratory bird seasons. Otherwise, the birds might be confused by the diffused light and fly into the building.

The Empire State cost almost $40 000 000 to build. Fifteen thousand people work there, and 35 000 visit it daily. A battery of 150 men and women wield the vacuum cleaner on off hours.

Visit. – Before going inside, walk a few yards along East 34th or 33rd Street, to obtain the dizzy effect of perspective.

Panoramic view from the Observatory ★★★. – *Enter the ticket office from Fifth Avenue. The Observatory is open 9:30 AM to Midnight; last ticket sold at 11:30 PM; hours vary December 24, December 25 and January 1; $3.50. Consult the visibility notice before buying your tickets.*

An average of 2 500 000 people visit every year. The express elevator will take you to the 80th floor in less than a minute. Take a second elevator to the 86th floor Observatory (snack bar, souvenir stands). Here a rectangular open platform permits you to enjoy, on a clear day, a magnificent **view** for 80 miles in each direction.

You may shudder to think that one July day, in 1945, a bomber crashed into the building at the level of the 78th and 79th floors.

For the full treatment, we advise you to take another elevator to the circular upper observatory (102nd floor) which is glass enclosed.

From 34th to 40th Streets (New York Public Library)

The section of Fifth Avenue between 34th and 40th Streets is bordered by several large department stores such as B. Altman and Co, famous for its floors of fashions and fine foods, and Lord and Taylor, known for fine clothing and its gaily decorated window displays during the Christmas season.

As you reach West 40th Street, the New York Public Library comes into view on your left.

New York Public Library ★★

The New York Public Library was founded in 1895 to house the Astor Library, Lenox Library and Tilden Trust all under one roof.

The library was opened in May 1911 with President Taft saying "this day crowns a work of national importance."

The famous marble lions, often called Patience and Fortitude, guard the entrance of the imposing Beaux Arts style building designed by Carrère and Hastings.

Behind the library is **Bryant Park** (p 46).

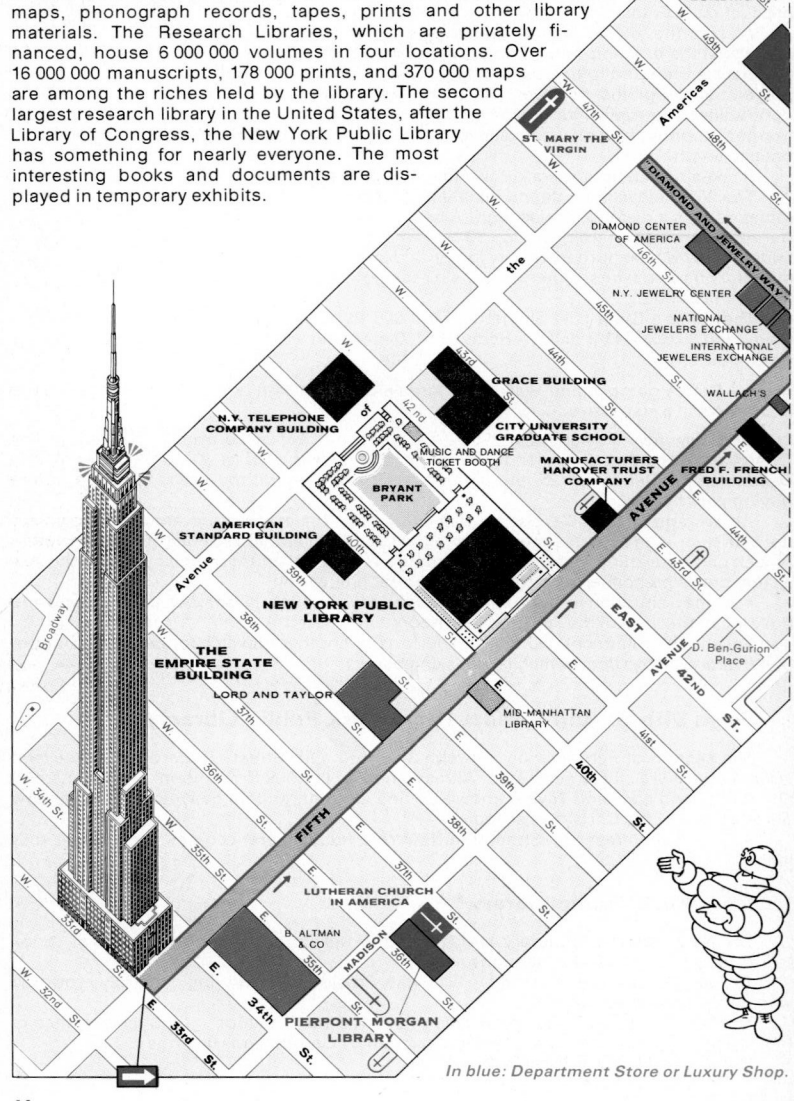

(From photo A. Devaney, New York.)

One of the Public Library lions.

A Popular Promenade. – In 1853 the first World's Fair in New York attracted crowds to the Murray Hill area, to gaze at three strange buildings. The first, on Fifth Avenue, dated back to 1842. Resembling a fort, it was topped by a walkway. Strollers could admire a large pool, for this pseudo-fort contained a reservoir supplied by water from Croton Lake in Westchester County. **The Croton Distribution Reservoir** remained in service until 1899, and was eventually replaced by the New York Public Library, completed in 1911.

The **Crystal Palace** was built for the New York Fair in imitation of the London Crystal Palace, built two years earlier. The iron and glass framework sheltered a large assortment of works of art and industrial products. A fire destroyed it in 1858, leaving the open space that would become Bryant Park.

Set back from 42nd Street, a pointed tower of timber braced with iron rose over 300ft high, a predecessor of the Eiffel Tower. The **Latting Observatory,** as it was called, had three levels of wooden platforms. From the highest one, there was a superb view of New York, with Croton Reservoir and the Crystal Palace in the foreground. The Latting Observatory, too, was short lived as it burned down in 1856.

Collections and Organization. – The Research and Branch Libraries contain over 9 000 000 books and over 22 000 000 manuscripts, maps, phonograph records, tapes, prints and other library materials. The Research Libraries, which are privately financed, house 6 000 000 volumes in four locations. Over 16 000 000 manuscripts, 178 000 prints, and 370 000 maps are among the riches held by the library. The second largest research library in the United States, after the Library of Congress, the New York Public Library has something for nearly everyone. The most interesting books and documents are displayed in temporary exhibits.

In blue: Department Store or Luxury Shop.

44

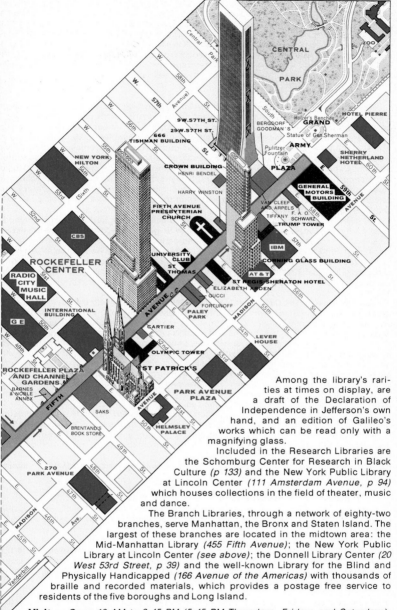

Among the library's rarities at times on display, are a draft of the Declaration of Independence in Jefferson's own hand, and an edition of Galileo's works which can be read only with a magnifying glass.

Included in the Research Libraries are the Schomburg Center for Research in Black Culture *(p 133)* and the New York Public Library at Lincoln Center *(111 Amsterdam Avenue, p 94)* which houses collections in the field of theater, music and dance.

The Branch Libraries, through a network of eighty-two branches, serve Manhattan, the Bronx and Staten Island. The largest of these branches are located in the midtown area: the Mid-Manhattan Library *(455 Fifth Avenue)*; the New York Public Library at Lincoln Center *(see above)*; the Donnell Library Center *(20 West 53rd Street, p 39)* and the well-known Library for the Blind and Physically Handicapped *(166 Avenue of the Americas)* with thousands of braille and recorded materials, which provides a postage free service to residents of the five boroughs and Long Island.

Visit. – *Open 10 AM to 8:45 PM (5:45 PM Thursdays, Fridays and Saturdays); closed Sundays and holidays.*

The grand, white marble entrance hall is on the first floor. Major temporary exhibits are held in **Gottesman Hall,** a handsome Beaux Arts room enhanced by graceful marble arches and a carved oak ceiling; in the south corridor is the richly paneled **DeWitt Wallace Periodical Room** containing a series of thirteen murals by Richard Haas. Take the elevator at the far north end of the corridor to the right, up to the third floor.

Along the walls are prints illustrating early views of the Americas. An exhibition room *(no 318)* displays interesting items

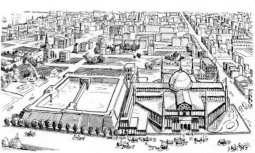

(From engraving, Museum of the City of New York.)

Site of the Public Library in 1850.

from the Berg Collection of English and American literature; on the walls are a number of portraits by noted American artists and printmakers. Rotating exhibits from the library's special collections are presented in the **Salomon Room,** a 19C picture gallery. Among the paintings on permanent display note the group of five portraits of George Washington on the west wall. The large central hall, **McGraw Rotunda,** is decorated with wood paneling and murals depicting the story of the Recorded Word. Facing the Salomon Room is the **Public Catalog Room** which consists of 800 retrospective volumes with 10 000 000 entries. Beyond are the main reading rooms which cover a half-acre.

Bryant Park

Bryant Park, a broad green space between 40th and 42nd Streets on the Avenue of the Americas, is named for William C. Bryant. Bryant, author of the poem "Thanatopsis," was editor and part owner of the *New York Evening Post,* an influential paper during the Civil War. In the summer the park is an oasis of coolness in sweltering Manhattan.

At lunch time, employees of nearby offices come to relax and enjoy concerts of live music and, on occasion, art exhibits. Passersby are also attracted by the flower vendors, bookstalls and the snack kiosks which operate during the warmer weather. At the Music and Dance Ticket Booth *(p 76)* on the 42nd Street side of the park, half price tickets to music and dance events *(not theater)* are sold the day of performance. *During the current program of construction and restoration the park is closed; reopening in 1991. The Music and Dance Ticket Booth continues to operate throughout this period.*

At 40 West 40th Street is the **American Standard Building** designed by Raymond Hood. Inspired by the Gothic tradition and adorned with gold terra-cotta trim, this was New York City's first skyscraper to be declared a landmark.

Two striking buildings can be seen from Bryant Park, to the west is the streamlined form of the **New York Telephone Company Building** with alternating columns of white marble and dark tinted glass. To the north, at 1114 Avenue of the Americas, is the **Grace Building,** the hyperbolic lines of its base merging without break into a 50-story tower of travertine and tinted glass.

Continue north. The **City University Graduate School,** at 33 West 42nd Street is one of 20 individual educational units within the City University of New York. The Mall, a pedestrian arcade running from 42nd to 43rd Street between Fifth Avenue and Avenue of the Americas is the site of art exhibitions and concerts *(free of charge).* At the corner of 43rd Street is a branch of **Manufacturers Hanover Trust Company,** one of the first banks constructed in glass designed by Skidmore, Owings & Merrill. For the public, accustomed to thick-walled buildings of masonry, it was surprising to see the interior of a bank so visible to passersby. One can even see the door of the vault through one of the windows. The bank is decorated with Macassar ebony furniture and Italian marble floors. The abstract sculpture may be more controversial – especially the spectacular composition, by Harry Bertoia, of metallic strips hanging from the ceiling.

Further up the avenue, as you approach the corner of 45th Street, look up to catch a glimpse of the attractive multicolored faience decoration on the upper stories of the **Fred F. French Building** *(551 Fifth Avenue).* Constructed of masonry, ornate, solid in appearance and rising 38 floors from a series of stories set back from the street, the French building is typical of the tall buildings of the 1920s.

At the southeast corner of 46th Street you will pass Wallach's, specializing in quality men's clothing and ladies sportswear.

Diamond and Jewelry Way ★

As you walk along 47th Street try to imagine that some 80 % of the diamond wholesale trade in America is transacted within this 750ft block. A bewildering variety of languages – Spanish and Yiddish interspersed with Flemish – serve to discuss carat, cut, color and clarity. The street is lined with shops, notably the International Jewelers Exchange, the National Jewelers Exchange, the Diamond Center of America, and the New York Jewelry Center, which display precious stones; but much of the trade is carried on in booths located on the upper floors and in the rear of the buildings. A sophisticated security system protects the dealers from unwelcome intruders.

The merchants carry their precious bounty in suitcases, unobtrusive packages or in their coat pockets. The exchanges take place either right on the sidewalk or in one of the two clubs; major transactions may be sealed simply by a handshake. Offenders transgressing this honor code are reportedly blacklisted throughout the diamond world.

Back to Fifth Avenue, between 48th and 49th Streets, is the Barnes and Noble Book Store, selling bestsellers at discount prices. Brentano's Book Store, across the avenue, has retained its handsome turn-of-the-century cast-iron facade and genteel interior.

Across 49th Street is Saks Fifth Avenue, an exclusive department store offering designer collections for men and women.

St Patrick's Cathedral ★★

The Roman Catholic Cathedral of New York, St Patrick's, is dedicated to the patron saint of the Irish, heavily represented in the city. The festivities of St Patrick's Day *(p 17)* demonstrate their veneration for the apostle of Ireland and even more for the "ould sod."

The cathedral was started in 1858 and opened in 1879, but its completion did not take place until 1906. At that time, churchgoers complained that it was too far out in the country, but it is now in the heart of midtown thanks to the northward growth of the city.

Designed by James Renwick, the cathedral was built of white marble and stone. Its Gothic architecture is patterned after the cathedral of Cologne, in particular the towers which rise over 330ft. However, the slender balanced proportions seem rather dwarfed by its neighbor across the street, the Olympic Tower, in whose glass wall the church is mirrored.

Three portals with fine bronze sculpted doors open into the nave, illuminated by stained glass windows of the Gothic type, with particularly intense blues. 30ft pillars support the cross-ribbed Gothic arches which rise 110ft above the nave. Note also the elegantly designed baldachin over the main altar, and the monumental organ.

Beyond 51st Street rise the 51 stories of **Olympic Tower**. This elegant brown tinted glass building houses shops, offices and luxury apartments in its upper stories. H. Stern Jewellers on the ground floor, enjoys a worldwide reputation for fine aquamarines, tourmalines, topazes, amethysts, emeralds and other colored gemstones primarily from Brazil. The indoor arcade **Olympic Place,** is a delightful public space with a reflecting waterfall, palm trees and plants, and a snack bar. *Entrance off of Fifth Avenue.*

On the same block is the French jewelry firm, Cartier, which acquired the building it presently occupies in 1917.

Across the street, at 666, the 39-story **Tishman Building (666)**★ was an original architectural efforts when it was built in 1957, with its facade of embossed aluminum panels. The inside is equally imaginative, with its unusual ceiling composed of thin wavy hanging strips, and a cascade fountain on one wall. On the top floor, a restaurant and lounge, "Top of the Sixes," offers a magnificent view over most of Manhattan.

St Thomas Church★

Open 7 AM to 6 PM, Saturdays 9 AM to 5 PM, Sundays 7 AM to 5:30 PM (2 PM June through September). Tours (time: 20 min) following 11 AM Sunday service. At other times by arrangement with the verger.

St Thomas Episcopal Church was completed in 1913 in French Flamboyant Gothic Revival style. Amidst the wealth of statues and delicate tracery on the facade are carved the words "Thou art the King of Glory, O Christ." In the middle of the portal, St Thomas welcomes the worshippers. Six of the apostles flank him, three on each side of the doors. The other apostles are arrayed centrally overhead in the tympanum. Below them are bas-reliefs of the legend of St Thomas. To the left of the main portal is the narrow "Brides' Entrance," decorated with symbolically joined hands.

On entering the nave you will be struck by the **reredos**★ of Dunville stone which rises to a height of 80 ft above the altar. Spotlighted, it forms a lighter contrast to the darker vault. Numerous recesses shelter statues of Christ, the Virgin Mary, the Apostles, and Saints of all denominations. After this highlight, the rest of the decoration and furnishings recede into the background but you should also notice the stained glass windows, in deep reds and blues, the pulpit and the sculptured organ case.

Organ recitals October through May Sundays 5:15 PM; October through May full choir and music Tuesdays and Thursdays 5:30 PM, Wednesdays 12:10 PM and Sundays 11 AM and 4 PM.

Opposite St Thomas Church, on the east side of Fifth Avenue, is the sleek stainless steel and glass exterior of Fortunoff, a 4-story jewelry and silverware emporium; next door is the Italian fashion and shoe boutique, Gucci. Between 54th and 55th Streets, adjacent to a second Gucci shop, is the well-known beauty and fashion salon of Elizabeth Arden. Here you will note, across the avenue, the imposing **University Club** (1899) designed by McKim, Mead and White in the Italian Renaissance style; carved into the building's granite exterior are the shields of major American universities. On the ground floor of the ornate Beaux Arts **St Regis-Sheraton Hotel,** will be found several specialty shops.

Fifth Avenue Presbyterian Church

One of the last churches built in brownstone *(p 30)*, the "Fifth Avenue Presbyterian" was built in 1875. The sanctuary, which has a seating capacity of 1 800, is noted for its magnificent organ casing as well as intricately carved ash-wood pulpit.

The southwest corner of 56th Street is occupied by the small Renaissance palace of the jeweler Harry Winston, whose specialty is diamonds and precious stones.

Standing, opposite, is the **Corning Glass Building**, New York City headquarters of one of the world's leading producers of specialty glass, including Steuben crystal. Built in 1959, the 28-story building is a handsome example of the skyscraper of the 50s and 60s, with its tinted glass exterior, neat, trim lines, and outdoor plaza with reflecting pool. The Steuben shop is on the ground floor. Here you will find exhibitions of new or historical designs, and examples of the American crystal often chosen as state gifts.

Trump Tower★

Rising 58 stories above street level is the exuberant, bronze mirror silhouette of Trump Tower (1983), a luxurious mixed-use structure containing commercial space, condominium apartments and retail stores. Designed by Der Scutt for Swanke, Hayden, Connell and Partners, this glass-sheathed tower, with its myriad of tiny setbacks and highly reflective exterior, is typical of the lively, innovative flair of the skyscraper style of the 1980s. Inside, the 6-story **atrium**★, an elegant pink marble shopping emporium with an 80ft high waterfall cascading down one side, has an array of fine boutiques and specialty shops such as Asprey and Charles Jourdan. From the atrium there is multi-level access to Bonwit Teller, the exclusive store for men and women.

Continue to the corner of 57th Street where you will notice Tiffany, the jewelry store, with its exquisite window displays. Inside, on the far left wall from the Fifth Avenue entrance, you may admire the **Tiffany Diamond,** a mere128 carats. On the same side of the avenue is the **Crown Building,** its château-like upper section richly embellished in 23 karat gold leaf; designed by Warren and Wetmore (1921) in the French Renaissance style, the building is named for the gilded crown at its pinnacle. I. Miller and Ferragamo, known for their fine shoes and leather accessories, occupy the street-level shops.

At 10 West 57th Street is Henri Bendel, the fashion store for the sophisticated shopper. Across the street from Bendel's rises the striking and controversial form of **9 West 57th Street ★** an elegant 50-story office building with tinted glass curtain walls and travertine edges. Unique in design and construction techniques, the building slopes down to plazas on 57th and 58th Streets. The use of travertine in the plazas is continued on the floors and walls of the lobby. The slightly distorted images of other buildings reflected in the sloping exterior walls produce unusual visual effects. Included in the project are a garage and a mini-park on 58th Street. The award-winning sculptured number nine sign on 57th Street was the work of Ivan Chermayeff. Before continuing, note the neighboring building, **29 West 57th Street**, adorned with a colorful sculpted relief of the French Cross of the *Légion d'Honneur*.

Located between 57th and 58th Streets, Bergdorf Goodman's is a bastion of haute couture. The jeweler's store Van Cleef and Arpels, close to Bergdorf Goodman, has a sparkling array of treasures, including the diamond tiara of the Empress Josephine.

On your way uptown stop, on the right, in the General Motors Building *(p 49)* to view the 28ft animated clock tower at the famous F.A.O. Schwarz toy store.

Admission prices and hours quoted in this guide
were accurate at the time of going to press

■ DAY 2 – FROM GRAND ARMY PLAZA (59th STREET) TO 86th STREET
(time includes the Frick Collection)

The section of Fifth Avenue bordering Central Park has long been New York's most prestigious residential area. Luxury apartment houses with spectacular views on the park, rise side by side with former mansions *(illustration p 50)*, most of which have now become museums, consulates, clubs or cultural institutions. The sidewalk is dotted with awnings, and uniformed doormen greet the residents of the skytop palaces as they step out of their chauffeur-driven limousines.

A BIT OF HISTORY

The Rush to the North. – During the last decade of the 19C, Fifth Avenue millionaires began to migrate from the 34th Street area toward the open space of Central Park. Here, massive stone mansions and palatial residences replaced the old-fashioned brownstones. The interiors were often decorated with tapestries and antique furniture acquired sometimes for a fortune in Europe, but sometimes for a song.

The boldest of these wealthy "migrants," Andrew Carnegie, moved all the way to 90th Street, while the haughty Mrs Astor *(p 42)* stopped at 65th Street. Nearby lived the families of the financier Gould (67th Street) and the Whitneys (at 68th and 72nd Streets). W.A. Clark, the copper king, built an edifice 150ft high at

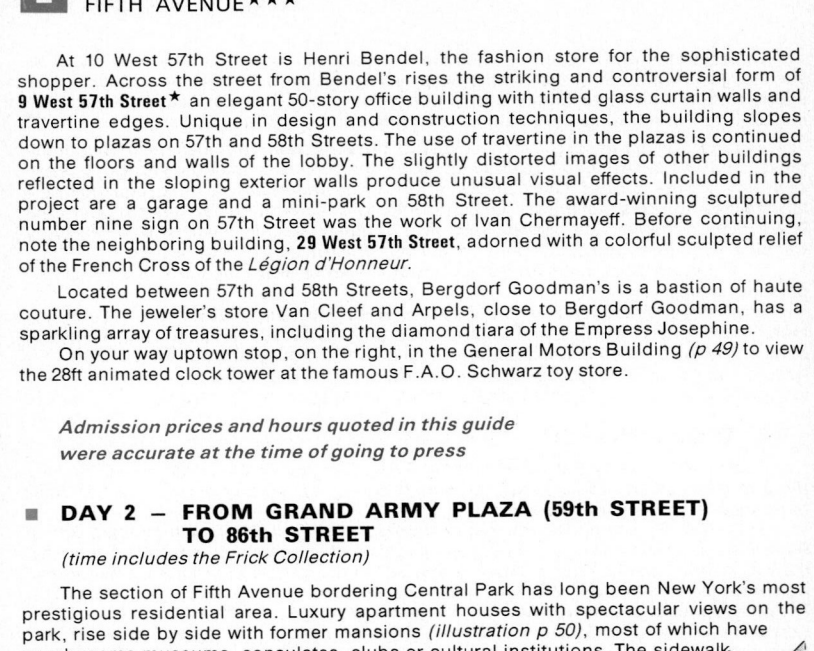

the corner of 77th Street. These magnates of finance flourished in their mini-palaces until the crash of 1929 forced a number of them to sell, making way for apartment houses.

Grand Army Plaza ★★

This square, a large and flowered breathing space sometimes referred to as "the Plaza" by New Yorkers, marks the division between the Fifth Avenue of luxury shopping and the fashionable residential section.

(map labels) RESERVOIR — GUGGENHEIM MUSEUM — THE METROPOLITAN MUSEUM OF ART — YIVO INSTITUTE FOR JEWISH RESEARCH — PARK AVE SYNAGOGUE — E. 86th St. — PARK AVE. CHRISTIAN CHURCH — ST IGNATIUS — Park Avenue — 998 — E. 80th St. — UKRAINIAN INSTITUTE OF AMERICA — 972 — CENTRAL — N.Y.U. INSTITUTE OF FINE ARTS — Statue of Alice in Wonderland — FIFTH AVENUE — HARKNESS HOUSE — CONSERVATORY POND — FRENCH CONSULATE — Madison — WHITNEY MUSEUM OF AMERICAN ART — E. 72nd — MADISON AVE. PRESBYTERIAN CHURCH — ST JAMES — ASIA HOUSE — East Drive

You may be tempted to take a ride in a horse-drawn carriage in Central Park *(a 1/2 hour's ride costs $17; $5.00 for every additional 15 min).*

Grand Army Plaza is surrounded by luxurious and distinguished hotels like the Pierre, the Sherry-Netherland and the Plaza, all of the continental type. The **Plaza** ★ (1907), designed by Hardenberg in the French Renaissance style, is a New York institution of elegance and standing where coming-out parties and charity balls draw the cream of New York society.

In front of the hotel, on the Fifth Avenue side, stands the figure of Abundance atop the Pulitzer Fountain with its gracefully cascading waters.

The fountain was built in 1915 and named for Joseph Pulitzer, the newspaper publisher who founded the literary prizes bearing his name. Just to the north, notice General Tecumseh Sherman on horseback (casting presented at 1900 Paris Exposition), a statue by Augustus Saint-Gaudens.

At the corner of Fifth Avenue and East 60th St in the Doris C. Freedman Plaza, black granite and white marble **benches** are carved with the amusing aphorisms of Jenny Holzer.

Nearly as celebrated as the Plaza, the Hotel Savoy stood in front of it, across the square, until 1966 when it was replaced by the **General Motors Building,** a 50-story tower clad in white Georgia marble.

In front of the building, the sunken General Motors Plaza, adorned with flowerbeds and fountains, contains an outdoor restaurant and is lined by shops and a gallery.

(From photo William Hubbell.)

Central Park South — Horse-drawn carriages.

49

The main floor showrooms display General Motors automobiles *(open 9 AM – 10 AM Saturdays – to 6 PM; closed Sundays and holidays).*

Across the street stands the **Sherry-Netherland Hotel,** its graceful tower overlooking the park. Built at about the same time as the Hotel Savoy and the Pierre, the Sherry-Netherland has a small richly furbished lobby.

On the north corner of 60th Street, the **Metropolitan Club,** an Italian Renaissance palace, stands next to the **Hotel Pierre,** one of the most elegant in New York; some of the rooms are occupied by permanent guests, but the hotel retains its continental style. Built in 1930, it is a sort of "40-story Versailles," with 600 rooms, topped by a tower in the form of the royal chapel designed by Mansart and Robert de Cotte. Presenting a complete contrast in style is **660 Madison Avenue,** the glass-paneled headquarters of Hertz which rises behind the Pierre. Turn into **62nd Street,** where town houses along either side are exemplary of the 19C architectural treasures of the residential streets which link Fifth Avenue to Madison and Park. The **Fifth Avenue Synagogue**

(From photo John B. Bayley, New York.)

Fifth Avenue. — A former millionaire's mansion.

with its modern facade, is a reminder of New York's large Jewish community.

Continuing up Fifth Avenue, on the south corner of 64th Street note the Tuscan Renaissance mansion built in 1896 for the coal baron, Edward J. Berwind. The Berwinds enjoyed equally splendid surroundings in Newport, at their summer home, The Elms *(see Michelin Green Guide to New England).* On the same street, at 3 East 64th Street, is the **New India House,** headquarters of the Consulate of India and the Indian delegation to the United Nations. Built in 1903 by Warren and Wetmore (architects of Grand Central Terminal-*p 82*) as a private residence, its exterior is an expression of elegance from the lavish entranceway and tall second-storied windows, to the dormered mansard roof.

On the other side of the avenue, in Central Park, is the former New York State **Arsenal.** Behind it is the Central Park Zoo *(p 129).*

At **no 47-49, East 65th street** is the double house commissioned by Sara Delano Roosevelt as a wedding present for her son, the future president Franklin Delano Roosevelt and his wife Eleanor. In 1921 after Franklin was struck with polio, he returned to this house at no 49 to begin his recovery. The elder Mrs Roosevelt lived at no 47 until her death in 1941.

Temple Emanu-El★

Open 10 AM (noon Saturdays) to 5 PM, guide available. Worship services Fridays 5:15 PM (organ recital at 5 PM) and Saturdays at 10:30 AM.

Occupying the site of Mrs Astor's (Caroline Schermerhorn) mansion, the leading Reform synagogue in New York, and the largest in the United States, Temple Emanu-El (God with us) was built in 1929 in Byzantine Romanesque style. The majestic nave can welcome 2 500 worshippers. The ceiling, the marble columns in low relief and the great arch covered with mosaics are reminiscent of the basilicas of the Near East. Traditional Jewish symbols decorate the stained glass windows. At the end of the nave, the sanctuary harbors the tabernacle, or Holy Ark, which contains the Torah scrolls. On either side of the sanctuary are placed the menorahs (seven-branched candlesticks).

Frick Collection★ ★ ★

Continue on Fifth Avenue to 70th Street where Henry C. Frick's former mansion, surrounded by terraced flower-beds, now houses, one of the most beautiful private museums in the world. *See description Walk 4.*

Strolling leisurely past the lovely town houses on East 70th Street, cross Madison Avenue and at 725 Park Avenue is Asia House.

Asia House★

Open 11 AM to 6 PM, Sundays noon to 5 PM; closed Mondays, and major holidays; $2.00.

The Asia Society was founded in 1956 under the guidance of John D. Rockefeller 3rd to promote an increased understanding and appreciation of Asian cultures. Rotating exhibits from the Mr and Mrs John D. Rockefeller 3rd's collection of Asian art, given to the society in 1979, are presented in the society's 8-story rose-colored granite headquarters (1981) designed by Edward Larrabee Barnes. The building houses an auditorium, library and offices as well as three exhibit galleries.

In the main gallery, the rich wood paneling and velvet wall coverings create an intimate setting for the lively animated Indian bronzes, Chinese and Japanese ceramics, paintings and sculpture, and examples of Southeast Asian art on view. An adjacent gallery contains three-dimensional and low-relief stone sculptures from Southeast Asia.

On the ground floor, a room is reserved for loan exhibits on specific themes in Asian art.

Before leaving Asia House, note among the monumental sculptures in the foyer, the elephant-headed Ganesha (8C), Hindu god of good luck; and the Chinese tympanum (6C) incised in low relief, showing the Buddha preaching.

Return to Fifth Avenue and the French Consulate, located at 934 Fifth Avenue, in an Italian Renaissance mansion.

Just north of 75th Street, an attractive wrought iron fence protects **Harkness House,** a "Roman" palace with ornate sculptured cornices. It was built in 1907 for Edward S.Harkness, a partner of John D. Rockefeller in the then Standard Oil Company of New Jersey. Today Harkness House serves as headquarters of The Commonwealth Fund, a foundation concerned with issues related to American medicine and health care.

At the corner of Madison Avenue and 75th Street is the Whitney Museum.

Whitney Museum of American Art ★★

Open 11 AM to 5 PM, Tuesdays 1 to 8 PM, Sundays noon to 6 PM; closed Mondays and national holidays; $4.50, free Tuesday evenings.

Designed by Marcel Breuer and Hamilton Smith, the museum grew out of the Greenwich Village studio of sculptress and art collector, Gertrude Vanderbilt Whitney. Its stark, cantilevered exterior, a striking example of minimalism, rises above a sunken sculpture garden.

Dedicated to the advancement of contemporary American art, the museum holds one of the world's foremost collections of 20C American art with works by such painters as Hopper, de Kooning, Kelly, Gorky, Prendergast, Demuth and Motherwell and by such sculptors as Calder, Nevelson, Noguchi and David Smith.

Selections from the permanent collection are displayed on the third floor. In addition, the museum conducts a frequently changing exhibition program. A special feature, on the main floor, is Alexander Calder's miniature animated Circus with its dozens of performers and animals; adjacent is a film showing Calder's last complete circus performance.

The Film and Video Department presents works by independent American film and video artists.

Return to Fifth Avenue going up Madison Avenue and turning left onto 76th Street.

N.Y.U. Institute of Fine Arts.– The institute, a division of New York University, is located in the James B. Duke House, built for one of the founders of the American Tobacco Company. Architect Horace Trumbauer's neoclassical design for the house was modeled after a Louis XV style residence in Bordeaux.

The institute offers courses in art, architecture, conservation and museum training, to graduate students.

At **972** Fifth Avenue, the cultural and press services of the French Embassy are housed in the former Payne Whitney home, designed by McKim, Mead and White.

The turreted mansion on the southeast corner of 79th Street is the former Stuyvesant Mansion. Built in Louis XII style by a descendant of the last Dutch governor of New Amsterdam *(p 131),* it now serves as the home of the **Ukrainian Institute of America.**

On the northeast corner of 80th Street is one of the most luxurious apartment houses on the avenue. It was built in 1910 by McKim, Mead and White in Italian style. Many of the apartments have two living rooms, four bedrooms, a dining room, kitchen, pantry, and six servants' rooms. Others are duplexes.

Continuing to 82nd Street, you will arrive at the main entrance to the **Metropolitan Museum of Art ★★★** *(p 52)* which houses some of the richest collections of fine art in the world.

Further on, at the southeast corner of 86th Street, is the "Louis XIII" Miller Mansion. First occupied by William S. Miller, it later belonged to Mrs Cornelius Vanderbilt III, one of the last to leave the "50s." After her death in 1953, it became the headquarters of the **Yivo Institute for Jewish Research.**

We end this walk on the west side of fifth Avenue; from here you will notice two blocks to the north the novel outlines of the **Guggenheim Museum ★★** *(p 114).*

MICHELIN GUIDES

The Red Guides *(hotels and restaurants)*

Benelux - Deutschland - España Portugal - main cities Europe - France - Great Britain and Ireland - Italia

The Green Guides
(beautiful scenery, buildings and scenic routes)

Austria - Canada - England: The West Country - Germany - Greece - Italy - London - Mexico - Netherland - New England - New York City - Portugal - Rome - Scotland - Spain - Switzerland

and 9 guides on France

Brittany - Châteaux of the Loire - Dordogne - French Riviera - Ile-de-France - Normandy Cotentin - Normandy Seine Valley - Paris - Provence

Richly endowed and supported, the Metropolitan Museum of Art is a veritable encyclopedia of the arts covering 5 000 years, from prehistory to the 20C.

The Growth of the Museum. – Founded April 13, 1870 by a group of New Yorkers, members of the Union League Club, the museum first opened in temporary quarters in 1872. The core of the collections was a gift of antiquities from General di Cesnola, a former consul in Cyprus, and a group of 174 paintings most of which were Dutch or Flemish.

The Building. – In 1880 the museum moved to its present location, into a building designed by **Calvert Vaux** (who, with Frederick Law Olmsted, also designed Central Park). It was a modest red brick structure and stood on land belonging to the City of New York. It still forms part of the present building. The southwest wing and facade were built in 1888; the monumental Renaissance facade, in gray Indiana limestone, was designed by Richard Morris Hunt and completed in 1902, although the sculptural decoration has never been finished. The Fifth Avenue side wings were designed by McKim, Mead and White and completed in 1906. In 1965 the privately endowed Thomas J. Watson Library, founded in 1881, was finished (designed by Brown, Lawford & Forbes). On the occasion of the museum's centennial celebrations in 1970 a comprehensive architectural plan was devised to bring the entire museum to physical completion. This master plan included a series of new wings: The American Wing, The Lila Acheson Wallace Galleries of Egyptian Art, The Temple of Dendur in the Sackler Wing, the Michael C. Rockefeller Wing, and the Lila Acheson Wallace Wing for 20C Art, all of which are open to the public, and a wing to house the museum's collection of European Sculpture and Decorative Art *(under construction).* Since 1975 Roche, Dinkeloo and Associates have designed among other additions, the American Wing and the Michael C. Rockefeller Wing.

The Benefactors. – Since the initial gift of General di Cesnola the collection has grown considerably either from purchases or from bequests and gifts of wealthy benefactors: Astor, Morgan, Rockefeller, Marquand, Hearn, Altman, Bache, Lehman, Wrightsman.

A Few Statistics. – The museum attracted 4 million visitors in 1988. About a fourth of the collection is on display at any one time: 236 galleries; over 2 000 European paintings and 3 000 European drawings; over 1 000 000 prints; 4 000 objects of medieval art; 3 000 American paintings and statues; 4 000 musical instruments.

General Information. – The main entrance of the "Met" is on Fifth Avenue, across from 82nd Street. You will enter the Great Hall around which are grouped various services: checkrooms, information desk, art book and gift shops. (Metropolitan Museum Christmas cards are very popular; the museum also sells reproductions of ancient jewelry and ceramics.) Recorded tours of the collections and special exhibitions are available for rent at a desk in the Great Hall and near special exhibition areas.

Beyond the Greek and Roman galleries, at the far left of the building, in the south wing, are a cafeteria and restaurant.

Special exhibitions, lectures, films, gallery talks and concerts are among the cultural activities of the museum.

For recorded information ☎ : 535-7710, for other information ☎ : 879-5500.

Principal sections of the museum. – We have organized the museum's 19 departments into 16 selected headings. *See the plan opposite.*

American Wing ★★★ *(p 54)*
Ancient Art ★★★ *(p 59)*
Medieval Art ★★★ *(p 62)*
European Sculpture and Decorative Arts ★★★ *(p 62)*
13-18C European Paintings ★★★ *(p 64)*
19C European Paintings and Sculpture ★★★ *(p 67)*
Lehman Pavilion ★★ *(p 68)*
Primitive Art ★★ *(p 69)*

Musical Instruments ★★ *(p 70)*
Asian Art ★ *(p 70)*
Islamic Art ★ *(p 70)*
Arms and Armor *(p 70)*
Costume Institute ★ *(p 71)*
20C Art ★ *(p 71)*
Drawings, Prints and Photographs *(p 71)*
Ruth and Harold D. Uris Center for Education *(p 71)*

VISIT

Open 9:30 AM to 5:15 PM (8:45 PM Fridays and Saturdays); closed Mondays and major holidays; suggested admission fee ($5.00) includes the Main Building and the Cloisters. Audio-guides are available for certain departments and temporary exhibitions. Certain galleries may be closed – inquire at the information desk in the Great Hall – and specific works of art may be exhibited in locations other than those indicated here.

We suggest you begin your visit at the Visitor Information Area in the Uris Center (ground floor). Large scale floor plans, an exhibition gallery, wall displays, and a slide program shown continuously in the Orientation Theater provide information on the museum, its collections, programs and special exhibits.

GREAT COLLECTORS AND THEIR TREASURE TROVES

Frick	*1 East 70th Street* *p 72*	*Frick Collection:* *European painting and decorative arts*
Guggenheim	*1071 5th Avenue* *p 114*	*Guggenheim Museum:* *contemporary works of art*
Hewitt	*9 East 90th Street* *p 130*	*Cooper-Hewitt Museum: contemporary and historical decorative arts*
Lehman	*Metropolitan Museum* *p 68*	*Lehman Pavilion: period rooms and European and American art*
Morgan	*29 East 36th Street* *p 122*	*Pierpont Morgan Library:* *manuscripts and works of art*

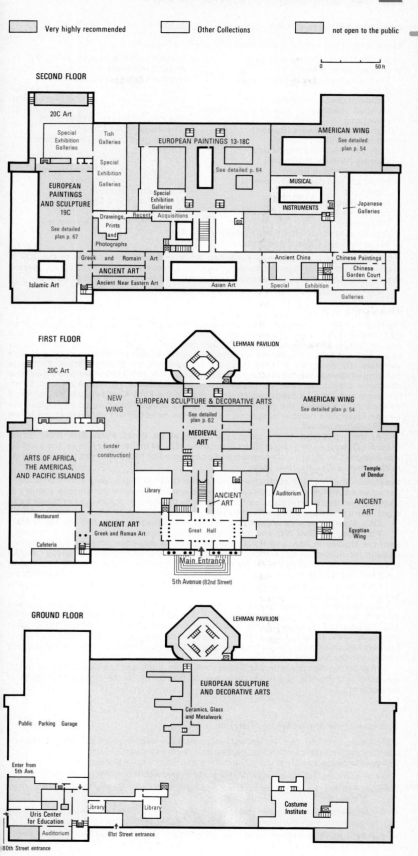

Very highly recommended   Other Collections   not open to the public

0 ____ 50 ft

SECOND FLOOR

20C Art

Special Exhibition Galleries

Tish Galleries

EUROPEAN PAINTINGS 13-18C

AMERICAN WING
See detailed plan p. 54

Special Exhibition Galleries

See detailed p. 64

MUSICAL

EUROPEAN PAINTINGS AND SCULPTURE 19C

See detailed plan p. 67

Special Exhibition Galleries

INSTRUMENTS

Japanese Galleries

Drawings, Prints and Photographs

Recent Acquisitions

Greek and Roman Art

ANCIENT ART

Ancient China

Chinese Paintings

Chinese Garden Court

Islamic Art

Ancient Near Eastern Art

Asian Art

Special Exhibition

Galleries

FIRST FLOOR

LEHMAN PAVILION

20C Art

NEW WING

EUROPEAN SCULPTURE & DECORATIVE ARTS

AMERICAN WING
See detailed plan p. 54

See detailed plan p. 62

MEDIEVAL ART

(under construction)

ARTS OF AFRICA, THE AMERICAS, AND PACIFIC ISLANDS

Library

ANCIENT ART

Auditorium

Temple of Dendur

ANCIENT ART

Restaurant

ANCIENT ART
Greek and Roman Art

Great Hall

Egyptian Wing

Cafeteria

Main Entrance

5th Avenue (82nd Street)

GROUND FLOOR

LEHMAN PAVILION

EUROPEAN SCULPTURE AND DECORATIVE ARTS

Ceramics, Glass and Metalwork

Public Parking Garage

Enter from 5th Ave.

Uris Center for Education

Library

Library

Costume Institute

Auditorium

81st Street entrance

80th Street entrance

AMERICAN WING★★★ *Time: 4 1/2 hours*

Major works presented in this department (see plan p 55)

- Tiffany stained glass windows
- Sullivan staircases
- Saint-Gaudens and La Farge mantelpiece
- facade of the United States Bank
- six-shell mahogany desk and bookcase (Newport)
- high chest of drawers (Boston)
- tall clock (William Clagett)
- Lady With Her Pets (Hathaway)
- animals (William Schimmel)
- Shakers' Retiring Room
- bookcase and desk (Baltimore)
- sideboard
- tea urn (Paul Revere)
- tea service (attributed to Christian Wiltberger)
- Adams gold vase (Tiffany and Company)
- Magnolia vase (Tiffany and Company)
- compote (Greenpoint Glass Works)
- art glass (Tiffany)
- George Washington (Stuart)
- View from Mount Holyoke, Massachusetts, after a Thunderstorm — The Oxbow (Cole)
- The Rocky Mountains (Bierstadt)
- The Aegean Sea (Church)
- Washington Crossing the Delaware (Leutze)
- Andrew Jackson (Powers)
- Prisoners From the Front (Homer)
- The Gulf Stream (Homer)
- Northeaster (Homer)
- Max Schmidt in a Single Scull (Eakins)
- The Bronco Buster (Remington)
- Madame X (Sargent)

The museum's collection of American art from the colonial period to the 20C is displayed on the three floors of the American Wing, recently expanded to contain period rooms, decorative arts galleries, and a section devoted to paintings and sculpture.

Entrance is through a garden court which looks out on Central Park.

The Court

The handsomely landscaped, glass-walled garden court conveys the genteel spirit of an earlier age. The works of well-known American artists and architects enhance the setting: **Tiffany stained-glass windows** (**A**) and the Islamic-inspired loggia fashioned by Louis Comfort Tiffany *(p 58)* for his Oyster Bay home; a pair of decorative cast-iron **staircases** (**B**) designed in 1893 by Louis Sullivan for the Chicago Stock Exchange Building which was demolished in 1972; Frank Lloyd Wright's triptych window made for a children's playhouse; and an imposing marble **mantelpiece** (**C**), by Augustus Saint-Gaudens and John La Farge, which once graced the Fifth Avenue home of Cornelius Vanderbilt. In addition, the selection of 19 and 20C sculptures arranged throughout the garden illustrate a number of stylistic trends in the development of American sculpture *(see Sculpture below)*.

At the north end of the court, the **facade of the United States Bank** (Wall Street branch - **D**) has been installed. Erected between 1822-24 in the Federal style, the building was designed by Martin E. Thompson and constructed of Tuckahoe marble from quarries in Westchester County, New York.

Sculpture. – The works of sculpture shown in the Court date primarily from the 1850s, a period when American artists traveling abroad were inspired by the antique statuary of Italy and the ideals of the classical world. Prior to this time sculpture was primarily trade signs, stern boards and ship's figureheads in wood.

Of a slightly later date is George Grey Barnard's *Struggle of the Two Natures of Man*. Following the Civil War and into the early 20C Augustus Saint-Gaudens, returning from his studies in Italy and Paris, exerted a strong influence on American sculptors through his numerous large-scale memorials and symbolic figures. The *Diana* covered in gilded copper gracing the center of the court, and the mantelpiece he executed in collaboration with John La Farge are examples of his work. Also by Saint-Gaudens are two small-scale figures: *Victory* and *The Puritan* which are on view in the Painting and Sculpture section *(p 58)*.

Equally famous was Daniel Chester French who, like Saint-Gaudens, earned numerous commissions for memorials and statues. Best remembered for his *Minute Man* in Concord, Massachusetts, and his impressive *Seated Lincoln* in the Lincoln Memorial (Washington, D.C.), French is represented here by replicas in marble of two of his works *(on the balcony – gallery 201 – overlooking the Court)*: the enigmatic *Mourning Victory* and the *Milmore Memorial*.

Impressive memorials in the Beaux Arts style, such as those executed by Saint-Gaudens and French, gradually gave way in popularity to the streamlined forms of modernism.

Services of the Metropolitan Museum:

Volunteers staffing the Visitor's Center provide information on the museum's collections, special exhibitions, guided and recorded tours.
***Wheelchairs** are available upon request in the Coat Check areas.*
*Special activities are arranged for the **sight-impaired;** ☏ 535-7710.*
*Information for the **hearing-impaired** is available by calling the Telephone for the Deaf; ☏ 879-0421.*
***Baby strollers** are allowed in most galleries during regular museum hours. They are not permitted on Sundays or in certain special exhibitions.*
*A museum **parking garage** located at 80th Street and Fifth Avenue is open seven days a week, 24 hours a day.*

AMERICAN WING

THIRD FLOOR

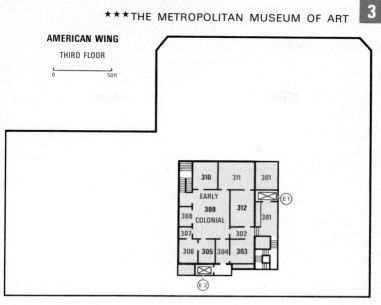

SECOND FLOOR

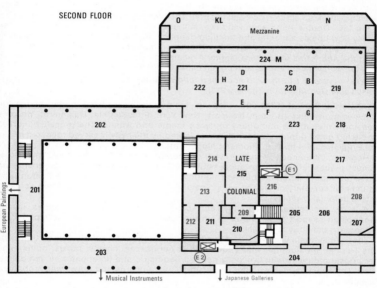

FIRST FLOOR

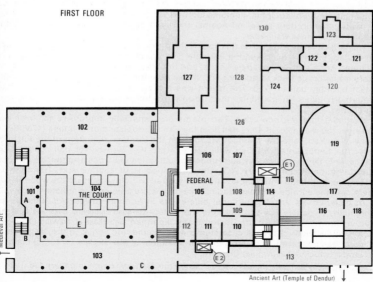

Interior Decoration

Beyond the facade of the United States Bank is a series of period rooms and decorative arts galleries illustrating the development of styles from the 17 to 20C. Although strongly marked by the English tradition, American decoration was also influenced by the Dutch and other continental styles.

To visit the period rooms and decorative arts galleries in chronological order, begin on the 3rd floor. Take elevator E2 from the 1st floor.

Early Colonial Period (1630-1730). – *3rd floor.* As you leave the elevator pass through the gallery of 17C furniture and into the small sparsely decorated Hart Room (1674) *(gallery 303)* from Ipswich, Massachusetts. The focus of the room is the huge fireplace around which the house was built. The plain, plaster walls, exposed hand-hewn beams, low ceiling and tiny casement windows are features common to this early date.

From the Hart Room, pause at the Newington Room *(gallery 305),* before proceeding to the main gallery, to view the decoratively painted furniture typical to the settlements of the Connecticut Valley.

The main gallery, the Meetinghouse Gallery *(gallery 309),* presents examples of 17 and early 18C furnishings which often recall the European styles brought over by the first settlers. The roof trusses of this gallery are inspired by those found in the Old Ship Meetinghouse in Hingham, Massachusetts. Built in 1681 by ship's carpenters, it spans a hall wider than the nave of any English Gothic cathedral.

The room *(gallery 310)* from the John Hewlett House (1740-60) on Long Island illustrates both a classical influence: in the fluted pilasters and heavy cornice; and the survival of the Dutch tradition: the Biblical fireplace tiles and the large cupboard painted in grisaille remind us that New York was once Nieuw Amsterdam.

Contrasting with the somber, modestly furnished Hart Room *(see above)* of an earlier date is the spacious John Wentworth Room (1695) *(gallery 312)* from Portsmouth, New Hampshire, an affluent colonial seaport. The Wentworth Room marks the transition into the 18C. Double-hung sash windows, still used today, make their appearance; the chimney now boasts a mantel and the pine paneling, framing the fireplace and covering an entire wall, adds a note of formality. The easy chair and high chest of drawers are among the new forms of furniture, lighter in scale, to appear; and furniture surfaces are decorated with veneers and japanning (an imitation of lacquer-ware).

Take elevator E1 to the 2nd floor then follow stairway to the old Wing. Begin in the Pennsylvania German Room (gallery 210).

Late Colonial Period (1730-90). – During this period the interiors, particularly in the wealthy seaport cities (Boston, Newport, New York, Philadelphia, Baltimore), become increasingly elegant as mahogany replaces maple and walnut. The gracefully curved cabriole leg gains popularity, then it is supplanted by the heavily carved rococo designs of the English cabinetmaker, Thomas Chippendale.

Regional differences in style prevail: the combination of blockfront and shell motif on chest pieces is used most successfully by Newport cabinetmakers Goddard and Townsend; superb japanned pieces (highboys, lowboys) are produced in Boston; and monumental secretaries heavily, yet gracefully carved, are among the finest achievements of colonial craftsmen.

A taste for refined decoration and comfort characterizes the homes in the cosmopolitan seaport cities; however, in the rural areas, simple styles interpreted by local artisans continue to persist.

The Pennsylvania German Room *(gallery 210)* attests to the colorful folk art traditions of the German immigrants, who adorned their cupboards, chests, boxes, pottery and other household items with brilliantly painted geometric and floral patterns and animal figures. The chest painted with red and white tulips, unicorns and doves was probably a dower chest.

Nearby, the Powel Room (1765-66) *(gallery 211)*, a parlor from the home of the last colonial mayor of Philadelphia, contains furniture made in that city. The highly polished, rich mahogany furniture is set off against the most striking feature of this room, the handpainted Chinese wallpaper.

The largest reconstitution on this floor is the Alexandria Ballroom (1792) *(gallery 215)* from Gadsby's Tavern in Alexandria, Virginia. The two chimneys, the musician's gallery, the Queen Anne and Chippendale chairs, and the brass chandeliers reflected in the old mirrors transport us back to another era: it was here that George Washington attended his last birthday ball in 1798. The tavern was a major coach stop on the route from the northern cities, in particular the nation's capital, Philadelphia, to the southern plantations.

Continue into the new wing. Two rooms are especially impressive for their wall coverings: the magnificent entry hall from the Van Rensselaer manor house (1765-69) in Albany, New York, and the Marmion Room from the Virginia plantation of the Fitzhugh family. The handpainted English wallpapers in the Van Rensselaer hall *(gallery 206)* depict scenic landscape panels surrounded by a flourish of scrolls and rococo designs. In the Marmion Room *(gallery 207)*, the decoration is of another sort. Handpainted landscapes, fruit-filled cornucopia, and urns topped with flowers cover the wooden wall panels; and the cornice, pilasters and bottom panels are painted to simulate marble.

In galleries 204 and 205 regional differences in furniture styles and fashions are highlighted. In gallery 204 you will note the stately **six-shell mahogany desk and bookcase** made in Newport (1760-90), the Boston-made japanned **high chest of drawers** (1730-60), and the cabinetwork of the tall case clocks which came into vogue in the 18C; note in particular, the concave block and shell door treatment of the **tall clock** (1740-50) made by the Newport clockmaker William Claggett.

From gallery 205 take the staircase down to the 1st floor; begin in gallery 116.

Folk Decoration. – Developing simultaneously with the high style decorative arts from the colonial period through the 19C, were the folk traditions of the untrained artisan and craftsman. Working primarily in the rural countryside, the folk artist painted portraits such as: **Lady With Her Pets** (Rufus Hathaway – 1790) flat in appearance and lacking perspective; and carved and decorated useful items for the home and farm.

In the section devoted to folk art you will also notice scrimshaw dating from the whaling era, and tiny gaily painted **animals** made by William Schimmel, an itinerant craftsman who carved toy animals in exchange for his room and board.

Dating from the same era is the neat, airy and sparsely furnished **Retiring Room** (gallery 118) of the **Shakers**, a religious sect that reached its peak in America in the 19C. The pure lines and superb craftsmanship of the chairs, tables and cupboards they made mirror the order and harmony that guided the lives of the members of this sect.

Stenciling, a decorative technique which uses precut stencils and paint, was used to embellish the furnishings, floors and walls of many homes. In gallery 117 a barber-writing chair in the museum's collection of painted furniture is an example of this early craft which remains popular even today.

Before leaving this section, enter gallery 119 where John Vanderlyn's panorama, painted between 1816 and 1819, transports the viewer to the gardens outside the palace of Versailles in the 19C.

Federal Period (1790-1820). – The light, delicate lines of the neoclassical style dominate the furniture and decoration of the Federal period, the decades of economic expansion following the Revolution. The leading exponents of this style were the Scottish architect-designers James and Robert Adam (p 63). Inspired by ancient art and architecture, the Adam brothers had an important impact on the furniture and building designs of their day in England, and ultimately in America.

In furniture, forms are lighter than those of the colonial period, and carving is subdued in favor of veneers and inlay and marquetry. Furniture made in Baltimore may be ornamented with oval panels of glass painted with classical figures or scenes. Painted glass panels are a feature of the **bookcase and desk** (gallery 105) made in Baltimore in 1811, and of the imposing **sideboard** (1795-1815) in the Baltimore Room (gallery 106). Elaborately carved and gilded looking glasses, and decorative shelf clocks made principally by New England clockmakers add a light note to the restrained classical interiors. Architecturally, the influence of the Adam brothers is seen in the use of classical motifs (urns, swags), slender pilasters and colonnettes, delicately adorned fireplace mantels and pastel tones. The overall effect is of understated elegance as in the Benkard Room (1811) (gallery 107) and the Haverhill Room (1805) (gallery 111).

The Richmond Room (1810) (gallery 110) is unusual for the period because of its heavy moldings, mahogany woodwork, and the massive proportions of its doorways. Furnishings made by the New York cabinetmakers Duncan Phyfe and Charles Honoré Lannuier, are set off by the scenic wallpaper depicting The Monuments of Paris.

The Revival Styles (1820-1870). – The neoclassical style which predominated during the early 19C gave way in later decades to a succession of revival styles: Gothic, Rococo, Renaissance, Louis XVI and Egyptian

Inspiration varied, giving rise to furniture fashions ranging from the elegant, refined Greek Revival forms of Duncan Phyfe (the Greek Revival Parlor: gallery 121) to the rich, heavily ornamental designs of John Henry Belter (the Rococo Revival Parlor: gallery 122).

Especially grand were the elaborate furnishings, architectural detailing and decoration of the Renaissance Revival style (the Renaissance Revival Parlor: gallery 124).

Further on, also on this floor, the contemporary style of the early 20C is exemplified by the living room from the Francis Little house (1912-1914) (gallery 127) designed by Frank Lloyd Wright (p 114). Decorated in warm earth tones and looking out on Central Park, the room is a harmonious extension of the outdoors.

Take the staircase adjacent to gallery 105 to the 2nd floor; turn left and begin in gallery 202.

Pewter, Silver, Glass, Ceramics. – Galleries 201, 202, 203. Major designs and stylistic trends in American pewter, silver, glass, and ceramics are illustrated by exhibits on the balcony overlooking the Court. Created in a variety of useful forms, these wares were often highly valued for their decorative qualities as well.

Galleries 202, 201. – In the 17 and 18C, pewter, a metal composed principally of tin with small amounts of lead and antimony, was transformed into a wide range of items to serve a variety of needs in the home, church and tavern. Because pewter was cast in molds, forms were standardized.

As you enter gallery 202 note, to the right, the tankard made by John Will (18C); a typical example of the popular drinking vessel of the period, this piece is prized for its delicate floral engraving. The many forms created and embellished by the American silversmiths of Boston, New York and Philadelphia from the colonial days through the early 20C, will be admired for their refined craftsmanship and style. Displayed in the second wall case is one of several works by the patriot-silversmith Paul Revere, owned by the museum: a large tankard topped with a pineapple finial. A **tea urn** fashioned by Paul Revere (1791) and engraved with the initials H.R., is also shown in this gallery.

Especially interesting is the close relationship between silver fashions of the period and furniture design trends: the simple, pear-shaped contours of the 18C teapot made by Peter van Dyck recalls the gracefully curved cabriole leg characteristic of the Queen Anne style; the eagle, adapted from the Great Seal of the United States, was a popular symbolic motif during the early years of the new Republic: eagle finials complement the refined engraving of the four-piece **tea service** (1799) attributed to Christian Wiltberger, and said to have been a wedding present given to Eleanor Custis on the occasion of her marriage to Lawrence Lewis, a nephew of George Washington.

Elaborate Rococo Revival tea services, such as those produced for Ball, Tompkins and Black (1850), are reminiscent of the richness of the intricately carved Chippendale pieces; and the exquisite one-of-a-kind pieces by Tiffany and Company: the **Adams gold vase**, encrusted with pearls and semiprecious stones, and the **Magnolia vase** (1893) covered with gold, enamels and opals, are hallmarks of America's "gilded age" of railroad kings, coal barons and financial tycoons.

(From photo Metropolitan Museum.)

The Adams Gold Vase.

Gallery 203. – In the section reserved for glass, the first group of cases features hand blown, cut, engraved and pressed glass. Craftsmen working in the traditional methods to create fine glassware, produced the hand cut and engraved **compote** ordered by Mrs Lincoln for the White House in 1861.

There are numerous examples of pressed glass, an American innovation which revolutionized the glass industry in the early 19C. Mechanically, rather than hand pressed into pattern molds, this type of glassware could be produced rapidly and at a low cost in a wide range of forms and patterns: a clear glass compote made in Pittsburgh in the 1860s illustrates the popular Thumbprint pattern. The new process made attractive tableware, candlesticks, paperweights, etc., previously a luxury only a few could afford, available in large quantities and at a reasonable price to the masses.

Nearby an exhibit focuses on blown-molded glass: the glass blown into a mold, is embossed with a pattern, then removed from the mold and blown into a larger shape: note the patterned flasks bearing patriotic themes – George Washington, the Flag; and subjects of national interest – the railroad, masonic orders.

Wall cases in this area describe and illustrate late 19C American art glass. Often opaque, with shaded coloring, a rich texture and elegant shape, this ornamental glass was known as Burmese (shaded coral pink to yellow), Peach blow (opaque white to rose), Amberina (pale amber to deep ruby), and Pomona (frosted appearance).

The highlight of the collection, however, is the beautiful irridescent **art glass** by **Louis Comfort Tiffany**, son of the founder of the New York silver store *(p 47)* which once catered to the carriage trade. A proponent of the Art Nouveau movement, Tiffany was one of the most influential innovators of his day. The luminous quality of his colors, and sensuous grace of his vases, lamps and other works brought him fame in his lifetime and continue to be regarded as masterpieces of American decorative art.

Among the remaining exhibits note the selection of American ceramics and pottery: in the center of the gallery a bust of Ulysses S. Grant, pitchers and statuettes of Parian ware, a white porcelain so named because it resembles the marble quarried on the Greek isle of Paros; Pennsylvania redware decorated in *sgraffito* technique (the design is cut through an outer coating to reveal the underlying red body); stoneware jugs decorated in cobalt blue; and a variety of items in Rockingham, an earthenware glazed a streaked brown color.

Painting and Sculpture

The approximately 400 works on display from the museum's collection are arranged chronologically constituting a survey from the colonial period to the early 20C.

Begin in gallery 217.

Galleries 217-221 and 223. – In the 18C a number of foreign-born and native portrait painters predominated in America. Born in Scotland, John Smibert *(Mrs Francis Brinley and Her Son Francis)* studied in Italy and settled in Boston in 1729, opening the era of professional painting in the colonies.

Particularly well-known were John Singleton Copley, who painted prominent personalities of his day, and Gilbert Stuart, best known for his portraits of **George Washington (A)**.

By the late 18C Americans were traveling abroad to study with their fellow countryman, Benjamin West, in London. West, a leader of the neoclassical movement, painted allegorical canvases: *The Triumph of Love (gallery 218)* and drew his subjects mainly from history and mythology. The grand manner and scale he favored inspired his student, John Trumbull, son of a Connecticut governor, to paint large historical canvases. In *The Sortie Made by the Garrison of Gibraltar*, Trumbull dramatizes an event that occurred during the siege of the English fortress by the French and Spanish. Among his other followers was Matthew Pratt, whose *American School* provides an interesting picture of artists at work in West's London studio.

Gallery 219. In the early 19C, portrait painting remained popular, reaching its peak in the hands of the Romantic painters Thomas Sully *(Mother and son)* and Samuel F.B. Morse *(The Muse)*, who is better known as the inventor of the telegraph.

In the meantime, other artists were turning their attention to genre scenes. William Sidney Mount portrayed everyday subjects of the common man, in the rural villages of Long Island *(Cider Making)*, while George Caleb Bingham **(Fur Traders Descending the Missouri - B)** transported the viewer further west to a land familiar to few. Landscape painting also flourished. The huge, lyrical canvases of the Hudson River School, America's first native school of landscape painting, depicted the grandeur and beauty of a vast, still largely unspoiled, American continent. The best known artists of the school were Thomas Cole **(View from Mount Holyoke, Massachusetts, after a Thunderstorm — The Oxbow - C)**, (note the portrait bust of Cole nearby), Asher B. Durand *(The Beeches)*, John F. Kensett *(Lake George)*, Albert Bierstadt **(The Rocky Mountains - D)**, and Frederic E. Church **(The Aegean Sea - E)**.

From gallery 221 proceed to gallery 223.

In the mid-19C pride in the nation's history and great geographical and economic expansion, inspired Emanuel Leutze to paint **Washington Crossing the Delaware (F)** recounting that historical moment when, on Christmas night, 1776, Washington made a surprise attack on the Hessians. At the far end of this gallery is a Hiram Powers' marble bust of **Andrew Jackson (G)**, a popular military hero who, like George Washington, rose to become President of the United States.

Galleries 222, 224 and Mezzanine. – *Return to gallery 222.*

Distinctly American in temperament were **Winslow Homer, Frederic Remington and Thomas Eakins.** Homer's experience as an illustrator is reflected in his early paintings which are realistic commentaries on the events of the time. His Civil War scenes **(Prisoners From the Front - H)** are straightforward yet sensitive. In later years Homer found inspiration in the powerful forces of the sea, and his vigorous interpretations **(The Gulf Stream - K** and **Northeaster - L,** *located in the Mezzanine)* made him a master of naturalism.

In the late 19 and early 20C, Frederic Remington immortalized the cowboy, scout, Indian, and cavalry of the Old West, and the vanishing frontier, in his action-filled bronzes **(The Bronco Buster - M).**

Take the stairs straight ahead down to the Mezzanine. Eakins, a contemporary of Homer, shared the latter's direct manner but preferred to paint people: *The Thinker: Portrait of Louis Kenton* reveals the influence of Velázquez, while *The Writing Master* reveals a familiarity with Rembrandt's technique. Predating Impressionism, his scenes of sports of the day are of interest for their brightly illuminated out-of-doors setting: **Max Schmidt in a Single Scull (N).**

At about the same time, many American painters spent a considerable part of their lives abroad. The fashionable portrait painter John Singer Sargent **(Madame X - O)** was trained in Paris as was Mary Cassatt *(Portrait of a Young Girl)*, a student of Degas and the only American to become a member of the Impressionist group, and James McNeill Whistler *(Arrangement in Flesh Colour and Black: Portrait of Theodore Duret)* who spent much of his career in England.

In the late 19C other American painters began to adopt the style of the Impressionists: the quick unbroken brushstrokes, uneven paint surfaces and bright colors that characterized the canvases of William Merritt Chase *(At the Seaside)* and Childe Hassam *(Winter in Union Square)* clearly show the influence of the French artists.

In the 20C the realistic vein was continued by The Eight including such artists as Arthur B. Davies, Robert Henri, John Sloan, George Bellows and Edward Hopper *(Office in a Small City)*. Meanwhile a gradual move toward abstraction was begun by John Marin and Arthur Dove. Finally Abstract Expressionism, an American movement, had its most powerful exponents in such figures as Jackson Pollock and Willem de Kooning *(see 20C Art p 71)*.

ANCIENT ART★★★ *Visit: 5 hours*

This section includes the Egyptian Wing, Greek and Roman Art and Ancient Near Eastern Art.

Major works presented in this section
   – Temple of Dendur   – Euphronios Krater

Egyptian Wing (1st Floor) *time: 3 hours*

Egyptian civilization, one of the earliest in the history of man, spans a period of more than 3 000 years. The life and customs of the ancient Egyptians were closely bound to religion. They believed that death was only a transition on the journey from this life to the eternal world, and built temples and tombs as dwelling places for the spirits of the dead. Most Egyptian art comes from these temples and tombs which were constructed to house the remains of the deceased and the many objects needed to ensure life in the next world.

Displayed in a series of galleries north of the Great Hall are ancient Egyptian sculpture, funerary objects, reliefs, and religious, personal and domestic artifacts dating from the Predynastic period (prior to 3 100 BC) to the close of the Coptic period (641 AD).

The **Temple of Dendur** *(gallery 25)* from the early Roman period, ca 15 BC, was a gift from the Egyptian government in the 1960's in recognition of American assistance in saving the temples of Nubia, including Abu Simbel from being submerged by the lake created by the Aswan Dam.

We suggest you visit the galleries in their chronological sequence by going to the right as you enter the Wing. The door jambs between galleries identify the time period.

Orientation Area. – *Gallery 1*. Comprehensive descriptions, a time line and a wall map, along with Predynastic objects, sculptures and a stone sarcophagus, introduce the visitor to the civilization of ancient Egypt.

Enter the mastaba (an Arabic designation for an above ground tomb) and chapel of Pernebi, the burial site of a dignitary of the Fifth Dynasty court at Memphis.

Dynasties 1-18. – *Galleries 2-15*. Presented in gallery 2 are examples of reliefs, sculpture, architecture and everyday objects from the 1st through the 10th Dynasties (3100-2040 BC), and reliefs from the famous Cheops Pyramid (4th Dynasty). The two figures, carved in stone, of a Bound Prisoner Kneeling (5th Dynasty) are portrayed with slanted eyes and deep facial furrows to indicate they are foreigners. Figures such as these were placed in the royal temples of the Old Kingdom to symbolize the king's control over disorder. Also from the 5th Dynasty are wood and stone statues of officials.

Dynasty 11 Models. – The 6th Dynasty was followed by a period of political strife. After two centuries of instability, a Theban king, Nebhepetra Mentuhotpe, reunited Egypt and established the golden age known as the Middle Kingdom. The objects in galleries 3-5 belonged to him, his family and the officials who served him. Outstanding is the group of models from the 11th Dynasty tomb of Mekutra, chancellor of Mentuhotpe. These small painted models showing workers in the bakery, the brewery, the slaughterhouse, etc. present a fascinating picture of daily activities in ancient Egypt. The boats along the back wall, and the colorful wooden figures in the Procession of Bearers and the Offering Bearer, nearby, are also from his tomb.

Proceeding to gallery 8, you will pass on the way the massive red granite offering table used in the funerary temple of Amenemhat I *(gallery 6)*, and the Stela of Montuwosre *(gallery 7)*, a stone tablet which has retained much of its original paint and is engraved with hieroglyphs describing Montuwosre's career as a king's steward.

The Lahun Treasure. – The high standards reached by artisans of the Middle Kingdom are exemplified by their achievements in portraiture and jewelry. Facing you on entering gallery 8 is a group of 12th Dynasty royal portraits. This group of portraits includes the small but sensitively carved representation of Senwosret III as a sphinx, and the highly expressive face of the same king in red quartzite. Displayed just beyond are the royal jewels of Princess Sithathoryunet excavated from her tomb at Lahun. Note the girdle of amethyst beads and gold spacers shaped like leopard heads which were designed to tinkle rhythmically as the princess walked. The gold pectoral of Senwosret II, a gift from her father, is inlaid with a myriad of tiny pieces of semiprecious stones; at the center of the design, a kneeling god supports the king's cartouche.

The Statues of Queen Hatshepsut. – The monumental statues of Queen Hatshepsut (early 18th Dynasty) displayed in gallery 12, are from her funerary complex at Deir el Bahri. The statues of the Queen are impressive for their great size and of interest for the varied manner in which she is portrayed: the colossal red granite kneeling statues show Hatshepsut in a rigid pose as a male, wearing the white crown of Upper Egypt or the *nemes* headdress; in sharp contrast is the graceful seated figure in white limestone which presents her, without a beard, as a ruler possessing more feminine qualities.

The funerary mask of Hatnofer *(gallery 13)*, covered in gold foil, is also from the early 18th Dynasty. The same fine workmanship is evident in the fragile gold sandals and falcon-headed collars *(gallery 14)* which served as funerary adornments to three royal wives.

The last group of antiquities in this section *(gallery 15)* is from the reign of Amenhotpe III. These works are of interest for the high quality of their sculptural detail in representing facial features, dress, etc. Note, in particular, the superbly preserved rendition, in faience, of Amenhotpe III as a sphinx. The four diorite statues in the center of the room represent Sekhmet, the lion-headed goddess of the desert and destruction, and the powerful protectress of the pharaoh.

Dynasties 18-30. – *Galleries 16-24, 26, 29*. This section covers the Amarna, Ramesside, and Late periods roughly about 1 000 years (1379-330 BC).

Reliefs, sculpture and funerary art from the reign of Akhenaton, who moved the capital of Egypt from Thebes to Amarna, and other 18th Dynasty kings: Tutankhamun, Ay and Haremhab are arranged in galleries 16-18. In gallery 17, royal statuary includes a head of the boy king Tutankhamun and a head of the god Amun. Also displayed here is a rare find: the materials from the embalming of Tutankhamun and the remains of the banquet held at the closing of his tomb. In a separate glass case, together with objects from a royal tomb in the Valley of the Kings, is an alabaster canopic jar with a lid carved in the form of a portrait head.

Entering the architectural hallway *(gallery 18)*, the central statue is of General Haremhab, who was later crowned king of Egypt.From this gallery, the Temple of Dendur can be seen.

Gallery 19, to the left, is devoted to the Ramesside period, named for the succession of 19th and 20th Dynasty pharaohs named Ramesses. Representations of two kings of the period include a kneeling statue of Sety I and the head of Amenmesse. The stela of Ptahmose bears four prayers and a representation of Ptahmose.

In the hallway of gallery 18, the limestone statue of Yuny, and the pair statue of Yuny and his wife are interesting for the details they provide of the garments and jewelry of the period. The funerary papyrus intended to assist the deceased in passing through the next world, and the granite doorjamb of Ramesses II are also of this period.

In gallery 20, note especially among the museum's extensive holdings from Dynasties 21 through 25, a tiny gold statuette of Amun holding the Ankh – symbol for life – and the group of magnificently painted ornamented coffins of the 21st Dynasty: the inner and outer coffins of Henettawy, Tabakmut, Menkheperra, and the mummy and cartonnage, as well as coffins, of Kharushere from the second half of the 22nd Dynasty.

The enormous basalt sarcophagus of Harkhebit *(gallery 18),* incised with his name and titles in hieroglyphs, dates from 664-525 BC.

Among the bronze and faience temple sculptures and small objects of the period in gallery 22, notice a bronze figure of Osiris with golden inlay and two decorative faience bottles inscribed with prayers for a happy new year. Along one wall, funerary material includes delicate gold foil mummy amulets and faience shawabtys, miniature servants intended to perform menial tasks for the deceased in the afterlife, and a choice assortment of scarabs and bijoux is displayed along one wall.

Of special interest are galleries 26 and 29 which have been set aside for the museum's rich collection of color facsimiles of tomb and temple paintings.

The last gallery *(gallery 23)* in this area focuses on Thirtieth Dynasty (380-342 BC) material: Prince Wennefer's massive sarcophagus; granite relief from the temples of the Delta; and the magnificent "Metternich Stela."

Ptolemaic Period; Roman - Coptic periods (30 BC-641 AD). – *Galleries 25, 27, 28, 31, 32.* Galleries 27 and 28 display stone sarcophagi, mummies and two long papyri (excerpts from a "Book of the Dead") all from the time of Alexander's conquest of Egypt (332 BC) to the death of Cleopatra (30 BC). In gallery 25 is the Temple of Dendur (time of Augustus) mentioned above. Gallery 31 contains a collection of Roman art from the time of Augustus (30-1 BC) to 4C AD; note here the remarkable "Fayum Portraits," eight portrait-panels painted in wax in 2C AD. Also shown in this section is a group of about 40 excellent pieces of Coptic Art (Egyptian Christian period, 2C AD-641AD) including a wide range of objects of everyday life as well as from monastic communities.

Greek and Roman Art (1st and 2nd Floors) *time: 1 hour*

On the 1st floor there are 9 galleries south of the Great Hall and 1 gallery north of the main staircase; on the 2nd floor there are 4 galleries south of the Great Hall balcony.

The large collection of Cypriot antiquities and Cycladic objects on the 1st floor show the variety of art created by these early centers of civilization.

The **Greek and Roman Treasury** *(north of the main staircase)* displays the museum's collection of ancient Greek and Roman gold and silver plate. Tableware and ceremonial vessels predominate. Note especially the gold libation bowl (3-4C BC) embellished with circles of acorns and beechnuts; and the archaic silver jugs and ladles (Greek, 6C BC).

The evolution of Greek pottery and sculpture is well represented by the rich collection. In sculpture the Geometric period produced works such as the bronze statuette of a horse (1C BC-1C AD) with pure and simplified lines. The search for form especially in the portrayal of the human body (Kouros, 7C BC) dominates in the Archaic period grave monuments and reliefs while the Classical period produced sculptures showing greater freedom. These are often represented by Roman copies of the Greek original. The Hellenistic period evolves toward greater diversity and realism, as can be seen by the portrayal of age in the *Peasant Woman* (2C BC).

The evolution of pottery followed a similar pattern with the geometric designs of the early period being superseded by human forms with scenes portraying mythological subjects of everyday life *(2nd floor galleries).* The black and red figure techniques are both represented. Outstanding is the **Euphronios Krater** from about 515 BC which is displayed in gallery IV. This red figured calyx-krater is signed by both the potter Euxitheos and the painter Euphronios and shows on one side the body of Sarpedon, son of Zeus, being lifted by Sleep and Death and on the other, an arming scene.

In the first gallery next to the Great Hall is an interesting collection of sarcophagi, and a group of portrait busts typical of the realism of expression of the later Roman period. In addition, a series of wall paintings have been installed from a villa at Boscoreale near Pompeii, which was buried by the eruption of Vesuvius in 79 AD. The paintings recall traditional theatrical scenery and prominently employ the characteristic Pompeian red. In the southeast corner of the Great Hall before entering the gallery, the bedroom (cubiculum) from the same villa has been even more greatly embellished by a 2C mosaic floor which probably originated in a bath near Rome.

Ancient Near Eastern Art (2nd Floor) *time: 1 hour*

The collections of this department come from a vast region of southwestern Asia reaching from Turkey to Afghanistan and the Indus Valley, and from the Caucasus Mountains in the north to the Arabian peninsula in the south. On view are sculptures, pottery and metalwork dating from the sixth millennium before Christ to the beginning of Islam with emphasis on the Sumerian and Assyrian civilizations of Mesopotamia and the prehistoric, the Achaemenian and the Sasanian civilizations of Iran.

Highlighting this section is a group of 20 large stone panels from the palace of Ashurnasirpal II, King of Assyria from 883-859 BC. Images of the king (holding a bow and bowl), bird-headed and human-headed deities, and the sacred tree, symbolizing fertility, are carved in low relief on the panels; inscriptions on the panels extol the king and the accomplishments of his reign. The two enormous five-legged, winged creatures, also in this gallery, adorned the palace entranceways. Many of the finely carved ivories (8C BC), nearby, were excavated at Nimrud, Iraq.

Notice also the glazed lion panels from the Ishtar Gate (6C BC) built in Babylon by Nebuchadnezzar II; the cylinder and stamp seals from Mesopotamia; stone sculptures from Sumeria; a group of bronze artifacts (8-7C BC) from cemetery sites at Luristan; and the painted pottery (5 000-4 000 BC), and silver and mercury gilding drinking horns (rhytons) and vessels (8C BC-6C AD) from Iran.

Michelin Green Guide are regularly updated. Make the most of your vacation by using the latest aditions.

MEDIEVAL ART★★★ (1st Floor) *time: 1 1/2 hours*

Major works presented in this section
- Romanesque Chapel
- Spanish Choir Screen

On the left side of the main staircase is the **Early Christian and Byzantine Corridor.** Byzantine art is represented by the Second Cyprus Treasure (7C) and ivories and enamels. Among the fine examples of metalwork from the Early Medieval period, note the chip-carved silver-gilt and niello pieces from the Vermand Treasure. Pass through an Italian Romanesque marble portal from San Gemini, in Umbria, to the **Medieval Tapestry Hall.** Under the staircase to the right is a chapel of Romanesque carvings.

Tapestries. – Woven principally in the workshops of Flanders (Arras, Brussels and Tournai), these tapestries date from the 14 to the early 16C. At that time, they were as practical as they were ornamental, serving to temper drafts and dampness.

The Annunciation, begun early in the 15C, is related to a painting by Melchior Broederlam, a court painter in Burgundy. An interesting series of tapestries, commissioned by Charles the Bold, Duke of Burgundy, shows the arming of Hector during the Trojan War. Late Gothic stained glass, with large panels from Cologne and from England, fills two walls of the gallery.

Medieval Sculpture Hall. – Built to suggest a church, with nave and side aisles. A splendid Baroque wrought iron **choir screen** is installed here. Begun in 1668 for the Cathedral of Valladolid, in Spain, the main part is 17C, and the upper part more recent. At Christmas, the museum exhibits a magnificent tree and an 18C Neapolitan creche in front of the choir screen.

A large collection of sculpture and bas-reliefs traces the development of Gothic sculpture from the 13 to the 16C. Most important are sculptures from Burgundy, Ile-de-France, Italy and Germany. Note especially the 15C Burgundian Virgin and Child from Poligny, France. In the same gallery is a rare group of panels representing Baptism, Marriage and Extreme Unction, from a tapestry depicting the Seven Sacraments.

Before leaving the hall note to the rear, in a glass case, an unusual German saddle of bone. The decoration, in very low relief, shows scenes of courtly love.

(From photo Metropolitan Museum.)

The Medieval Hall and Spanish Choir Screen.

Medieval Treasury. – In addition to the portable shrines, reliquary caskets and sacramental objects, the Treasury also contains two fine sculptural groups (French, early 16C) of the Entombment and Pietà, from the private chapel of the Château of Biron.

In the wall and central cases are precious objects: an Ottonian ivory situla (holy water bucket), a 13C Limoges enamel shrine with scenes from the life of Christ in copper-gilt, the silver reliquary head of St Yrieix (Limousin, 13C) which once held fragments of his skull, and a processional cross covered in silver (Spanish, 12C). The richness of the collection of Romanesque and Gothic enamels rivals that of the French ivories of the 13C to 15C, including a rosary with beads in the form of skulls.

EUROPEAN SCULPTURE AND DECORATIVE ARTS★★★ *time: 3 hours*

Ceramics, Glass and Metalwork (Ground Floor)

Ceramics. – This term includes all objects of baked clay; distinctions are made between several types of pottery and porcelain on the basis of the kinds of clay and glaze used. Shown on a changing basis are examples of pottery encompassing 16C German stonewares and the earthenwares developed by Josiah Wedgwood (18C). Selections from the large collection of faience include Italian maiolica from Urbino, Gubbio and Deruta (16C) as well as later productions of the Delft and French workshops (Nevers, Rouen, Sceaux, Marseilles, Strasbourg). Porcelain is represented by examples from English and Continental factories, interspersed with examples of silver and glass. China Trade porcelain made for European markets is shown in Gallery 49.

Metalwork, Collector's Items. – Gallery 39 displays French Provincial and Parisian silver of the 17 and 18C, including objects by N. Besnier, F.-T. Germain, E.P. Balzac and J.-N. Roettiers. In addition, there are galleries devoted to English silver and to Continental European metalwork and glass. Pause in gallery 39 where Renaissance goldsmiths' work and enamels from Limoges and Venice are displayed together with snuffboxes, toilet sets and dance cards of the 18 and 19C.

Renaissance clockmaking is represented in gallery 40 by the richly decorated clock of gilded bronze (1568), signed by the Viennese clockmaker Caspar Behaim.

Decorative Arts (1st Floor)

Blumenthal Patio (Vélez Blanco). – To the left of the main staircase is the Renaissance patio (reconstructed here in 1964) from the castle of Vélez Blanco in Andalusia. The white marble galleries and the fine bas-relief decoration by Lombard sculptors create a Mediterranean ambiance. The capitals, arches and balustrades reflect Italian Renaissance motifs. The Latin inscription beneath the cornice gives the name of the owner: Pedro Fajardo and the dates of construction: 1506-15.

Northern Renaissance Galleries. *Galleries 1-5.* – These include the chapel with marquetry paneling from the Château de la Bastie d'Urfé (French, 1550); the Elizabethan "Nelson Room" from the Star Hotel, Great Yarmouth (Norfolk); and a paneled room with ceramic stove from Flims in Switzerland.

Italian Galleries. *Galleries 8-10, and 57.* – Further on, a vestibule provides an entrance to the rococo bedroom from the Sagredo Palace in Venice (early 18C). In gallery 57, adjacent to the Blumenthal Patio, there are examples of Italian bronze statuettes by the masters of this art from 15 to 18C (Bellano, Riccio, Antico, Giovanni Bologna, Vittoria).

English Galleries. *Galleries 14-20.* – To follow the development of English decorative arts from 1660 to 1840, start with gallery 19.

A staircase from Cassiobury Park, Hertfordshire, by Gibbons, represents the decorative arts of the 17C. The rococo style of mid-18C is reflected in the stucco decoration of a dining room from Kirtlington Park, Oxfordshire, now arranged as a drawing room.

The Tapestry Room, formerly at Croome Court, Warwickshire was designed by the architect Robert Adam (1728-92), who gave his name to a style reminiscent of ancient motifs. The crimson wall coverings and upholstery, ordered by the owner Lord Coventry, were made at the Gobelins factory and designed by François Boucher.

Also designed by Adam is the dining room from Lansdowne House, London. Pastel colors, pilasters, niches for ancient statues, and "Pompeian" stucco decoration all contribute to the refinement of the setting, in delicate contrast to the deep tones of the mahogany table and chairs. The Lamerie silver and an elaborate chandelier complete the arrangement.

In galleries 15 and 18 note the varied collection of 18C English decorative arts.

French Galleries. *Galleries 21-26, 29 and 32-35.* – These galleries of 18C period rooms and settings present a full and rich panorama of the French decorative arts.

The introductory gallery *(gallery 33)* contains a Paris shopfront of 1775. Embellished with pilasters and fancifully carved garlands, this charming boutique facade is typical of the Louis XVI style. In its windows are displayed outstanding examples of Paris silver.

Opposite, and side by side are two elegant small rooms. The rococo boudoir from the Hôtel de Crillon is graced with pieces of furniture from the Château de St-Cloud, including a daybed made for Marie-Antoinette. The Bordeaux Room is a delicately paneled circular salon decorated and furnished in the neoclassical style.

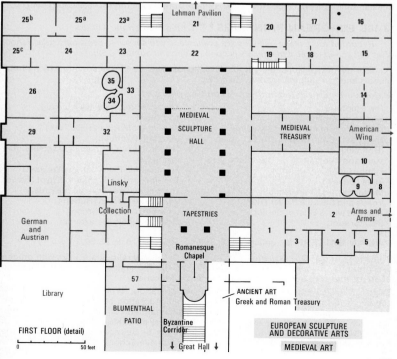

Hung in the Louis XV room *(gallery 23)* is the famous *Portrait of Louis XV as a Young Boy* painted by Rigaud, a replica of the original at Versailles. Among the porcelain in the Sèvres Alcove Gallery is a unique vase in the form of a ship and pieces from the Rohan service in the delicate turquoise-blue for which Sèvres was famous. Beyond the alcove is a graceful room from the Hôtel Lauzun, the setting for an exquisite collection of French furniture inlaid with Sèvres porcelain plaques. Masterpieces by the cabinetmakers Carlin, Weisweiler and Bernard II van Risenburgh (B.V.R.B.) are also displayed. The bronze and marble clock in the form of a Black woman is by André Furet, watchmaker to Louis XVI; when one of the figure's earrings is pulled, the hours and minutes appear as numbers in her eyes *(gallery 23a)*.

The focal point of the Louis XVI gallery *(gallery 24)* is a pair of upright secretaries in black and gold Japanese lacquer signed by Weisweiler. Four 18C rooms open into the gallery. The white and gold paneled salon *(gallery 25a)* from the Hôtel de Varengeville has magnificent Louis XV furniture, particularly the king's own desk from his study at Versailles. In the room from the Palais Paar in Vienna *(gallery 25b)* a late rococo room in blue and gold tones, are exquisite pieces of furniture, among them a writing table and *commode en console* both by Van Risenburgh and a rock-crystal chandelier.

The neoclassical, oak-paneled salon *(gallery 25c)* from the Hôtel de Cabris in Grasse still retains the original gilding on the paneling. Among the treasures in the room is a *nécessaire de voyage,* a collapsible table used for traveling, dressing and eating.

The Hôtel de Tessé room *(gallery 26)* with its gray and gold neoclassical paneling was the grand salon of the Comtesse de Tesse's residence. The room displays a rare 17C Savonnerie carpet and furniture made for Marie-Antoinette by Jean-Henry Riesener.

The final two galleries are devoted to French 17C art from the reigns of Louis XIII and Louis XIV. The Louis XIV style State Bedchamber displays a set of hangings embroidered with allegories of the *Seasons* and the *Elements*; several pieces of furniture by André-Charles Boulle, appointed cabinetmaker to the King in 1672; and a monumental carved chimneypiece after designs by Jean le Pautre.

German and Austrian Galleries. Ceramics here include 18C faience pottery, Meissen stoneware and enamelled Zwischengold glass (1730) from Bohemia. The floral garden room furniture was commissioned by Prince Bishop Adam Friedrich von Seinsheim for his Franckenstein Pavilion.

The Linsky Collection* (1st Floor). The approximately 375 works of art which comprise the collection are displayed in seven rooms designed to create an intimate setting suggesting a private residence. Paintings by early European masters, Renaissance and Baroque bronzes, European procelains, 18C French furniture, jewelry, and examples of goldsmith's work are among this group of objects admired for their beauty as well as quality. The Italian, Flemish, French, Dutch and German schools of painting are represented. The *Madonna and Child* by the Venetian Carlo Crivelli (15C) impresses by its elaborately tooled gold background. The collection includes the earliest dated work (1597) by Rubens, a portrait painted on copper of an architect or geographer.

Expressive bronzes (*Monk-Scribe on a Dragon*, 12C; Antico's *Satyr*, 16C) along with enameled gold pendants are displayed together with the paintings. Equally noteworthy are an 18C commode by David Roentgen, marquetried with scenes of the Italian Comedy; and a writing table (18C) with exquisite marquetry made by Jean-François Oeben for Mme de Pompadour. In the last room note the porcelain figures depicting Russian national types made at the Imperial Porcelain Manufactory (St Petersburg – late 18C).

13-18C EUROPEAN PAINTINGS★★★ (2nd Floor) *time: 4 hours*

Recorded tours of the galleries are available. If you set out to see a particular school of art call ahead to see if the gallery is open (telephone number p 52).

This department occupies some 40 galleries. The works are arranged by national schools and in roughly chronological order.

Major works presented in this section (see plan p 67)

- The Epiphany (Giotto or his workshop)
- The Journey of the Magi (Sassetta)
- The Last Communion of St Jerome (Botticelli)
- Man and Woman at a Casement (Fra Filippo Lippi)
- Pietà (Crivelli)
- Madonna and Child (Bellini)
- Venus and the Lute Player (Titian)
- Aristotle with a Bust of Homer (Rembrandt)
- Young Woman with a Water Jug (Vermeer)
- Repentant Magdalen (La Tour)
- Mezzetin (Watteau)
- The Crucifixion and Last Judgment (Jan van Eyck)
- Francesco d'Este (Van der Weyden)
- The Rest on the Flight Into Egypt (David)
- The Harvesters (Bruegel the Elder)
- Venus and Adonis (Rubens)
- View of Toledo (El Greco)
- Juan de Pareja (Velázquez)

ITALIAN GALLERIES – galleries 1, 2, 3, 4, 4a, 4b, 5, 6, 7, 8, 9, 22, 30.

Primitives and 15C. – *Galleries 3, 4, 4a, 4b, 5, 6.* Usually religious scenes with golden backgrounds, painted on wood. However, with the Florentine Giotto or the Sienese Sassetta, there is a beginning of modeling and landscape.

Gallery 3. — **The Epiphany**, from Giotto or his workshop, brings together the Angel appearing to the Shepherds, the Nativity and the Adoration of the Magi. Like Giotto, Sassetta is especially important for his careful treatment of landscape and human approach to his subjects, as exemplified in **The Journey of the Magi.** Works by Giovanni di Paolo (*Madonna and Child with Saints*) and Segna di Buonaventura (*Saint John the Evangelist*), in addition to Sassetta, illustrate the Sienese School.

Gallery 4. – This gallery is devoted to 15C secular painting. Above the *cassone* (marriage chest) ornamented with a battle scene, is hung a Fra Filippo Lippi painting of a **Man and Woman at a Casement**; the portrait of a woman, nearby, may be the work of Giovanni di Francesco. Also represented is the Florentine Ghirlandaio: *Francesco Sassetti and His Son Teodoro;* note the contrast between the firm features of the man and the soft features of his son.

Gallery 4a (Pinturicchio Room). – The ceiling of a Sienese palace, painted by Pinturicchio (1454-1513) has been remounted here. Notice the allegorical and mythological scenes (*Triumphs* after Petrarch, the *Three Graces* and the *Judgment of Paris*). Also on display are 15C secular paintings from Florence and Siena.

Gallery 4b. – The Florentine School is represented by Botticelli and his masterpiece **The Last Communion of St Jerome** and the glazed terracotta sculpture *Madonna and Child with Scroll* by Luca Della Robbia.

Gallery 5. – Among the Northern Italian paintings will be found a **Pietà** from an altarpiece by the Venetian Carlo Crivelli, a **Madonna and Child** by Bellini, Cosimo Tura's *The Flight into Egypt,* and Mantegna's *The Adoration of the Shepherds.*

Gallery 6. – In this room are works from the Florentine School: note the exquisite *Birth of the Virgin* (15C) in a classical setting, attributed to the Master of the Barberini Panels.

Renaissance (16C). – *Galleries 7, 8, 9.* High Renaissance paintings are represented by the Venetian School which is characterized by vivid colors, large foreground figures and backgrounds often depicting real landscapes.

Gallery 7. – Highlighting the religious paintings in this gallery is Raphael's *Madonna and Child Enthroned with the Young Baptist and Saints Peter, Catherine, Lucy and Paul,* an altarpiece completed in 1505 for a convent at Perugia. Note also *The Agony in the Garden,* a small panel from the predella of the above altarpiece.

Gallery 8. – Decorative canvases by Tintoretto *(The Miracle of the Loaves and Fishes)* and Titian **(Venus and the Lute Player)** are hung in this gallery. Also worth noticing is Titian's large portrait of Filippo Archinto, Archbishop of Milan, and Lorenzo Lotto's *Venus and Cupid.*

Gallery 9. – Works by comparatively minor artists are also of interest: for example, the soberly executed portrait, by Moretto da Brescia, *The Entombment,* and Solario's *Salome with the Head of Saint John the Baptist.* The large canvas of *Saints Peter, Martha, Mary Magdalen, and Leonard* is by Correggio, the leading painter of Parma.

17C. – *Gallery 30.* Among the works exhibited in this gallery are Caravaggio's *The Musicians* with their sensuous and effeminate features, *The Coronation of the Virgin* by Annibale Caracci and his pupil Reni's *Charity.*

18C. – *Galleries 1, 2 and 22.* Gallery 1 is devoted to the 18C Venetian master Giovanni Battista Tiepolo. His canvases, painted in luminous colors, depict scenes filled with turbulent movement.

In the center of gallery 2 stands a monumental table inlaid with alabaster and semiprecious stones. It was designed by the architect Jacopo Barozzi da Vignola for the Farnese Palace in Rome in the 16C. Nearby are two paintings of the same period by Pannini: *Ancient Rome* and *Modern Rome* illustrating the monuments of Rome; note Michelangelo's *Moses* in the center of the latter painting.

Gallery 22 exhibits an additional work by Tiepolo *A Dance in the Country,* and contains two other great Venetians at the height of 18C Baroque style: Francesco Guardi with his views of Venice; and Pietro Longhi, whose intimate scenes, drawn with minute care, depict the daily life of the Venetian nobility.

DUTCH GALLERIES – galleries 12, 13, 14, 15.

The collection concentrates on works of the 17C artists: the "golden age" of Dutch painting. The Met owns 33 of **Rembrandt's** works covering all phases of his career. Using light with great ingenuity, the painter gave careful attention to the hands, jewels, collars and cuffs of his subjects. In gallery 15, among his earlier portraits are *Portrait of a Lady with a Fan* and *Man in Oriental Costume (The Noble Slav),* dating from the 1630s. The high point of this collection is Rembrandt's celebrated **Aristotle with a Bust of Homer,** a symbol of philosophic reflection. This imaginary portrait was signed and dated 1653. Contrasting with these introspective portraits is the lively activity in Jan Steen's *Merry Company on a Terrace (gallery 12).* Also in this gallery and gallery 13 are the later Dutch paintings showing serene interior scenes, seascapes and landscapes with vast skies. A masterpiece by Vermeer, **Young Woman with a Water Jug,** bathed in a soft light, immediately attracts the eye. Note also the graceful and refined figures in *Curiosity* by Ter Borch.

Rembrandt's later works comprising a self-portrait and portraits of his fellow citizens reveal the painter's deep psychological insight. In gallery 14 the vivacious and colorful group portraits by Frans Hals record a different aspect of the life of the burghers as in *Merrymakers at Shrovetide.* Also in this gallery, you should not overlook Rembrandt's *Toilet of Bathsheba,* notable for its uncompromising realism; and *Young Man and Woman in an Inn* by Frans Hals.

FRENCH GALLERIES – galleries 10, 11, 18, 21.

17C. – *Galleries 10,11.* An impressive **Repentant Magdalen** *(gallery 11)* by Georges de la Tour illustrates the restraint and strength of expression of the French School.

Of the two "Roman" French painters, Claude Lorrain and Nicolas Poussin, Poussin is represented by *The Rape of the Sabine Women (gallery 10).* Claude in *View of La Cresenza* created a classical type of landscape combined with subtle luminosity. His *Trojan Women Setting Fire to their Fleet* nearby depicts a passage from Virgil's *Aeneid.*

18C. – *Galleries 18, 21.* Portraits are displayed showing the French interest in outward appearance and in psychological analysis. In gallery 18 you can follow the development of the art of the portraitist, from the polished figures by Drouais *(Madame Favart)* to the sober works of Duplessis *(Madame de Saint-Maurice).*

Along the way, in gallery 18, the *Self-Portrait with Two Pupils* by Adélaïde Labille-Guiard has been interpreted as the artist's feminist reaction to the practice of limiting the number of women who could become members of the French Royal Academy. Two works by Chardin move by their frank simplicity: *The Silver Tureen* and *Boy Blowing Bubbles.* *The Broken Eggs* by Greuze reflects his Italian training and the influence of Dutch genre painting on his style.

In gallery 21 along the walls is arranged a succession of "fêtes galantes," which were popular during the reign of Louis XV. Among them are the tender and sad **Mezzetin** – a character from the *Commedia dell'Arte* – a small but celebrated work by Watteau; and the *Dispatch of the Messenger,* a pastoral scene by Boucher. Handsome genre paintings by Fragonard are also exhibited including *The Italian Family,* a lively sketch, and *The Stolen Kiss.*

ENGLISH GALLERIES – galleries 2, 16.

18C (The Age of Reason). – In these galleries are hung a number of portraits brilliantly executed in fresh colors, but somewhat superficial in their charm. Two artists in gallery 2 are Thomas Gainsborough *(Mrs Grace Dalrymple Elliott* and Sir Joshua Reynolds *(Hon. Henry Fane with His Guardians* and *Colonel George Coussmater).*

FLEMISH AND GERMAN GALLERIES – galleries 23-28.

15C. – *Gallery 23.* This room contains paintings of the 15C in Flanders. Depicting sacred subjects and portraits almost exclusively, these works are characterized by a taste for the picturesque and familiar details. Jan van Eyck is represented by **The Crucifixion** and **Last Judgment.** These dramatic scenes may have been designed as side panels of a triptych, whose central panel has disappeared. By his contemporary, Petrus Christus, there is a *Portrait of a Carthusian. The Annunciation,* with a luminous landscape, is also attributed to Jan van Eyck. The works by Rogier van der Weyden (*Christ Appearing to His Mother* and *Francesco d'Este*), Gerard David (**The Rest On the Flight Into Egypt,** the *Crucifixion*), and the *Portrait of a Man* by Hugo van der Goes reveal a different style in Flemish art.

15-16C. – *Galleries 24-26.* Gallery 24 contains religious works by Gerard David *(The Nativity with Donors and Saints Jerome and Vincent; The Annunciation,* part of a polyptych from a church near Genoa), and a *Virgin and Child* by Jan Gossart called Mabuse. The theme of the Adoration of the Magi is treated by the Flemish painters Quentin Massys, Hieronymus Bosch and Joos Van Ghent. In the center of this gallery is *The Annunciation* formerly attributed to Memling and now to Van der Weyden, which is set in the room of the Virgin; the figures occupy most of the foreground and the tunic of the angel Gabriel, with its fine gold embroidery, is especially striking.

The Flemish and German Schools are represented in gallery 25 by Dürer's *Salvator Mundi* (Saviour of the World), *Saint John on Patmos* by Baldung, and portraits of German and English personalities by Holbein.

Gallery 26 is of special interest with several works by Lucas Cranach the Elder *(The Judgment of Paris, The Martyrdom of St Barbara, Samson and Delilah),* a triptych by Patinir *(The Penitence of St Jerome),* and a masterpiece by Bruegel the Elder: **The Harvesters.**

17C. – *Galleries 27 and 28.* These two galleries present Rubens and his circle. Notice Rubens's flamboyant **Venus and Adonis** and several portraits by Van Dyck, who served as an assistant to Rubens and went on to become one of the leading 17C Flemish painters. In gallery 28 you will see *The Triumph of Henry IV,* a preparatory oil sketch for one of the paintings commissioned by Marie de Medici.

SPANISH GALLERIES
galleries 29-32.

The Spanish character, grave, mystic and passionate, is expressed by such great painters as El Greco, Velázquez, Murillo and Ribera.

Gallery 29 contains the works of El Greco: **View of Toledo,** his only extant landscape, and a portrait of the *Cardinal Guevara, Grand Inquisitor.*

Among the four works by Velázquez in gallery 31 are two early works: *Supper at Emmaus* and the *Portrait of Philip IV, King of Spain.* Outstanding, however, is the portrait of **Juan de Pareja,** Velázquez's assistant and traveling companion. This masterpiece, an example of the artist's mature style, is astounding for its vitality and lifelike appearance.

Note, in gallery 30, Ribera's *Holy Family with St Anne and St Catherine of Alexandria.*

EUROPEAN PAINTINGS

SECOND FLOOR

0   50 ft

20C ART   Special Exhibition Galleries

C

H   G   D
F   E   B
I

19 C PAINTINGS
AND SCULPTURE

J   X   Y   A

K   L   M   N

Ancient Art (Greek and Roman Art) ↓

19C EUROPEAN PAINTINGS AND SCULPTURE★★★ *time: 2 1/2 hours*

The collection of 19C European paintings and sculpture, one of the museum's great strengths, is displayed in the 14 André Meyer galleries on the second floor of the Michael C. Rockefeller Wing.

An overall view of the 19C is presented, from the academic, conservative works of the French Salon to the avant-garde canvases of the Impressionists and Post-Impressionists.

Major works presented in this section *(see plan p 66)*

- The Death of Socrates (David)
- Madame Leblanc (Ingres)
- Abduction of Rebecca (Delacroix)
- Majas on a Balcony (Goya)
- Grand Canal, Venice (Turner)
- Woman with a Parrot (Courbet)
- Autumn Landscape with a Flock of Turkeys (Millet)
- Hand of God (Rodin)

- Terrace at Sainte-Adresse (Monet)
- La Grenouillère (Monet)
- Madame Charpentier and Her Children (Renoir)
- Sunflowers (Van Gogh)
- Cypresses (Van Gogh)
- Mont Sainte-Victoire (Cézanne)
- 14-year old Little Dancer (Degas)
- Woman with Chrysanthemums (Degas)

The galleries in this section of the museum have been given alphabetical letter designations in this guide in order to facilitate locations of major works.

Neoclassicism, Romanticism, Realism. — *Galleries N, A, B.* In the section devoted to the early 19C, the Neoclassical School, inspired by the art of ancient Greece and Rome, is represented by David's stoical and severe **The Death of Socrates.** David's follower, Ingres, was a master of the elegant, pure line (portraits of *Monsieur Leblanc* and **Madame Leblanc**). The graceful *Portrait of a Young Woman, Melle Charlotte du Val d'Ognes,* formerly attributed to David, may have been painted by another of his followers.

In **Grand Canal, Venice** as well as in one of his later works, *Whale Ship,* the English painter Joseph Turner places great emphasis on light and color in a manner that anticipates Impressionism.

In a more romantic vein, are Delacroix's **Abduction of Rebecca** inspired by Sir Walter Scott's novel *Ivanhoe,* and Goya's flamboyant **Majas on a Balcony.** Goya won recognition for his portraits of children *(Manuel Osorio)* and Spanish nobility and dignitaries: *Ignacio Garcini y Querait.*

Rebelling against the established conventions of the academic painters, Courbet executed his hunting scenes, landscapes *(Source of the Loue)* and pictures of the sea, with vigorous realism. His nudes **(Woman with a Parrot),** represented without mythological pretext, caused quite a stir at the time.

The Barbizon School, The Salon, Millet. — *Galleries D, E, F, G, H.* Reacting against the idealized rendering of classical landscape painting, the members of the Barbizon School painted directly from nature (Theodore Rousseau: *Forest in Winter at Sunset;* Daubigny: *Apple Blossom*).

Corot's feathery, gray-green landscapes, were much in favor during his lifetime; today many prefer his human figures *(Woman Reading, Sybille),* attractive in their simplicity of expression and attitude.

Among the painters showing their devotion to the Dutch School, Millet is known for his somber landscapes extolling the life of the peasant **(Autumn Landscape with a Flock of Turkeys).**

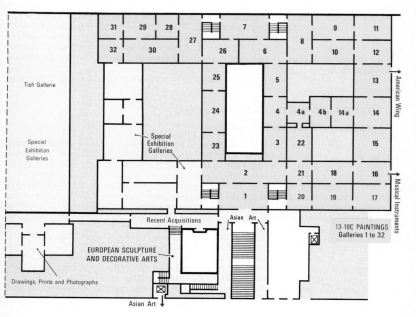

Adjacent areas contain works in the established academic tradition, as upheld by the Paris Salon of the French Academy. A variety of subjects are treated: exotic, romantic, mythological, idyllic and historical (Bastien-Lepage: *Joan of Arc*), Ernest Meissonier: *Friedland*).

The large canvas by Rosa Bonheur, *The Horse Fair*, a masterpiece in its time, was purchased by Cornelius Vanderbilt and presented to the museum in 1887. Inspired by ancient frescoes, allegorical in content, Puvis de Chavanne's mural panels located in the Rodin gallery celebrate such virtues as family and country *(Cider and the River)*.

In the next gallery, among the marble sculptures by Carpeaux, is the monumental, dramatic composition *Ugolino and His Sons*.

Rodin. – *Gallery J.* In the sculpture gallery beyond will be found works in marble, bronze and terra-cotta by Rodin. Rodin's fascination with the hands as a means of expression can be seen in his **Hand of God** and the models of hands in a glass case nearby. Impressed by the powerful figures of Michelangelo, Rodin created his large-size bronze representations of *Adam* and *Eve*.

Also of interest are the busts of *Countess Anne de Noailles* – called "Madame X" (marble) – *St John the Baptist* (bronze) and *Balzac* (terra-cotta).

Impressionists, Post-Impressionists. – *Gallery X.* Manet, a precursor, was greatly indebted to Spanish masters. Among the 18 Manets in the collection are *The Spanish Singer, Woman With a Parrot,* and the somber *Dead Christ, with Angels.* His later association with the Impressionists is seen in *Boating.*

Impressionism took its name from a canvas painted by Claude Monet: *Impression: Soleil Levant* (Sunrise) *(not in the museum's collection).* Painting outdoors, the members of the group sought to render visual transitory impressions gathered from nature and everyday life, and to capture the fleeting effects of light by juxtaposing pure tones of color.

There are a large number of landscapes by Monet in the collection. Note the cheerful **Terrace at Sainte-Adresse,** the luminous **La Grenouillère** with its rippling waters, and the dramatic rendering of the cliffs and sea at Etretat *(The Manneporte, Etretat I* and *II).* A shimmering light flickers across the views of Vétheuil *(Vétheuil in Summer).* The *Rouen Cathedral* is perceived in blazing midday sun, whereas *The Houses of Parliament* are veiled in a mist which tends to dissolve all solid forms. *The Bridge Over a Pool of Water Lilies* is one of a series of views of this subject which Monet painted.

Van Gogh's personal expression is shown in portraits *(Self-Portrait with a Straw Hat, Mme Ginoux – "l'Arlésienne"),* landscapes and still lifes. In his *Irises,* **Sunflowers,** and **Cypresses,** swirling lines and vehement brushstrokes are used to express intense emotion.

Renoir's delicate palette is revealed in his landscapes *(In the Meadow)* and most notably in his portraits of graceful young women *(By the Seashore).* The intimate family portrait of **Madame Charpentier and Her Children** was exhibited at the Paris Salon in 1879, and marked the beginning of Renoir's success as an artist.

All facets of Cézanne's art encompassing classical and modern concepts can be admired here – landscapes: *Gulf of Marseilles Seen from l'Estaque,* **Mont Sainte-Victoire;** and almost geometrical paintings of still life, suggesting the first hints of cubism, and figures: *The Cardplayers, Madame Cézanne in a Red Dress.*

La Parade or *Invitation to the Sideshow* (Seurat) and *View of the Port of Marseilles* (Signac) acquaint the viewer with the pointillist technique developed by these two artists.

Among the Post-Impressionists are Toulouse-Lautrec, who portrayed the dissolute, sometimes dark, sides of Parisian lifestyle *(The Sofa)* and Gauguin who depicted the beauty of the South Seas with bold colors and statuesque figures *(Two Tahitian Women).* *Galleries K, L, M.* – Exhibited in three galleries are works in several media, demonstrating Degas's interest in the study of body movement. Degas portrayed ballet dancers in a variety of poses in paintings *(The Dance Class, The Rehearsal of the Ballet on the Stage),* pastels *(Dancers Practicing at the Bar),* and in bronze: the statuette of a **14-year old Little Dancer.** The small bronzes in the glass case echo the movements of the dancers depicted on the canvases. Scenes painted from everyday life include *A Woman Ironing* and **Woman with Chrysanthemums.**

The collection of bronze horses bears witness to Degas's admiration for the energy and grace of horses in motion.

OTHER DEPARTMENTS (see plan p 53)

LEHMAN PAVILION★★ (1st Floor)

The Robert Lehman Collection can be seen in this pavilion, where a series of period rooms and galleries built around a garden court have been designed to house the encyclopedic collection of some 3 000 works of art. The period rooms contain magnificent examples of the decorative arts: tapestries, furniture, bronzes, enamels, etc.

The collection is famous for its Italian paintings of the 14 and 15C. The Sienese School is represented by Sassetta *(St Anthony in the Wilderness),* di Paolo *(Expulsion from Paradise),* and others. The Florentine School is exemplified by Botticelli *(Annunciation)* and the Venetian School by Bellini *(Madonna and Child)* and Crivelli *(Madonna and Child).*

Among a distinguished group of works by painters of the Northern Renaissance is *St Eligius as a Goldsmith* by Petrus Christus; also shown are panels by Gerard David, Memling and Cranach the Elder. Later period painting is exemplified by El Greco *(Christ Carrying the Cross)* and portraits by Rembrandt and Goya. Also featured are French paintings of the 19C (Ingres's *Portrait of the Princesse de Broglie)* and 20C.

On the lower level, a selection from the collection of drawings and decorative arts, ranging widely in the history of European art, is usually on view.

PRIMITIVE ART ★ ★ ★ (1st Floor) *time: 1 1/2 hours*

The galleries displaying Primitive Art are located in the Michael C. Rockefeller Wing, the south wing of the museum. The core of the collection, approximately 3 500 works of art from the former collection of the Museum of Primitive Art founded by Nelson A. Rockefeller, was donated to the MMA by Mr Rockefeller in the late 1970s. Together with the collection gathered by the museum over the years, the department now owns about 8 000 objects spanning a period of 3 000 years.

The wing is named in honor of Mr Rockefeller's son, Michael, who died while on an expedition to the island of New Guinea in 1961. Among the most impressive objects on display are the towering memorial poles *(mbis)* and attractively decorated shields of the Asmat of Irian Jaya (Western New Guinea) collected by Michael Rockefeller.

The galleries are divided into three sections, representing the three major divisions of the collection: Africa, the Pacific Islands and the Americas.

Africa. – Sculpture, primarily masks and figures carved in wood, dominates the art of Africa which is essentially religious. The first gallery contains a collection of monumental sculpture by the Dogon of Mali: the 7ft high elongated male figure stands with arms raised, in a pose characteristic of other Dogon figures carved in the round and in relief. A wooden container on the same platform has the head and tail of a horse and was used to hold sacrificial meat during ceremonies held to commemorate the myth of creation.

Adapting animal traits to headdresses and masks, the Bamana people created antelope headdresses with extremely slender vertical lines, while the ferocious-looking Senufo helmet masks incorporate the jaws and teeth of a crocodile, the horns of an antelope, and the tusks of the warthog. To the rear, among the Bamana figures, you will see a Mother and Child, one of several in the collection.

In the adjacent exhibit area are figures, masks and the chief's ceremonial stool carved by the Buli Master; the small ivories and wooden figures from Zaire, notably an ivory mask from the Lega people, are of interest. The serene Fang reliquary head was carved to protect a box that contained the skulls of honored ancestors.

Highlighting this area is a collection of dark brass (called bronze) items: plaques, animals, figures and heads, from the royal court of Benin. Dating from the 16 to 19C the heads are adorned with caps and chokers of the type still worn by the king today. A precious ivory mask, a royal ornament also from Benin, is displayed in a separate case. Carved into the hair of the mask are mudfish, symbolic of wealth and royalty, and faces that represent the Portuguese merchants who arrived in Nigeria in the 15C.

Leaving this section, on the right, pause to view the naturalistic double headdress of the Ekoi of Nigeria, and the wooden mask (from a triple mask) carved by the Ibibio people, perhaps portraits direct from life.

(From photo Metropolitan Museum.)

Belt Mask from the Court of Benin

Pacific Islands. – The arts of the Pacific Islands are varied, and include sculpture and painted and carved objects for ritual and daily use. The masterfully carved tall drum from the Austral Islands, and the ceremonial shield inlaid with shell (Solomon Islands) reflect the ornamental as well as utilitarian purpose these objects often served.

The largest and most diverse group of works in this section are from New Guinea. Paintings on sheets of bark, recreating the roof of a ceremonial house, are displayed overhead in the first gallery to the right, where elaborately decorated shields, and masks, fence posts, ceremonial boards and slit-gongs (drums) are on view.

The last gallery in this section, a long spacious glass-walled hall, has as its focal point a remarkable group of nine delicately carved poles *(mbis)* ranging up to 20ft in height. These Asmat *mbis* serve as a centerpiece for the other objects arranged in this hall: carvings with intricate openwork from New Ireland, figures sculpted from fern wood and a standing slit-gong from New Hebrides, and a 25ft long crocodile effigy (from Papua New Guinea).

Americas. – Entering the galleries devoted to the Americas, you will be drawn immediately to the Treasury, where exhibits of gold ornaments, vessels and masks from South and Central America include a pair of Mochica shell and stone mosaic ear spools (3-6C), a pendant (Colombia, 13-16C) in the form of a figure wearing an elaborate headdress which combines animal and bird heads and spirals, and a boldly painted Paracas funerary mask (Peru, 3-ICBC). Also from Peru is the luxurious yellow and blue feather hanging (late 7-8C) on the far right wall, a group of silver vessels, and ancient Peruvian pottery.

The adjacent gallery features the arts of Mesoamerica. Here, note especially the Mayan seated figure (6C), one of the few extant three-dimensional Mayan pieces in wood. Cases mounted along the wall contain "smiling figures" (7-8C) from Vera Cruz, characterized by their broad faces and wide grins; and ornamented stone objects (yokes, palmas, hachas) associated with the ancient ritual ball game. Finally, the superb relief carving of the Maya is exemplified by a stone stela from Mexico.

As you leave, note to the right, the jade mask, a refined example of the artistry of the ancient Olmec civilization (1200-400 BC) of Mexico.

Information regarding new installations at the museum and revised floor plans may be obtained at the information desk in the Great Hall.

ARMS AND ARMOR (1st Floor)

The Arms and Armor galleries are in the process of rearrangement and are scheduled to be reopened in the spring of 1991. The new arrangement will display a wide array of arms from all over the world, particularly the Far East and Japan.

Side Galleries. – Do not miss the examples of parade armor, and finely chiselled and embossed arms. In the first side gallery to the right are arms and armor predating the 16C, including pieces from the Crusades, a helmet said to be Joan of Arc's, and a group of shields for battle and tournament. The most arresting armor pieces are the parade helmet of Francis the First, by the great Milanese armorer Filippo Negroli, the shield and helmet of Claude Gouffier, Master of the Horse of Henry II, and the three quarter armor of Anne de Montmorency, High Constable under the same king.

Arms of tempered steel, often made in Toledo, Spain, include daggers, swords and rapiers, halberds, lances and pikes: especially handsome is the sword with the chiselled cup hilt, which belonged to the Marquis of Spinola (16C). Among the firearms are matchlock and wheel lock pistols, as well as flintlock muskets and pistols (note the double-barreled pistol which belonged to Charles V).

You will also see the embossed shield designed for Henry II of France, by Etienne Delaune (1555), a gilded helmet of Cosimo II de Medici and in the side gallery on the left, devoted to firearms from Europe and America, a flintlock garniture made at Versailles by Nicolas Noël Boutet, Napoleon's artist. A double-barreled pistol by Peter Pech of Munich made for Emperor Charles V (c 1540) is one of the earliest in existence.

MUSICAL INSTRUMENTS★★ (2nd Floor) time: 1 hour

Audio equipment ($3.00) enables the visitor to hear the instruments play period music. Available at Recorded Tour Desk, 1st floor.

This section presents an original and rare collection of more than 4 000 musical instruments from all periods and all parts of the world. You should not miss the three Stradivarius violins, made by the famous violin maker of Cremona; 2 classical guitars of Andres Segovia of rosewood, spruce and mahogany; and an outstanding series of keyboard instruments decorated with marquetry, sculpture and paintings including the spinet made in 1540 in Venice for the Duchess of Urbino. Other interesting instruments include a Flemish double virginal of the 16C decorated with musical scenes; lutes, zithers and guitars from the 17C; and wind instruments made of shell, bone, goatskin and meissen. In addition there are Near and Far Eastern, American and African instruments, many of which are in working order and are used for occasional concerts.

ISLAMIC ART★ (2nd Floor) time: 1 hour

A map and descriptions introduce the visitor to the culture of Islam which flourished during 12 centuries in a huge region ranging from Central Asia to Spain.

The opulence of an 18C Syrian house appears in the richly paneled reception room decorated with an ornamented ceiling, painted and gilded walls, stained glass windows and a magnificent marble floor. Gallery 2, devoted to the museum's excavations in Nishapur, a thriving Persian city from the early 9 to the 12C, contains rare wall paintings and a collection of objects in metal, stone, ceramics and glass. Inscriptions and the famous arabesques appear already on some of the pottery.

As the centuries unfold, the treasures exhibited gain in refinement. On display in successive galleries are tile panels, intricate wood and metalwork from the Mamluk period *(gallery 5),* ivory carvings, artfully painted ceramic bowls, decorated glass mosque lamps, bottles and jugs from Iran, jade vessels and jewelry from 17C India. In gallery 4c notice the pages from the Koran reflecting the artistry of the calligraphers. Because of their sacred character prayer niches were decorated with meticulous care. The mihrab or indicator of the direction of Mecca, is an exquisite 11 ft high mosaic from Isfahan which is composed of glazed ceramic tiles in geometric and floral patterns and inscriptions from the Koran.

An array of sumptuous carpets attests to the importance of carpet weaving brought to perfection in the workshops of Egypt, Persia, Turkey and India.

The early 16C wood ceiling in gallery 5 comes from Moorish Spain. A pair of doors (Egypt, 14C) bearing a kaleidoscopic pattern carved in wood and ivory illustrate the Muslim mastery of intricate design. Note the beautiful 15C Egyptian carpet.

Painting, which found a lively expression in the illustration of manuscripts, is represented by the delicate art of miniatures as practiced in Persia, India and Ottoman Turkey. The collection is highlighted by the miniatures depicting episodes from the great Persian literary work known as the "Shah Nameh" or "Book of Kings" *(gallery 6).*

ASIAN ART★ (2nd Floor) time: 1 hour

Around the main stairway and the balcony above the Great Hall, you can trace the development of Chinese ceramics. There are also Korean ceramics and metalwork and examples of Indian Southeast Asian sculpture.

A gallery to the north of the Great Hall features Chinese Buddhist sculpture of the 5 and 6C; a huge mural from Shansi in northern China (14C) forms a magnificent background: it depicts Buddha and his assembly.

Ancient Chinese art is displayed in galleries which begin at the left of the wall mural. Spanning the period from the Neolithic (early 2nd millenia BC) through the T'ang dynasty (10C AD), these galleries include jades, ceramics, bronze ritual vessels, tomb art, and Buddhist sculpture. You will exit into the galleries for Chinese painting and the Chinese garden court. *(Also accessible by elevator or stairway in the Egyptian Wing).*

Chinese Garden Court. – The garden court is a reproduction of a Ming Dynasty court-yard and scholar's study in Soochow, China. Set apart from the mainstream of museum traffic, and meticulously landscaped with Chinese plantings, the court recreates a setting similar to that in which Chinese artists and intellectuals once worked. The princi-pal features of the courtyard are best viewed from the irregular stone steps: the moon-viewing terrace facing the garden entrance, the half pavilion to the left and the walkway opposite, and the south wall with its latticed windows and formal rock arrangement.

On either side of the courtyard are galleries of Chinese paintings from the museum's collection. Rotating exhibits span four dynasties: Sung (960-1279), Yuan (1279-1368), Ming (1368-1644), Ching (1644-1911), as well as the modern era and illustrate a wide range of subject matter from landscapes and flower paintings, to Buddhist and Taoist themes.

West of the Chinese galleries are the galleries for **Japanese Art.** Changing exhibitions feature paintings, sculpture, lacquer, woodblock prints and Edo period scrolls from the museum's collection. Note, also, in this section the central altar from a 12C temple; a shoin-style meditation room modeled on a room in the Onjo-ji temple (17C) outside Kyoto; and *Water Stone*, a sculpture by Isamu Noguchi.

COSTUME INSTITUTE★ (Ground Floor)

The Costume Institute, a center for costume research and study, has a vast collection – almost 40 000 articles – of western and regional costumes from five centuries and five continents. Included in the collection are costumes from the wardrobes of royalty and society, and fashions by the most distinguished contemporary American and French couturiers. *Changing exhibitions run from mid-December to mid-April and mid-June to the Sunday before Labor Day; the galleries are closed the remainder of the year.*

20C ART★ *time: 1 1/2 hours*

The galleries of 20C art are located in the new 3-story Lila Acheson Wallace Wing. Paintings, sculpture and works on paper from 1900 to the present are displayed on the three floors, and sculpture is exhibited in the skylit sculpture court on the mezzanine level, as well as in the **rooftop garden** *(open May through November)*. The collection is strong in American art, particularly that of the New York School *(p 31)*.

Included among the early 20C paintings are Pablo Picasso's *Gertrude Stein*, with the first cubic forms; and Marsden Hartley's *Portrait of a German Officer*. Georgia O'Keeffe, one of the most original artists of this century, is represented by *Cow's Skull: Red, White and Blue*.

In the postwar period (1946) New York was the center of the art world and witnessed the development of Abstract Expressionism with such artists as Jackson Pollock *(Autumn Rhythm)*, Willem de Kooning *(Easter Monday)* and Mark Rothko *(Untitled Number 13)*. More recent works in the collection by Roy Lichtenstein *(Stepping Out)*, James Rosenquist *(House of Fire)*, David Hockney, Frank Stella, Ellsworth Kelly and other important American and European painters continue the survey of 20C art through the 1970s and into the 1980s.

DRAWINGS, PRINTS AND PHOTOGRAPHS (2nd Floor) *time: 1 hour*

At the top of the main staircase, to the left. Presented in the form of temporary exhibits.

Drawings. – The collection includes important works by masters from Italy (Michelan-gelo with a study for the Libyan Sibyl, Parmigianino, Pietro da Cortona, Pordenone, Romanino di Brescia); France (Poussin, Claude Lorrain, Vouet, David, Ingres, Dela-croix); Holland and Flanders (Rubens, Rembrandt, Lievens, Breenbergh) and Spain (Goya). Of the 4 000 drawings, one of the finest is by Raphaël: on one side is the Madonna and Child with the infant John the Baptist, and on the other a study of a nude male figure. Others of special interest are the *Redemption of the World* by Veronese, and the *Garden of Love* by Rubens.

Prints. – All techniques are included: woodcuts, lithographs and all forms of engraving.

Among the most memorable we should mention: for the Renaissance, a *Battle of the Ten Naked Men* by Antonio Pollaiuolo; *Bacchanal with a Wine Vat* by Andrea Mantegna; *The Four Horsemen of the Apocalypse* by Albrecht Dürer; *Summer*, after Pieter Bruegel.

For the 17C: *Time, Apollo and the Seasons* by Claude Lorrain; Rembrandt's *Faust in His Study,* and *Christ Preaching;* and a landscape by Seghers, also a Dutch painter.

The 18C artists represented include the Englishman Hogarth, the Roman Piranesi, the Frenchman Fragonard and the Spaniard Goya. Particularly noteworthy among 19C artists are Daumier *(Rue Transnonain)* and Toulouse-Lautrec *(Aristide Bruant)*.

RUTH AND HAROLD D. URIS CENTER FOR EDUCATION (Ground Floor)

The Metropolitan's comprehensive education program of classes, gallery tours, lectures, courses and films is administered through the Division of Education Services headquartered in the Uris Center. Information on all programs is available in the Visitor Information Area.

Business Hours:
Banks: 9 AM to 3 PM — Shops: 10 AM to 5 PM (or 6 PM)
Shopping Centers: 9 AM (or 10 AM) to 9 PM (or 10 PM)
Post Offices: 8 AM to 5 PM (1 PM Saturdays)

For those who love the Old Masters, as well as for those who simply like beautiful things, the Frick Collection, at 1 East 70th Street, is one of the highlights of a visit to New York. Here, the visitor may enjoy a glimpse of life in a luxurious private home as well as the rich collection of masterpieces.

The Mansion. – Designed in 1913 for Henry Clay Frick (1849-1919), a Pittsburgh industrialist, the mansion contains a collection of furnishings, works of art, and decorative arts acquired by Mr. Frick over a period of forty years.

It was transformed into a museum and opened in 1935.

VISIT*time: 1 1/2 hours*

Open 10 AM (1 PM Sundays and holidays - Election Day, Veterans' Day) to 6 PM; closed Mondays and January 1, July 4, Thanksgiving Day, December 24 and 25; $3.00, $1.50 students and senior citizens. Children under 10 are not admitted; those under 16 must be accompanied by an adult.

On occasional Sunday afternoons and on three Wednesday afternoons during the summer, there are chamber music concerts *(tickets are necessary; they are free but must be applied for by mail, for information ☏ 288-0700).* Also October through May, illustrated lectures are given *(no tickets required).*

Works of art may occasionally be relocated or removed from exhibition.

Entrance Hall. – In a niche on the right is displayed a bust of *Henry Clay Frick* by Malvina Hoffman.

Boucher Room. – You are carried back in time to an 18C French boudoir, with its intimate and refined atmosphere. The woodwork frames eight Boucher paintings commissioned by Madame de Pompadour. They represent the *Arts and Sciences.*

Among the 18C French furniture are pieces by Martin Carlin, Riesener and Malle.

Anteroom. – This room is reserved for rotating exhibitions of drawings and prints from the collection.

Dining Room. – Decorated with English 18C paintings in delicate colors: portraits by Hogarth, Romney and Reynolds, and *The Mall in St James's Park* by Gainsborough. The silver is 18C English.

West Vestibule. – Here are displayed the series of the *Four Seasons* (Boucher, 1755).

Fragonard Room. – The room is named for the eleven decorative paintings by Fragonard, a work of inimitable grace that is a hymn to love. Four of the large panels were commissioned by Madame du Barry, mistress of Louis XV. They recount the various stages of a romantic encounter: *The Pursuit, The Meeting, Love Letters* and *Lover Crowned.*

Exquisite furnishings add to the total effect: sofas and armchairs covered in Beauvais tapestry designed by Boucher and Oudry; a Louis XVI commode by La Croix; two delicate porcelain tables; Sèvres porcelains, etc.

South Hall. – Foremost, among the furniture, we should mention a Louis XVI secretary desk made for Marie-Antoinette and signed by Riesener. Among the paintings, notice the *Portrait of His Wife* by Boucher (1743, signed twice) and two small Vermeers, one of which, the *Officer and Girl,* is remarkable for its radiant luminosity. At the foot of the stairs is a thirty-day Louis XV calendar clock which also contains a barometer.

Living Hall. – Furnished with a desk by André Boulle and two cabinets in the style of this famous 17C French cabinetmaker, this room displays 16C masterpieces. The Venetian School is represented by Giovanni Bellini's *Saint Francis in Ecstasy*, set against a finely rendered landscape; and by two Titian portraits, one depicting the sensual features of a young man in a red cap. The commanding figure of *St Jerome* as Cardinal, by El Greco, represents the Spanish School. Typical of the best of the German School are two celebrated portraits by Hans Holbein the Younger: with great psychological perception he has depicted *Sir Thomas More* and *Thomas Cromwell*.

Library. – Henry Clay Frick looks down from a portrait in this room which is decorated with lovely examples of Chinese porcelain on black backgrounds and with small Italian and French bronzes of the 16 and 17C.

You will also notice the terracotta bust of the Swedish miniature painter Peter Adolf Hall, done by the French sculptor Boizot in 1787, the marble bust of an Italian lady by Francesco Laurana (15C), and a whole series of English paintings of the 18 and 19C.

(From photo Frick Collection.)

Henry Clay Frick's Living Hall.

North Hall. – Above the blue marble Louis XVI table hangs Ingres's portrait of the *Comtesse d'Haussonville*. The marble bust by Houdon represents the *Marquis de Miromesnil*, Keeper of the Seals under Louis XVI. There is a spirited Baroque sketch by Tiepolo of *Perseus and Andromeda* (Venetian, 18C), a charming Chardin, *The Lady with a Bird Organ* and a Monet, *Vétheuil in Winter*.

West Gallery. – In this room, decorated with 16C Italian furniture and Persian carpets, are portraits and landscapes of the Dutch, French, Spanish and British Schools.

Among the portraits notice *Lodovico Capponi,* a page in the court of Duke Cosimo I de Medici, by Bronzino (Florence, 16C); an El Greco of the Italian period *(Vincenzo Anastagi, a Knight of Malta);* works by Frans Hals; three splendid Rembrandts of a great intensity of expression *(Portrait of Himself, Nicolaes Rutz,* and *Polish Rider);* two famous works by Van Dyck: the Antwerp painter of still life *Frans Snyders,* and his wife; *Philip IV of Spain,* by Velázquez. There is also the well-known *The Forge* by Goya.

You may particularly admire, among the landscapes, the van Ruisdael, the Hobbema (Dutch, 17C), and *The Harbor of Dieppe* by Turner. A work by Georges de la Tour (French, 17C): *The Education of the Virgin,* a typical example of this painter from Lorraine, also deserves special attention.

Enamel Room. – A beautiful collection of Limoges painted enamels of the 16 and 17C in intense blues and greens accompanies a *St Simon the Apostle* (mid-15C) by Piero della Francesca and a *Madonna and Child with Saints Lawrence and Julian* by Gentile da Fabriano.

There are also a few Italian Primitives and examples of Renaissance sculpture.

Oval Room. – A life-size terra-cotta figure of *Diana the Huntress* by Houdon (French, 18C) graces this gallery. It is a version of a statue executed for the Duke of Saxe-Gotha and acquired by the Russian Empress, Catherine the Great.

East Gallery. – An assortment of paintings from different schools and periods, all of fine quality. Claude Lorrain's dramatic *Sermon on the Mount* dominates the gallery. Other works on display are: Greuze's genre painting *The Wool Winder; Amsterdam*, by Jacob van Ruisdael (Dutch, 17C), where the sail of the boat on the left seems to capture all the light; a portrait by Jacques Louis David of *Countess Daru*, the wife of Napoleon's Quartermaster General; and Degas *The Rehearsal*. Four portraits by Whistler, including the striking *Mrs Frederick R. Leyland* and two portraits by Van Dyck complete the collection.

Court. – One of the most delightful parts of the museum, the court is a cool haven in summertime thanks to its marble floor, fountain and pool, tropical plants and flowers. From the south colonnade you can view the entire court and the statue of *Diana*, by Houdon, in the Oval Room beyond. Among the other sculptures, there is a 15C bronze *Angel* by Jean Barbet.

Two suggested programs for a short visit to New York City will be found on pp 18-21.

Distance: about 1 mile – Time: about 3 hours.

Divided by a series of islands covered with shrubs and flowers, Park Avenue has a certain elegance which has made it one of

the desirable residential and business addresses of the city. Colorful in summer, it is also attractive at Christmas when the trees are decorated with fairy lights.

A Masterpiece of Urban Design. – Park Avenue has not always been such an attractive street. Until the early 20C the open railroad tracks ran straight down it and bridges carried the crosstown traffic. The smoke and noise made the area almost unbearable.

Then the New York Central Railroad Company built Grand Central Station *(p 82)* and sank the tracks below street level. New engineering techniques made it possible to isolate buildings from railroad vibrations allowing the company to develop the real estate above both the tracks and the fan-shaped train yards which stretch as far as 50th Street. The newly named Park Avenue was quickly lined with apartment buildings and the whole scheme was hailed as one of the great pieces of urban design of the early 20C.

Today, between the terminal and 60th Street, the original apartment houses have given way to high-rise offices of varying styles, home to many banks. North of 60th Street, the ten- and twelve- story structures built in the 20s and 30s remain, their slightly monotonous facades broken only by their colorful awnings stretching to the street and the uniforms of their doormen.

From the Helmsley Building to 60th Street

Behind the Helmsley Building are Grand Central Terminal and the Pan Am Building *(p 82).*

Helmsley Building ★. – Built as the headquarters of the New York Central Railroad in 1929 by Warren and Wetmore, this building stands in the center of Park Avenue. The tower with its pyramidal roof and cupola is today dwarfed by the Pan Am Building *(illustration p 31)*. The structure is pierced by two tunnels through which the traffic passes, and the monumental main entrance is on the north side.

The lobby is elegant with travertine walls and gilt decorations.

270 Park Avenue. – Built in 1960 for the Union Carbide Company by Skidmore, Owings & Merrill, this tower of contrasting black and white steel and shining glass windows rises 52 stories. It is set back from the avenue behind a pedestrian plaza paved in pink marble-chip terrazzo.

Like many of the buildings near Grand Central Station, the main lobby and elevators are located on the 2nd floor *(reached by escalator)* because there is no room for the elevator shafts below ground.

Chemical Bank Building. – This silver gray tower built in 1963 rises 50 stories on the east side of the street, balancing no 270. A three-story atrium protruding toward the street forms a glass enclosed park called **Chemcourt** with shrubs and fountains.

Waldorf Astoria ★. – This world famous hotel built in 1931 *(p 42)* was designed by Schultze and Weaver in a sedate version of the Art Deco style. It has twin towers rising 42 stories and an elegant interior. Note in particular the main lobby with its clock at the center.

A staff of 1700 serve the more than 1 692 guest rooms, including luxury apartments and suites occupied by a succession of celebrities. A protocol service has been organized to decide delicate questions of precedence and etiquette. Thus certain dignitaries who stay at the Waldorf are entitled to see their national flags flying in front of the hotel. The private apartments have been occupied by such notables as every U.S. president since President Hoover, General MacArthur, Adlai Stevenson, the Duke of Windsor and Henry Kissinger. Several suites are reserved for presidents or heads of state.

St Bartholomew's Church★. – *Chapel and church open 8 AM to 6 PM; guided tours (time: 1/2 hour) following the 11 AM service on Sunday. Concerts most Tuesdays at 6 PM and Sundays at 3 PM (October through May). ☎ for information 751-1616.*

This Episcopal church erected in 1918 is generally Byzantine in style with its multi-colored dome, salmon pink brick and gray limestone walls. The Romanesque front portal comes from Stanford White's original St. Bartholomew's Church which stood on Madison Avenue from 1902-1918. Its richly sculptured bronze doors were donated by the Vanderbilts. This ensemble contrasts curiously with the surrounding modern style skyscrapers. The interior is interesting with a mosaic of the Transfiguration in the apse above alabaster windows.

On Lexington Avenue immediately behind the Church is the **General Electric Building ★**, its reddish-orange spire topped by a spiky crown. The building was constructed for RCA Victor Company in 1931. Decorative features include rays, lightning bolts and flashes, which are particularly appropriate to the building's tenants; A whimsical GE-logo clock surmounts the main entrance. The building is a fine example of Art Deco ornamentation.

Continuing up the avenue, note the skyscraper at **345 Park Avenue** with its pool, fountain and sculpture in a plaza beside the building.

Seagram Building ★★. – The headquarters of Joseph E. Seagram & Sons Inc., located at 375 Park Avenue, was designed in 1958 by **Mies van der Rohe** and **Philip Johnson**. Perfectly proportioned, the 38-story tower is set back half an acre on a granite plaza with twin fountains. The subtle color scheme of the exterior bronze panels and the bronze colored windows, and the refinement of the interior lobby, with its travertine walls and the continuation of the granite plaza floor, give an air of classic distinction to the building.

Just inside the restaurant The Four Seasons, on the ground floor, is a huge Picasso painting *(visible from the lobby)*. This was executed in 1919 as a stage curtain for the ballet "Le Tricorne." *Guided tours of the building Tuesdays 3 PM (☎ 572-7000).*

Park Avenue Plaza★★. – This unusual 15-sided green mirror glass structure rises up behind the 1918 Italian Renaissance palace of the exclusive Racquet and Tennis Club. Designed by Skidmore, Owings & Merrill and opened in 1981, the building features a 30ft high pedestrian shopping arcade between 52nd and 53rd Streets. An attractive café and fountain, almost a wall of water, enhance the light and airy interior.

Turn right on 53rd Street, past the Citibank Building, to Citicorp on Lexington Avenue.

Citicorp★★. – The headquarters of Citicorp, parent company of Citibank, is housed in a spectacular aluminum and glass sheathed tower whose top is sliced off at a 45° angle, making it not only Manhattan's fourth tallest building but one of its most conspic-uous landmarks. The 900ft tower stands on four colossal columns, each 9 stories or 115ft high and 22ft square, set not traditionally at the corners of the building but in the cen-ter of each wall. Beneath these canti-levered corners, which extend 72ft from the central columns, nestle the St. Peter's Church and a separate 7-story structure housing the Market, which is entered by a sunken plaza. The success of the complex designed by Hugh Stubbins & Associates and opened in 1977, has led to a surge of high-rise construction in the area on Lexington and Third Avenues.

St Peter's Church. – This Lutheran church sold its land to Citicorp on the understanding that a new church in-tegrated with the complex be con-structed. The result is a comparative-ly tiny structure whose roof lines repeat the angle of the tower above. The interior *(viewed from street level gallery)* is dramatic and simple. Roof

(From photo Citibank.)

Citicorp interior

and side wall skylights bring natural light into the structure but excellent soundproofing makes it an oasis of silence in this noisy corner of Manhattan. The altar, lectern, platform, steps and pews are constructed simply of red oak and are easily movable.

The church also contains the lovely **Erol Beker Chapel of the Good Shepherd ★** designed by Louise Nevelson for the purpose of creating a "place of purity" in Manhattan.

The Market. – *Illustration p 75.* This attractive arrangement of shops and restaurants on three levels is set around a landscaped atrium rising the full seven stories of the building. Beneath the vast skylight, through which the main tower can be glimpsed, café tables have been placed among trees and shrubs. Popular and full of vitality, the atrium is often the scene of exhibitions, concerts and other activities.

Return to Park Avenue.

Lever House★. – Designed by Skidmore, Owings & Merrill and much influenced by the architectural concepts of Le Corbusier, Lever House was considered avant-garde when it opened in 1952. The graceful 21-story tower of blue-green glass and stainless steel rising from a two-story base was an exciting contrast with the concrete and stone apartment buildings which lined the Avenue in 1952.

Changing art exhibits can be viewed in the main lobby *(Mondays through Fridays 10 AM – 5 PM; Sundays and holidays – 5 PM; closed Saturdays except May and December, Sundays and holidays June to Labor Day, and January 1, July 4, Thanksgiving Day and December 25 ☎ 906-4685).*

Continuing along Park Avenue, note the **Mercedes-Benz showroom** at no 430. Designed in 1955 by Frank Lloyd Wright, it is a symphony of ramp and reflection.

At the corner of 57th Street is the Ritz Tower, a typical Park Avenue apartment building. The legendary Le Pavillon restaurant once occuped space on the ground floor.

Between 58th and 59th Streets at **499 Park Avenue,** a black glass and aluminum tower housing the Banque Nationale de Paris can be seen. Designed by I.M. Pei, it opened in 1981.

At this point, on either side of the street, the **view★★** toward the Pan Am Building is resplendent.

Rising behind 500 Park Avenue (1960) is **500 Park Tower,** a slender 40-story mixed-use building designed by James Stewart Polshek & Partners in association with Schuman, Lichtenstein, Claman, Efron. Though recently constructed (1984), the Tower is pleasingly compatible with its 11-story neighbor: the upper stories are partly cantilevered and its granite, glass and aluminium skin blends well with the exterior of the earlier structure. The interior is given over to commercial space on the lower floors and luxury condominium apartments on the floors above.

On the corner of 59th Street is Christie's, fine art auctioneers since 1766.

Beyond 60th Street, Park Avenue becomes residential and one of the most fashionable addresses in the city, as a short stroll uptown will soon make obvious.

Half-Price Tickets

Tickets are sold on the day of performance to Broadway, Off-Broadway, Lincoln Center and other performing arts events at half-price plus a small service charge.

The Times Square Theatre Centre — Duffy Square, Broadway and 47th Street, 354-5800
> *evening performance tickets are sold Mondays through Saturdays 3 PM to 8 PM*
> *matinee tickets are sold Wednesdays and Saturdays 10 AM to 2 PM*
> *matinee and evening tickets are sold Sundays noon to 8 PM.*

The Lower Manhattan Theatre Centre — Two World Trade Center, mezzanine, 354-5800
> *evening performance tickets are sold Mondays through Fridays 11 AM to 5:30 PM; Saturdays 11:30 AM to 3:30 PM*
> *matinee and Sunday tickets are sold one day prior to performance 11 AM to 8 PM.*

The Music & Dance Booth - Bryant Park, near the corner of 42nd Street and Avenue of the Americas, 382-2323
> *music and dance tickets only are sold Sundays noon to 6 PM*
> *Tuesdays, Thursdays and Fridays noon to 2 PM and 3 PM to 7 PM*
> *Wednesdays and Saturdays 11 AM to 2 PM and 3 PM to 7 PM*
> *matinee tickets are sold day of performance*
> *Monday tickets are sold one day prior to performance.*

Brooklyn Information/TKTS map p 147 - Court and Montague Streets, Brooklyn, (718) 625-5015
> *evening performance tickets are sold Tuesdays through Saturdays 11 AM to 5:30 PM; Saturdays 11 AM to 3:30 PM*
> *matinee and Sunday tickets are sold one day prior to performance.*

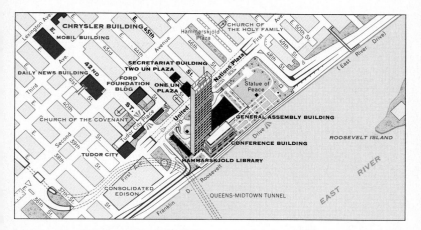

Situated on the banks of the East River, the headquarters of the United Nations is dominated by the Secretariat Building, a tall, slender structure which rises toward the sky above the surrounding building and sculpture studded gardens.

A Philanthropist. – The Charter of the United Nations was drafted at the founding conference in San Francisco in 1945. The following year, the General Assembly and Security Council met for the first time in London where the decision was made to locate the permanent headquarters in the United States. Later that year, the General Assembly met at Hunter College in the Bronx, and then finally at Flushing Meadow in Queens *(p 156)*.

In December 1946, John D. Rockefeller, Jr. *(p 36)* offered the United Nations a gift of $8 500 000 in order to acquire the present site on the East River, between 42nd and 48th Streets. This area, known as Turtle Bay, consisted mainly of slums, slaughter houses and breweries. The construction of the UN headquarters, coupled with renovation projects by the city of New York, has revitalized the area. The UN buildings were designed under the direction of the American architect Wallace K. Harrison.

Building the UN. – The construction program cost about $67 000 000. The government of the United States made available an interest-free loan of $65 000 000, which is being reimbursed by annual payments. The balance was met from the regular United Nations budget. Among the numerous architects consulted on the project were Le Corbusier (France) and Oscar Niemeyer (Brazil).

The Secretariat Building was occupied in 1950, and two years later the first meetings of the Security Council and the General Assembly could be held at the permanent site. The new Dag Hammarskjöld Memorial Library was completed in 1962. The entire group of buildings and gardens, occupying 18 acres of land, enjoy extraterritorial status.

The Organs of the UN. – The United Nations, governed by a charter of 111 articles, is composed of six principal organs and a number of subsidiary organs. Working closely with the UN are 15 specialized international agencies such as UNESCO (in Paris) in the fields of science, education and culture, the FAO (in Rome) dealing with food and agriculture, and the IMF (in Washington, D.C.) which helps to stabilize exchange rates. The UN and these specialized agencies comprise what is known as "the United Nations family."

The Secretary General, at present Javier Pérez de Cuéllar of Peru, is the chief administrative officer of the Organization. He performs such functions as are necessary to carry out decisions or recommendations adopted by the General Assembly and the Councils.

■ THE COMPLEX

Exterior

From the corner of 45th Street and First Avenue, there is a view of the buildings, with the flags of member states (160 as of April 1990; there were 51 original members). These flags are arranged in alphabetical order according to the English spelling, the same order in which delegations are seated in the General Assembly. Beneath the lawn to the north of the building, three underground levels are occupied by printing facilities.

Hammarskjöld Library. – The library, a gift of the Ford Foundation *(p 81)*, is dedicated to the memory of the second Secretary General, **Dag Hammarskjöld,** killed in 1961 in a plane crash during his peace-keeping mission to the Congo.

Its marble walls enclose 380 000 volumes for the use of UN delegates, Secretariat staff members and scholars. In addition, there are newspapers, reading rooms, a collection of 80 000 maps, a microfilm laboratory, tape recording services and an auditorium.

Secretariat Building. – *Not open to the public.* Constructed entirely of white Vermont marble and glass and aluminium panels, the building is architecturally striking for its pure, clean lines. The simple grid-like pattern of the exterior rises 39 floors without a break. In front of it is a circular marble pool donated by American schoolchildren, with black and white stones collected by the children of the Greek island of Rhodes; set in the pool is *Single Form*, an abstract sculpture by Barbara Hepworth of Great Britain.

The 5 155 international civil servants and other employees who work here are drawn from many of the member nations, and include interpreters and translators, experts in international law and econo mics, press officers, print ers, librarians, statisticians, 235 United Nations guards and other supporting staff. Young people in uniform or their native dress serve as tour guides for the approxi mately half a million visitors who come each year.

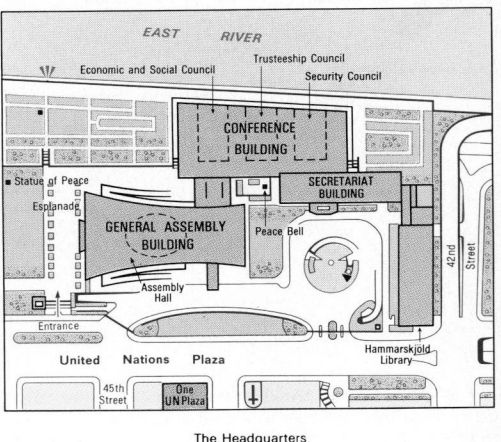

The Headquarters

Conference Building. – Thus named because of its council and committee meeting rooms, this build ing links the Secretariat and the Assembly build ings. The meetings of the Security Council, the Econ omic and Social Council, and the Trusteeship Coun cil are held here. The main facade faces the East River.

General Assembly Building. – A long, low-lying structure with an elegantly curved roof, this building contains the Assembly Hall, which is covered by a central dome.

Diagonally across from the UN Secretariat and General Assembly Buildings, at the northwest corner of 44th Street and First Avenue, rise the dual spires of **United Nations Plaza** (1976), sheathed entirely in green reflecting glass. Designed by Kevin Roche, John Dinkeloo and Associates (architects of the Ford Foundation Building, Lehman Pavilion and other recent additions at the Metropolitan Museum of Art). One and Two UN Plaza complement the Secretariat Building.

Continue to the north of the buildings on the esplanade in front of the visitors entrance. From here you have an attractive view of the gardens. The bronze equestrian statue, *Peace,* was a gift from Yugoslavia. A nearby stairway leads to a lower terrace with a riverside promenade, providing good views of the UN complex, the river and buildings along the bank.

Interior

The Conference Building and parts of the General Assembly Building may be visited only by guided tour daily except January 1 and December 25. Tour (1 hour) includes visits to the main meeting rooms and leaves every 15 min from 9 AM to 4:45 PM.
Purchase tickets ($5.50) at the Tour Desk at the south end of the General Assembly Building's main lobby. Appropriate attire is required. Children under 5 are not admitted.
Tours conducted in Arabic, Chinese, English, French, Russian, Spanish and other languages (if guides are available). Reservations advised for foreign language tours (☎ 963-4440). The Information Desk in the center of the lobby distributes free tickets to open meetings.

General Assembly Building. – The building is the heart of the United Nations.

Main Lobby. – Enter through one of the seven doors donated by Canada and turn around. Notice that the exterior wall of concrete and glass, which seemed opaque from the outside, now appears translucent.

Beyond the **Information Desk** is the curved wall of the Conference Room. To the right of the entrance is the **Meditation Room,** dedicated to those who have died in the name of peace. The room is high lighted by a stained glass window by Chagall. Unveiled in 1964 as a memorial to Dag Hammarskjöld, the window was contributed by the members of the UN staff and the artist.

Assembly Hall. – Lighted from above, the oval Assembly Hall measures 165ft by 115ft and is 75ft high. The speaker's rostrum is surmounted by a dais on which sits the President of the General Assembly flanked by the Secretary General and the Under Secretary General for Political and General Assembly Affairs. Above the dais, the emblem of the United Nations hangs between the illuminated boards which indicate members, votes. On either side are glass-enclosed booths for radio and television, and for the interpreters who work in the six official UN languages: English, French, Spanish, Russian, Arabic and Chinese. The side walls are decorated with murals designed by the French artist Fernand Léger and executed by his student Bruce Gregory.

The General Assembly regularly meets in an annual three-month session which starts on the third Tuesday in September. Special sessions may be called at the request of the Security Council or of a majority of the Member States.

The Assembly may discuss any matters within the scope of the Charter, except those under consideration by the Security Council. It also receives and discusses annual reports from the other organs and votes on the UN budget. Decisions on important questions are made by a two-thirds majority of members present and voting; a simple majority suffices for other matters. Member nations are required to obey only those decisions of the Assembly concerning the UN budget. The Assembly may pass resolutions, initiate studies and make recommendations for the maintenance of peace.

and security and the promotion of international cooperation. It also elects its own president and vice-presidents, admits new members on the recommendation of the Security Council and chooses the non-permanent members of the Security Council.

Conference Building. – The five stories of the Conference Building house, from the basement up, technical installations (air conditioning, printing presses, television and recording studios, photographic dark rooms), Conference Rooms, Council Chambers, Delegates' Lounges, the Delegates' Dining Room and the cafeteria for the members of the Secretariat.

A number of works of art, gifts of member nations, may be seen during the tour: a Persian carpet, a mosaic from Morocco, a huge Belgian Tapestry, two Brazilian murals depicting Peace and War, a painting by Rouault: *Christ Crucified,* an ivory carving from China illustrating the Chengtu-Kunming Railway and a scale model of a Thai royal barge. In the garden, in front of the Conference Building and the Secretariat, is a Japanese peace bell, made of copper coins and metals donated by the people of 60 countries.

Security Council. – The chamber, donated by Norway, is decorated with gold and blue hangings, and a mural by Norwegian artist Per Krohg symbolizing Peace and Liberty, Equality and Fraternity. There are seats for 200 people in the public gallery.

The primary responsibility for the maintenance of international peace and security lies with the Security Council. Amendments which were adopted by the General Assembly and came into force in 1965 have increased the number of members of the Security Council from 11 to 15; 10 are elected for two year terms , and the other 5 (China, France, United Kingdom, USSR, United States) are permanent. Votes on procedural matters require an affirmative vote of 9 members, and for important questions, these 9 must include the 5 permanent members. This rule of unanimity for the "great powers" is better known as the veto, but an abstention by a permanent member does not in practice prevent a decision from being adopted. The members of the Security Council preside in rotation; the president changes every month.

Trusteeship Council. – The furnishings in this room were the gift of Denmark. Precious woods cover the walls and provide the backdrop for a large teak statue of a woman releasing a bluebird, which symbolizes Hope and Independence.

The Trusteeship Council supervises the Trust Territories administered by Member States. Only one territory remains which has not become independent: the U.S. Strategic Trust Territory of the Pacific Islands, which includes the Marshalls, the Carolines and the Mariana Islands, except Guam.

Economic and Social Council. – This functional room was decorated with funds contributed by Sweden. The plain walls and exposed heating apparatus contrast with the vivid colors of the large "window wall."

The council coordinates the efforts and resources of various UN and affiliated organizations towards the alleviation of economic and social problems. Subjects under consideration include the environment, population, women's rights, health, transportation, human rights, crime prevention and freedom of information. All the decisions of the Council are subject to the approval of the General Assembly.

View of the United Nations from the East River.

Distance: about 1/2 mile – Time: about 2 hours.

Slicing across Manhattan from the East River to the Hudson, Forty-Second Street is New York's major crosstown artery. Its eastern section between the United Nations and Fifth Avenue contains a magnificent assortment of distinguished buildings reflecting changing architectural styles since 1900.

A BIT OF HISTORY

From the Shanties to the Skyscrapers. – Forty-Second Street was officially opened to settlement in 1836 by the mayor, in an attempt to encourage people to move uptown and enjoy the pure clean air. However, in 1860 it was an area of shanties where newly arrived immigrants eked out an existence among their pigs and goats. As the city grew, the municipal government had some difficulty removing these people.

(From documents, Library of the Boston Athenaeum.)

The site of 42nd Street in 1850.

Thus the development of Forty-Second Street as a hub of activity began only in the 20C when the land, once rocky and sloping, was leveled and Grand Central Terminal built, followed gradually by its neighbors.

■ TUDOR CITY

This group of buildings constructed (1925-28) in Tudor Gothic style stands on the site of Corcoran's Roost, the hideout of one Paddy Corcoran, a notorious bandit.

The complex was developed as a self-contained city with 3 000 apartments, a hotel, shops, and private park along its own street – Tudor City Place. The twelve brick buildings enjoy a relative calm and isolation rare in New York. They face onto the park and are almost windowless on their east side because in the 1920s, the chic plaza where the United Nations stands today *(p 77)* was an industrial area of breweries, slaughterhouses, glue factories, and a gas works.

From Tudor City Place, which crosses East Forty-Second Street by a bridge *(access by steps from Forty-Second Street or from 43rd Street)*, there is a fine view of East Forty-Second Street and of the United Nations to the east.

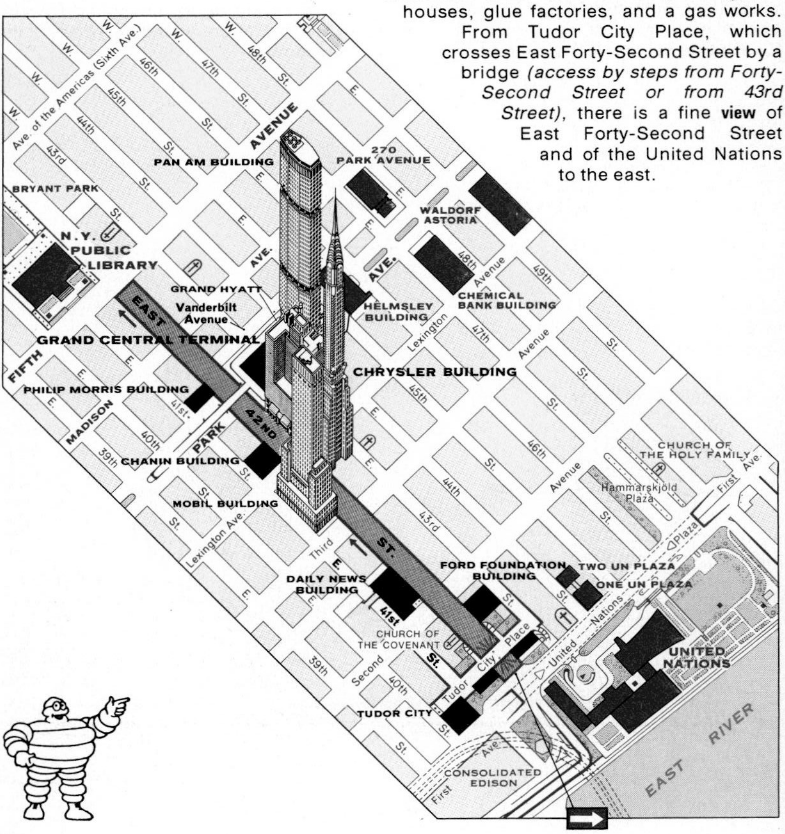

■ FORD FOUNDATION BUILDING ★

Main entrance on 43rd Street – building open Mondays through Fridays 9 AM to 5 PM but can be viewed from East Forty-Second Street. This elegant 12-story glass box anchored by granite pillars was designed by Roche, Dinkeloo and Associates and opened in 1967. It reversed the trend of the 60s to build in the center of a plaza and instead encompassed the plaza in the building. This **plaza**, 10 stories in height, covering 1/3 acre and enclosed by a skylight, forms a magnificent glass house containing trees, shrubs, flowering plants and a pool. Offices at the sides and top of the building overlook the garden.

The building forms an appropriate home for this private, non-profit making institution established in 1936 by Henry Ford and Edsel Ford. Foundation funds support research, training and other activities in the fields of urban poverty, rural poverty, human rights, public policy, education, culture, and international affairs. To date, the Ford Foundation has assisted more than 9 000 organizations all over the United States and in many foreign countries.

■ DAILY NEWS BUILDING

The original News Building was designed by Howells and Hood and constructed in 1930. White brick piers alternate built with patterned red and black brick spandrels and windows to give the tower a vertical striped look and an illusion of height greater than its actual 37 stories, which made it remarkable in 1930. The more recent annex (1958) stretching to Second Avenue has conserved this striped look.

Above the main entrance *(220 East Forty-Second Street)* note the embellishments typical of the stylized decorative designs of the 30s.

The lobby is famed for its huge revolving globe (12ft in diameter) and the clock showing differences in time in 17 time zones. The floor is laid out as a giant compass indicating most of the principal cities of the United States and the world and their distance, by air, from New York City.

The Daily News is a tabloid with the largest circulation of any metropolitan newspaper in the United States (more than 1.2 million copies daily, 1.6 million on Sundays).

■ MOBIL BUILDING ★

Not open to the public. When built in 1955 this massive 45-story structure at 150 East Forty-Second Street was the largest metal clad office building in the world and an attempt by the steel industry to show that glass and aluminum were not the trends of the future. The stainless steel "skin" is about 1/3 of an inch thick (it is backed by a masonry wall) and it is embossed with a design which makes it self-cleaning – the wind scours the splayed pattern and prevents dirt building up. It was also the largest centrally air conditioned structure ever built.

■ CHRYSLER BUILDING ★★★

This building with its distinctive spire of radiant stainless steel arches which glimmer in sunlight and are illuminated at night, is one of New York's famous landmarks. Designed by William Van Alen and completed in 1930, it was briefly the tallest building in the world (the Empire State Building was opened in 1931). It was also one of the first buildings to have exposed metal as an essential part of its design. The decoration on the masonry walls below the spire changes with every setback but always has an automotive theme. Note in particular the huge radiator cap gargoyles (from the 1929 Chrysler) at the fourth level.

The **lobby**, a fine example of "high" Art Deco, is faced with African marble and boasts elevators with ornate elevator doors and richly paneled interiors. Chrysler no longer has offices in the building.

Con Edison, the New York power corporation, has a permanent display on conservation on the ground floor *(entrance on Lexington Ave; open 9 AM to 5 PM; closed Sundays, Mondays and major holidays).*

■ CHANIN BUILDING ★

A prime example of the Art Deco style, this building designed by Sloan and Robertson was opened in 1929. Note the frieze of floral bas-reliefs on the exterior and the intricately detailed lobby with its ornamented door frames, elaborate convector grilles and mailboxes.

■ GRAND HYATT HOTEL ★

This immense structure of silver mirror glass, 30 stories high and H-shaped, was opened in 1980. Designed by Gruzen and Partners with Der Scutt, it is a total contrast to its neighbors – Grand Central Terminal and the Chrysler Building, both of which are reflected in it.

This rather flashy exterior – it is rare for a hotel to have so much glass – contains an elegant and cosmopolitan interior.

From the entrance foyer *(on East Forty-Second Street)* with its waterfall, Italian marble and bronze-sheathed columns, an escalator takes visitors up into the 275ft long lobby enclosed within a 4-story high atrium. Here, shops and restaurants surround a fountain, plants, lounge and a brass rod sculpture by Peter Lobello. Natural light filters into this area from the Sun Garden – a sort of second floor sidewalk café which is cantilevered over East Forty-Second Street offering interesting views.

■ GRAND CENTRAL TERMINAL★★

This famous railroad terminal, one of the two major stations in New York *(Penn Station p 125)*, is a symbol of the city and a masterpiece of urban planning. From street level there is virtually no evidence that a vast railroad terminal exists at all. The trains carrying 190 000 daily commuters in addition to long distance travelers arrive and depart via a subterranean tunnel along Park Avenue.

From Depot to Terminal. – The first steam trains in New York chugged down Fourth Avenue (now Park) to a depot at 23rd Street. Then horses pulled the coaches to the end of the line near City Hall. An 1854 ordinance banned steam locomotives south of Forty-Second Street because of air and noise pollution, and so **Commodore Cornelius Vanderbilt**, who had acquired and consolidated all the city's railroad companies by 1869, built a huge iron and glass terminal at the present site.

A 1902 state order banned steam locomotives from the city altogether leaving the railroad company (New York Central) with the choice of relocating outside city limits or electrifying the line. Under the direction of chief engineer, William J. Wilgus, they chose the latter, deciding to cover the tracks and bring trains in on two levels. The engineering firm of Reed and Stem and architects Warren and Wetmore designed the new terminal.

(From photo Ewing Galloway.)

Grand Central Terminal.

The Terminal Building. – The sumptuous façade of this classic Beaux Arts structure, completed in 1913, faces south down Park Avenue and features three massive arched windows separated by pairs of columns. Surmounting all is a clock and sculpture by Jules Coutan, which incorporates the figure of Mercury (Commerce) flanked by Hercules (Physical Energy) and Minerva (Moral Energy). Below the sculpture stands a statue of Commodore Vanderbilt.

Inside, the cavernous **main concourse** is 275 ft long, 120 ft wide and 125 ft high, topped by a vaulted ceiling decorated with the signs of the zodiac. The elegant spaces below are appointed with melon chandeliers, terrazo floors in the north balcony, and a central clock of brass and white onyx. Continuous streams of people flood past shops and service concessions which line the two levels of ramps leading to the tracks. The terminal is connected to many of the neighboring buildings underground.

Walk through the concourse to the Pan Am Building.

■ PAN AM BUILDING★

The vast behemoth of the Pan Am Building rises up behind Grand Central Terminal to the north, dwarfing all around it. Conceived by a group of architects including **Walter Gropius** of the Bauhaus School, its nonconforming design and the fact that it blocked the formerly unobstructed view down Park Avenue raised a storm of protest which still rumbles occasionally today. With 2 400 000sq ft of office space, it was one of the largest office buildings in the world when built (exceeded only by the Pentagon). Its octagonal tower of precast concrete rises 59 stories and is broken only by two floors of mechanical equipment.

In the lobby *(street level, Vanderbilt Avenue side)*, redesigned and refurbished in the late 1980s, note the grand curving stairway that rises to the mezzanine. The building is best viewed from Park Avenue to the north *(illustration p 31)*.

■ PHILIP MORRIS WORLD HEADQUARTERS

This 26-story tower, designed by Ulrich Franzen and Associates, is distinguished by its two different facades. On the Park Avenue side, vertical strips of granite run up the building above the classically inspired main entrance. The East Forty-Second Street facade, however, is simpler and less ornamented in design. Surmounting the Park Avenue entrance is an enormous medallion of the Philip Morris corporate insignia.

On the ground floor will be found a branch of the Whitney Museum of American Art *(p 51) (open 11 AM to 6 PM - 7:30 PM Thursdays; closed Sundays and most holidays)*, its refined and inviting atmosphere a welcome respite from the crowded sidewalks and traffic-clogged streets. Large 20C American sculptures are displayed in the 42ft high enclosed sculpture court *(open 7:30 AM to 9:30 PM, Sundays 11 AM to 7 PM)*, and an adjacent gallery serves for temporary exhibitions covering the entire range of American art.

For security reasons visitors may not be permitted to enter certain buildings, especially office buildings. This situation changes constantly, thus we hope our readers will understand if they are unable to enter a sight described in the guide due to circumstances unknown to us at press time.

Distance: 1 1/4 miles – Time: about 4 1/2 hours (visits not included).

Gigantic skyscrapers, as close together as trees in a forest, are typical of the Financial District, feverishly busy during the week and deserted on weekends. Along with Broad Street, Wall Street is the most famous: its name a symbol of the financial power of the United States.

It is best to visit weekday mornings.

A BIT OF HISTORY

New York's Dutch Days. – The general area we now call the Financial District was the center of Dutch power in the middle of the 17C, when the town was still called Nieuw Amsterdam. The Dutch town occupied a limited area, protected to the south by a fort and to the north by a wooden wall (the origin of the name of Wall Street) from the Hudson River to the East River.

About 1 000 persons occupied the 120 houses made of wood or brick, with characteristic Dutch gables and tile roofs. The windmill and a canal, "The Ditch," in the middle of Broad Street, made the town seem really Dutch. At the end of "The Ditch" on the East River, where Indians paddled their canoes, sailing ships of various sizes anchored, sheltered by the tip of Manhattan.

The inhabitants were of varied origins; in 1642, when the first Stadhuis (became City Hall in 1653) was built at 71 Pearl Street, no less than 18 languages were spoken in Nieuw Amsterdam.

Governing the town was first a commercial agent of the Company, and later a succession of governors. The most famous, Peter Stuyvesant *(p 131)* founded the noble body of chimney inspectors in 1648. Fires then, as now, were a constant concern of the municipal authorities.

Under the Cross of St George. – When the British occupied Nieuw Amsterdam in 1664, the town changed very little. Pigs still roamed the muddy streets, haphazardly solving the garbage problem and occasionally biting passersby. But Breetweg became Broadway, "The Ditch" was filled in, the wall was torn down and, from the beginning of the 18C, colonial Georgian houses *(p 30)* like Fraunces Tavern *(p 86)* began to replace the narrow Dutch dwellings.

The press had its difficulties. Eight years after **William Bradford** founded the first New York newspaper, the *Gazette,* another printer, **John Peter Zenger**, started the New York *Weekly Journal* (in 1733), in which he attacked the governor. The furious official had the offensive issues burned by the sheriff's men in the middle of Wall Street, and Zenger was thrown into prison where he languished for a year, still managing to publish his newspaper. Finally the trial began at the colonial City Hall (at the site of the present **Federal Hall National Memorial,** *p 89*); brilliantly defended by Andrew Hamilton, Zenger was acquitted. Fifty years before England, New York was well on the way to achieving a free press.

The Blacks, Africans or West Indians increased in numbers, forming one-fifth of New York's population by the middle of the 18C. A number of freed slaves settled at the end of Wall Street, near the slave market.

Two fires, in 1776 and 1835, devastated the area, without affecting its role in finance.

■ THE WORLD TRADE CENTER★★

Occupying a 16-acre site, the buildings of the World Trade Center are grouped around a plaza which appears as a vast, open space in this densely developed section of Manhattan. The idea for such a trade center was proposed in 1960 and legislation was passed in 1962 authorizing the Port Authority to realize such a project.

Plans were drawn up by the architects Minoru Yamasaki and Associates and Emery Roth and Sons; construction started in August 1966. The first tenants of this project opened their offices in late 1970 and it is estimated that 60 000 people work here and a further 90 000 businessmen and other visitors come to the center daily.

The role of the trade center is the advancement and expansion of international trade and it has already been called a "United Nations of Commerce." All international business services are concentrated here – exporters, importers, American and overseas manufacturers, freight forwarders, Custom House brokers, international banks, federal, state and overseas trade development agencies, trade associations and transportation lines – making this the central market of international trade.

The Buildings

The complex includes two 110-story high buildings, twin towers (1 and 2 WTC), a U.S. Customhouse (6 WTC), two plaza buildings (4 and 5 WTC) and an international hotel (3 WTC), all surrounding the central plaza; a 47-story tower (7 WTC) connected to the central plaza by a walkway that passes over Vesey Street; a PATH (Port Authority Trans-Hudson) railroad terminal, parking for 2 000 cars, truck dock, storage areas, access to the New York subways and 8 acres of shops and services on the concourse.

The Plaza. – This sweeping 5-acre plaza links the various buildings of the center and interconnects with other pedestrian systems in the area. In the fountain-pool is a slowly revolving huge bronze sculptured globe by the German, Fritz Koenig.

From this point pause and look across to the **twin towers;** allow your eyes to travel slowly from the lower to upper stories. Peering upward as though from the bottom of a deep well, you will experience the dizzy effect of perspective and wonder if the ground is actually moving beneath your feet, or is this sensation merely an illusion.

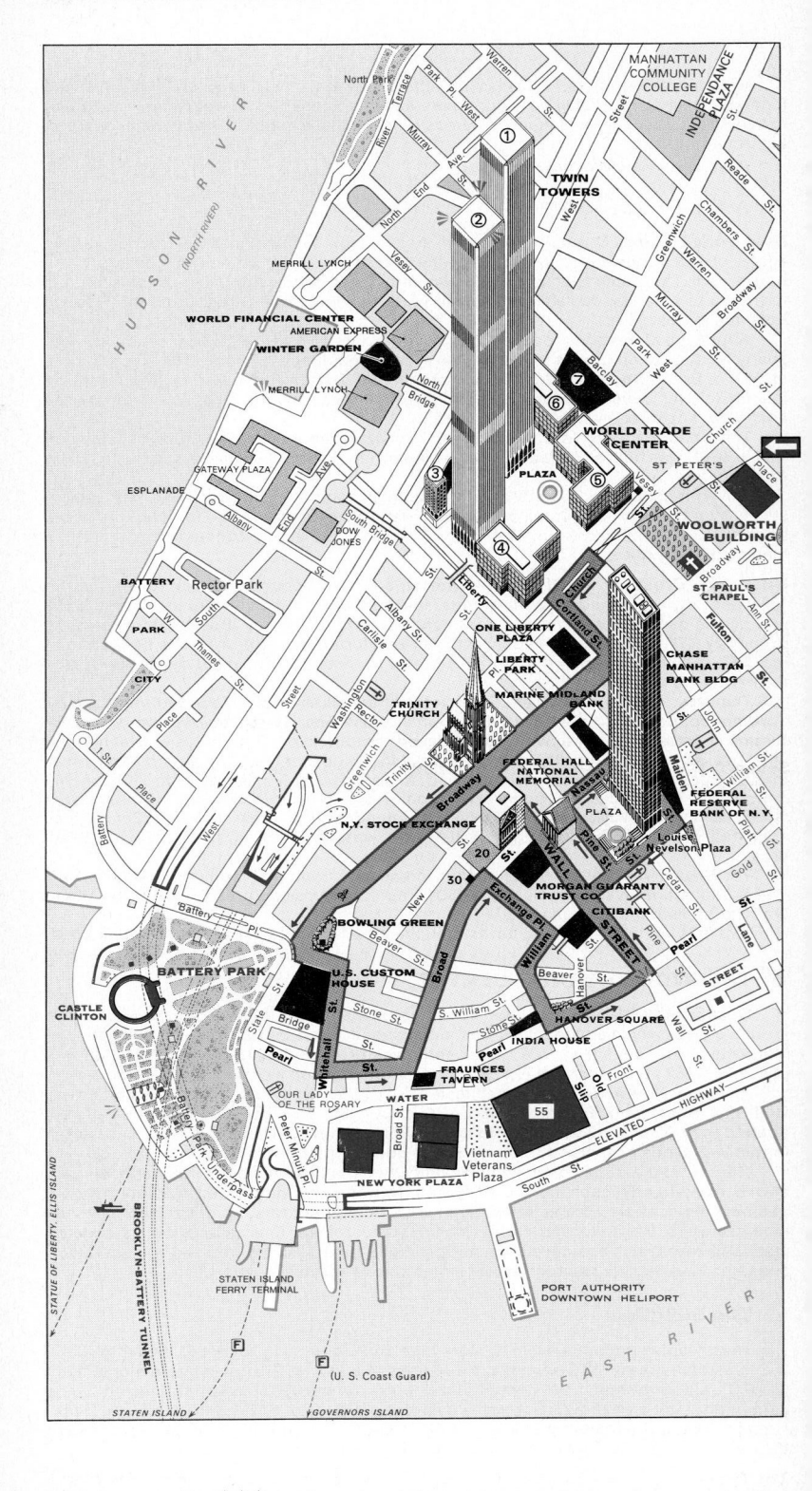

Twin Towers (1,2)★★★. – These two 110-story tower buildings, the second tallest buildings in the nation after the Sears Roebuck Building in Chicago, rise upwards to 1 350ft to add an additional landmark to the Manhattan skyline.

The problem of laying foundations in wet landfill terrain without disrupting existing communications and surrounding buildings was solved by using the "slurry wall" foundation system, whereby an underground concrete wall was built around the site.

With the wall in place, excavation work began within this "bath tub" area, without danger of subsidence due to water pumping. The excavated material was used to create 23 acres of landfill for Battery Park City.

The conventional skyscraper is built with a maze of interior columns. In the towers, a new structural design was used in which the exterior walls bear most of the load, providing the maximum of open column-free floor space. These outer walls consist of closely spaced vertical columns of steel, tied together by massive horizontal spandrel beams which girdle the towers at every floor. The columns are covered with a thin skin of aluminum, and separated by tinted floor to ceiling windows recessed 10in.

The introduction of the "skylobby" system minimizes the floor space occupied by elevator shaftways. Each building is divided into 3 zones: 1 – 43rd; 44 – 77; 78 – 110th. The 44th and 78th are the skylobbies which are connected to the ground floor lobby by express elevators, traveling 1 600ft per minute. A battery of local elevators then serves all floors within each zone. There are, therefore, three "locals" operating in each shaft.

One World Trade Center contains the **World Trade Institute** *(55th floor)* which offers practical courses in all aspects of world trade, as well as modern conference facilities.

Panorama ★ ★ ★ . – Observation deck on 107th floor of Two WTC. Open 9:30 AM to 9:30 PM; hours vary on Thanksgiving Day, December 24, 25, 31 and January 1 ☎ 466-7397. $3.50, children $1.75

The glass-enclosed observation deck of Two WTC offers a spectacular view of the entire metropolitan area from a downtown vantage point. Weather permitting, it is also possible to take an escalator up to the 110th floor to the rooftop "promenade" for a stroll at a quarter of a mile in the sky. On the 107th floor of One WTC, the view can be enjoyed from the Windows of the World restaurant. Numerous shops, cocktail lounges, restaurants and snack bars are found throughout the complex.

Plaza Buildings (4, 5). – These two 9-story buildings flank the main entrance at Church Street. Four WTC serves as headquarters for four exchanges: the New York Cotton Exchange, the New York Coffee, Sugar and Cocoa Exchange, the Commodity Exchange, Inc. and the New York Mercantile Exchange, and their Commodities Exchange Center trading floor. *Trading activities may be observed from the visitors gallery (Commodities Exchange Center: 4 WTC, 9th floor) 9:30 AM to 3 PM Mondays through Fridays.*

Five WTC contains the offices of a variety of international trade and financial firms.

U.S. Customhouse (6). – Bordering the northwest corner of the site, this 8-story building consolidates all intricate customs functions relating to the movement of commerce in and out of the port, in one convenient location.

Seven WTC. – This 47-story office tower clad in insulated glass and polished red granite is the most recent addition to the World Trade Center complex. The building's trapezoidal shape reflects the irregular site on which it stands, bounded by Vesey, Church and Barclay Streets and West Broadway. An open plaza and a covered walkway link the upper lobby level of 7 WTC to the main plaza of the World Trade Center.

Vista International Hotel (3). – Designed by Skidmore, Owings & Merrill, the Vista International (1981) has the distinction of being the first major hotel in almost 150 years to be built in the downtown area. The Vista is a modern 22-story hostelry catering primarily to a clientele with business dealings in the World Trade Center.

Take the stairway between One WTC and the Vista Hotel down to West Street. Across West Street is Battery Park City.

■ BATTERY PARK CITY

This vast commercial-residential complex adjoining the Financial District rises on 92 acres of landfill edged by the Hudson River. An extension of lower Manhattan, Battery Park City will when completed *(scheduled completion late 1990s)* have a working population of about 40 000 and a residential population of almost 25 000.

Development. – The idea to create Battery Park City was first conceived by Governor Nelson Rockefeller in the late 1960s. The landfill and infrastructure were completed in the mid-1970s, then work at the site came to a halt. The fate of the project remained uncertain until, in 1979, during the administrations of Mayor Ed Koch and Governor Hugh Carey, a new plan to develop the area was adopted. Construction once more began.

The Complex. – The commercial heart of Battery Park City is the **World Financial Center** designed by Cesar Pelli Associates. Its four glass and granite-sheathed office towers extending from Vesey Street to Albany Street are home to some of the nation's most prestigious brokerage and financial services firms: American Express Company, Dow Jones, Merrill Lynch. Marked by setbacks and notches, topped with copper roofs, and solid in appearance, the buildings of the World Financial Center are a graceful blend of traditional design elements which harmonize well with the earlier structures of lower Manhattan. Set amidst the WFC and looking out on North Cove is the **Winter Garden** ★ , a vaulted glass and steel structure reminiscent of the crystal palaces of the 19C. The Winter Garden is the site of performing arts programs and events, and houses shops and a variety of restaurants. Inside, the grand central staircase is as versatile as it is handsome, serving as a stage and providing additional seating space when necessary.

On the fringe of the WFC are the buildings of Gateway Plaza (1982), the first of Battery Park City's residential developments which will eventually stretch north to Chambers Street and down to the Battery. Just to the south lies the architectural pleasing Rector Place area, with ten buildings containing 2 200 residential units.

Landscaped parks, public plazas and open spaces, too, are a part of this enormous complex. Especially pleasant is the riverside esplanade *(access from Liberty Street)* with its benches, trees, flowering shrubs and **views** ★ ★ of the harbor.

Turn right on Liberty Street. Cross Church street and continue on Liberty street.

■ FROM LIBERTY PLAZA TO HANOVER SQUARE

One Liberty Plaza. – This 54-story building (1974) of dark gray painted steel and tinted gray windows was designed by Skidmore, Owings & Merrill.

The surrounding plaza and Liberty Park to the south of Liberty Street, form an important link in the pedestrian system reaching from the World Trade Center eastward to the financial district.

At Broadway turn right and note, on the left, the **Marine Midland Bank**. A tall, dark, glass-curtained tower, this 55-story building rises straight up without setbacks. Its smooth unbroken exterior is characteristic of the buildings erected in the 1960s and later.

The sculpture in the plaza fronting the bank is a reddish-orange **cube** (actually a rhomboid) by Isamu Noguchi. Resting solely on one corner, the sharply angled, bright colored cube is an ideal foil for the elegant and reserved bank building.

Trinity Church★ . – On Broadway, at the beginning of Wall Street, stands Trinity Church now dwarfed by the surrounding buildings, but the highest building in New York for nearly 50 years. Around the church is the churchyard where a number of famous New Yorkers are buried.

The First Anglican Parish of New York. – An Episcopal church, Trinity was founded by a charter granted by William III in 1697. Influential local citizens aided in its construction. Among them was **Captain Kidd**, the famous pirate-privateer who lived at nearby Hanover Square, and who was hanged for piracy in London in 1701.

The first church building looked like a country chapel with a spire and narrow spear-shaped windows. In 1754 King's College, which was to become Columbia University (p 116), occupied a schoolhouse next door to the church.

This first building burned in the great fire of 1776 and was replaced by another, the roof of which collapsed in 1839. The present building, designed by Richard Upjohn in the Gothic Revival style, was completed in 1846 except for part of the choir (1877), All Saints Chapel (1913) and the Bishop Manning Memorial Wing (1966).

Before the Revolution, Trinity was one of New York's most fashionable parishes.

The Church. – The most interesting part of the exterior is the bell tower with its 280ft spire, which towered above the nearby houses when it was built. The tower contains ten bells including three of the original eight bells dating from 1797. Handsome bronze doors, inspired by those of the Baptistry at Florence, lead to the interior. Notice the highly colored stained glass windows, the white marble altar erected in 1877, and the wooden screen of the Chapel of All Saints (1913) at the right of the choir.

To the left of the chancel is **Trinity Museum** *(open 9 to 11:45 AM and 1 to 3:45 PM - Saturdays 10 AM to 3:45 PM, Sundays 1 to 3:45 PM)* with exhibits portraying the history of Trinity Church and its interrelationship with the city of New York from colonial days to the present.

Free classical music programs (time: 40 min) are given at 12:45 PM Tuesdays.

The Cemetery. – This parcel of land occupied by the Cemetery is worth several million dollars, at the going rate in the area. There are many old tombstones, including some Dutch names: the oldest marks the grave of Richard Churcher, who died in 1681. Notice also the graves of the publisher William Bradford, Jr. (near the entrance, to the right of the church), Robert Fulton, the inventor of the steamboat (left of the church), two Secretaries of the Treasury, Alexander Hamilton (near the fence on Rector Street), and Albert Gallatin, and Francis Lewis, a New York signer of the Declaration of Independence.

After visiting Trinity Church and the cemetery continue south along Broadway.

Bowling Green. – An egg-shaped green with its 1771 wrought iron fence still intact, Bowling Green was named for the lawn where colonial gentlemen played bowls for the modest annual fee of one peppercorn. The prosperous residences which surrounded Bowling Green have disappeared since the middle of the 19C, making way for office buildings.

U.S. Custom House★ . – *On Bowling Green*. Built in 1907 by Cass Gilbert in the Beaux Arts style, the Custom House presents a monumental facade, where white Tennessee marble sculpture adorns the gray Maine granite walls. The lower series, sculpted by Daniel Chester French (who did the statue of Lincoln in the Lincoln Memorial in Washington, D.C.), depicts Asia, America, Europe and Africa. The statues above are curious representations of the most famous trading cities and nations of the world: notice, to the left of the central shield, a woman representing Lisbon, by Augustus Saint-Gaudens, and the doge with a death's head representing Venice.

The customs offices have been transferred to the new U.S. customs building 6 World Trade Center (p 85). The Custom House occupies the site of an early fort and later the former Government House, where the state governors resided: this majestic building with columns and pediment was torn down in 1815 and replaced by a row of handsome buildings later called Steamship Row.

From Bowling Green, continue south on Whitehall Street, behind the Custom House. Turn left on Pearl Street. This very old street originally ran along the shoreline, where a few neoclassical houses remain.

Fraunces Tavern★ . – *Open 10 AM to 4 PM, Sundays noon to 5 PM; closed Saturdays and major holidays. Free admission on Thursdays, other times contribution suggested.*

This handsome brick house, with its slate roof and cream-colored portico and balcony, is a good example of neo-Georgian architecture. It was built in 1719 (restored in 1907) as the home of Etienne de Lancey. He was the first of a family prominent in New York history, which gave its name to Delancey Street (p 131).

The house became a tavern in 1762 when Samuel Fraunces bought the building. He later became President Washington's steward. Governor Clinton *(p 111)* gave a dinner here, celebrating the British evacuation of New York in 1783, and on December 4 of the same year the tavern was also the scene of Washington's farewell to his officers.

Fraunces Tavern has been preserved by the Sons of the Revolution. A restaurant occupies the main floor. A wooden stairway leads to the museum on the upper two floors where permanent and changing exhibitions treat the early history of New York City and the Revolutionary War, and American decorative arts are displayed in period settings.

From Fraunces Tavern walk north on **Broad Street,** the slight curve of which follows the line of the old canal. Broad Street used to be the main street in New York; the activity here is still intense during the week. At no 30 was the *Wall Street Journal* building. The famous business and financial daily now located at 200 Liberty Street in the World Financial Center has a circulation of 2 000 000. Turn right on Exchange Place, and again on William Street for two blocks; then continue one block to the east to reach Hanover Square.

Hanover Square. – This quiet little square planted with trees, gives an idea of what old New York must have been like. The waters of the East River extended up the Old Slip, to lap the foundations of the southeast side of the square. Here and in Pearl Street were numerous shops. Note **India House,** on the south side of Hanover Square, a handsome classical edifice built in 1837.

Walk north on Pearl Street and turn left on Wall Street: you will be struck by the **view★** of the celebrated "canyon" which ends with the tiny dark silhouette of Trinity Church *(p 86).* Pearl Street follows the original shoreline.

■ WALL STREET★★

Center of high finance, Wall Street winds its narrow way in the shadows of the skyscrapers which enclose it. They hide the sunlight from the busy crowds below, which are so thick between 9 AM and 5 PM, and especially at lunch hour, that they almost manage to stop all traffic – quite an exploit in New York!

The Wall and the Street. – In 1653, the Dutch Governor Peter Stuyvesant ordered the construction of a wall of thick planks between the Hudson and the East Rivers to protect the town from marauding Indians. In fact, the protection was rather symbolic, since

(From engraving, Museum of City of New York.)

Wall Street, early 19C.

the inhabitants regularly dismantled the wall, taking the planks to shore up their houses or even to heat their homes.

Completely dismantled by the English in 1699, the wall was replaced by a new street where, on the corner of Broad Street, the new City Hall was built. Wall Street became an administrative and residential street, with rows of fine homes ornamented with Georgian pilasters and porticoes.

After the Revolution, the east end of the street harbored a series of coffee warehouses and taverns. One of the most famous was the **Tontine Coffee House,** built in 1792 at the corner of Water Street; it was the first home of the New York Stock Exchange.

Business Takes Over. – In the 1840s merchants, warehouses, stores and banks occupied buildings rapidly reconstructed after the 1835 fire, which destroyed 700 houses in the area.

But speculation flourished, especially after 1860. Thus **Jay Gould** (1836-92) tried to corner the gold market with an associate, James Fisk; when Fisk left him to work on his own, Gould sold out and brought about the financial panic of September 24, 1869, "Black Friday."

The father of thirteen children, **Cornelius Vanderbilt** (1794-1877) was nicknamed the "Commodore" because he was first engaged in shipping. Beginning in 1862, he extended his activities to the railroads. First the owner of small lines (the Harlem, Hudson, and New York Central), in 1873 he launched the New York – Buffalo line.

J. Pierpont Morgan (1837-1913), a banker, financed the great new industries: steel, oil and railroads. Generous, but a ruthless businessman, the founder of the famous Morgan Library *(p 122)* was succeeded by his son John Pierpont Morgan, Jr., who was the target of an assassination attempt in 1920; on September 16 a bomb exploded in a cart near the bank, missing Morgan, Jr. but killing 38 innocent people caught in the noonday rush.

(From photo Andreas Feininger, New York.)

Wall Street today.

The business activities and interests of the Vanderbilts, Goulds, Morgans and later other financiers, contributed to the leading position gained by New York in the 20s. Wall Street replaced London as the financial capital of the world and has maintained this role despite the Crash of 1929.

From the intersection of Wall and Pearl Streets, continue toward Trinity Church. Turn right on William Street to reach the Chase Manhattan Bank.

Chase Manhattan Bank. — Born of the merger between the Chase National Bank and the Bank of the Manhattan Company, the Chase Manhattan Bank became, in 1961, the first bank to occupy a prestigious modern building in Lower Manhattan. The stately glass and aluminum structure, designed by Skidmore, Owings & Merrill, rises from a paved plaza which offers access to Nassau and Pine Streets.

The Manhattan Company: from dolors to dollars. – In 1798, a yellow fever epidemic broke out in New York. The inhabitants (55 000 at that time) attributed it to polluted water. The following year, the Manhattan Company was founded to provide and distribute drinking water to the city. They laid down a network of hollow pine log pipes, which still come to light occasionally during excavations.

At the same time, the Manhattan Company, with the encouragement of one of its founders, **Aaron Burr,** decided to expand its activities to the realm of banking and finance, a possibility included in the original charter of the Company granted by the State of New York. Thus, on September 1, 1799, the Manhattan Company opened its first office of discount and deposit. The extension of its activities was a serious blow to the political and financial interests of another founder, **Alexander Hamilton,** who was interested in the two banks then operating in New York. The two men's financial differences reinforced by their longstanding political rivalry finally led Burr to challenge Hamilton to a duel on July 11, 1804, in which Hamilton was fatally wounded.

The Chase National Bank: Salmon P. Chase, father of the modern banking system. – The Chase Bank was founded in 1877 by John Thompson and his son, who named it in honor of **Salmon P. Chase** (1808-73). Chase, U.S. Senator and Governor of Ohio, was later Lincoln's Secretary of the Treasury and Chief Justice of the U.S. Supreme Court. He drafted a bill which was enacted by the Congress as the National Currency Act of 1863, establishing a national currency and the present Federal banking system. The portrait of Chase appears on the largest bill in circulation ($10 000).

Construction. – The tract of land originally purchased by the Chase Manhattan Bank was large, but unfortunately cut in two by a street. This problem was solved when, under an agreement with the city, the bank was able to acquire the part of the street connecting the two parcels.

On this 2 1/2 acre parcel of land, the most expensive in the world, the bank decided to build a single high-rise building, leaving a wide open space for the esplanade which circumscribes the bank. Almost five years were required for the completion of this building, a steel frame structure covered with a glass curtain wall.

Note, on the plaza, Dubuffet's striking sculpture *Group of Four Trees* which is composed of fiber glass materials, yet has the appearance of *papier mâché*.

A Few Figures. – One of the largest office buildings constructed in the last 30 years, the Chase Manhattan building is 813ft high and contains 65 stories (including 5 below street level) and 8 800 windows. An average of 6 000 people work here, more than half for the bank itself, which occupies the five basement floors (90ft of foundations), the first 35 stories and the top floor; the rest is rented to other firms. The interior telephone system links 7 000 extensions.

To the left of the lobby, on the concourse the Plaza Banking Office is curved around the sunken Japanese water garden (designed by the sculptor Isamu Noguchi), where fountains play in the summer.

Located in the fifth basement, the Bank vault is reputed to be the world's largest: longer than a football field, it weighs 985 tons and has 6 doors, each 20in. thick (four of them weigh 45 tons a piece and the other two 30 tons).

Federal Reserve Bank of New York. – Across from the Chase Manhattan Bank, on the Liberty Street side, is the Federal Reserve Bank of New York, an imposing 14-story masonry establishment completed in 1924. The design for this structure was inspired by several 15C Italian Renaissance palaces which were built to house the wealthiest banking and merchant families in Florence. Inside the building, at a depth of 80ft below the street level, is the Federal Reserve's gold vault. Approximately half the length of a football field, this chamber contains the gold reserves of 80 foreign nations, thought to be the largest accumulation of gold in the world: about 338 million troy ounces, with a market value (1989) of nearly $122 billion.

Tours allow the public to view the gold vault and an exhibit on cash processing, including many examples of old currency and coins. Tours (time: 1 hour) by reservation only (at least one week in advance) Mondays through Fridays 10 and 11 AM and 1 and 2 PM; closed bank holidays. Contact the Public Information in writing: 33 Liberty Street, New York, N.Y. 10045; or ℡(212) 720-6130.

Return to William Street. In the small park, Louise Nevelson Plaza, at the triangle formed by William and Pine Streets and Maiden Lane, note the huge black, welded steel sculptures (as high as 70ft) by **Louise Nevelson.** Following William Street, turn right at Wall Street.

Citibank. – This financial establishment, dating from 1812, succeeded the first bank founded in New York by Alexander Hamilton ten years earlier. Its branch at 55 Wall Street occupies a massive classical style building designed in 1842, by Isaiah Rogers, as the Second Merchants Exchange, and enlarged and renovated by McKim, Mead and White in 1907. The main feature of the exterior is a double colonnade: the first tier erected as part of the original structure, the second added in 1907.

Especially impressive is the ornate interior which has been restored to its earlier classic appearance. The Great Hall, embellished with Roman arches and colonnades and marble and travertine, is topped by a 72ft high coffered and domed ceiling.

Continuing west, you arrive at the intersection of Wall and Nassau Streets, with the Federal Hall National Memorial to the northeast, the Morgan Guaranty Trust Company to the southeast, and the New York Stock Exchange to the southwest.

Federal Hall National Memorial★. – Administered by the National Park Service, built of Westchester marble, and reminiscent of a Doric temple, the Federal Hall Memorial occupies the site of one of the most important buildings in old New York. It was originally New York's City Hall and was later (in 1788) remodeled to serve as Federal Hall, the country's first capitol.

Construction of the first English City Hall was started in 1699 on land donated by Abraham de Peyster, and in 1703 the city government moved in. In front of it were placed the pillory where minor offenders were exposed to public derision, and the stake to which they were bound for flogging. The first City Hall also served as a courthouse and a debtor's prison. It was here in 1735 that John Peter Zenger was tried and acquitted of seditious libel *(p 83)*. The Stamp Act Congress met in the same place 30 years later to oppose English colonial policy.

Reconstructed in 1788-89 under the supervision of **Major Charles Pierre L'Enfant**, the French engineer and architect who designed the master plan of Washington, D.C., the building became Federal Hall, the first capitol of the United States under the Constitution. George Washington took the oath of office as the first President on the balcony of Federal Hall on April 30, 1789. The towering statue of Washington by George Q. A. Ward commemorates this event. The Federal Government was transferred to Philadelphia the following year, and the building was used for state and city offices, to be sold for salvage in 1812 for $425.

The present building dates from 1842 and served as the United States Custom House until 1862, when it became the United States Subtreasury. Later the site of a number of government offices, it was designated as an Historic Site in 1939 and a National Memorial in 1955.

The **interior** *(open Mondays through Fridays 9 AM to 5 PM)* is arranged around a large dome resting on sixteen marble columns: mementos of George Washington are displayed and there is an exhibit on the constitution. In the section devoted to the history of the building and New York, several dioramas depict the three buildings which have stood on this site.

In addition, there are changing exhibits in the balcony galleries of Federal Hall year round.

Morgan Guaranty Trust Company. – The exterior of this marble building, which sheltered J. Pierpont Morgan and his fortune, still shows the traces of the explosion of 1920 *(p 87)*. A huge crystal chandelier is visible through the ground floor windows of the 23 Wall Street building.

New York Stock Exchange★. – The facade, with its Corinthian columns and sculpted figures on the pediment symbolizing Commerce, is on the Broad Street side of the building. In front of the entrance, a tree recalls the buttonwood tree at Wall and William Streets where 24 brokers met to found the forerunner of the New York Stock Exchange in 1792. The traders dealt in stocks and bonds issued by the government and a few private companies; a handshake or a tap on the shoulder sealed a bargain.

Today 1 366 Exchange members trade the shares of more than 1 600 leading companies which are listed on the Stock Exchange. These companies are the leaders of American industry and include virtually all of the automobile manufacturing industry and almost 90 % of the electricity producers. One American in five is a shareholder.

The present 17-story building dates from 1903. *On the ground floor is the actual exchange where trading takes place Mondays through Fridays 9:30 AM to 4 PM.*

Visitors Center. – *Entrance 20 Broad Street, 3rd floor; open Mondays through Fridays 9:15 AM to 4 PM; closed major holidays. Admittance is free but tickets to the Gallery are limited. Tickets should be picked up at least an hour before the visit is anticipated.* The public may visit exhibits which show the history of the New York Stock Exchange, and present the workings of the Stock Market and the workings of the financial organization of companies listed. The **Visitors Gallery** *(3rd floor)* overlooks the hectic pace of activity on the trading floor below; a taped explanation on the Exchange may be heard here in English, French, German, Japanese and Spanish. Visitors Center staff are available to answer questions.

Continue west along Wall Street, returning to Trinity Church.

The **Michelin Green Tourist Guide** to New England
Beautiful scenery,
Buildings,
Geography,
Economy,
History, Art,
Scenic routes,
Automobile tours,
Plans of towns and buildings

An indispensable guide for your vacation.

At the entrance to New York harbor stands the Statue of Liberty, her upraised torch lighting the world with the promise of freedom and justice for all. This symbolic gesture has warmed the hearts of countless numbers of immigrants who challenged the unknown to realize their dreams of a better life in a new place. A dignified, emotionally moving reminder of the ideals upon which the nation is founded, this "grandest lady in the world" has been welcoming travelers arriving by sea for more than a century.

Nearby in the harbor is **Ellis Island** *(p 92)*, the immigration station and entry point for millions during the peak years of immigration.

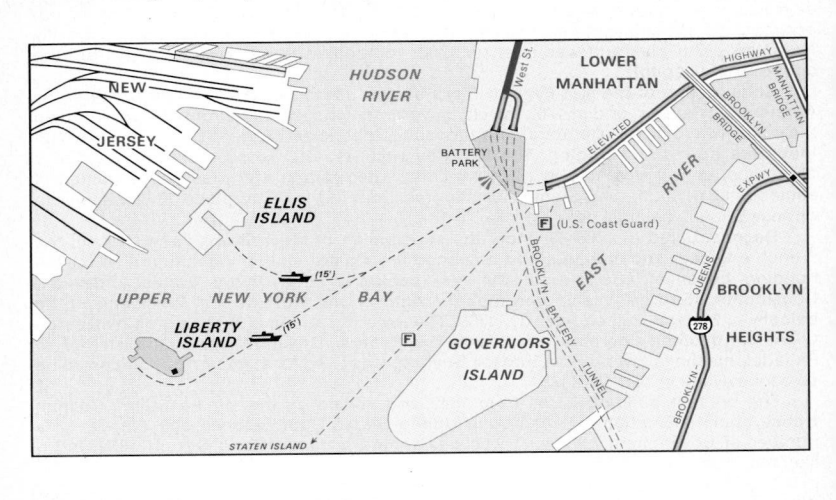

■ THE STATUE OF LIBERTY★★★

The Birth of an Idea. – In 1865 the historian Edouard de Laboulaye hosted a dinner party at his home in France. It was at this party that the idea was first conceived to present the American people with a memorial commemorating the friendship of France and the United States, a friendship which dated back to the alliance between the two nations during the American Revolution.

To further explore the idea, a committee was formed under the chairmanship of De Laboulaye in 1871. A young Alsatian sculptor, **Frédéric-Auguste Bartholdi** was then selected by the committee to travel to America for the purpose of studying and promoting the project.

The Inspiration. – Bartholdi had attended the opening ceremonies of the Suez Canal in 1869, in hopes of securing a commission for a huge statue-lighthouse at the entrance to the new canal. Unsuccessful in obtaining the commission, he now, two years later, turned his energy to creating a similar monument in the United States.

Entering New York harbor, he was overwhelmed by the view he encountered: "The picture... is marvelous; when, after some days of voyaging... is revealed the magnificent spectacle of those immense cities (New York and Brooklyn), of those rivers extending as far as the eye can reach.... It is thrilling. It is, indeed, the New World, which appears in its majestic expanse...." Inspired by the grandeur of the scene before him, and its significance as the main gateway to the New World, the sculptor's imagination soared. Then and there he knew that the monument he would create would be a figure of Liberty, and one of the tiny harbor islands in this breathtaking setting would be the ideal place for the statue to stand.

A Franco-American Union was established, with De Laboulaye as president, to raise funds and coordinate all matters regarding the statue. The French committee in Paris was under the direction of **Ferdinand de Lesseps**, builder of the Suez Canal, and the American committee was headed by the Boston-born jurist **William Evarts**. The project was to be a joint effort reflecting the shared commitment of both nations: the French would underwrite the statue itself, and the Americans, the pedestal. A private subscription of $250 000 was planned.

The Difficulties: technical... . – In 1874 Bartholdi began to work. Using his mother as a model, he first made a clay figure 4ft high, and then three successively larger working models in plaster which were corrected and refined before the final dimensions were achieved. Turning his attention to the framework which would support the statue, the sculptor called upon the skill and knowledge of the inventive French engineer **Gustave Eiffel**, who was later to build the Eiffel Tower. Foreshadowing the construction techniques of the skyscrapers of the 1880s, Eiffel designed, for the statue, an intricate iron and steel skeletal frame to which the 300 copper plates (each 3/32in. thick), forming the skin of Liberty, were applied.

... and financial. – With the technical problems solved, the financial difficulties assumed an increasing urgency. The cost of construction had almost doubled – from $250 000 to $400 000 – since work on the statue had begun. To reach its goal, the French committee launched a fund drive featuring a variety of special benefits and events which included a presentation of Gounod's *Liberty Cantata*, written especially for the occasion. The response was favorable and by 1884 the French had met their commitment, and the statue was complete.

At a special ceremony held July 4, 1884, the statue was presented to the ambassador of the United States as a gift from the people of France. Following the festivities, Liberty was dismantled and packed in 214 crates, specially marked for reassembly, in preparation for the ocean voyage to her permanent home across the Atlantic.

In the meantime, in the United States little progress had been made in collecting the money necessary for the construction of the pedestal. At the American centennial exhibition in Philadelphia in 1876 the statue's forearm and torch were displayed to the delight of numerous visitors who took great pleasure in being photographed on its balcony; but purse strings were slow to open. Benefit balls, theatrical and sporting events, even a poetry contest were held to support the pedestal campaign. Inspired by the spirit of liberty and affected by the persecutions then taking place in Russia, **Emma Lazarus** wrote her poem *The New Colossus* (1883) which was later engraved on the pedestal of the statue.

Included were the memorable lines:
"Give me your tired, your poor,
Your huddled masses yearning to breathe free,
The wretched refuse of your teeming shore.
Send these, the homeless, tempest-tost to me,
I lift my lamp beside the golden door!"

By 1885, with the statue awaiting shipment to the U.S. and contributions still not forthcoming, the committee once again acted. An urgent "appeal to patriotism" was issued stating: "If the money is not now forthcoming the statue must return to its donors, to the everlasting disgrace of the American people." As a result, numerous donations were received.

However, in the end, the success of the project was due largely to the fund raising campaign of **Joseph Pulitzer**, the publisher of the New York *World*. In front page editorials Pulitzer criticized the rich for not providing the mere "pittance" required, and encouraged all Americans to contribute to the project as the masses of French people had. In addition, he promised to publish in his newspaper the names of every donor, no matter how small the amount of the gift. With this, the drive rapidly assumed a new impetus and contributions began to pour in daily!

The Dedication. – With the arrival of spring 1885, the French warship *Isère,* carrying its precious cargo, set sail from Rouen and approximately one month later dropped anchor in New York harbor. The pedestal was still far from complete, yet owing to the persistence of Pulitzer more than the necessary amount had been collected.

Bartholdi traveled once more to New York, this time to confer with the engineers and the architect chosen to design the pedestal, **Richard Morris Hunt**. Hunt was acknowledged as one of the leading American architects of the day. Having obtained commissions for many commercial and cultural projects, he was also well known for the opulent summer "cottages" he had built for Newport's wealthy set *(see Michelin Green Guide to New England)*. Hunt's final design for the pedestal, judged handsome and architecturally sophisticated with its Doric columned gallery, blended in character and scale to form an integrated unity with the statue.

Declared an official holiday in New York City, the festivities took place October 28, 1886. Presiding over the unveiling of the statue on Bedloe's Island (renamed Liberty Island in 1956) was **President Grover Cleveland** who had arrived by boat, accompanied by a 300 ship escort. National and international dignitaries huddled together at the foot of the statue while speech after speech was heard. The excitement that had been mounting throughout the day eventually reached a climax as the statue was unveiled. At that moment cries of emotion filled the air, and as fog horns bellowed, the roar of a 21-gun salute sounded from nearby batteries. Liberty's torch was illuminated simultaneously, symbolizing prophetically the beacon of hope she would be to the millions who would one day soon begin to flock to these shores.

VISIT *time: 3 hours*

Ferries leave from the Battery every hour 9 AM to 4 PM; July and August every 1/2 hour starting 10:30 AM; closed December 25; $3.25, children $1.50 – round trip including admission to the statue and museum. Tickets sold only at Castle Clinton Monument (p 111). For additional information ☎ Circle Line: 269-5755.

During the brief crossing *(15 min)* you will have magnificent **views**: of the Lower Manhattan skyline gradually receding into the background; and of the Statue of Liberty as the nearer the boat draws, the more majestic and massive she appears. The statue, a National Monument administered by the National Park Service, is placed at one end of the island, above the star-shaped walls of Fort Wood (1808-11) and receives about 3 million visitors a year.

Weighing 225 tons, Liberty represents a crowned woman trampling beneath her feet the broken shackles of tyranny; the seven points in her crown signify liberty radiating to the seven continents and the seven seas. In her left hand she holds a tablet representing the Declaration of Independence and bearing the date of its proclamation, July 4, 1776. Her right hand raises the symbolic torch 305ft above sea level. The torch and the crown are lighted in the evening. It is especially from the base of the statue that the enormous size of the monument is apparent.

A Few Figures. – The statue is 151ft high and the head is 10ft by 17ft. The right arm, holding the torch, measures 42ft long with a diameter of 12ft and the index finger is 8ft long.

Entrance to the statue is gained by walking up a*landscaped mall to the main lobby. From there visitors may proceed directly to the statue or to one of two exhibit areas: the **Immigration Exhibit**, or the **Statue of Liberty Exhibit**, where the poem written by Emma Lazarus in 1883 *(p 91)* is inscribed on a bronze plaque.

Immigration Exhibit★. – *3rd floor in the pedestal.*

The museum uses photographs, drawings, native costumes and other artifacts arranged chronologically and by nation to present the history of immigration in America. These displays tell of immigrants who rose to prominence in the fields of science, politics (Alexander Hamilton was a native West Indian), education and the arts, and emphasize the enormous contributions made by those who shared in the building of their adopted nation.

From the Immigration Exhibit, an observation deck at the top of Fort Wood provides views of Manhattan and the harbor.

Statue of Liberty Exhibit. – *2nd level in the pedestal.*

The badly corroded torch which was eventually replaced in 1986 is featured in this exhibit which recounts the history of the statue from de Laboulaye's conception to the present. Bartholdi's working models of the statue illustrate the evolution of his ideas, and a cutaway model provides an excellent view of the complex inner structure. The repousse technique which was used in forming the copper exterior is explained in a continuous videotape, and a substantial collection of postcards and souvenirs depict the statue's role as a symbol of liberty both in America and abroad.

(From photo National Park Service, Washington, D.C.)

The Statue of Liberty.

Panorama★★★. – *Observation deck at the top of the pedestal.*

An elevator from the main entrance accesses this four-sided balcony which provides spectacular views of New York Harbor, southern Manhattan and the Financial District, the Verrazano-Narrows Bridge and New Jersey.

Climb to the Crown. – The 364-step climb from the ground to the crown begins just inside the main entrance. A narrow, circular metal staircase *(visitors with claustrophobia are advised to proceed with caution)* winds its way up through the statue's interior, culminating in a narrow platform from which a view of New York Harbor is visible through the openings in the crown.

Before taking the ferry to return to the Battery stroll along the promenade above the island's ledges. Glancing across the harbor you will note the contrast between modern high-rise Manhattan and, in Brooklyn, the older lower-scale buildings.

■ ELLIS ISLAND

Ferry Service to island by Circle Line. Statue of Liberty Ferry, Inc. Call 269-5755 for schedule and fares.

Situated a short distance from the Statue of Liberty in Upper New York Bay is Ellis Island, a 27.5 acre patch of land which, as a major entry point for millions of immigrants in the 19 and first half of the 20C, played an important role in the drama of American immigration. A teeming tower of Babel during those decades when the air was filled with the cacophony of languages of different nationalities, the island and its buildings, vacated in the 1950s, now lie silent.

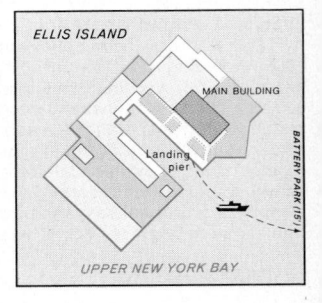

Ellis Island was opened in 1892 as a processing station for immigrants, to replace Castle Garden *(p 111)*. Facilities at Castle Garden were no longer sufficient to handle the successive waves of newcomers who had begun to enter through the Port of New York in growing numbers since the 1850s. Boatloads arrived daily: first from Germany, Ireland, Scandinavia and Central Europe; later to be followed by large groups of Italians, Poles, Czechs, Slavs, Russians and Jews. Estimates are that between 1892 and 1954 approximately 12 million of the "huddled masses" entered the United States through the center at Ellis Island. The memories of the hopes and dreams of the immigrants, the terror they felt at the possibility of being denied admission, and the great joy they experienced when finally receiving a landing card are indelibly inscribed in the story of America's people.

The principal structure on the island is the imposing red brick Main Building where, in the Great Hall, frightened and confused, an average of 2 000 persons a day passed before the stern, scrutinizing eyes of the examiners. During the center's peak year (1907) more than 1 million immigrants passed through here.

Closed in 1954 as an immigration center, Ellis Island was added to the Statue of Liberty National Monument by Presidential Proclamation in 1965.

Distance: 1/2 mile – Time: 2 hours.

At the intersection of Broadway and Columbus Avenue, the Lincoln Center for the Performing Arts, a harmonious architectural group constructed between 1959 and 1969, is comprised of six buildings devoted to theater, music and dance, in an area of 14 acres.

Just to the south of Lincoln Center, Fordham University has established a campus *(p 138).*

A BIT OF HISTORY

It was in 1955 that the original conception of a great cultural center in New York, where ballets, plays, operas, operettas and concerts could take place at the same time, was first discussed. A committee under the chairmanship of John D. Rockefeller III was formed in 1956, and the following year the City of New York bought the necessary land between West 62nd and 66th Streets, Columbus Avenue, Broadway, and Amsterdam Avenue.

In May 1958, the committee chose the architects headed by **Wallace K. Harrison,** who had also participated in the design of Rockefeller Center, the United Nations and the John F. Kennedy International Airport. Harrison began by creating an expert commission which was to visit 60 concert halls and theaters in 20 different countries to analyze their strong points and weaknesses.

In order to tailor the seats in the halls to their occupants, the architects even studied the dimensions of the average American, to find that the size of the hips, for example, had distinctly increased in the last 50 years.

The total budget, an estimated $185 000 000, was largely met by private contributions; public support accounted for only about a quarter of this sum.

Gifts ranged from $5 (for 118 bricks) to $5 000 000 (an entrance lobby); for $1 000 a donor could have his name inscribed on a seat in Philharmonic Hall (Avery Fisher Hall), for $100 000 his name would appear on a plaque in the lobby.

■ VISIT

Avery Fisher Hall, the New York State Theater, the Metropolitan Opera House, the New York Public Library at Lincoln Center, the Vivian Beaumont Theater, Mitzi E. Newhouse Theater, Alice Tully Hall and The Juilliard School constitute a cultural unit which can accommodate 13 666 spectators at a time.

The buildings are very classical in inspiration: the rectangular floor plan, peristyle, and flat or terraced roofs are reminiscent of antiquity, and are all covered with Italian travertine.

The interior is designed for maximum comfort and excellence in the performing arts.

Guided tours (time: approximately 1 hour) are available daily 10 AM to 5 PM; $6.25. For information: ☏ 877-1800.

Tours leave from the concourse level under the Metropolitan Opera House and visit the Opera House, the New York State Theater and Avery Fisher Hall. Do not miss the New York Public Library at Lincoln Center, a library and museum of the performing arts, which is open without charge.

For box office information: ☏ 877-2011.

Bird's eye view of Lincoln Center

① Avery Fisher Hall
② New York State Theater
③ Guggenheim Bandshell
④ Metropolitan Opera House
⑤ New York Public Library at Lincoln Center
⑥ Vivian Beaumont Theater & Mitzi E. Newhouse Theater
⑦ The Juilliard School
⑧ Alice Tully Hall

Free midday and evening performances held outdoors in summer, are a marvelous way to enjoy the combination of fine music, theater and dance, and the open spaces of Lincoln Center.

The Plaza. – Surrounded by the three principal buildings of the Center, this pleasant flagged esplanade is decorated with an attractive fountain in black marble.

A restaurant with a café terrace *(summer only)* borders one side of the plaza.

Free midday and evening performances in the summer.

Avery Fisher Hall (1). – Formerly Philharmonic Hall, the hall was renamed Avery Fisher Hall in 1973 in recognition of a generous gift made by Avery Fisher, the founder of Fisher Radio. Designed by Max Abramovitz, it was, in 1962, the first building finished. Somewhat resembling a Greek temple, it has a peristyle of 44 columns, seven stories high.

The lobbies and corridors are decorated with works of art: a bust of the Austrian composer *Gustav Mahler* (1860-1911) by Rodin, a bust of *Beethoven* by Bourdelle and, suspended from the ceiling of the Grand Promenade foyer, two spectacular scintillating figures composed of polished metal strips: *Orpheus* and *Apollo,* by Richard Lippold.

The auditorium was totally reconstructed in 1976 by the architects Philip Johnson and John Burgee, in association with Cyril M. Harris as acoustical consultant.

Seating 2 742 it includes the orchestra level and three balconies, called tiers. The stage, enlarged and reshaped for better sound projection, is framed by a proscenium adorned with gold leaf designs. The antique-white painted walls and ceiling, the oak floor and the velvet upholstery are in the classical tradition. A profusion of lights adds to the magnificence of the hall.

Avery Fisher Hall is the home of the New York Philharmonic Orchestra, the oldest in America, which previously played at Carnegie Hall *(p 141)*. Zubin Mehta is Music Director of the New York Philharmonic, which has had such distinguished predecessors as Arturo Toscanini, Leopold Stokowski, Leonard Bernstein (also well-known as the composer of *West Side Story)*, Pierre Boulez and others.

In addition to regularly scheduled performances, Philharmonic rehearsals are open to the public at very modest admission prices on Thursdays at 9:45 AM during the season. In the summer, the *Mostly Mozart* concert series is performed here.

New York State Theater (2). – Facing Avery Fisher Hall, this theater which can hold 2 792 spectators was designed by Philip Johnson and completed in 1964.

Behind a glass façade, the three-level foyer is decorated with bronze grill work, each panel having been individually executed by Meshekoff. Round jewel-like lights face the rounded balconies known as "rings" and 23 carat gold leaf covers the ceiling of the Promenade. The open spaces of this hall make it an ideal setting for large dinners and receptions, and its sumptuous decor has earned it the nickname of the "Jewel Box".

The New York State Theater is the home of the New York City Ballet and the New York City Opera. The theater is owned by the City of New York and is operated by the City Center of Music and Drama, under whose auspices the Ballet and Opera companies operate.

Guggenheim Bandshell (3). – Located to the left of the Metropolitan Opera House, in Damrosch Park, this open-air theater with its bandshell is used for free concerts where 3 500 can be seated. To the north, beyond a plaza with a reflecting pool displaying a bronze figure by Henry Moore and Alexander Calder's steel sculpture *Le Guichet,* the Vivian Beaumont Theater appears.

Metropolitan Opera House (4). – Opened in September 1966 with Samuel Barber's *Antony and Cleopatra,* it seats 3 788 persons. Designed by Wallace K. Harrison, it replaced the celebrated "Met" at the corner of Broadway and 39th Street, which closed on April 17, 1966 with a nostalgic farewell gala.

The facade, with a marble colonnade ten stories high, forms the background of the Plaza. In the lobby hang large murals by Chagall, the *Sources of Music* and the *Triumph of Music.* The stunning double staircase carpeted in red is accentuated by crystal chandeliers, gifts from the Austrian government, which rise toward the gilded ceiling when the performance is about to begin.

The huge stage is equipped with rolling platforms to change elaborate sets. There are also 7 rehearsal halls, and space for scenery for 15 operas. Significant works of art include sculptures by Mary Callery, Maillol and Lehmbruck.

The Metropolitan Opera Season is from mid-September to early May. Distinguished visitors such as the American Ballet Theatre appear during the other months.

New York Public Library at Lincoln Center (5). – *Open Mondays and Thursdays 10 AM to 8 PM, Tuesdays, Wednesdays and Fridays noon to 6 PM, Saturdays 10 AM to 6 PM. Closed Sundays and holidays and 6 PM in summer.*

This unique institution, both a library and museum of the performing arts, is truly a cultural center as well as an attractive and ultramodern specialized library. One can spend several hours enjoying the various free facilities provided here (films, concerts, exhibits, etc.). Not included in the original plans, the intentionally unobtrusive building designed by Skidmore, Owings & Merrill, houses an extensive collection of circulating books and records and a Research Library on theater, music, dance and recorded sound.

Enter the building from the Plaza to the left of the Vivian Beaumont Theater. A stairway leads to the 2nd floor where you will see the Children's Library surrounding the Heckscher Oval, designed for puppet shows, children's films and story hours. Turn left to browse in the spacious Main Gallery. This floor also includes the Vincent Astor Gallery which presents temporary exhibits pertaining to the Research Collections. The Collections themselves are on the floor above.

Take the elevator down to the Amsterdam Avenue level. Here is another gallery, as well as an auditorium for 200 people.

Vivian Beaumont Theater and Mitzi E. Newhouse Theater (6). – Built according to plans drawn by the late Eero Saarinen shortly before his death, the Vivian Beaumont Theater was opened in 1965. It has an original architectural form with a projecting terraced roof. Seating 1 000 to 1 089, it is intended for repertory theater.

The Mitzi E. Newhouse Theater is a much smaller amphitheater with 280 seats.

The theaters are the home of the Lincoln Center Theater, which opened its first season in 1980.

The Juilliard School (7). – On the other side of 66th Street, the Juilliard building (designed by Pietro Belluschi, and Catalano and Westermann) is linked to the rest of Lincoln Center by a footbridge.

The Juilliard School moved here from its site at 120 Claremont Avenue, thus adding a center of training for musicians, actors and dancers.

Recitals, concerts, drama and dance events are presented in the four auditoriums.

Alice Tully Hall (8). – Lincoln Center's smaller concert hall is the home of The Chamber Music Society of Lincoln Center, and is used by recitalists and chamber music groups and The Film Society of Lincoln Center.

Outstanding institutions, the American Museum of Natural History and the Hayden Planetarium are located on Central Park West, between 77th and 81st Streets. At 170 Central Park between 76th and 77th Streets is The New-York Historical Society.

■ AMERICAN MUSEUM OF NATURAL HISTORY★★★ *time: 4 hours*

The museum, among the most venerated New York establishments, is the largest of its kind in the world.

The Building. – The construction of this colossus began in 1874, when General Ulysses S. Grant, then President, laid the cornerstone. It was formally opened three years later by his successor, Rutherford B. Hayes. Its architecture is a curious mixture of styles, the result of a program directed by different architects. On the Central Park side is the main entrance, part of a majestic facade 800ft long. The Ionic colonnade bears the statues of explorers and naturalists: Boone, Audubon *(p 96),* Lewis and Clark.

The Collections. – Before occupying its present site, the museum was temporarily installed in the Arsenal *(p 129).* The collections include more than 36 000 000 artifacts and specimens. There are 40 exhibition halls currently on view on four different floors. The displays, dealing with all facets of natural history, include life-size dioramas of animals shown in their natural habitats: the ground and vegetation are faithfully reproduced, and the background scenes are effectively painted by artists using sketches made at the original sites. The lighting contributes to the realism of the scenes.

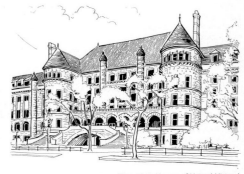

(From photo Museum of Natural History.)

The American Museum of Natural History.

Visit. – *Open 10 AM to 5:45 PM (9 PM Wednesdays, Fridays and Saturdays); closed Thanksgiving Day and December 25; suggested admission: $4.00, children $2.00. Naturemax Theater: $4.00, children $2.00 each film (time: about 1/2 hour each film). For schedule ☎ 769-5650.*

Films on several different subjects are shown in the Naturemax Theater (1st floor), a 600-seat auditorium equipped with a gigantic movie screen 4 stories high and 66ft wide.

We mention only the most famous highlights of the museum below, since a thorough visit would require several days.

The museum is often under renovation; some halls may be closed.

First Floor. – *Enter from West 77th Street.* In the foyer, you will see a seagoing Haida war canoe from the Queen Charlotte Islands, in British Columbia, complete with suitable warriors. In the section of this floor devoted to the North American continent, visit the halls presenting Indians of the Northwest Coast with superb totem poles, American Indian and Inuit tools and handicrafts. You should also visit the halls of North American Mammals – from the bear to the bunny – and of North American Forests.

The 2-story Hall of Ocean Life and Biology of Fishes contains among other exhibits, an immense (94ft long) model of a blue whale suspended in a dive position.

To the left of the 77th Street foyer is the unusually designed hall, Mollusks and Mankind; it covers the many uses of mollusks and their shells by past and present cultures around the world. The section Meteorites, Minerals and Gems houses more than 6 000 rubies, emeralds and diamonds as well as the Star of India, the world's largest star sapphire (weight: 563 carats). The 34-ton meteorite, Ahnighito, and the Brazilian Princess Topaz are among the other highlights of the collection. The Biology and Evolution Gallery is scheduled to open in late 1991.

Second Floor. – The Hall of Man in Africa shows the development of complex human culture on the African continent. The Hall of Mexico and Central America displays one of the finest pre-Columbian collections. Of special interest are the exhibits related to the Aztec and Mayan civilizations, the gold ornaments of the Americas dating from 2 500 years ago, and clay sculptures from central Veracruz. The Hall of South American Peoples exhibits Andean and Amazonic treasures, including the 2 300-year-old Paracas mantle, which are testimony to the religious beliefs and social organization of the ancient, existing and recently extinct cultures of this continent.

The most spectacular hall (African Mammals) is just west of the entrance foyer on Central Park West. In the center is an impressive herd of African elephants on the alert, and along the walls, groups of zebras, antelopes, gorillas, lions and gazelles are shown in their natural surroundings. In the galleries on the Third Floor level of this hall, other dioramas show different species of monkeys, rhinoceroses, leopards and hyenas. Another attraction on the Second Floor is the Hall of Oceanic Birds, to the north of the Central Park West entrance. Overhead, a group of birds fly by, set off by the sky blue ceiling.

The Hall of Asian Peoples features a comprehensive exhibit of life from prehistoric times to the late 19C when Western technology began to influence the traditions of the Orient. Daily life in Asian cities and villages from Arabia to Japan and Siberia to India, and colorful ceremonies and rituals are portrayed by dioramas and life-size displays.

Third Floor. – Here is the fascinating Hall of Reptiles and Amphibians, featuring the world's largest living lizards: the Komodo Dragon. The Hall of the Biology of Primates displays animals from the same biological order as man, starting with the tree shrew. To the west of Primates are displays on the lifestyles of the Indians of the Eastern woodlands and plains; also of interest is the Hall of North American Birds.

The Hall of the Pacific Peoples, inspired by the work and ideas of Dr Margaret Mead, contains exhibits related to six cultural areas of the Pacific: Australia, Indonesia, the Philippines, Melanesia, Micronesia and Polynesia. A large display case toward the center of the hall holds sacred masks, carved figures, boldly decorated shields illustrating the rich and diverse art of the peoples of the Sepik River Basin.

Fourth Floor. – The Early and Late Dinosaur Halls form the most popular exhibit on this floor. The dinosaurs, giant land reptiles, lived during the Mesozoic era which spanned the period from 225 million to 65 million years ago. Included in the museum's displays is the skeleton of a huge brontosaur which must have weighed about 35 tons alive, as well as a triceratops, a stegosaurus, and a tyrannosaur. In the Late Mammals Hall, a lineup of mastodons and mammoths are reminders of the origins of present day elephants.

Proceeding west is the John Lindsley Hall of Earth History. A 10 min audiovisual presentation introduces visitors to the story of the earth, the subject of the exhibits in this hall.

Hayden Planetarium★★

The Hayden Planetarium is the astronomy department of the Museum of Natural History. From the outside, the huge dome somewhat resembles an observatory.

The Show. – *Time: 45 min. Open Mondays through Fridays 12:30 to 5 PM, Saturdays 10 AM to 6 PM and Sundays noon to 6 PM (July through September Saturdays and Sundays noon to 5 PM); $4.00, children $2.00 (includes admission to the Museum of Natural History. For show times ℡ 769-5900).*

The Guggenheim Space Theater. – The space theater shows an exciting series, presented in sight and sound on the 360 degree space-screen covering such topics as the "Earth," "Moon," "Solar System" and "Rocketry." The ceiling is an animated model of the solar system 40ft in diameter. Around the central sun move six of the planets simultaneously rotating on their axes. They are the Earth, Mercury, Venus, Mars, Jupiter and Saturn with its rings; Mars, Jupiter and the Earth are accompanied by their moons. The three outer planets, Uranus, Neptune and Pluto, are not represented, due to the huge distances involved and because they cannot be seen by the naked eye from the Earth. The model is lighted so that each planet and satellite has "daytime" on the side facing the sun.

The Planetarium. – Go upstairs to the Sky Theatre in which a new projector has been installed. The Sky Show is changed three times a year and features such subjects as "Seven Wonders of the Universe", "Destination Mars," "The Star of Wonder," etc.

The "screen" is the hemispherical dome 75ft in diameter and 48ft from the floor at its highest point. The spectators are placed all around the projector which weighs 2 1/2 tons and is 12ft long. At either end are large globes which project images of the fixed stars of the northern hemisphere and the southern hemisphere. The sun, moon and planets are projected from the cylinder which supports the globes.

On the second floor is the "Hall of the Sun" devoted entirely to the sun. It includes how the sun affects our planet, the sun in the universe and a mini-theater with a short film.

Surrounding Corridors. – Two galleries, on the same floors as the Space Theater and the Planetarium, contain exhibits illustrating the history and progress of astronomy. Among the astronomical murals is the 35ft, scientifically accurate representation of the surface of the Moon, rockets, artificial satellites and an interactive display.

■ THE NEW-YORK HISTORICAL SOCIETY★★ *time: 2 hours*

The New-York Historical Society, founded in 1804, is a museum and library of American history and art.

Visit. – *Open 10 AM to 5 PM Tuesdays through Sundays; closed Mondays and holidays; $2.00. The library is open Tuesdays through Saturdays 10 AM to 5 PM in winter; Mondays through Fridays 10 AM to 5 PM in summer.*

First Floor. – The first floor exhibits 17, 18 and 19C objects in silver, mainly by New York craftsmen. In the other 1st floor galleries the Society holds temporary exhibits on New York history and American folk art.

Second Floor. – A stunning collection of stained glass lamps by Louis Comfort Tiffany traces the progression of this art from the simplest one-piece blown glass shades to those whose beauty rivals nature's in their exquisite floral form and color. This floor also houses a permanent and extensive collection of paperweights from America, England and France.

Third floor. – Closed to public.

Fourth floor. – These galleries are opened on a rotating basis and include 19C American landscape paintings by Asher B. Durand, Albert Bierstadt and John Trumbull and genre paintings by Eastman Johnson and George Henry Boughton. Of particular interest are the original watercolors by John James Audubon for his "Birds of America", a study which took the artist on journeys throughout North America for two decades in the early 19C. In the collection of eighteenth century American furniture are pieces from Federal Hall including the mahogany desk used by members of the first U.S. Congress in 1789. Portraits from this period are by Gilbert Stuart and Charles Wilson Peale. The Colonial Dutch and American portraits hung in the hallway are works by Lawrence Kilburn, John Durand and Abraham Delanoy, Jr.

Distance: about 1 mile – Time: 5 hours

This walk combines the pleasures of being out-of-doors in Fort Tryon Park *(p 101)*, with the artistic joys of the treasures displayed in The Cloisters.

To reach The Cloisters take bus no 4, *"Fort Tryon Park – The Cloisters,"* on Madison Ave or the subway *"190th Street – Overlook Terrace,"* (A line) and the no 4 bus or walk.

Isolated on a hill in Fort Tryon Park, The Cloisters looks like a fortified monastery, a part of the Old World transplanted to the New. Its collections enjoy an unrivaled reputation among lovers of medieval art.

A BIT OF HISTORY

Rockefeller to the Rescue. – John D. Rockefeller, Jr. was largely responsible for this extraordinary institution.

The core of the collection is made up of medieval sculptures and architectural remains assembled by the sculptor **George Grey Barnard** during his frequent trips to Europe. When the collection was opened to the public in 1914, in a special brick building on Fort Washington Avenue, it already included large sections of the cloisters of Saint-Michel-de-Cuxa, Saint-Guilhem-le-Désert, Bonnefont-en-Comminges and Trie, all from southern France.

In 1925, Rockefeller donated a large sum to the Metropolitan Museum to purchase the Barnard collection and to improve its presentation. When the first Cloisters opened in 1926 in the old brick building, as an annex of the Met, the Rockefellers also added a number of sculptures.

It was in 1930, when Rockefeller decided to give to the City of New York an estate he owned in the area which is now Fort Tryon Park, that he reserved the northern part for the new Cloisters.

(From photo Metropolitan Museum.)

The Cloisters.

The building, designed in 1935 by **Charles Collens** of Boston, was completed in 1938. Considerably enriched by gifts and acquisitions, the museum has remained administratively a part of the Metropolitan Museum of Art.

■ THE CLOISTERS ★★★ *time: 4 hours*

Open 9:30 AM to 5:15 PM (4:45 PM November through February); closed Mondays and January 1, Thanksgiving Day and December 25; suggested admission fee $5.00, includes same day admission to the Metropolitan Museum of Art (p 52).

Recorded concerts of medieval music daily. There are live concerts on selected Sunday afternoons: tickets available by mail order only – The Cloisters, Fort Tryon Park, New York, N.Y. 10040 – Attention: Concerts. These musical events help to create a peaceful and meditative atmosphere.

The **building** is arranged around a square tower inspired by that of Saint-Michel-de-Cuxa. This group of cloisters, chapels and halls resembles an ancient monastery. There is little unity of style since both Romanesque and Gothic elements are incorporated, as was also often the case in European monasteries, but the weathered stone and pleasing proportions create a certain harmony.

One part of the construction is a rampart wall. Walk along this parapet to enjoy different views of the building, as well as of the park and the Hudson. On the east side of the building, a postern serves as the entrance. Leave The Cloisters by a driveway paved with Belgian blocks, originally from New York streets, and reminiscent of European cobblestones.

Main floor

Fuentidueña Chapel. – This "chapel" is largely devoted to Spanish Romanesque art. The apse comes from the church of San Martin at Fuentidueña in Old Castile (Spain), and dates from about 1160.

Notice the illustrative capitals (to the right, Daniel in the Lion's Den, and to the left, the Adoration of the Magi) and pier figures of Saint Martin, Bishop of Tours (to the left), and the Annunciation (to the right). The two niches in the wall probably served for the cruets of water and wine used in the Mass, and held the ewer for the priest's ceremonial handwashing.

The semi-dome bears a fresco of the Virgin and Child with the three Magi and the archangels Michael and Gabriel. This originally was in the apse of a small Catalan church, San Juan de Tredos (Spanish Pyrenees).

In the nave of the chapel is an Italian Romanesque doorway from San Leonardo al Frigido in Tuscany (Italy), carved from Carrara marble in about 1175. Just to its left a Tuscan cream-colored marble holy water font, depicts Raynerius, patron saint of Pisa, who performed miracles such as separating water from wine. The font was carved in 1160, the year of Raynerius' death. On the left wall of the nave hangs a 12C crucifix from the Convent of Santa Clara (Spain). In an excellent state of preservation, the figure is a fine example of Romanesque sculpture.

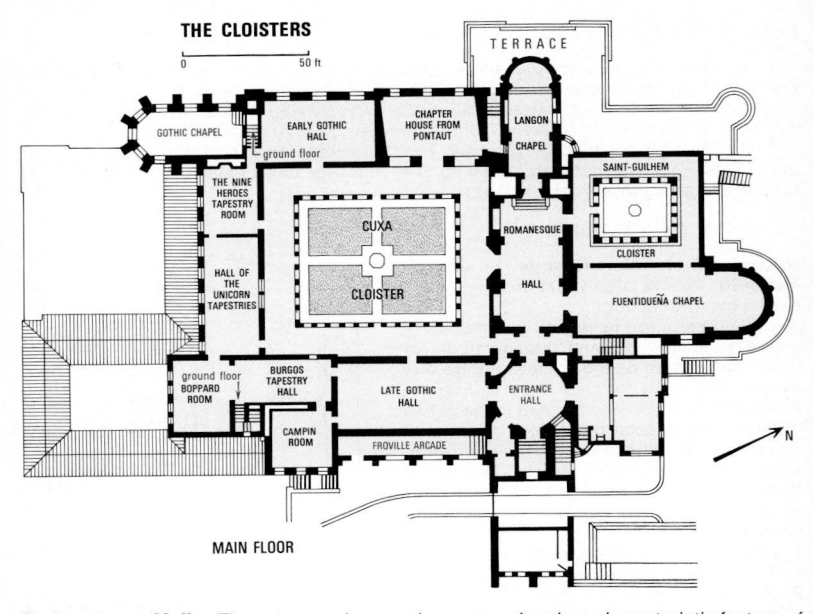

THE CLOISTERS

0   50 ft

TERRACE

GOTHIC CHAPEL

EARLY GOTHIC HALL
ground floor

CHAPTER HOUSE FROM PONTAUT
ground floor

LANGON

CHAPEL

SAINT-GUILHEM

THE NINE HEROES TAPESTRY ROOM

CUXA

ROMANESQUE

CLOISTER

HALL OF THE UNICORN TAPESTRIES

CLOISTER

HALL

FUENTIDUEÑA CHAPEL

ground floor
BOPPARD ROOM

BURGOS TAPESTRY HALL

LATE GOTHIC HALL

ENTRANCE HALL

CAMPIN ROOM

FROVILLE ARCADE

N

MAIN FLOOR

Romanesque Hall. – The entrance doorway has a round arch, a characteristic feature of the Romanesque style. On the left side the capitals are carved with graceful birds feeding upon acanthus plants. The capitals on the right bear imaginary animals surmounted by a delicate acanthus motif. The doorway is believed to come from Poitou in France.

Note the two early Gothic French portals: the one on the right, leading to the Saint-Guilhem Cloister, is from a church in Reugny in the upper Loire Valley, and dates from the late 12C; the other, leading to the Langon Chapel, is 13C: it was the entrance to a transept of the former abbey of Moutiers-Saint-Jean in Burgundy. Notice the statues representing, on the left, Clovis, the first Christian French king, and on the right, Clothar, who protected the abbey after its foundation by his father at the end of the 5C.

On the right wall can be found the Torso of Christ (12C), a fragment of a Deposition group, whose head is one of the treasures of the Louvre in Paris.

Saint-Guilhem Cloister. – This cloister contains a magnificent series of columns and capitals from the Benedictine abbey of Saint-Guilhem-le-Désert, near Montpellier (France). The property was sold during the French Revolution, and some of the columns were being used to support grape vines, when George Barnard acquired them in 1906.

Admire the vigor and freedom of execution of the capitals (12-13C), with the intricate carving of plants and figures; a number of the capitals bear the mark of Roman inspiration. Several columns are also carved with geometric patterns of vegetation.

The fountain in the center of the cloister was once a Romanesque capital in the church of Saint-Sauveur in southwestern France. The grotesque corbels supporting the ribs and cornice of the gallery vaults are from the Abbey of Sauve, near Bordeaux.

Langon Chapel. – The original parts of this chapel came from the choir of the Romanesque church of Notre-Dame du Bourg at Langon, near Bordeaux, used as a Jacobin Club during the French Revolution, and later a dance hall and movie theater. A 12C Italian marble ciborium (tabernacle) symbolically protects a poignant 12C Virgin in birch from Autun, Burgundy. Another 12C Virgin and Child (near the door) from Auvergne creates an interesting contrast.

Chapter House from Pontaut. – Notre-Dame-de-Pontaut was first a Benedictine and later a Cistercian abbey in Gascony (France). The chapter house, where the monks met every morning to discuss community affairs, is a magnificent example of the late Romanesque style and the transition to Gothic with rounded-arch windows and doors, and a rib-vaulted ceiling. On the other side of the open arches the lay brothers gathered in the cloister to follow the debates, while the monks were seated along the wall. The capitals are particularly worth noting for the simple but forceful carving of ornamental geometric or plant forms.

Cuxa Cloister. – Although the largest cloister in the museum, it is only half its original size. The various elements came from the Benedictine monastery of Saint-Michel-de-Cuxa, near Prades, in the French Pyrenees, one of the most active centers of art and learning in the Roussillon. Abandoned during the French Revolution, the monastery was sold in three parts; during the 19C, its elements were widely scattered. In 1913, Barnard was able to bring together about half of the original Romanesque capitals, 12 columns, 25 bases and 7 arches. Rose-colored Languedoc marble was cut from original quarries to complete the restoration. You will notice the vigorously carved capitals, with their plants, grotesque personages and fantastic animals possibly inspired by motifs from the Near East; curiously, there are very few which bear a clear religious significance.

Early Gothic Hall. – This room features several fine examples of early stained glass, which played such an important role in Gothic design. There are also a number of interesting statues in this hall, including a 13C Virgin (on the wall) from the former choir screen of Strasbourg Cathedral, with its original paint.

The Nine Heroes Tapestry Room. – The doorway from the Cuxa Cloister is capped by ornemental ogee arches, exemplary of the Flamboyant Gothic style. Contained within is a large part of a set of **tapestries** which is among the oldest known to survive (1385), along with the Apocalypse tapestries at Angers (France). The theme of the nine heroes, very popular in the Middle Ages, includes 3 pagans (Hector, Alexander, Julius Caesar), 3 Hebrews (David, Joshua, Judas Maccabeus) and 3 Christians (Arthur, Charlemagne, Godfrey of Bouillon). Their feminine counterparts were the Nine Heroines.

(From photo Metropolitan Museum)

An Angel with the "Rheims Smile"

The surviving tapestries on display depict 5 of the 9 Heroes. David is recognizable by his golden harp, and Arthur from his banner with 3 crowns representing England, Scotland and Brittany. Joshua, Alexander and Caesar are also portrayed. A number of lesser personages escort the Heroes, giving an edifying view of the medieval social structure.

The arms of Berry, with golden fleurs-de-lis on the tapestries depicting the Hebrew heroes, indicate that the set may have been woven for Jean, Duke of Berry, a patron of the arts and brother of the French king Charles V. Before continuing into the next room, pause to admire the Gothic doorway (16C) of volcanic stone, from the Auvergne, carved with unicorns.

Hall of the Unicorn Tapestries. – Finely executed, realistic in expression and attitude, precise in detail, harmonious in color, the **Unicorn tapestries** are among the most exceptional of the golden age of tapestry, at the end of the 15 and the beginning of the 16C. To be admired is the fine craftsmanship, keen sense of observation, and attention to detail with which the artist has depicted the people and animals (dogs, birds, etc.), their expressions and poses. The set includes seven tapestries which hung in the Château of Verteuil in Charente (southwestern France), the home of the well-known La Rochefoucauld family, when they were bought by John D. Rockefeller, Jr. in 1920. A narwhal tusk, strongly resembling a unicorns horn leans against a 15C limestone fireplace from Alençon, France.

Boppard Room. – This room is named for the town of Boppard on the Rhine, where the six stained glass panels were created for the Carmelite Church (late 15C). There is also a Spanish alabaster retable (15C), and a brass eagle lectern (16C) from Belgium.

Burgos Tapestry Hall. – Large tapestries (1495) are hung in this hall. One is a Glorification of King Charles VIII of France, after his accession to the throne in 1483. The young king appears at least five times and can be identified by his crown. His sister, Anne de Beaujeu, the regent during his minority, and his fiancée, Margaret of Austria, are also represented. Other scenes in the complicated iconographic scheme include the story of Esther and Ahasuerus, the Emperor Augustus, the three Christian Heroes and Adam and Eve.

Campin Room. – This room, with its painted Spanish ceiling, has been furnished with medieval domestic objects in order to recreate the atmosphere of that period: table and benches, bronze chandelier, and 15C iron birdcage (the only one known to have survived from the Middle Ages).

Above the chest is the famous **Annunciation altarpiece** by Robert Campin. The central panel represents the Annunciation. The side panels depict the donors, on the left, and on the right St Joseph in his workshop: notice the mousetrap on St Joseph's workbench, and the painstakingly reproduced details of the town square in the background.

Late Gothic Hall. – This large gallery designed to resemble a monastery refectory is lighted by four 15C windows from the convent of the Dominicans at Sens. There is a remarkable example of a Spanish 15C altarpiece, in painted wood, carved and gilded. You will also admire the pure lines of a Virgin kneeling (Italy, late 15C) and the adoration of the Three Kings (Ulm, Germany, late 15C). In an effort to recreate the original positioning and perspective, the statue of St Michael (Spanish, 16C) has been placed above the doorway.

Cloisters are covered passages around an open space connecting the church to the chapter house, refectory and other parts of the monastery.

The plan of the Cloisters in New York City was developed around architectural elements (12 to 15C) from:

Saint-Guilhem-le-Désert — Benedictine abbey; founded in 804; intricate carved capitals and sculptures.

Saint-Michel-de-Cuxa — Benedictine monastery; founded in 878; vigorously carved capitals.

Bonnefont-en-Comminges — Cistercian abbey; founded in 1136; double carved capitals.

Trie — Romanesque convent; destroyed in 1571 (Wars of Religion); decorated capitals.

Froville — Benedictine priory; founded in 1091; arcade (14-15C).

Ground Floor

Gothic Chapel. – Inspired by a chapel in the church of Saint-Nazaire at Carcassonne and by the church at Monsempron, both located in France, this modern setting forms the perfect background for an interesting collection of tomb effigies and slabs. Among the former note the effigy of Jean d'Alluye (13C) and four monumental Catalan sarcophagi of the Counts of Urgel (13C). The tombs come from the Premonstratensian monastery of Santa Maria de Bellpuig de las Avellanas, north of Lérida in Spain. The apsidal windows are now glazed with 14C Austrian stained glass, mostly from the pilgrimage church of St Leonhard in Lavanthal.

Bonnefont Cloister. – This cloister is bordered on two sides by twin columns. Their double capitals in gray-white marble, from the quarries of Saint-Béat, are from the cloister (13-14C) of the former Cistercian abbey at Bonnefont-en-Comminges in southern France.

The other two sides of the cloister form terraces with a view on Fort Tryon Park and the Hudson. A medieval garden of herbs and flowers adds to the charm of this spot.

Trie Cloister. – Because of its small size, this cloister evokes in an especially pleasant manner the atmosphere of serenity and meditation associated with a monastery. Its capitals, dating from the late 15C, are decorated with coats of arms or religious scenes; notice those on the south arcade which illustrate the Life of Christ.

The central fountain is a composite of two 15-16C limestone fountains discovered in France's Vosges region.

Glass Gallery. – This room is named for the roundels and panels of stained glass (15-16C) representing scenes from the Old and New Testaments. A fine selection of 15 and 16C statues in wood, alabaster, stone and ivory is gathered here along with a fine Nativity altarpiece painted by a follower of Rogier van der Weyden (Flanders, late 15C). At the far end of the gallery are intricately carved wood panels which surrounded the courtyard staircase of a 16C house in Abbeville.

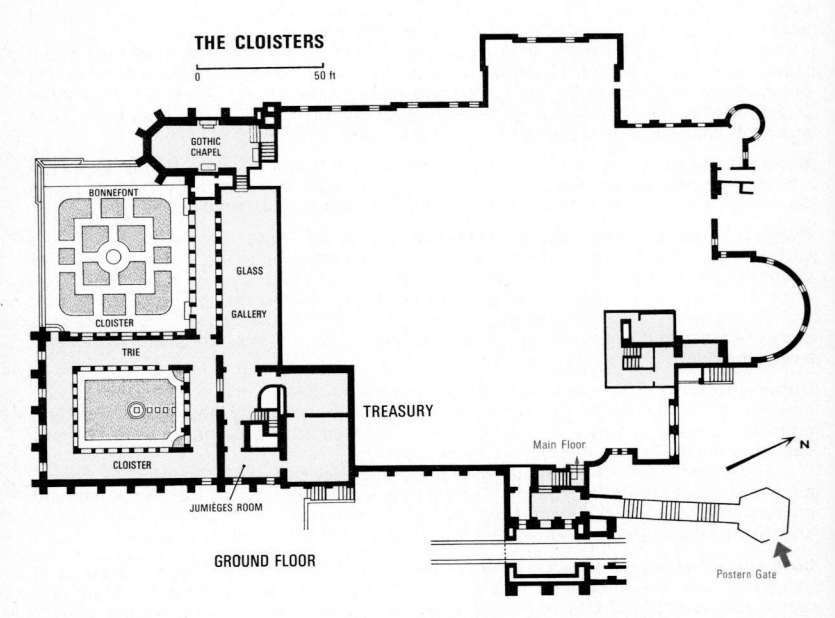

THE CLOISTERS

GROUND FLOOR

Jumièges Room. – The group of 37 carved wooden panels is believed to have been part of choir stalls, probably from the royal abbey of Jumièges in Normandy (early 16C); the panels are decorated in late Gothic style with scenes from the life of the Virgin and Christ. The wall case contains the *Belles Heures* (Book of Hours) which belonged to Jean, Duke of Berry who also commissioned the Nine Heroes Tapestries.

Treasury. – The Cloisters collection of smaller objects of exceptionally fine quality is displayed in the room adjacent to the Jumieges Room.

The most outstanding piece is the 12C walrus-ivory Bury St Edmund's Cross, which has been traced to the monastery of Bury St Edmund's in Suffolk, England. Both the front and back surfaces of the Cross are covered with figures, inscriptions and miniscule scenes from the Old and New Testaments, which have been skillfully carved with great attention to detail; note the expressiveness of the hands, and on the back of the Cross, the individuality of the twelve figures set in frames: the facial expressions of each figure is different, and no two figures hold the scroll in the same manner.

Also of interest are the enamels (Limoges, 13C) and reliquaries used for personal devotions, and a rosary bead of boxwood, with a tiny representation of the Passion inside (Germany, 15C).

Superb wallhangings embroidered with silk and gold threads depict Biblical scenes. Note the late 14C German hanging with scenes from the Life of Christ and the Old Testament.

■ FORT TRYON PARK★★ *time: 1 hour*

Covering 62 acres of wooded hills above the Hudson, this park is peaceful and green, giving the visitor the impression of being miles away from the bustle of the heart of the city. Although fairly small, the terrain is varied, with its hills and dales and cleverly arranged terraces overlooking the river. In the 19C, the area was covered with farms and pastures, replacing earlier Indian camps.

A lookout built upon the site of Revolutionary **Fort Tryon** caps a hill 250ft above the river. The fort, named for the last English civil governor of New York, William Tryon, was an outpost of Fort Washington, which was the last to resist the British invasion of Manhattan. It was here that Margaret Corbin replaced her husband killed in action, and fought until severely wounded. With the fall of Fort Washington on November 16, 1776, the British occupied all of New York City, which remained in their hands for seven years. Not long ago, it was still possible to find cannon balls and Revolutionary buttons and belt buckles.

The lookout point affords a magnificent view of the Hudson River and the George Washington Bridge to the west, and the East River to the east.

Between Fort Tryon and Margaret Corbin Plaza to the south, is the three-acre Heather Garden planted with colorful and ornamental flower beds based on 1930's designs by the Olmsted brothers.

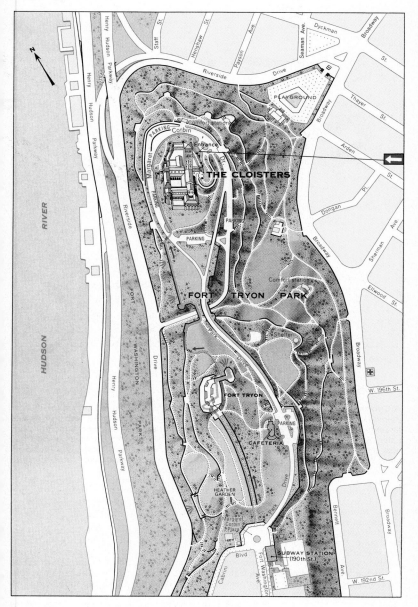

If you want to plan your own visit to New York,
please consult the map of walks and main sights pp 9-12.

Distance: about 1 mile – Time: 2 hours.

Greenwich Village occupies approximately the region bounded by Spring Street in the south and 14th Street in the north between Greenwich Street and Broadway. Its heart, however, is Washington Square and the area just to the west of it. Here Federal and Greek Revival town houses line crooked streets which play havoc with the grid system prevalent elsewhere in Manhattan. Restaurants and coffee houses abound interspersed with craft shops, boutiques, theaters and galleries.

But, like Janus, Greenwich Village has two faces. During the day, a serene small-town atmosphere pervades, enlivened on Sunday afternoons by strollers who gather to hear street musicians or have their portrait painted. The night, however, reveals a countenance reminiscent of Montmartre and St Germain des Prés in Paris: a cosmopolitan tourist crowd rubs shoulders with artists, intellectuals and students. People flock to theaters and movie houses, and folk, rock and jazz musicians perform in dimly lit night clubs and cafés.

In green: Legitimate Theater   In blue: Movie Theater

A BIT OF HISTORY

A Country Village. – When Henry Hudson sailed up the river named for him in 1609, the countryside, which was to become Greenwich Village, was covered with woods and streams abounding with fish, and sheltered an Indian settlement called Sapohanickan. Later, British colonists settled here and in 1696 a village sprung up which was named after the English town Greenwich (actually, the name "Greenwich Village" is redundant, since "wich" means village or town). Between rows of wooden houses ran Greenwich Street, then the main street of the village overlooking the Hudson.

During the 18C, wealthy landowners such as the De Lanceys and Van Cortlandts, Sir Peter Warren and Abraham Mortier had estates in the area, and it became a settled and well-known part of the city, with good taverns and even a road that led directly out of town. Thomas Paine, the famous revolutionary figure and pamphleteer, lived in Greenwich Village for a time.

The early 19C saw recurrent smallpox and yellow fever epidemics ravaging the downtown New York area, and residents, thus, sought the healthy country air of Greenwich Village. The present Bank Street, in the northern part of the Village, was named for the Wall Street banks which took refuge here, in 1822, along with other businesses.

In the 1830s, the area became fashionable and prominent families built town houses here, but they moved further north when industry developed near the waterfront. Irish and Chinese immigrants came to live in the Village and "Little Italy" sprouted up around Bleecker and MacDougal Streets. Lower rents attracted artists and writers, following the example of **Edgar Allan Poe** who took up residence at 85 West 3rd Street in 1845, where he wrote *Gordon Pym* and *The Fall of the House of Usher*.

Village Bohemia. – The early years of the 20C saw Greenwich Village become New York's Bohemia. Intellectuals, social reformers and radicals descended in droves to join the writers and artists, and it seemed as though the entire avant-garde of the United States was concentrated in these few streets. *The Masses*, a publication founded in 1910, was the mouthpiece of the radicals who attacked the complacency of American society and its Victorian morality, wanting to replace it with "free love." The favorite haunt of the Village rebels was the **Liberal Club,** frequented by such social critics as **Upton Sinclair.** At its headquarters, 137 MacDougal Street, the club organized cubist art exhibits, lectures and debates, and all-night dances called "Pagan Routs;" there were soon so many Pagans that the festivities had to be moved to other quarters. Polly Holliday's restaurant, located below the Liberal Club, became the favorite meeting place of anarchists.

Ferment also swept the arts. A new group of painters known as **"The Eight"** or sometimes as the "Ash Can School" challenged established academic concepts. Literary salons helped to create an intellectual climate in the village which stimulated such writers as Walt Whitman, Mark Twain and Henry James. Theodore Dreiser, O'Henry and Stephen Crane lived there for a certain time. Not surprisingly, the Village attracted the theater. In 1915, the **Washington Square Players,** later to become the Theater Guild, was founded at the Liberal Club. In the following year, the Provincetown Players made their New York debut on the ground floor of a bottling plant, after a summer season in Provincetown, Cape Cod. Among the members of the company was the poetess and playwright Edna St Vincent Millay. It was here that Eugene O'Neill first gained recognition. The jazz age of the 20s touched off a wave of eccentricity with **F. Scott Fitzgerald,** the main actor of the Lost Generation scene.

Today, Greenwich Village is still a hive of non-conformism and originality. It is not as radical, Bohemian and avant-garde as it once was. High rents have driven away struggling and would-be artists to cheaper areas (such as the East Village *p 132* and Tribeca *p 139*). Nonetheless, scattered among the small houses in the winding streets, high-rise buildings accommodate New Yorkers who prefer the liveliness of the Village to the conventionality of suburbia or residential uptown. They are attracted by a community which welcomes talent, offers serious and light entertainment, caters to the bibliophile and to the gourmet and cherishes diversity of lifestyle. They, as well as their neighbors, are deeply committed to preserving the character of their unique neighborhood.

VISIT

This walk links the most typical parts of the Village. We advise you to follow it twice, once during the day and once at night.

For a description of NYU see p 120.

Leaving Washington Square, first take Sullivan Street, and turn right on 3rd Street, then right again on MacDougal Street: at no 133 is the **Provincetown Playhouse,** one of the oldest Off-Broadway theaters.

Continue on Washington Square West before turning right on MacDougal Alley *(p 119).* Then visit 8th Street, where a diversity of shops (jewelry, clothes, books, records) are interspersed with pizzerias and other eating places. Turn right on Avenue of the Americas and note the extraordinary structure on the corner of West 10th Street. The red brick **Jefferson Market Library,** built in 1877 as a courthouse, is generally considered to be Victorian Gothic. But with its pinnacles, gables, turrets, arches, etc., it seems to reflect a variety of architectural styles.

Return along Avenue of the Americas and turn right on Waverly Place and right again to Gay Street. At no 14 lived Ruth McKenney and her sister, who inspired the best seller *My Sister Eileen,* later adapted for stage and screen. At the end of this little street, lined with brick houses, turn left on Christopher Street. At the next intersection is the **Northern Dispensary,** a brick building erected in 1831 to dispense free medical care to the poor. Follow West 4th Street, between Seventh Avenue and Avenue of the Americas; it is jammed with a succession of restaurants, coffee houses and craft shops.

Walk along Cornelia and Leroy Streets into **St Luke's Place.** This attractive row of houses from the 1860s is shaded by fine trees. It was here, at no 16, that Theodore Dreiser wrote *An American Tragedy.* South of this area, near Charlton and Vandam Streets, was an elegant estate, Richmond Hill, which served as a headquarters for General Washington, and later as a residence of both John Adams and Aaron Burr.

Continue on Hudson Street and Morton Street, with its fine Federal houses, to Bedford Street. No 75 1/2 is reputed to be the narrowest house in the city. Edna St Vincent Millay and John Barrymore are thought to have lived there. Turn left into Commerce Street where an old barn, no 38, has been used since the 1920s as an Off-Broadway theater; the **Cherry Lane** has seen the American premieres of plays by Beckett, Ionesco and Edward Albee. Across the street are two handsome brick houses, "The Twin Sisters;" it is said that these were built by a sea captain for his two daughters who could not live together under the same roof.

On Hudson Street, between Barrow and Christopher Streets, stands **St Luke in the Fields Church,** built in 1822 and reconstructed following a fire in 1981. Turn right on Grove Street; a few steps further, where the street turns a corner, note the gate of **Grove Court★** on the right. This attractive V-shaped court contains brick fronted Federal houses of the 1850s. A wooden house, unusual for New York, is on the northern corner of Grove and Bedford Streets (no 17). Grove, like Bedford, is a peaceful byway which seems miles away from feverish Manhattan.

The scene changes at **Bleecker Street,** one of the hubs of **"Little Italy",** and with 8th Street and MacDougal Street, one of the most active commercially in the Village. Notice the displays of fruits and vegetables, the specialized grocery stores and pastry shops, and the coffee houses for espresso lovers.

Return to Washington Square along MacDougal Street.

Time: 1 1/2 hours.

Colorful Chinatown seems to be a city within a city, isolated at the heart of New York. The narrow streets are lined with Oriental shops and restaurants, all teeming with people, particularly on weekends. However, the area really comes to life with a bang for the **Chinese New Year** *(the first full moon after January 19)*, when dragons dance down the streets accompanied by banner-carrying attendants while evil spirits are driven away by displays of fireworks.

Trains and Tongs. – The first Chinese to settle in New York came from the California gold fields and from jobs building the transcontinental railroad. The majority were men who had no intention of staying, unlike other immigrants. They just wished to make their fortunes and return to a life of luxury in China. By the 1880s, the community numbered about 10 000. Then restrictive legislation stopped further immigration, and growth was effectively halted. By the turn of the century, Chinese immigrants began to form "tongs" or associations designed to ease their adaptation to American culture. Organized gambling and prostitution eventually sprang up in Chinatown, and the tongs fell into conflict with each other. During the resulting tong wars, accounts were often settled with hatchets and revolvers, from which comes the term "hatchetmen".

Present-day Chinatown. – Since the 60s, when the restrictive legislation was removed, many new immigrants from Taiwan and Hong Kong, as well as from mainland China, have arrived. New York's Chinatown has expanded. Once bounded by Baxter, Canal, the Bowery and Worth Streets, it is now encroaching on "Little Italy" and the formely Jewish Lower East Side *(p 131)*. The present day Asian community of New York has been estimated at 481 000, of which roughly three-forths are Chinese.

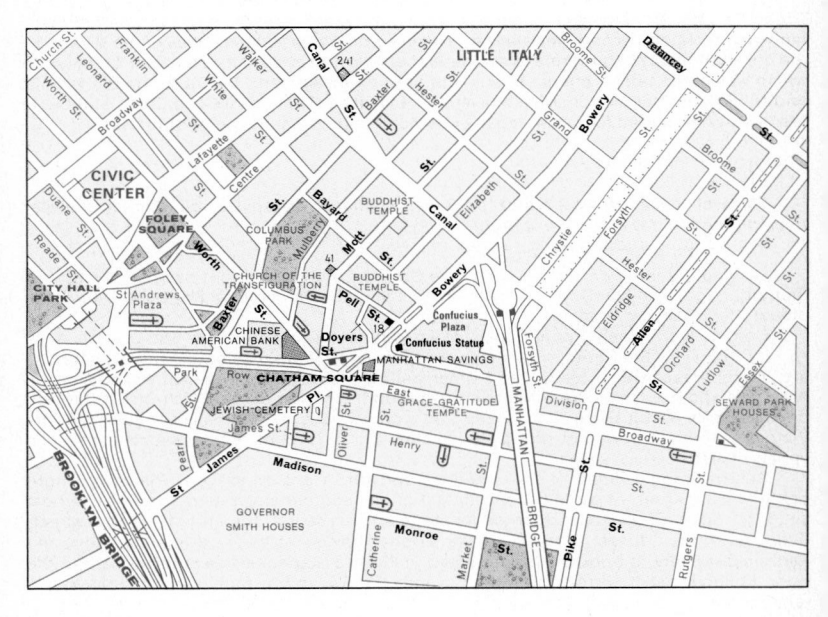

VISIT

The main streets of Chinatown are Canal, Mott, Bayard and Pell. Visitors should stroll noting the stalls and shop windows piled high with exotic displays of herbs and condiments, snow peas, bean curd, dried fungi, duck eggs, real birds' nests for soup. Bundles of Chinese mushrooms resemble strange marine plants, and ducks are strung up as if in a shooting gallery. Other shops offer jade and ivory carvings, brocade dresses, silks, fans, "Chinese" lanterns and tea sets. The streets are full of colorful banners and signs in Chinese calligraphy, elements of Chinese architecture adorn the otherwise undistinguished tenement buildings, and several telephone booths sport mini-pagoda roofs *(illustration p 171)*. Note the building at 41 Mott Street with its pagoda roof, and the gaily ornamented pagoda-roofed structure at 241 Canal Street.

At the corner of Bowery and Division streets, adjacent to Confucius Plaza, stands a bronze **statue** of the Chinese philosopher (551-479 BC). Just across the intersection, traffic flows past the Kim Lay Memorial, which honors those Chinese killed in defense of freedom. The Chinese culture is kept alive here by a number of Chinese film theaters, by Buddhist Temples and by the local cultural center. Visitors entering either the Grace Gratitude Temple on East Broadway or the Buddhist Temple on Pell Street will be struck by their serenity.

At no 18 the Bowery stands the **Edward Mooney House;** the red brick building is the earliest surviving row house in Manhattan. Dating from the Revolutionary era (1785-89) it reflects both Georgian and Federal styles.

A visit to Chinatown is of course not complete without a meal in a Chinese restaurant. The cuisine of China is as varied as the country is large and many different regional specialties (Cantonese, Hunan, Mandarin, Szechuan, etc.) are available.

Time: about 2 hours.

SoHo (for *south* of *Houston* – pronounced *How*ston – Street) is today an international art center and a haven of the avant-garde in America. During the 19C, industry flourished in this area bounded by Canal, Sullivan, Broadway and West Houston Streets. Today the quarter, once known as Hell's Hundred Acres because of its many warehouse fires, retains an industrial flavor despite its undeniably chic reputation. The SoHo area sports a unique concentration of buildings which are partially or totally constructed of cast iron. This type of building is thought to be America's one great contribution to 19C architecture.

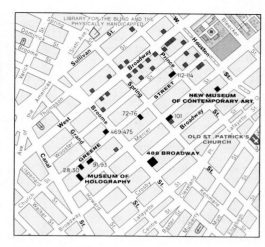

In green : Art Gallery

Construction in Cast-Iron. – As a building material, cast-iron was first used in England in the 18C for a bridge over the Severn River. This was followed by its use in the construction of textile mills, railroad stations and, most famous of all, Joseph Paxton's Crystal Palace for the Great Exhibition of 1851. Built within 6 months, Paxton's building of prefabricated elements of sheet glass and iron was an important innovation in mass production of standardized materials. However, cast-iron achieved its greatest popularity in the United States between 1860 and 1890. Buildings of this type can still be found in the old business districts of modern cities, yet more buildings were constructed of it in New York City than anywhere else. Soho's collection of buildings is so important that the area was declared a historic district in 1973.

The foundations of cast iron's popularity were the beams which eliminated the need for massive, load bearing walls. Thus, cast-iron buildings were lighter and cheaper than stone; could be mass produced from standardized molds when painted; required little upkeep and made possible more interior space with larger windows (an important factor in the days of gaslight).

Cast-iron façade patterns could be ordered from catalogs, and might include fluted columns, pilasters, elaborate cornices and balustrades, in styles freely borrowed from the Italian Renaissance, the French Second Empire and Ancient Greece. In general the buildings were simple, quick to erect, and inexpensive, putting almost every architectural style within reach of developers and merchants.

By the 1880s, however, cast-iron went out of fashion as structural steel replaced it and skyscrapers became the mode.

Note: not all the buildings have cast-iron facades although they may look as though they do. Later builders copied cast-iron's delicacy in stone! Also, some buildings are of masonry construction with cast-iron ground floors or decoration. Apart from tell-tale signs of rust, the only sure way of identifying cast-iron is to carry a magnet.

Metamorphosis of an Area. – In the 1950's, many of the industrial concerns relocated to the boroughs. They left vast, empty warehouses full of light and space, ideal for studios. Artists moved in, although not until 1971 did changes in the zoning law allow them to live and work in the same space. Even today, strictly residential occupancy is illegal and prospective residents are required to be certified as a professional artist by the New York City Department of Cultural Affairs, before they can live in Soho. It is hoped this will prevent the area from becoming too expensive for artists to afford, as has happened to Greenwich Village *(p 102).* Where artists moved in, galleries, boutiques

*(By permission of
Dover Publications, Inc., New York.)*

427 Broadway.

and restaurants followed. Now the prestigious uptown galleries have branches in SoHo side by side with very avant-garde establishments. Shops offer antiques, folk art, ceramics, home furnishings, woodwork, jewelry, clothes and unique handcrafted objects from countries around the world. Eating and drinking establishments abound.

Although Soho has blossomed, it is still an area in transition. Some of the original light manufacturing companies remain, and visitors are often surprised to discover how many warehouses and loading docks are still in use as warehouses and loading docks. In sum, SoHo is a somewhat incongruous place, which is perhaps part of its charm.

488 Broadway★. – The **Haughwout Building,** constructed in 1857, is a classic of the genre. It resembles a Venetian palace with its arches and columns. The basic design of a key-stoned arch resting on colonnettes flanked by taller Corinthian columns is repeated 92 times.

Museum of Holography★. – *11 Mercer Street. Open 11 AM to 6 PM, closed Mondays and major holidays; $3.50.*

This amazing museum, located in a building with a handsome cast-iron facade, is devoted to the art of holography or the use of laser light in exposing photographic film in order to achieve three-dimensional images.

A permanent display presenting the historical development of holography is supplemented by changing exhibitions which use pieces from the extensive permanent collection to present the application of this art form in scientific, technological and business applications.

(By permission of Dover Publications, Inc., New York)

Haughwout Building.

Greene Street★. – This street has the most remarkable collection of cast-iron facades. Most of the buildings between Canal and Grand Streets and between Grand and Broome Streets are exemplary of this type.

The "Queen" of Greene Street is found at **no 28-30**. This fine Second Empire facade with its immense mansard roof was designed by Isaac Duckworth in 1872. Around the corner at **no 91-93 Grand Street** stand two houses apparently built of stone blocks. In fact, large rectangular plates of iron were pinned onto a brick front so precisely that the seams cannot be seen from the street. False grooves were added for a faithful resemblance to stone. On the corner of Greene and Broome Streets, at **no 469-475 Broome,** stands the Gunther Building a unique structure with a curved corner and curved window panes. At **no 72-76 Greene** stands the "King" of Greene Street, another Duckworth building. Its projecting porch of Corinthian columns rises the full five stories of the building to a pedimented cornice. The building at **no 112-114 Prince Street** has a trompe-l'œil mural by Richard Haas of a cast-iron facade painted on a brick wall complete with a cat on a windowsill.

Finally, **no 101 Spring Street** is worth a visit. This 1870 masterpiece of cast-iron has delicate columns on two sides of the building and huge expanses of glass.

The New Museum of Contemporary Art. – *583 Broadway. Open noon to 6 PM (8 PM Fridays and Saturdays), closed Mondays, Tuesdays and holidays; $3.50.*

This museum, founded in 1977, is devoted to exhibiting art of the last ten years by contemporary artists not yet having received public exposure or acceptance. Located formerly on Fifth Avenue in the New School for Social Research, the museum moved in 1983 to its present, permanent home, a renovated building in Soho with large, high-ceilinged spaces of the type generally associated with the buildings in this district.

West Broadway. – Many though not all the galleries are located on West Broadway. *They are generally open Tuesdays through Saturdays 11 AM to 6 PM although there are many individual variations; Saturday afternoons are the most lively times.*

A FEW FILMS EVOKING THE NEW YORK SCENE

A Tree Grows in Brooklyn	1945	Elia Kazan
On the Waterfront	1954	Elia Kazan
West Side Story	1961	R. Wise and J. Robbins
Midnight Cowboy	1969	J. Schlesinger
Next Stop: Greenwich Village	1975	Paul Mazursky
Manhattan	1978	Woody Allen
Ragtime	1981	Milos Forman
The Cotton Club	1984	Francis Coppola

Distance: 3/4 mile – Time: about 3 hours.

Foley Square and City Hall Park at the foot of the Brooklyn Bridge form the area known as the Civic Center. A large number of government offices are located here, federal and state as well as municipal.

■ CIVIC CENTER ★

Foley Square ★. – This square was once part of a large pond called The Collect which was drained in 1811. In 1796, John Field tried out a prototype of the steamboat on this pond. The square is surrounded by government buildings.

Jacob K. Javits Federal Building and U.S. Court of International Trade. – This 1967 high-rise, somewhat resembling a checkerboard, is attached by a bridge to a smaller glass building (the Court) which is suspended from concrete beams.

New York County Courthouse. – This hexagon-shaped neoclassical monument with its Corinthian colonnade was built in 1926. The interior is imposing; in the central hall under the dome, note the rich polychrome marble floor with copper medallions representing the signs of the zodiac.

United States Courthouse. – This building is a curious architectural mixture. A "modern" style (1936) tower with a pyramid top bursts through the roof of a neoclassical temple. It was designed by Cass Gilbert.

Note, to the south of the building, the attractive St Andrew's Plaza, particularly pleasant in summer, with its tables, umbrellas and food stalls.

Walk along Lafayette Street.

Municipal Building. – The unusual shape of this building is due to the fact that it spans Chambers Street *(now closed to traffic)*. Built in 1914, it rises 40 stories from a classical colonnade. Note the statue of Civic Fame at the top of the tower.

The pedestrian way leads to Police Plaza and the red brick and concrete Police Headquarters building; in the center of the plaza is Bernard Rosenthal's imposing steel sculpture, *Five in One*.

Surrogate's Court. – This richly ornamented Beaux Arts structure was erected in 1911 to house the Hall of Records – the city archives.

City Hall ★★. – Surrounded by a pleasant park, this handsome building contains the office of the Mayor and the City Council Chamber.

(From engraving, photo City of New York.)

City Hall, early 19C.

The "new" City Hall. – The present building is New York's third City Hall. The Dutch established their "Stadt Huys" in 1653 in a former tavern on Pearl Street (their city council consisted of two burgomasters, a public attorney and five magistrates). During the 18C the English City Hall was at the corner of Wall and Broad Streets (the present site of Federal Hall National Memorial, *p 89*).

Today's City Hall was built from 1803-12 at a cost of about half a million dollars. A competition for the design and a prize of $350 were won by French architect **Joseph F. Mangin** and **John McComb, Jr.** Solemnly inaugurated on May 5, 1812, City Hall has been the scene of many memorable events. In 1824 the Revolutionary War hero Lafayette was officially entertained here during his triumphal return to America. The first parades up Broadway for visiting dignitaries began at that time.

In the middle of the night of April 9, 1865 City Hall learned of General Lee's surrender at Appomattox, and the next day the city was draped with flags. The gaiety was brief for, less than a week later, **Abraham Lincoln's** assassination plunged the nation into sadness. Lincoln's body lay in state at City Hall while 120 000 grief-stricken New Yorkers filed past. Then, on April 25, the hearse, pulled by 16 black horses, proceeded slowly up Broadway to the Hudson River Railroad where the coffin was placed in a special train for Springfield, Illinois, Lincoln's home.

The 1860s witnessed less solemn and dignified proceedings at City Hall and nearby Tammany Hall (at the corner of Park Row and Frankfort Street). The Tammany political machine founded by Aaron Burr at the beginning of the century, flourished under the leadership of "Boss" **William M. Tweed.** Its fierce tiger-head emblem came from one painted on the *Americus,* a fire engine, because Tweed rose to power from the ranks of the volunteer firemen. The pendulum swung against him during the 1870s; discontented city officials, aided by the incisive cartoons of Thomas Nast, brought about his downfall and imprisonment.

City Hall was restored in 1956 (at a cost of about $2 000 000) and rededicated. It remains the focus of welcoming ceremonies for visiting dignitaries and the starting point of ticker tape parades during which the honoree is deluged with tons of paper shreds.

The Building. – *Open Mondays through Fridays 10 AM to 4 PM.* With its French neoclassical facade, Renaissance style lantern and Georgian interior, City Hall is among New York's most elegant buildings. It was originally constructed of marble on its downtown side and brownstone on the uptown face. The City Fathers in an economy drive decided that because practically nobody lived north of Chambers Street, practically nobody would notice! City Hall was refaced with Alabama limestone in 1956 – on both sides.

In the main lobby, the bronze statue of Washington is a replica of the original marble by Jean Antoine Houdon; a fine double curved stairway leads to the second floor. The gallery is ringed with Corinthian columns and a wrought iron railing. The Council Chamber (to the left) and the Board of Estimate Room (to the right; *open only if public sessions are being held*) are on this level. The former has a statue of Jefferson by David D'Angers and a portrait of Lafayette by Samuel F.B. Morse, the inventor of the telegraph.

The **Governor's Room** *(open same hours as building if sufficient staff is available)* at the top of the stairs is actually a suite of three rooms once used by the Governor on official visits. Today it houses a small museum of furniture (note the 18C writing desk used by G. Washington) and paintings (note John Trumbull's portraits of Washington and George Clinton).

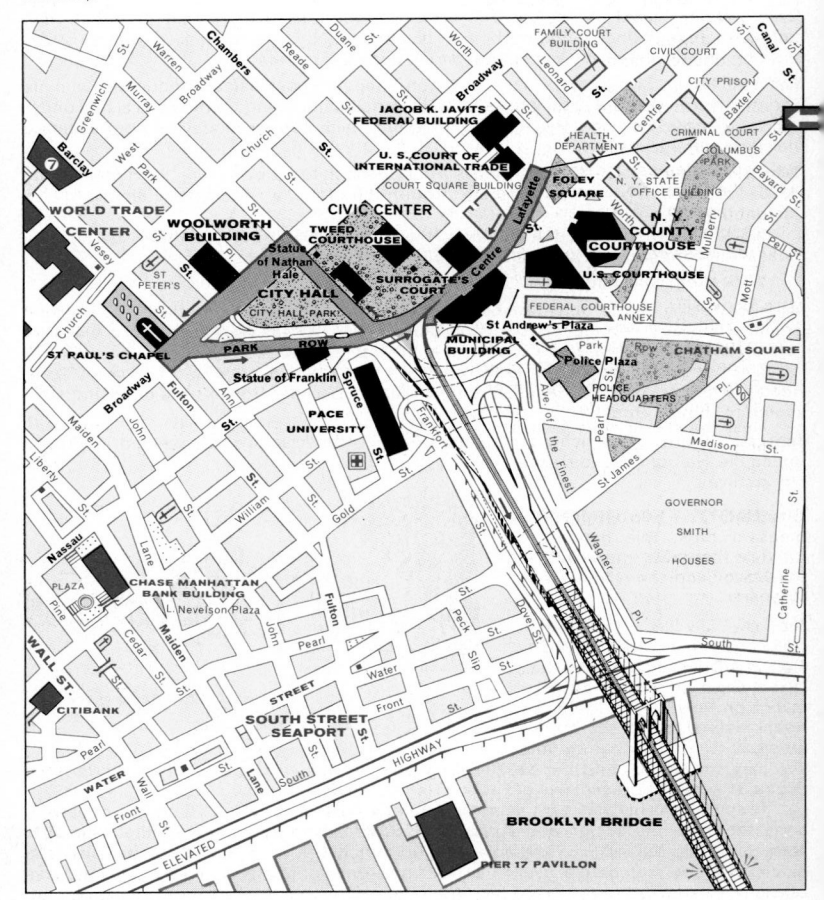

The Park. – Before the Revolution, this area was a common planted with apple trees. Liberty poles were erected here by the Sons of Liberty, and in July 1776 the Declaration of Independence was read in the presence of Washington, his troops and other patriots. Afterward the crowd rushed down Bowling Green to attack the statue of the king.

When the English returned a few weeks later, the scene changed and the apple trees were converted into gallows. A statue, erected on the Broadway side of City Hall Park, commemorates **Nathan Hale,** one of the heroes of this period. A captain of 21, he was hanged for having spied on the English disguised as a schoolmaster. His last words: "I regret that I have but one life to lose for my country" have thus entered American History. A statue of Horace Greeley and a plaque to Joseph Pulitzer are reminders that this was once the center of newspaper publishing in New York *(p 109)*.

Behind them, the old New York County Courthouse, now known as the **Tweed Courthouse,** stands as a monument to "Boss" Tweed *(p 107)* who allegedly pocketed some $10 million of the building's $14 million construction cost!

Pass in front of City Hall and turn left into Broadway.

Woolworth Building★★★. – This 1913 skyscraper, the tallest in the world until the Chrysler Building was completed in 1930 *(p 81)*, soars toward the sky like a Gothic cathedral of commerce. Cass Gilbert's masterpiece for F.W. Woolworth (the founder of the ubiquitous five-and-ten-cent store) cost more than $13.5 million for which Woolworth paid cash. At the highlight of the opening ceremony, President Woodcrow Wilson pressed a button in Washington that lit up 80 000 light bulbs on the building.

The cathedral theme is continued inside. An ornate entrance leads to the **lobby★★,** one of the most elegant in New York. Three stories high, its vaulted ceiling is covered with Byzantine-style mosaics and its second floor balconies are decorated with frescoes.

A marble stairway and ornate gilt decoration complete the picture, with small caricatures of Woolworth (counting his nickels and dimes) and Gilbert (clutching a model of the building) under the supporting crossbeams on the Barclay Street side.

St Paul's Chapel★. – A dependency of Trinity Parish *(p 86)*, this small chapel of native New York stone is the oldest church in Manhattan. Completed in 1766, it resembles St Martin-in-the-Fields in Trafalgar Square, London, possibly because its architect, Thomas McBean, studied under James Gibbs who was responsible for St Martin's. The lovely spire, which contrasts so well with the twin towers of the World Trade Center behind it, and the portico on Broadway were added in 1794. This portico *(not the main entrance although it looks like it)* with its Palladian window contains a memorial to Major-General Montgomery who was killed at Quebec in 1775 *(for details see Michelin Green Guide to Canada)*.

The chapel stands in its own cemetery – a delightful spot full of trees and 18C tombstones.

Interior. – The chapel has a surprisingly elegant Georgian interior. Painted in pastel colors and lit by Waterford crystal chandeliers, it was remodeled in the 1790s by Pierre L'Enfant, who later laid out Washington, D.C. Above the cream and gold pulpit, the feathers of the Prince of Wales can be seen reminding visitors that this was the "Established" church before the Revolution. Despite this fact, Washington worshipped here regularly after his inauguration *(p 89)*. His pew can be seen in the north aisle, and that of Governor Clinton in the south aisle (the arms of the State of New York hang on the wall beside it).

Free classical music programs (time: 40 min) are given in the chapel on Mondays and Thursdays at 12:10 PM. ☎ 402-0747 *for program schedule.*

Park Row. – The stretch of road from St Paul's to the Municipal Building along the edge of City Hall Park was a fashionable promenade in the 19C. It became known as Newspaper Row at the end of the century because so many newspapers had their offices there. The intersection with Nassau Street *(p 141)* was called Printing-House Square. Park Row is no longer the center of journalism in the city, and today only three of New York's one time 19 daily newspapers remain.

Near the statue of Franklin stands **Pace University** (Civic Center Campus). The main building which is adorned with a copper-relief sculpture is built around a garden and pool *(visible from Spruce Street)*.

■ BROOKLYN BRIDGE★★ *15 min walk to the middle*

The first bridge to link Manhattan and Brooklyn, Brooklyn Bridge was one of the great engineering triumphs of the 19C and the longest suspension bridge in the world for 20 years (and then the Ambassador Bridge at Detroit exceeded it by only 250ft). Its graceful silhouette set against the New York skyline has inspired many artists, writers and poets.

Construction. – In 1869, German-born **John Augustus Roebling,** a pioneer bridge builder responsible for the Niagara Falls Railroad Suspension Bridge, was commissioned to design a bridge linking Manhattan and Brooklyn. Shortly after approval of the plans, Roebling's foot was crushed while he was taking measurements for the piers. Despite an amputation, gangrene set in and he died three weeks later. His son, Washington Roebling, carried on his work, adopting new methods in pneumatic foundations which he had studied in Europe.

To construct the foundations, workers used caissons immersed in water and then filled with compressed air to prevent water from infiltrating them. In order to adapt to the air pressure, the workmen underwent periods of gradual compression before going down to work, and decompression afterward. Despite these precautions, a few had burst eardrums or developed the "bends" which cause convulsions and can bring on partial or total paralysis. Washington Roebling himself was stricken with the "caisson disease." Confined to his sickbed he, nevertheless, continued to direct the operation from his window overlooking the bridge. Finished in 1883, the bridge cost $25 000 000.

History and Legend. – The Brooklyn Bridge immediately became the busy thorough-fare its planners had foreseen. On opening day, 150 000 people walked across the bridge. However, less than a week after its inauguration by President Arthur, tragedy struck. A woman fell on the stairway; her screams set off a panic killing 12 persons and injuring many more.

Monumental and awe-inspiring, the Brooklyn Bridge has fascinated, obsessed and haunted New Yorkers. Some people have felt compelled to jump from the bridge, not all of them in despair. A character named Steve Brody who purportedly jumped off Brooklyn Bridge without harm, later gained fame as an actor on Broadway.

Since the end of the 19C, the bridge has provided an opportunity for confidencemen to fleece strangers to the city by extorting exorbitant "tolls" (the original toll, now abolished, was one cent for pedestrians), or by actually "selling" it to the gullible.

Characteristics. – The bridge and its approaches have a total length of 6 775ft. The central suspended span between the two stone towers with their neo-Gothic arches is 1 595ft long. The span is made of steel – the first time this metal was used for such a mammoth undertaking, and it is supported by four huge cables (15 3/4in. thick) interconnected by a vast network of wires.

Visit. – *The pedestrian walkway can be reached by crossing Park Row from City Hall Park, or from the "Brooklyn Bridge – City Hall" subway station. The Brooklyn side is accessible from the "High Street – Brooklyn Bridge" subway station.*

This is one of the most dramatic walks in New York. The view★★ of the city and harbor through the filigree of cables is magnificent, especially as the sun sets.

Distance: about 1 mile – Time: 2 1/4 hours.

At the southern tip of Manhattan, the maze of stone and steel monoliths which dominate the Financial District give way to a vast expanse of greenery: Battery Park. Here, strolling along the waterfront promenade, visitors may enjoy one of the finest panoramas on the eastern seaboard.

A BIT OF HISTORY

The *Dauphine* had sailed from Rouen in May 1523 with three other ships to discover the legendary passage to India and at the same time to trade with the natives. Small and stubby, the modest four-master weighing about 100 tons was named in honor of the Dauphin, son of Francis I, born in 1518. The hazards of navigation caused the loss of her companion ships. After long delays en route, the *Dauphine* finally sighted the coast of Florida and headed north. In April 1524 the anchor was dropped near the island of Manhattan. The fifty-man crew was commanded by Antoine de Conflans but the real head of the expedition was the pilot, **Giovanni da Verrazano,** a Florentine merchant in the service of France. Returning to Dieppe on July 8, 1524, Verrazano addressed a report to the French king; four copies of the report still exist, one of them annotated in Verrazano's hand.

Today, a statue and the giant bridge which was opened in 1964 *(p 150)* commemorate the first recorded sighting of New York and its harbor, 85 years before Hudson's exploration.

■ BATTERY PARK★★

Lying at the southern tip of Manhattan, with the skyscrapers of the Financial District as a backdrop, is Battery Park, an open area of 21 acres extending from Bowling Green *(p 86)* to the junction of the Hudson and the East Rivers. The view of New York Bay, animated by the movement of boats of all sizes entering and leaving the harbor, attracts large numbers of tourists to this spot year round.

Under Battery Park passes the **Brooklyn-Battery Tunnel** (about two miles long) which links Manhattan to Brooklyn.

Man-Made Land. – During the 17 and 18C the shore followed the lines of Greenwich Street, Bowling Green and Pearl Street. The British built a fort in 1693 on a rocky island offshore.

Early in the 19C the West Battery was built, giving its name to the present park, and in 1870 the land was filled in between the island and Manhattan proper.

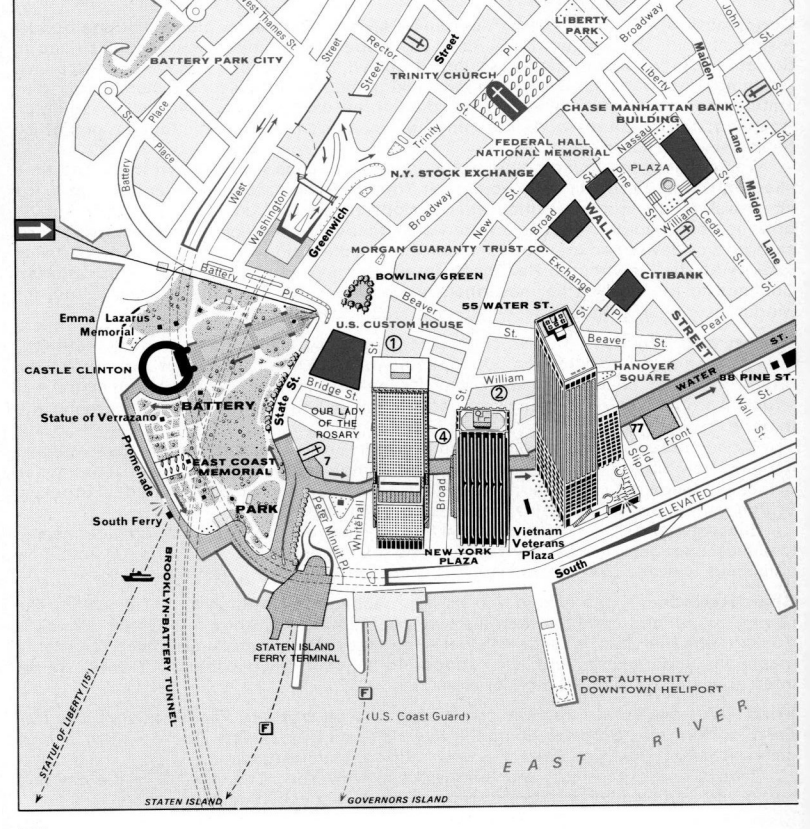

From Bowling Green to State Street

We suggest the following walk starting from Bowling Green, where you enter Battery Park. This park is dotted with **commemorative monuments** among which is one dedicated to the memory of Emma Lazarus *(p 91)*. From the entrance to Battery Park, there is an attractive view across green lawns and walks to the dark mass of Castle Clinton.

Castle Clinton National Monument. – *Open 9 AM to 5 PM, closed December 25. The Monument contains an Information Center and sales counter where tickets for the Statue of Liberty ferry (p 91) are sold.*

Built on a small island from 1808 to 1811, Fort Clinton went the way of a number of fortifications since Dutch times; it never had to be used for its original purpose.

In 1824 it was transformed into Castle Garden, and used for entertainment and opera. It could be reached from Manhattan by a covered footbridge. That same year a gala evening was held there in honor of **Lafayette.** James Fenimore Cooper described the occasion in an article: "nearly five thousand persons, it is estimated, were brought together.... . The General walked several times around the area and the galleries of the Castle, receiving the eager pressure of fair hands...." On another grand occasion in 1850, Castle Garden was the setting for a concert by the "Swedish Nightingale," **Jenny Lind.** The concert was promoted by P. T. Barnum and tickets were worth up to $225. It was here, also, that Samuel Morse demonstrated his new invention, the telegraph.

Between 1855 and 1890 the former fort and opera house once again was transformed, this time into an immigrant landing depot through which many immigrants passed. Over 7 million passed through Castle Garden. Later the New York Aquarium – now in Coney Island *(p 150)* – occupied the building until 1941. Designated as a National Monument in 1950, the structure was restored and reopened to the public in 1975.

Today, **Castle Clinton,** named for De Witt Clinton, governor of New York State in the early 19C, is once more the severe, circular red sandstone building of the last century. The 8ft thick walls are pierced with gun-ports for cannons, and the entrance is framed by pilasters. The interior contains a large courtyard, the very spot which served as a ballroom (roofed with a tent) when Lafayette was entertained.

To the left of the fort, is the **statue of Verrazano,** erected in 1909; nearby an air vent from the Brooklyn-Battery Tunnel is visible.

From Castle Clinton to the Ferry Terminal where the famous Staten Island ferries dock, the walk winds pleasantly along the shore of New York Bay. Sunny, thanks to its southern exposure, and protected from north winds by the buildings of the Financial District, it is an agreeable walk in winter. In summer, too, New Yorkers come to enjoy the sea breeze. From South Ferry you can take the ferry to the Statue of Liberty. Nearby is the **East Coast Memorial,** dedicated to those who died in the Western Atlantic during World War II. The powerful statue of a landing eagle with outspread wings, faces Liberty Island; on either side leading down to the water there are four granite columns inscribed with names.

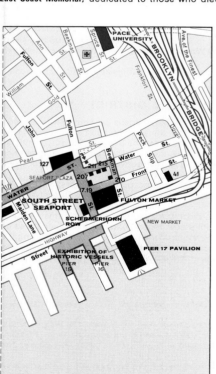

View★★★. – *Plan p 90.* The bay is animated by a constant succession of ferries and railroad barges, tankers, tugs, motor boats and an occasional cruise ship, while helicopters chop the air. The view extends in three directions. From Jersey City on the right to Brooklyn, you will see in the foreground:

– **Jersey City** with its Colgate clock, one of the largest in the world. Despite the distance, you can easily read it.

– **Ellis Island,** the former processing center for immigration *(p 92)*.

– **Liberty Island,** formerly known as Bedloe's Island, with the colossal Statue of Liberty.

– **Governors Island,** known in Dutch times as Nutten's Island, because of the many nut trees which grew there. The island possesses spectacular views of Manhattan and Brooklyn, and is the site of two pre-1800 structures: the Governor's House and Fort Jay. Another fort, Castle Williams, was built there at the beginning of the 19C, at the same time as Castle Clinton. Since then, the island has remained a military reservation. *Group visits can be arranged by writing the U.S. Coast Guard Support Center, Governors Island, NY 10004.*

— **Brooklyn,** with its docks at the foot of Brooklyn Heights.

Further in the background are Bayonne, New Jersey, with its oil refineries and its naval port, the hills of Staten Island, the Narrows and the cobweb of cables of the Verrazano-Narrows Bridge, half hidden by Governors Island.

Continue to the Ferry Terminal. Returning in the direction of Bowling Green by State Street note on the left, at no 7 State Street, the handsome Federal style chapel and Parish House of Our Lady of the Rosary. The part of the building on the right, the former James Watson House, dates from 1792; the graceful colonnade was added in 1806.

■ WATER STREET★

Water Street epitomizes the astonishing pace of development which has occurred in lower Manhattan since the late 1960s, due principally to the creation of new office space. Here progressive planning has re-established the human and recreational elements in the architectural landscape. Laid out on landfill, Water Street is lined with new office buildings of a variety of shapes, colors and construction materials, greatly altering the skyline of this seafront area. *Visit on a weekday.*

The buildings of **New York Plaza,** nos 1, 2 and 4, form a fascinating, highly varied grouping, linked by plazas and a ground level concourse lined with shops and restaurants. The 22-story red brick building of 4 New York Plaza with its narrow slit windows houses the electronic accounting unit of Manufacturers Hanover Trust.

At Vietnam Veterans Plaza, a street level plaza, pause to view the **Vietnam Veterans Memorial,** a granite and glass block wall inscribed with excerpts from writings by Americans during the Vietnam era. The memorial is dedicated to the nation's men and women who died in combat, and its veterans who returned home safely. Especially moving are the passages from letters, diary entries and poems written by American soldiers describing their thoughts, feelings of pride, fear, isolation, comradeship and reactions to the war experience.

On the north side of this plaza is **55 Water Street** where the two buildings, north and south, flank a raised plaza *(access by escalator)*; from the plaza there is an expansive **view**★★ across the East River to Brooklyn Heights.

Continuing along Water Street pass the Chemical Bank at 55 Water North, then the welcoming plaza of 77 Water Street, Bennett Park, where pools, fountains, sculpture and benches have been thoughtfully provided.

The northwest corner of Wall and Water Streets, was the site of the Tontine Coffee House *(p 87)*, which was the first home of the Stock Exchange.

In the plaza of **88 Pine Street,** designed by I.M. Pei, is Yu Yu Yang's tantalizing two-part sculpture which encourages pedestrians to pass through its large central opening and be mirrored in the nearby reflective disc. Just beside, the **Queen Elizabeth I Memorial,** a plaque embedded in the plaza surface, describes the *R.M.S. Elizabeth*, the largest and fastest ocean liner ever built.

Passing other office blocks, continue to Maiden Lane; look westward up this street to catch a glimpse of the twin towers of the World Trade Center and the Chase Manhattan Bank Building.

127 John Street with its digital clock, colored chairs, tables and awnings, provides a pleasant touch in the urban landscape.

■ SOUTH STREET SEAPORT HISTORIC DISTRICT ★★

Fronting the East River and south of the Brooklyn Bridge is the South Street Seaport Historic District, an 11-block district which was, in the 19C, the heart of the port of New York and the center of its world-wide shipping activities. The South Street port eventually declined as shipping moved to the deepwater piers on the Hudson River, and its once busy countinghouses, shops and warehouses, at first converted to a variety of uses, were later abandoned and left to decay.

In the 1960s, efforts to preserve the port's historic buildings, piers, streets and vessels led to the establishment of the South Street Seaport Historic District and the South Street Seaport Museum.

Interest in the area continued, and in the 1980s a large-scale development project was launched to revitalize the Seaport, with a new 3-story Fulton Market building as its centerpiece. Extensive restoration and new construction have resulted, transforming the area bounded by John, South, Water and Beekman Streets into a complex of pedestrian malls, restaurants, shops and boutiques animated with a vitality reminiscent of the district's days as a major seaport.

VISIT

Free admission to the South Street Historic District, its shops, restaurants, piers and the Fulton Market.

A general admission fee ($5.00) covers admission to the Gallery, the historic ships, the Museum's special programs (films, etc.) and guided tours of the Seaport (11 AM to 4 PM, time: 50 min). Tickets may be purchased at the Visitor's Center (see below) and Pier 16 ticketbooth.

The major points of interest are described below. We suggest you begin your visit with The Seaport Experience *(p 113)*, a multimedia presentation of the history of the Seaport and its influence on present-day New York.

Museum Block. – A group of fourteen 18 and 19C buildings in the block bounded by Fulton, Front, Beekman and Water Streets. The **Visitor's Center** *(open 10 AM to 6 PM - 5 PM in winter; closed January 1, Thanksgiving Day and December 25)*, located at 12 Fulton Street, has a permanent exhibition on the history of the seaport.

The Seaport Experience. – *Trans-Lux Seaport Theater, 210 Front Street. Open 10:30 AM to 3:30 PM (6:30 PM Saturdays, Sundays and holidays); closed early September to mid-March; $5.25, children $4.25. Time: 60 min.* Viewers experience moments from the Seaport's past and present during this sight and sound experience which uses a combination of loudspeakers, special lighting and effects (fireworks, fog, sea mist, etc.), and dozens of projectors flashing images on the main screen and screens hidden in dioramas along the walls.

The Gallery. – *213 Water Street. Same hours as the Visitor's Center.* Changing exhibitions related to the history of the South Street district and the New York waterfront.

Bowne & Co. Stationers. – *211 Water Street. Same hours as the Visitor's Center.* A re-creation of a 19C printing and stationery shop *(daily demonstrations).*

New "Bogardus" Building. – *17-19 Fulton Street.* A steel and glass low-rise structure (1983) inspired by the cast-iron buildings of James Bogardus *(p 30).*

Schermerhorn Row. – A handsome group of 19C Georgian Federal style buildings unified by a red brick facade and sloping roof. Constructed for the shipchandler and developer Peter Schermerhorn between 1811 and 1813, the row was occupied by a string of countinghouses and warehouses during South Street's heyday. Today these buildings house a number of speciality shops as do the Greek Revival structures across the street in Cannon's Walk Block.

The Fulton Market Building. – This new brick and granite market (1983) designed by Benjamin Thompson and Associates, is the fourth market to be built on this site since 1822. A hub of activity both day and night, the market houses an assortment of food stalls and restaurants which serve a variety of international cuisine as well as ice cream, hot dogs and other favorites. The marketplace is a splendid spot for people-watching and enjoying the festive atmosphere of the Seaport.

The South Street side of the building incorporates stalls of the **Fulton Fish Market** which has been operating at this waterfront site for more than a century and a half. *Guided tours (time: 2 hours) of the Fulton Fish Market complex April through October 6 AM on alternate Thursday mornings; prepaid reservations required ☏ 669-9400; $10.00.*

Pier 17 Pavilion. – Rising from a pier that reaches 400ft into the East River, the Pavilion (designed by Benjamin Thompson and Associates) is a 3-story glass and steel structure with more than 100 shops, restaurants and cafés. The spacious public promenade decks overlook the river on three sides, creating for the viewer the marvelous illusion of being on board a ship. The **vistas**★★ are magnificent: north to the Brooklyn Bridge, opposite to Brooklyn Heights and the Brooklyn waterfront, and south to New York harbor.

Exhibition of Historic Vessels. – *Pier 16. Same hours as the Visitor's Center. For admission see p 112.*

Moored at piers 15 and 16 along South Street is the fleet of historic ships: the *Peking,* a square-rigged, four-masted barque (1911); the *Wavertree,* a square-rigger built (1885) for the jute trade between India and Europe; the *Ambrose,* the first lightship to serve as a guide to vessels approaching the entrance to Ambrose Channel in New York harbor; and the *Lettie G. Howard* (1893), one of the last extant Gloucester fishing schooners.

Harbor Cruises. – *Pier 16.* Cruises of New York harbor aboard the replica sidewheeler, the *Andrew Fletcher* or the replica steamship, the *Dewitt Clinton* or by sail, aboard the schooner *Pioneer. The* Andrew Fletcher *and the* Dewitt Clinton *operate late March to late October; time 1 1/2 hours; $13.00 ☏ 669-9400. The* Pioneer *operates May through September; 2 hour cruise $15.00, 3 hour cruise $22.00 ☏ 669-9416.*

Before leaving the Seaport, notice at **no 41 Peck Slip** the *trompe l'œil* painting *The Brooklyn Bridge,* one of several outdoor murals in the city by Richard Haas *(p 106).*

NEW YORK IS FOR CHILDREN

Museums: American Museum of Natural History; Brooklyn Children's Museum; New York City Fire Museum; Hayden Planetarium; Staten Island Children's Museum; Whaling Museum in Cold Spring Harbor.

Walks: Central Park; Jamaica Bay Wildlife Refuge; Old Bethpage Restoration Village on Long Island; Richmondtown Restoration on Staten Island; South Street Seaport; Statue of Liberty; Stony Brook on Long Island.

Views: Circle Line Tour around Manhattan; Empire State Building; World Trade Center.

Amusement: Coney Island; Jones Beach State Park on Long Island; Montauk State Park on Long Island; Radio City Music Hall Entertainment Center; Robert Moses State Park on Fire Island; Sunken Meadow State Park on Long Island.

Zoos: Bronx Zoo; New York Aquarium; Staten Island Zoo.

Time: about 1 hour.

The museum is closed for construction and renovation until November 1991.

Located on Fifth Avenue, between 88th and 89th Streets, The Solomon R. Guggenheim Museum is particularly interesting, both for its original architecture and the works of contemporary art it displays.

Two Innovators. – **Solomon R. Guggenheim** (1861-1949), a copper magnate, was fascinated by modern painting. An enthusiastic collector, he established the Solomon R. Guggenheim Foundation to promote non-objective art and art education. In 1943 he commissioned Frank Lloyd Wright to design a museum and set aside the sum of two million dollars for this purpose.

Frank Lloyd Wright (1867-1959) participated in the Chicago School which pioneered contemporary architecture at the turn of the century. He designed more than 600 buildings, including the Johnson Wax Company Laboratory Towers in Wisconsin and the Kaufmann house "Falling Water" in Pennsylvania.

The Building ★★. – The museum is one of Wright's most controversial works. To those who criticized his "corkscrew," or "monstrous mushroom," he replied that "one should no more judge a building from the outside than a car by its color."

Exterior. – From the Central Park side of Fifth Avenue you can see the entire building, constructed in cream-colored concrete. The Thannhauser building on the left is a four-story rounded structure joined by a sweeping concrete overhang to the museum proper. This latter building is a cone composed of a four-layer spiral, which becomes larger as it rises. In addition, each section is inclined outward toward the top.

Interior. – *Open 11 AM to 4:45 PM (7:45 PM Tuesdays); closed Mondays and holidays; $4.50.*

Enter the main gallery. The continuous spiral ramp,

(From photo Ezra Stoller.)

Guggenheim Museum. — Exterior.

over a quarter of a mile long, rises gradually to the glass dome, 92ft high. Frank Lloyd Wright designed a dome completely covered with glass, but planning authorities required the addition of concrete arches and the reduction of the dimensions.

Although the diameter of the museum increases as it rises, this is not evident from here, since the ramp becomes wider as it ascends. The oval basin, compared to a seedpod by the architect, has a central unifying value: its form is repeated in the shape of the galleries and the elevators, and in the decorative pattern of the floor, as well as in the sidewalk outside the museum.

Take the elevator to the top floor and make your way down slowly, passing in front of sculpture and paintings. These are attached to the circular outside wall and to the side panels, which form separate compartments, a sort of vast chambered nautilus. Wright had wanted the paintings to be displayed as if on an artist's easel and illuminated by natural light from windows in the ceilings immediately above, changing with the movement of the sun and the seasons. Although the lighting in the museum now comes from spot lights and fluorescent tubes in the ceiling above the paintings, Wright's concept continues to prevail and the paintings are hung unframed, or with frames which are simple and uniform directly on the walls.

Collections. – The core is composed of works left to the museum by Solomon Guggenheim. Among the 6 000 works are the largest Kandinsky collection in the world, over 70 Klees and important groups by Chagall, Delaunay, Léger and others. A permanent display of 20C pioneer abstractionists has been installed in a gallery off the fourth ramp, with emphasis on such masters as Feininger, Gris, Léger, Delaunay, Mondrian, Kandinsky and Klee. In addition, the museum offers a wide range of temporary exhibits.

Modern Masters in the Thannhauser Wing. – Presented on the second floor just off the central ramp, this collection is the bequest of Justin K. Thannhauser who died in 1976. It includes some of the most significant works of the past 100 years, from the Impressionists to Picasso. Among the Impressionists, the best represented are Pissarro *(Les Coteaux de l'Hermitage à Pontoise)*, Renoir *(Woman with a Parrot),* and Manet *(Before the Mirror).* Other highlights are works by Cézanne (still lifes), Van Gogh *(The Viaduct, Mountains at Saint-Rémy),* Gauguin, Toulouse-Lautrec *(Au Salon),* Matisse *(The Italian Woman),* Degas, Modigliani and Vuillard's two-panel scene of the Place Vintimille in Paris. Canvases by Braque, executed in a severe palette of browns, black and ocher *(Piano and Mandola, Le Buffet, Violin and Palette)* reflect the artist's Cubist tendencies.

Picasso is most bountifully represented: notice his early works, *The End of the Road, Le Moulin de la Galette* and *The Fourteenth of July,* as well as the brightly colored *Pitcher and Bowl of Fruit* painted later, in 1931. *Woman Ironing, The Harlequins,* the still lifes, the doves and the portraits of Dora Mar and Françoise Gilot illustrate the classic and restrained side of his artistic temperament.

Distance: 1 1/2 miles – Time: 2 1/2 hours.

This walk which leads from church to university, two pillars of American life, is relatively brief. But it will allow you to visit the area known as Morningside Heights, originally called **Harlem Heights.** The Battle of Harlem Heights took place here in 1776 when, for the first time, American troops commanded by Washington successfully resisted the British.

■ CATHEDRAL CHURCH OF ST JOHN THE DIVINE★★
Visit: 1 hour

The Cathedral Church of the Episcopal Diocese of New York rises impressively on Amsterdam Avenue at West 112th Street. "The largest Gothic cathedral in the world" can welcome 10 000 worshippers at any one time.

A Challenging Task. – The idea of building the largest religious edifice in the United States orig- inated with the sixth Episcopal Bishop of New York (1861-87), **Horatio Potter.** However, it was only in 1892 that his nephew and successor, Henry Codman Potter, bought the necessary land; the cornerstone was laid on December 27 of that year, the Feast of St John.

Model of the Cathedral
as it will appear when completed.

The first architects, Heins and La Farge, were inspired by the European Romanesque style which is reflected in the exist- ence of a narthex and, above all, in the choir and sanctuary. How- ever, beginning in 1911, the Gothic style was adopted, and has come to dominate the pre- sent conception of the cathed- ral. The crossing, the choir and the sanctuary were completed in 1916.

In 1924 a national campaign raised $15 000 000, including $500 000 donated by John D. Rockefeller, Jr., although he was a Baptist. A year later, the foundation stone of the nave was laid. The first service in the completed nave was held in March, 1939.

At the present time, nearly one-third of the cathedral is yet to be completed: the towers of the West Front, the north and south transepts, the central dome and tower, the chapter house and the sacristy building. The carving of the figures of the central and south portals of the West Front is underway. Apprentices on the project, many of them neighborhood youth, have been trained by and work with master craftsmen, skilled in the traditional methods of stone cutting and carving which were used in building the great cathedrals of the Middle Ages. *Visitors may view these activities in the stoneyard adjacent to the cathedral.*

Exterior. – The wide West Front (207ft) is flanked by two towers which will be 266ft high when completed (the towers of Notre Dame in Paris are 225ft high). The five portals, corresponding to the five interior naves, have not yet been entirely finished; however, Burmese teak doors are installed in four of them. The central portal has bronze doors, cast and fabricated in Paris by Ferdinand Barbedienne, who also cast the Statue of Liberty; each door weighs about 3 tons and contains scenes from the Old and New Tes- taments. The central pillar bears a statue of St John the Divine; above, in the tym- panum is the Majestas, a carving representing the Lord in Glory. The great rose window above the main portal measures 40ft in diameter and contains 10 000 pieces of glass.

Interior. – Enter the narthex, which contains two of the finest stained glass windows in the cathedral; on the left is the Creation, and on the right scenes symbolizing elements of Christian doctrine. Note also the Greek icons and a Virgin and Child (15C).

Taken together, the naves are 150ft wide and 250ft long; the central nave is as wide as 112th Street. The arches rise 124ft above (Notre Dame: 115ft high.). The floor, known as the Pilgrims' Pavement, is decorated with medallions representing great Christian pilgrimages and episodes from the life of Christ.

At the crossing, the pulpit of Knoxville marble is also decorated with scenes from the life of Christ; figures of Isaiah and John the Baptist are placed on the newel posts. Notice the large dimensions of the crossing which is surmounted by an impressive dome.

The Romanesque sanctuary is enclosed by a majestic semicircular arrangement of eight granite columns, each 55ft high and weighing 130 tons. Notice the choir stalls in carved oak and the episcopal throne. This is surrounded by a white marble Historical Parapet. Niches are provided for statues of notable figures of the Christian Era, from St Paul to Washington and Lincoln; the 20C is temporarily represented by a stone block to be carved. Behind the high altar of white Vermont marble is the tomb of Horatio Potter.

To the north of the choir, the baptistry has a vaulted dome and octagonal lantern. The figures along the wall represent personages from the history of the Netherlands, including Peter Stuyvesant *(p 131).* The font is a copy of that from the baptistry of St John in Siena, a work by Jacopo della Quercia (15C).

Works of Art. – Among the old tapestries hung in the cathedral are Scenes from the New Testament (17C) patterned after a design by Raphael. In the north transept a model of the completed cathedral is displayed. In the ambulatory you may admire paintings of the 16C Italian school, a glazed terra-cotta Annunciation (Della Robbia School, 15C) and a 16C cloth embellished with an Adoration of the Magi. The central chapel of the Savior contains interesting icons.

A passage leading from the south transept takes you to a large room where religious art is displayed. On the cathedral grounds are a **Biblical Garden** containing only trees and plants mentioned in the Bible and several neo-Gothic buildings which serve as offices, the Bishop's House, the cathedral school and the Synod house.

Leaving the cathedral, take 113th Street to the east. On the north side of this street is St Luke's Hospital, administered by the Episcopal Church. You will reach **Morningside Drive**, which follows the crest of the hills above Harlem. Between 114th and 115th Streets is the Grotto Church of **Notre Dame**, a Roman Catholic church of baroque inspiration with portico and dome, built in 1915. Its choir is a representation of the grotto of Lourdes.

Continue on Morningside Drive to 116th Street. At the northwest corner is the **residence of the President** of Columbia University; General Eisenhower lived there for several years.

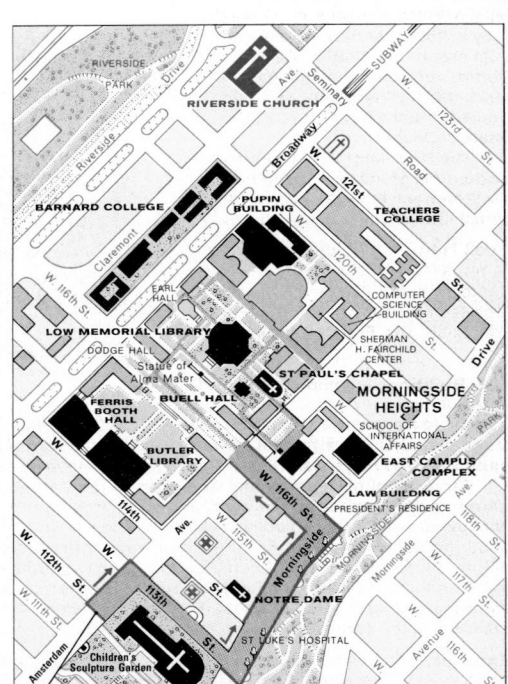

■ **COLUMBIA UNIVERSITY** ★

Visit: 1 hour

Enjoying a worldwide reputation, Columbia University is one of the oldest, largest and richest private universities in the United States. Its campus occupies a large area reaching from 114th Street to 121st Street between Broadway and Amsterdam Avenue.

A BIT OF HISTORY

From King's College to Columbia University. – Founded in October 1754, by charter from His Gracious Majesty George II, King's College was first established close to Trinity Church *(p 86).*

At the beginning of the Revolution, during the battle of Harlem Heights, the British were repulsed by Washington's troops after a struggle which took place on the present site of the Barnard College campus on September 16, 1776 in what was then a buckwheat covered field.

In 1784, King's College reopened under a new name – Columbia College. A hundred years later, the college had but 80 professors and 1 600 students; in 1897 it moved to the present site after 40 years at a Madison and 49th Street location.

A Galaxy of Celebrities. – Among the first graduates of King's College were a number of noted public figures: **Alexander Hamilton,** aide de camp to General Washington, one of the authors of *The Federalist* and later Secretary of the Treasury; **John Jay,** also a co-author of *The Federalist* and first Chief Justice of the United States; **Robert R. Livingston,** the Chancellor of New York State, who administered the oath of office to Washington in 1789 and later, as U.S. Minister to France, negotiated the Louisiana Purchase; **Gouverneur Morris,** also Minister of the United States to France, where he remained during the Reign of Terror. Another great administrator and alumnus of Columbia was **De Witt Clinton,** untiring promoter of the Erie Canal, opened in 1825, while he was governor of New York State. More recently, both **Theodore** and **Franklin D. Roosevelt** attended Columbia Law School, although each left before graduation to begin his political career.

It was a Columbia professor, **Harold C. Urey,** who discovered heavy water, earning a Nobel Prize in 1934. Finally, we should mention that General Eisenhower was President of Columbia University from 1948-52.

Profile. – Encompassing a variety of academic disciplines, Columbia University is particularly known for its Law and Medical Schools, Teachers College, the School of International Affairs, the School of Journalism, Columbia College (coed since 1983), and Barnard College, an affiliated liberal arts school for women. Columbia has an endowment at present of approximately $1.4 billion.

The coeducational private university has a student population of about 18 900 and a teaching and research faculty of about 5 000.

The School of General Studies admits students with or without college credits or, in some cases, a high school diploma. Students under 21 who work and cannot study full time are also admitted. More than 1 300 liberal arts courses are offered each year. Campus sports facilities are supplemented by Baker Field, the Columbia University athletics complex for intercollegiate competition, located at the northern tip of Manhattan.

VISIT

You may stroll about the campus as you like. However, a guided tour (free) enabling you to see the interior of many of the buildings is available at 2 PM late May through August, and at 3 PM during the academic year; it leaves from Room 201 Dodge Hall, corner of 116th Street and Broadway.

For a visit of the principal buildings, we suggest the following walk (plan p 116). Begin at Dodge Hall.

Campus. – The lawns and walks form a harmonious open space between Butler Library (1934) to the south, and Low Memorial Library (1896).

Low Memorial Library. – Originally the university library, now occupied by administrative offices, this monumental edifice with its colonnade and 130ft tall dome is built on a Roman mold; it was designed by Charles McKim. In front of the majestic staircase, stands the statue of the *Alma Mater*. The central rotunda serves as an assembly room or for exhibitions.

Buell Hall. – The oldest building on campus (1878); it serves as the Buell Center for the Study of American Architecture and houses the Maison Française, the French cultural center.

Law Building. – Completed in 1961, this building now houses the Law School. In front of the building is the monumental Lipchitz bronze *Bellerophon Taming Pegasus*.

(From photo Constance M. Jacobs, New York.)

Low Memorial Library.

The School of International and Public Affairs consists of the renowned W. Averell Harriman Institute for Advanced Study of the Soviet Union and other regional institutes occupying the modern building at 118th Street and Amsterdam Avenue.

St Paul's Chapel ★. – Predominantly neoclassic in style this chapel is open for worship and organ recitals; the interior has finely crafted woodwork.

The campus has also recently been enriched by a modern building of striking originality, the Sherman H. Fairchild Center for the Life Sciences, designed by a Columbia architecture professor. The Computer Building (1983) on the other side of Uris Business School symbolizes Columbia's important role in the field of computer research since the 1930s.

Pupin Building. – Across the terrace of the underground Marcellus Hartley Dodge Physical Fitness Center is the 13-story red brick Pupin Physics Laboratories (1927). It was here that the maser (forerunner of the laser) was invented, heavy water was discovered, properties of atomic nuclei were explained and the development of atomic energy in this country – the Manhattan Project – was begun. A total of 20 Nobel Prizes in physics has been won by researchers who have taught or studied at Columbia. To the east of Pupin is the new Center for Engineering and Physical Science Research.

Returning in the direction of Low Memorial Library note Earl Hall, neoclassic in inspiration, which serves student groups and religious organizations.

Barnard College. – Founded in 1889, Barnard College, affiliated with Columbia University, is an independent college for women.It has its own campus, across Broadway from Columbia, ranging in architecture from the late 1880s to 1988. Barnard was among the pioneers in the late 19C crusade to make higher education available for young women. Barnard's anthropology department, founded during World War I, is one of the oldest in the U.S. Perhaps the department's best known student and scholar is Margaret Mead, who began her fieldwork in Samoa in the mid-20s.

Butler Library. – This building houses the central university library, the Rare Book and Manuscript Library, and the School of Library Service, the oldest in the country. The university libraries possess a distinguished collection of over 5 700 000 volumes.

Ferris Booth Hall. – A modern building, it serves as a student union and recreation center providing rooms for relaxation or informal discussion, lecture and reading rooms, bowling alleys, shooting galleries and ping-pong rooms.

Distance: about 3/4 mile – Time: 1 1/2 hours.

These two squares within easy walking distance of midtown come as pleasant surprises in an otherwise undistinguished area of the city.

Gramercy Park ★. – This attractive square and its immediate surroundings form an elegant and tranquil residential enclave in a largely commercial area of the city. It was laid out in 1831 by Samuel Ruggles who drained an old marsh (Gramercy is a corruption of the Dutch for "crooked little swamp") and patterned it after the London residential squares. He sold the lots around it on the understanding that each would have access to the public park at the center.

Today, surrounded by a cast-iron fence, Gramercy Park remains private, the only such square in New York. The lack of through traffic keeps the area quiet and it has long attracted artists and intellectuals as residents. A statue of the actor Edwin Booth dressed in his favorite role of Hamlet stands at its center.

Walk around the park.

Gramercy Park West is the most attractive side of the square with its red brick town houses (nos 1, 2, 3, 4). Nos 3 and 4 have elaborate cast-iron porches, and "Mayor's lamps" stand outside no 4, the former home of James Harper, Mayor of New York in 1844.

The present site of the National Arts Club at no 15 was the home of Samuel Tilden, an opponent of Tammany Hall *(p 107)*, Governor of New York State 1874-76, and unsuccessful contender for the Democratic nomination for the Presidency in 1876. Next door at no 16 Edwin Booth founded the Players Club in 1888. Note the ornate street lamps and the elaborate ironwork of the second floor balcony. No 19 was the domain of Mrs Stuyvesant Fish, leader of New York society (succeeding Mrs William Astor, *p 42*), whose innovations included reducing the time for a formal dinner from several hours to 50 minutes.

At the east end of the square stand two apartment buildings. No 34 dates from 1883 and is red brick with an octagonal turret corner. No 36, next door, is neo-Gothic in style, built of white terra-cotta (1908) with two concrete knights in armor outside.

Follow East 20th Street and cross Park Avenue South.

Theodore Roosevelt Birthplace. – *28 East 20th Street. Guided tours (time: 30 min) Wednesdays through Sundays 9 AM to 5 PM; closed holidays and Wednesdays following Monday holidays; $1.00.*

This reconstructed Victorian brownstone was the home of **Theodore Roosevelt** (1858-1919) until he was 14 years of age. A National Historic Site, the house has been filled with appropriate furnishings, mostly donated by the family, and numerous memorabilia.

Harvard graduate, rancher in the Dakota Territory, Colonel in the Rough Riders, hunter-naturalist on three continents, Theodore Roosevelt was a colorful personality and a dynamic force in U.S. politics for 40 years. McKinley's Vice President in 1901, he succeeded to the Oval Office on the assassination of the President a few months later. Elected in his own right in 1904, he finally retired in 1909, after having received the Nobel Peace Prize for his mediating efforts between Russia and Japan.

"Teddy," who gave his name to Teddy Bears, was the uncle of Eleanor Roosevelt, future wife of another U.S. President, her distant cousin Franklin Delano Roosevelt.

Return to Park Avenue South and turn left on East 19th Street.

Between Irving Place and Third Avenue, East 19th Street is known as the "block beautiful." Lined with graceful trees, the houses are harmonious yet original. Note in particular nos 129 and 135, and also no 141 with its jockey hitching posts.

Turn right on Third Avenue and left on East 17th Street.

Stuyvesant Square. – A gift to the city from Peter Stuyvesant *(p 131)*, this was an elegant residential quarter in the 19C. Today, the square is cut in two by Second Avenue. Hospitals surround the east side, and the towers of Stuyvesant Town, a middle-income housing project built by the Metropolitan Life Insurance Company, are visible beyond.

The west side, however, retains a little of its 19C elegance. The red brick **Friends' Meeting House** and Seminary (1860) on Rutherford Place with the neighboring **St George's Episcopal Church** give a village green look to the square. St George's, a Romanesque brownstone built in 1856, was known as "Morgan's Church" because the elder J.P. Morgan *(p 87)* was a parishioner here. A bronze statue of Stuyvesant, easily recognizable by his peg leg, stands in the square in front of the church.

Time: about 1 1/2 hours.

This area of the city has a very special character because of the existence of New York University. A visit late in the afternoon or in the evening is recommended so that the atmosphere and local color can be enjoyed to the fullest.

■ WASHINGTON SQUARE★★

The heart of present day Greenwich Village *(p 102)*, this large square is the main gathering place for Villagers and visitors alike. It stands at the beginning of Fifth Avenue, its arch making a fitting start to this famous street. On fine days, it is a people watchers' paradise. Young people throng here, there are impromptu performers, soapbox orators, skateboard and frisbee enthusiasts, and hordes of exhibitionists of all kinds in a wide range of weird and wonderful outfits.

Twice a year for three weeks *(see A New York City Calendar p 17)*, the square and surrounding streets are the scene of the **Washington Square Outdoor Art Exhibit.** More than 500 emerging artists display their work, many for the first time.

The Ashes of the Past. – Originally a marshland and favorite hunting ground of the early colonists, Washington Square became a potter's field in the 18C (skeletons of about 1 000 early New Yorkers were found during the renovation of the square in the 60s). It was also popular as a dueling ground and the site of public hangings. The 19C saw it become a military parade ground and later a fashionable residential area with the construction of elegant red brick town houses around it. **Henry James**'s novel *Washington Square,* later adapted for stage and screen as *The Heiress,* depicts the life of the local aristocracy. Mark Twain, O'Henry, Walt Whitman and the painter Edward Hopper also frequented Washington Square and evoked it in their works.

After the founding of New York University *(p 120),* Washington Square became the unofficial university campus, and today a large number of the buildings around it belong to the university.

> *At the official opening of Washington Square as a public park in 1828, hearty New Yorkers consumed two whole oxen, 200 hams and the contents of a quarter mile of back-to-back beer barrels.*

VISIT

Washington Arch★. – Designed by Stanford White in 1892, this white marble triumphal arch replaced a temporary one commemorating the centenary of Washington's inauguration *(p 89)*. The arch, 30ft across and 47ft high, is best viewed from Fifth Avenue. Gracing this side are two sculptures of Washington – as a soldier by Herman Atkins Mac Neil and as a civilian by A. Sterling Calder, father of the creator of "mobiles." On the south side, note the frieze with the American eagle and the "W's" for Washington at the center, and the trumpet blowing statues of fame.

Statue of Garibaldi. – Erected in 1888, this statue forms a rallying point for the inhabitants of nearby "Little Italy" *(p 131)*. A hero of the Italian struggle for independence, Garibaldi visited New York in 1850. NYU students claim that the statue turns its head whenever a virtuous girl walks past – but no one has actually seen this happen ... .

Washington Square North★. – This is the most attractive side of the square. Two rows of red brick town houses (nos 1-13, and 21-26) remain from the 1830s, suggesting what the entire square once looked like. John Dos Passos wrote *Manhattan Transfer* in no 3. Doric or Ionic columns grace the entrances topped by flat lintels, and cast-iron railings separate the houses from the sidewalk. Some (nos 7-13) are only facades as the interiors have been gutted and they are part of the complex behind.

Washington Mews and MacDougal Alley. – Behind Washington Square North, two picturesque alleys have survived which once contained stables and servants' quarters for the town houses. The charm and intimacy of these streets with their whitewashed or brick facades, climbing trees, gas lights and, in the Mews, cobblestone pavement have long attracted artists, writers and actors. In the early 1900s, MacDougal Alley was inhabited by sculptress Gertrude Vanderbilt Whitney, who opened a gallery in a converted stable that was to be the precursor of the Whitney Museum *(p 51)*.

(From photo Seymour Linden.)

Washington Mews.

■ NEW YORK UNIVERSITY

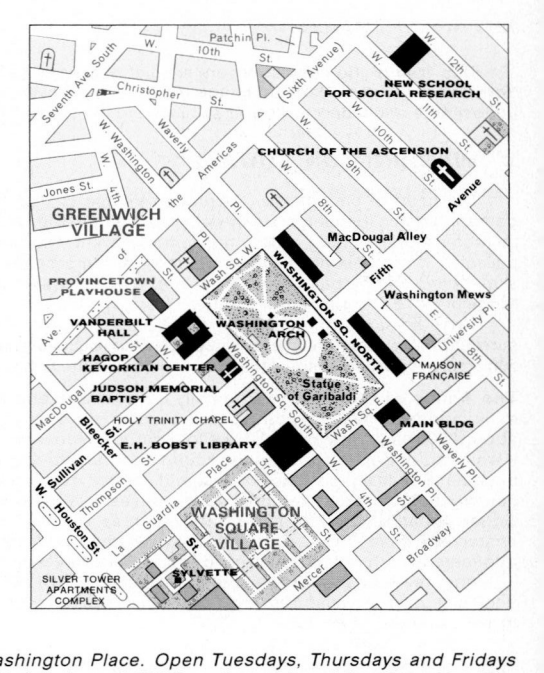

The largest private university in the United States, NYU was founded by **Albert Gallatin**, Secretary of the Treasury under Jefferson, in 1831.

Today, NYU has 14 colleges and nearly 46 000 students. The principal campuses are: Washington Square (Sciences, Arts and Letters, Business, Law, Education), the NYU Medical Center on First Avenue *(p 137)* (Medicine and Dentistry), the Stern School of Business on Trinity Place in the Wall Street area, and the Institute of Fine Arts on Fifth Avenue and 78th Street.

The following buildings surround Washington Square:

Main Building. – Built 1894, this neoclassical structure replaced the original building erected in 1836. Its ground floor houses the **Grey Art Gallery.** — *Entrance on Washington Place. Open Tuesdays, Thursdays and Fridays 11 AM to 6:30 PM, 8:30 PM Wednesdays, 5 PM Saturdays; closed Sundays, Mondays and holidays*. This pleasant gallery features changing exhibits of high quality.

Elmer Holmes Bobst Library. – This huge red sandstone cube on the southeast corner of the square was designed by Philip Johnson and Richard Foster in 1973. It houses 2 million books *(not open to the general public)*.

Walk past the Loeb Student Center and Holy Trinity Chapel with its modern stained glass windows.

Judson Memorial Baptist Church. – Making a marked contrast with the Roman Catholic Chapel, this Romanesque Revival structure of yellow brick has a separate campanile. Built in 1892, it was designed by Stanford White. Note the stained glass windows of John La Farge inside.

Hagop Kevorkian Center for Near Eastern Studies. — This stark modern building on a small corner lot was designed by Philip Johnson and Richard Foster in 1972. It contains a surprising and delightful **entrance hall**★ *(Sullivan Street)* which is a reconstruction of a Syrian courtyard complete with tiled floor, fountain, moldings and door panels. These pieces came from a merchant's house in Damascus built in 1797.

Vanderbilt Hall (School of Law). – This red brick neo-Georgian structure (1951) has a courtyard and exterior arcade.

> *Famous NYU professors include Samuel F.B. Morse,*
> *inventor of the telegraph; the composer Percy Grainger;*
> *the poet Walt Whitman; the painter Winslow Homer;*
> *the writers Joyce Kilmer and Thomas Wolfe;*
> *the mathematician Richard Courant; the philosopher Sidney Hook;*
> *and the economist Wassily Leontief, 1973 Nobel Prize Winner.*

■ ADDITIONAL SIGHTS

Sylvette. – Between Bleeker and West Houston Streets in the center of the Silver Towers Apartment complex (designed for NYU by I.M. Pei in 1966) stands this 36ft high bust of Sylvette. The original Picasso sculpture was enlarged in concrete and stone by Carl Nesjar.

Church of the Ascension. – *36-38 Fifth Avenue*. This Gothic Revival Episcopal church was designed in 1841 by Richard Upjohn in brownstone. The interior was remodeled in 1888 by Stanford White. Note the John La Farge mural of the Ascension over the altar, the stained glass windows and the box pews.

The New School for Social Research. – *Main building 66 West 12th Street*.

The New School for Social Research, founded in 1919 by economists Thorstein Vebleu and Alvin Johnson, educational philosopher John Dewey and historian Charles Beard, was originally conceived as a small informal center for adults where a broad range of economic and political issues could be discussed. Over the years the New School has evolved into a diversified institution of higher learning and today, with its seven divisions and total enrollment of more than 40 000 students, it is one of the nation's leading universities.

Distance: 1 1/2 miles – Time: 6 hours

For many people, the name of Madison Avenue evokes the image of advertising executives, figures in conservative gray flannel and pin-striped suits who exert their powerful influence to shape the tastes of consumers. But for the casual visitor, this activity is nearly invisible. A few name plates, casually dressed business people and

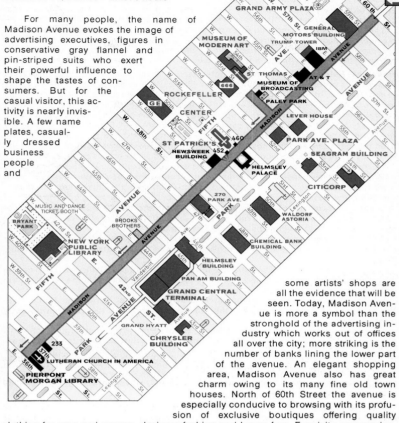

some artists' shops are all the evidence that will be seen. Today, Madison Avenue is more a symbol than the stronghold of the advertising industry which works out of offices all over the city; more striking is the number of banks lining the lower part of the avenue. An elegant shopping area, Madison Avenue also has great charm owing to its many fine old town houses. North of 60th Street the avenue is especially conducive to browsing with its profusion of exclusive boutiques offering quality clothing for men and women, designer fashion and luxury furs. Exquisite accessories, precious rugs and other Oriental imports, dinnerware and rare gifts are tastefully displayed. The proximity of great museums has attracted the abundance of art galleries and antique dealers found between 57th and 90th Streets.

From 60th to 36th Street

The first section of this walk is dominated by a series of high-rise office buildings of very recent construction which reflect architectural trends of the 80s. One, the General Motors Building *(p 49)*, is of an earlier date.

IBM Building. – This five-sided 43-story tower (1983) designed by Edward Larrabee Barnes has a polished green granite skin. Strips of windows set flush with the smooth stone exterior wrap around the building, creating a pattern of horizontal bands. The building has a recessed main entrance on the corner of 57th Street; cross Madison Avenue and from the southeast corner, opposite, note the effect created by the tower's mass which appears to rise unsupported above the corner of the building.

Special features include two public spaces: a 4-story "greenhouse" **plaza** with trees, refreshment kiosk, tables and chairs; and the **IBM Gallery of Science and Art★** *(open Tuesdays through Saturdays 11 AM to 6 PM, closed Sunday, holidays and between exhibitions)* which mounts noteworthy exhibitions on art, science and technology.

AT & T Headquarters★. – This striking tower(1983), a radical departure from the boxlike forms erected in the 1960s and 70s, has caused comment since the plans were unveiled in 1977. Designed by Philip Johnson and John Burgee in association with Henry Simmons, the 40-story building has an unusual roof reminiscent of Colonial furniture design (a triangle split at the peak by a concave hollow), and at its base a huge arched entrance, 110ft high, flanked by columns; to conserve energy only a third of its pink granite exterior is covered with windows.

In the vaulted main lobby note the gilded bronze statue of the *Spirit of Communication* or "Golden Boy," the symbol of AT & T for more than half a century.

The tower is the main element of the headquarters complex which also includes a pedestrian plaza, a through block galleria, and a 4-story annex housing the **AT & T InfoQuest Center★** *(open 10 AM to 6 PM - 9 PM Tuesdays; closed Mondays and holidays)*, a permanent exhibit which allows visitors to explore the technologies of the Information Age through computerized hands-on activities, an audio-visual presentation and other educational and fun-filled displays.

Paley Park. – This "vest pocket" park on East 53rd Street provides a tiny island of tranquillity. Office workers and visitors alike can relax under the trees beside the waterfall which mutes the city noises. *(Closed Sundays, major holidays and January.)*

Museum of Broadcasting. – *1 East 53rd Street. Open noon to 5 PM (8 PM Tuesdays); closed Mondays and major holidays; $4.00.* The first of its kind in the world, this museum contains tapes of over 50 000 radio and television programs and commercials. These are available for viewing in individual consoles. Major public events from war reportage to presidential elections are represented as well as dramatic and comedy productions from the previous fifty years of broadcasting. The museum also mounts programs on changing themes in its theater and videotheque.

Helmsley Palace. – This hotel has integrated a modern skyscraper with **the Villard Houses**★★, a group of six mansions built in 1885 by McKim, Mead and White for Henry Villard, founder of the Northern Pacific Railroad. The Renaissance-style brownstones, modeled after the Palazzo Cancelleria in Rome appear to be one mansion built around a central courtyard. Villard went bankrupt before completion of the residences, which were eventually bought individually by several New York notables including Mrs. Whitelaw Reid, wife of the *New York Tribune* editor. Following World War II several companies used the mansions as office space, until the Archdiocese of New York sold them to the Helmsley chain on the condition that they be preserved as the hotel's public rooms.

Enter the pedestrian courtyard (formerly a carriage yard) through wrought iron gates on Madison Avenue. Inside the building, the second floor lobby is dominated by a red marble fireplace designed by Augustus Saint-Gaudens; the figures on the mantel represent Joy, Hospitality and Moderation. The public rooms have been luxuriously restored, particularly the **Gold Room** *(open 2-5 PM for afternoon tea and 5 PM-1 AM for cocktails; gentlemen are required to wear jackets)* with its barrel-vaulted ceiling, musicians' gallery and lunette paintings by John Lafarge.

The great hallway and staircase beyond the Gold Room feature Venetian mosaics, a gilt-and-marble zodiac clock by Saint-Gaudens; and stained glass windows by Louis Comfort Tiffany.

On the west side of Madison Avenue, the apse of St Patrick's Cathedral *(p 46)* can be seen flanked on either side by a small town house. **No 460 Madison** is the rectory of the cathedral, **no 452** the residence of the archbishop.

From the corner of 50th Street, there is a good **view** of Rockefeller Center. The **Newsweek Building** on the west side of the avenue is the home of the well-known weekly news magazine.

On the northwest corner of 44th Street is Brooks Brothers, the stronghold of men's and boys' clothing for more than 150 years. Today it also carries exclusive items for women.

Murray Hill. – The final blocks of this walk show evidence of the era when Madison Avenue rivaled Fifth Avenue as a fashionable residential area. It was named for Robert Murray, whose country estate once stood where East 37th Street crosses Park Avenue. It was here that Murray's wife is rumored to have served tea to British General Howe and his staff while Washington's troops escaped to the north.

No 233 Madison, a magnificent house with a mansard roof, today houses the Polish Consulate. It was built in 1905 for Dutch sea captain, De Lamar. Across the street at no 231 stands a branch of the **Lutheran Church in America**. This free-standing brownstone residence constructed in 1852 was formerly the home of J.P. Morgan, Jr.

Pierpont Morgan Library★★. – A cultural treasure trove, the Morgan Library houses rich collections of rare books, manuscripts, drawings, engravings and works of art assembled by **J. Pierpont Morgan** (1837-1913) *(p 87)* which have been preserved and expanded since his death. Morgan, an inveterate collector whose interest in art, literature and history resulted in an unusually broad and varied accumulation of objects, wished to make his possessions accessible to the public following his death. The result is not only a fine art museum but also an outstanding research library filled with rare and exemplary items from the development of Western civilizations.

The Italian Renaissance-style main building on 36th Street was completed in 1906 after several tempestuous tugs-of-war between Morgan and designer Charles McKim. The annex on the corner of Madison Avenue (on the site of Morgan's former residence) was added by his son in 1928. The main building on 36th Street was designed by Charles McKim in 1906 in Italian Renaissance style. Steps lead to the main entrance *(not the public entrance)* guarded by two crouching lionesses. The annex on the corner of Madison Avenue was added in 1928 on the site of Morgan's house by his son.

The Library and the Museum★★. – *Open 10:30 AM (1 PM Sundays) to 5 PM; closed Mondays and holidays; $ 3.00.*

The vestibule is resplendent in marble polychrome. On the left is the main Exhibition Hall for rotating exhibitions and on the right a reading room open to accredited scholars *(open weekdays 9:30 AM to 4:45 PM; closed the last two weeks in August).*

The West Room. – The opulence of Mr Morgan's former study is enhanced by painted and carved Italian ceiling (16C), a red damask hangings, and massive black wood furniture.

Paintings and statuettes, enamels and metalwork of the Middle Ages and the Renaissance, and Swiss stained glass of the 16 and 17C blend harmoniously with the decoration. Above the Florentine marble mantel (15C) is a portrait of Morgan himself. Among the paintings, notice two small Bohemian panels of the 14C: *The Adoration of the Magi* and *The Death of the Virgin*, *Portrait of a Moor* (1570) by Tintoretto and the wedding portraits of Martin Luther and his wife by Lucas Cranach the Elder (Germany, 16C).

Among the sculpture are a number of small Florentine marbles of the 15C, such as the bust of *Marietta Strozzi* by Desiderio da Settignano. Among the enamels and goldwork note the 12C ciborium from England.

The East Room. – This library is decorated with a Flemish tapestry (16C) representing the Triumph of Avarice. There are changing exhibitions of books, manuscripts, letters and illuminated manuscripts. A copy of the Gutenberg Bible and an illuminated manuscript of an Antiphonary are permanently displayed.

"The longest street in the world," Broadway has given its name to this famous area of pleasure and entertainment. Times Square is its center, but the theater district extends approximately from 40th to 53rd Streets. Best seen at night, Broadway lights up when a colorful crowd throngs beneath its huge illuminated billboards.

■ **TIMES SQUARE** ★ *Time: 2 hours, preferably after dark.*

Located at the intersection of Broadway and Seventh Avenue (called with some justification the "Crossroads of the World"), Times Square takes its name from the *New York Times,* which moved here in 1905.

Yesterday. – At the end of the 19C the Times Square area, then known as Longacre Square, was a center for livery stables and harness makers. The American Horse Exchange remained at 50th Street and Broadway, the present site of the Winter Garden Theater, until 1910.

(From photo John B. Bayley, New York.)

The old Times Building.

On the southeast corner of Broadway and 42nd Street, was the ornate **Knickerbocker Hotel,** since converted into an office building *(142 West 42nd Street).* At the turn of the century, its "free lunch," offering such delicacies as lobster Newburg, was very popular.

The Hotel Astor, one of the grandest in New York, was opened in 1904 on the west side of the square between 44th and 45th Streets and replaced in 1968 by an office building. To the north, on Duffy Square, are to be found the statues of Father Francis Duffy, the chaplain of the "Fighting 69th" during World War I, and George M. Cohan, the famous song and dance man.

In the 20s the rise of the film industry was reflected in the number of movie palaces which began to appear in the area. The **Paramount Building,** located between 43rd and 44th Streets, was erected to house a movie theater and offices. The theater no longer exists, but the building, its symmetrical silhouette culminating in a clock tower crowned with a glass ball, remains as a monument to the movie era.

Times Square is often, for various reasons, the setting for huge gatherings: election returns, scenes of mass enthusiasm such as the record turnout on VE Day (May 8, 1945), or the annual vigil to celebrate the twelfth stroke of midnight on New Year's Eve.

Today. – Noisy and congested, lined with movie houses, discount and record shops which are interspersed with bars, "adult" bookstores and other tawdry establishments, Times Square by day reveals little of its former grandeur.

However, Times Square after dark still generates great excitement; it is here that the quick pulse of the city can best be felt. A good time to visit Times Square is in the evening when the milling theater crowds merge with the thousands strolling under the flashing neon signs.

Present efforts to revitalize Times Square follow on the renewal in the mid-1970s of West 42nd and 43rd Streets between 8th and 10th Avenues. The construction of **Manhattan Plaza** (1977): a complex of shops, restaurants and two residential towers; and the renovation of tenements between 10th and Dyer Avenues into **Theater Row,** a series of Off-Off Broadway theaters, have upgraded the westerly fringe of Times Square. More recently, the completion of the Marriott Marquis Hotel *(see below)* and the new construction at a number of sites at the north end of Times Square, have heralded the long-awaited rebirth of the Great White Way.

Marriott Marquis Hotel. – The futuristic profile of the Marriott Marquis Hotel (1985), a 50-story glass and concrete structure that is the second largest hotel in Manhattan, towers above Times Square.

Conventions and seminars are held at the Marriott which is located a short walk from the Jacob K. Javits Convention Center *(p 137).* Designed by John C. Portman and Associates, the 1 874-room hotel has as its centerpiece a 37-story landscaped **atrium.** Note, on the Broadway facade, the 4-story electronic billboard.

One Times Square. – The Times Tower's 25 stories seemed prodigiously high at the time it was erected (1904). Demolished except for its steel framework in 1964, the building was remodeled into a marble clad structure and known as the Allied Chemical Tower until 1975 when it was renamed One Times Square. The moving electric news sign so long associated with the Times Tower is once again in operation, following a period of darkness in the late 1970s and early 1980s; while the lighted ball which falls to mark the arrival of the New Year has been replaced by -- a big apple! In addition a giant electronic billboard flashes news, weather reports and advertisements from 6 AM to midnight year round. The Times itself has now consolidated all its operations in a building at 229 West 43rd Street, just west of Times Square.

■ BROADWAY★★ (Theater District)

For ticket information see pp 16 and 146.

One of the first "Broadway" theaters was opened by Oscar Hammerstein in 1892 at 42nd Street and Seventh Avenue. This far-sighted gentleman was the grandfather of Oscar Hammerstein II, well-known for the musicals *Oklahoma* and *South Pacific*, among others. Many of these early theaters in the Broadway area specialized in vaudeville or burlesque.

Today Broadway offers a far wider range of diversions, with its world-renowned legitimate theaters, its movies, night spots and bars offering entertainment. In recent years the number of legitimate theaters has increased due to a large extent to the growth of Off and Off-Off Broadway theaters and companies on Broadway, in Greenwich Village and SoHo, as well as in other sections of Manhattan.

The major concentration of bigger theaters is between 40th and 57th Streets, Avenue of the Americas and Eighth Avenue, an area which has been designated a special theater district to protect its exceptional character. Incentives are offered to future developers who provide a theater in new office buildings (e.g. the Gershwin, Minskoff and Circle in the Square Theaters).

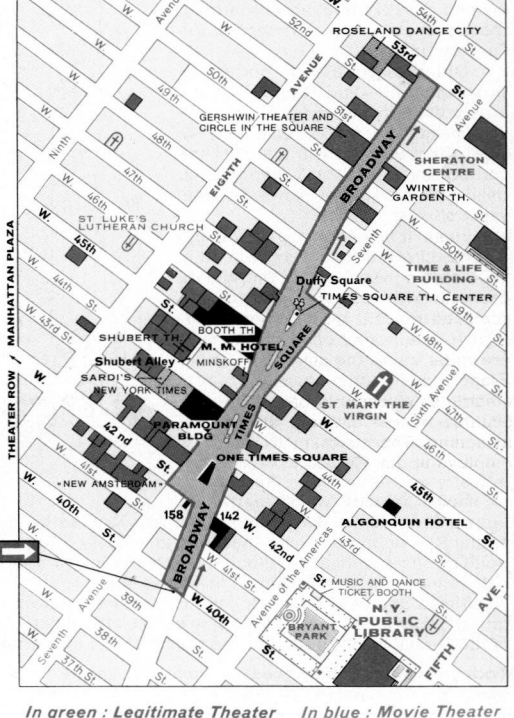

In green : Legitimate Theater   In blue : Movie Theater

Movie Theaters. – Scores of movie theaters are concentrated in the Broadway area, including some "grinds" open 24 hours a day, showing second-run films. Along 42nd Street, between Seventh and Eighth Avenues, there is a whole series of converted legitimate theaters, virtually a solid row of marquees. The once magnificent New Amsterdam, built in 1903, welcomed such stars as Maurice Chevalier and the Italian actress Eleonora Duse, and offered "Midnight Folies" on its roof during the summer.

Further north on Seventh Avenue, or Broadway, larger movie houses were originally built to accommodate two to three thousand spectators at a sitting. On their screens passed such famous figures as Shirley Temple, Deanna Durbin, Gary Cooper, Irene Dunne, Clark Gable, Doris Day, James Dean and Marilyn Monroe. Most of these giant prewar houses have since been demolished or transformed into multiscreen cinemas.

Legitimate Theaters. – Approximately forty theaters remain in the theater district, many of them grouped around 45th Street. One of their glories is the musical, which often runs many years to sold-out houses.

Just next to Broadway, behind the former Hotel Astor site, is the heart of the theater district, **Shubert Alley.** This short private street, reserved for pedestrians, was laid down in 1913, between 44th and 45th Streets and extended to 46th Street during the construction of the Marriott Marquis Hotel *(p 123).*

The Shubert Brothers built the Booth and Shubert Theaters, and were required to leave this passage as a fire exit. At intermission or after the show, many theatergoers drop into Sardi's nearby. This restaurant becomes a show-business headquarters on opening nights, and is well-known for the caricatures of celebrated theatrical personalities lining the walls, and their more or less famous successors who gather in the bar or the restaurant.

On 44th Street, between Fifth Avenue and Avenue of the Americas, is a landmark of the theatrical and literary world – the **Algonquin Hotel.** Here, in the 20s, Alexander Woollcott organized the famous "Round Table," which counted Robert Benchley, Dorothy Parker and Robert Sherwood among its regulars. Some of the old aura of the period, and virtually the entire original decoration remain. The Algonquin is now noted for its after-theater suppers and bar.

Night Clubs and Bars. – There is a variety of night clubs and bars in this area. The celebrated Roseland Dance City, for years a haven for devotees of ballroom dancing, now attracts dance aficionados of all ages and tastes. Featured are an American orchestra, a Latin band, and disco music.

Distance: 1 1/2 miles – Time: 1 1/2 hours.

This walk does not show the tourist any notable sights, rather it is an introduction to some of the activities characteristic of New York, and to some of the busiest public buildings in the city.

"Clothes Make the Woman".

– The area between Broadway and Ninth Avenue, south of 40th Street, is devoted to the manufacture and finishing of clothing, especially for women and children; it is known as the **Garment Center**. Workshops, warehouses, factories and showrooms line the streets jammed with trucks; and delivery boys push racks of clothes on handtrucks at dizzy speeds between main factories and subcontractors, who often assemble the garments or add finishing touches. Adding to this hubbub are the rush hour and the mass exodus at quitting time; then within a short while, the area is deserted.

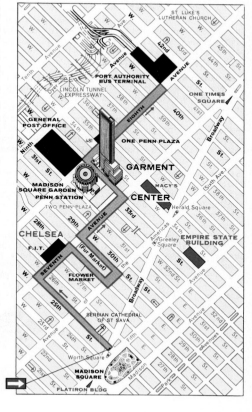

Despite competition from imports, the Garment Center continues to manufacture one-seventh of the clothing made in the United States, outfitting American women with dresses, coats, hats and furs produced in highly specialized workshops. The most modern equipment is used: a number of shops have electric saws capable of cutting 500 thicknesses of some fabrics at a time. The Garment Center employs about 100 000 workers.

From Madison Square to 42nd Street

Leaving Madison Square *(p 142)*, take West 25th Street. Along this street are second-hand stores selling sewing, button-making and overcasting machines and other tools of the trade. You pass the Serbian Cathedral of St Sava (1855), in English Gothic style.

Turn right and walk north on Seventh Avenue. On the west side of the avenue between 26th and 28th Streets, are the buildings of the **Fashion Institute of Technology**, commonly known as **F.I.T.** Programs offered by F.I.T. train young men and women aspiring to careers in the fashion or garment industry.

Turn right at 28th Street into the center of the colorful wholesale **Flower Market** ★ especially busy during the morning hours with the coming and going of delivery trucks and retail dealers from outlying areas.

Returning to Seventh Avenue at 29th Street you will find yourself in the heart of the largest **Fur Market** in the world. Beyond these storefronts, New York furriers create luxurious hats, coats and jackets in the latest designer styles.

Madison Square Garden and Pennsylvania Station. – On this spot, from 1910 to 1964, stood the imposing bulk of the old **Pennsylvania Station**. Now Penn Station spreads out below street level, accommodating three railroads: Amtrak, New Jersey Transit and the Long Island Rail Road. About 750 trains are scheduled daily, entering or leaving New York through tunnels under the Hudson and the East Rivers. Above ground, the present group of buildings includes a high-rise office building along Seventh Avenue, the round Madison Square Garden Sports Center and other facilities.

Madison Square Garden is the sports and entertainment capital for over five million people annually. Since its opening in 1968, Madison Square Garden, located on the upper five tiers of the 9-story complex, has been a worthy successor to the three previous Gardens, beginning with the first at 26th Street and Madison Avenue in 1879. The Garden is the home of the New York Knickerbockers (basketball team) and the New York Rangers (ice hockey team), and the traditional site for major attractions: the Ice Capades, the Westminster Club Dog Show, rock concerts, the circus, boxing, tennis, etc. *(see A New York City Calendar p 17)*.

Walking west on the south side of 33rd Street, pause before reaching Eighth Avenue; you will have an interesting view to the north of two contrasting building styles: to the left, the former New Yorker Hotel (1930) at **481 Eighth Avenue**, is a huge 43-story cluster of neat setbacks appearing as though it were composed of a set of children's building blocks; to the right, the more recently completed **One Penn Plaza** (1972), is a streamline reflecting tower rising almost uninterruptedly from the ground level to its upper stories. Continue to the corner of 33rd Street and Eighth Avenue, across from the General Post Office.

General Post Office (James A. Farley Building). – Covering two square blocks, between Eighth and Ninth Avenues and 31st and 33rd Streets, this huge neoclassic building bears on its colossal Corinthian facade the well-known inscription: "Neither snow nor rain nor heat nor gloom of night stays these couriers from the swift completion of their appointed rounds." It is a rather free translation from the Greek historian Herodotus and, ideally, describes the round-the-clock task of the post office.

Continue north on Eighth Avenue. During the second half of the last century and the first quarter of the present century, the entire area between 30th and 58th Streets, west of Eighth Avenue, was known as Hell's Kitchen. This tenement area was rife with crime, serving as the home base for ferocious gangs such as the Gophers, the Gorillas and the Kitchen Mob. There were 500 Gophers alone in 1910.

Port Authority Bus Terminal. – Built by the Port Authority *(p 29)* in 1951, this is one of the largest bus terminals in the world. It is a functionally designed building, linked directly to the Lincoln Tunnel with access roads to major New Jersey cities, and has underground passageways to subway lines. In 1983, a new wing was added to the existing structure, extending the terminal north to 42nd Street. The Port Authority Bus Terminal is the principal destination daily for approximately 6 800 buses from 34 bus companies serving commuters and long distance travelers. More than 60 stores and restaurants provide a variety of consumer services, and direct bus service is available to all three metropolitan area airports.

The Triumph of Virtue. – At the beginning of the 20C, West 42nd Street harbored a number of saloons, including one belonging to the prize-fighter **John L. Sullivan,** who was as feared as he was well-known. In 1901 a celebrated incident took place in his saloon. **Carry Nation,** who led the crusade against intemperance and debauchery, had taken to destroying suspect establishments in the Middle West. When John L. Sullivan heard about her rampages, he declared that he would toss Carry into the gutter if she tried it with his saloon. When Carry Nation heard Sullivan's challenge, she decided to go to New York.

A week later she appeared, was surrounded by newspaper reporters, and headed straight for Sullivan's saloon. When she arrived, he was calmly drinking a beer, but when he spied her face illuminated with righteous indignation and her hand brandishing a deadly instrument, he turned and fled, stopping to reflect on his humiliation only when he had barricaded himself in the furthest corner of the cellar. Sullivan never quite recovered from the embarrassment of his hasty retreat.

Toll Tunnels and Bridges

Name	Toll Rates (per passenger car)	See map page
Bayonne Bridge	$3.00 *(1)*	158
Bear Mountain Bridge	50¢ *(1)*	161
Bronx-Whitestone Bridge	$2.50	23, 145, 155
Brooklyn-Battery Tunnel	$2.50	23, 150
Cross Bay Parkway Bridge	$1.25	23
George Washington Bridge	$3.00 *(1)*	23
Goethals Bridge	$3.00 *(1)*	158
Henry Hudson Bridge	$1.25	23
Holland Tunnel	$3.00 *(1)*	23, 150
Lincoln Tunnel	$3.00 *(1)*	23, 150
Marine Parkway Bridge	$1.25	23, 151
Outerbridge Crossing	$3.00 *(1)*	159
Queens-Midtown Tunnel	$2.50	23, 154
Tappan Zee Bridge	$2.50 *(1)*	161
Throgs Neck Bridge	$2.50	23, 145, 155
Triborough Bridge	$2.50	23, 144, 154
Verrazano-Narrows Bridge	$5.00 *(2)*	23, 150, 158

(1) Charge paid only on eastbound crossings.
(2) Charge paid only on westbound crossing.

Distance: 1 1/2 miles – Time: 6 hours.

A haven of greenery, light and air in the heart of Manhattan, Central Park covers 840 acres, and is 2 1/2 miles long and 1/2 mile wide. More than 14 million people visit the park each year. Framed by the silhouettes of surrounding buildings, its lawns, trees and shrubs create a quiet oasis which offers many opportunities for recreation.

A BIT OF HISTORY AND GEOGRAPHY

An Idea Takes Shape. – Foreseeing the need for recreational open spaces in the fast-growing city, the journalist and poet **William Cullen Bryant** launched the idea of Central Park in 1850 through a press campaign in his newspaper, the *New York Post*. With the aid of two well-known authors, Washington Irving and George Bancroft, and other public-minded New Yorkers he urged the city government to acquire, well beyond 42nd Street, where the city ended, a "waste land, ugly and repulsive." It was in fact a swamp inhabited by squatters who raised pigs and goats.

After acquiring the land, the city held a design competition and the $2 000 prize was awarded to **Frederick Law Olmsted** and **Calvert Vaux**. Clearing began in 1857 with a labor force of 3 000 mostly unemployed Irish workers, and 400 horses.

In spite of fierce resistance by the squatters who bombarded the workers with stones, the project got underway and proceeded at a steady pace. A billion cubic feet of earth were moved, and after years of extensive drainage, planting, road and bridge building and ingenious landscaping, the park emerged essentially as we now know it.

Carriages, Horses, Bicycles. – From its beginnings, Central Park enjoyed great popularity among New Yorkers. Soon after its completion, Central Park became the testing ground for the finest equipages. On sunny afternoons, carriages lined up at the park entrance were avidly eyed by the populace. Victorias, broughams, phaetons and barouches carried society ladies in elegant attire who pitilessly judged the rigs of their rivals.

Trotters were in great favor, and they whipped through the park to the speedways of Harlem. Around 1875, it became fashionable for gentlemen to drive their own four-in-hands. In 1876, Leonard Jerome, the maternal grandfather of Sir Winston Churchill, founded the select Coaching Club together with the financier and sportsman August Belmont. Bicycle riding, which became popular in the 1890s, was denounced as unbecoming for young ladies because of undue freedom of dress and movement. But the trend was too strong to resist, and before long the curved paths of Central Park were teeming with cycling women.

An Unfortunate Interlude. – In the early 1930s, Central Park served as a camping ground for victims of the depression; the emptied reservoir sheltered "Hooverville," a cluster of shanties.

Design of Central Park. – Using nature as their main source of inspiration, the designers of the park skillfully blended natural and man-made elements to create a diversely landscaped garden in the style which was highly favored in the 19C. Sparse vegetation in parts of the park, where the thin layer of top soil barely covers outcropping rocks, accentuates the rugged character of the topography. In the northern part, hills and dales, rocky crags, trees, bushes and shrubs produce a landscape of great scenic beauty. Wide open spaces and meadows where sheep grazed until 1934 give other sections a pastoral charm, unimpaired by asphalt-covered roads. 185 acres were set aside by the designers for lakes and ponds. A formal atmosphere prevails at the Mall and in the Conservatory Garden.

RECREATION

Visitor Information Center. – The Visitor Information Center for the park is located in the **Dairy** *(open 11 AM to 5 PM - 4 PM mid-October to mid-February; closed Mondays and January 1, July 4, Thanksgiving Day and December 25)*, a restored Victorian Gothic structure located at 65th Street, between the zoo and the Carousel. Maps, a seasonal calendar of events, and other materials may be obtained here as well as at the Arsenal *(p 129 – open Mondays through Fridays 9 AM to 5 PM)*. The seasonal calendar of events can also be obtained by sending a self-addressed envelope to: *The Arsenal, Room 103, 830 Fifth Avenue, New York, NY 10021. For recorded information on events currently being held in the park ☎ 360-1333.* Central Park has two zoos, skating rinks, tennis courts, various athletic fields and other recreational facilities. Guided walks and talks *(time: 90 min)* on the history, geology, wildlife and botany of the park are conducted regularly by Urban Park Rangers. For schedule and topics consult the seasonal calendar of events *(see above)* ☎ 397-3080.

In summer the Parks Administration offers opera, symphony concerts and a variety of light entertainment. One of the great attractions, the annual "Shakespeare in the Park" festival, is held at the Delacorte Theater *(see A New York City Calendar p 17)*.

In addition one can boat on the lake, ride horseback on the 5 miles of bridle paths, cycle on the several miles of bicycle paths *(you may rent a bicycle at the Loeb Boathouse March through November; $6.00 first hour, $3.00 each additional half hour, $100 deposit or proof of identity required ☎ 861-4137)*, jog on the 1 1/2 mile running track around the Reservoir, join lively roller skaters near the Mall or play quieter games at the Chess and Checker House.

Park drives are closed to vehicular traffic to permit safe cycling: Mondays through Fridays 10 AM to 3 PM and evenings Mondays through Thursdays 7 to 10 PM; weekends beginning 7 PM Fridays to 6 AM Mondays. In winter closed weekends and holidays only.

In addition to the stylish Tavern on the Green there is a cafeteria at the zoo, with tables outdoors, and a snack bar at the Loeb Boathouse.

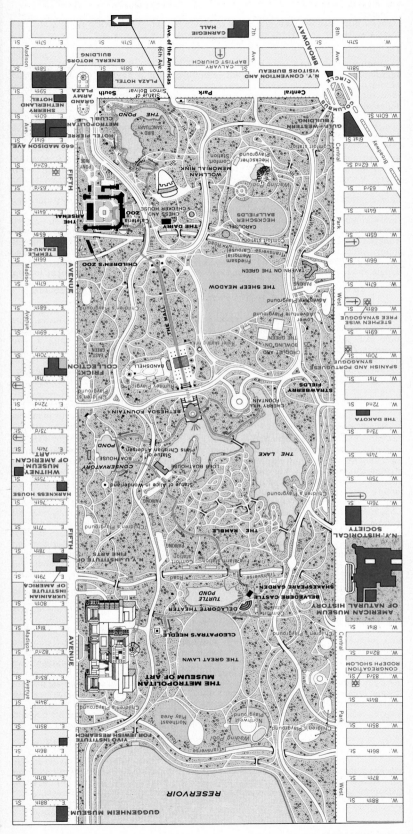

25 CENTRAL PARK★

For children, there are the Children's Zoo *(open 10 AM to 4:30 PM; 10¢)* donated by the late Governor Herbert H. Lehman, a marionette theater, fishing and other recreational facilities. Natural history exhibits, and children's programs and entertainment are offered at the Central Park Learning Center *(see Belvedere Castle below: open same hours as the Visitor Center p 127; ☎ 772-0210).* There is storytelling in summer on fine Saturdays *(11 AM),* in front of the statue of Hans Christian Andersen, not far from the statue of Alice in Wonderland (and friends) on a giant toadstool.

You may hire a horse-drawn carriage for a ride in Central Park, at the southeast corner, near the Plaza Hotel ($17.50 per half hour, $5.00 each additional 15 min).

VISIT

The park is open every day from a half hour before sunrise to midnight. The section south of the Reservoir is the most interesting. The park is most lively on Sundays.

From Central Park South to the Metropolitan Museum of Art

Enter through the "Artist's Gate" across from Avenue of the Americas on Central Park South. The statue of Simon Bolivar overlooks this entrance. Turn right, taking the path leading down to **the pond,** which winds among green shores. Continue around the pond to your right, noticing the flocks of birds, and head northwest to the Wollman Memorial Rink which is used for ice skating in the winter. Turn eastward toward the zoo.

Central Park Zoo ★. – *Open 10 AM to 5 PM Mondays through Fridays, 10 AM to 5:30 PM Saturdays, Sundays and holidays from April through October; Tuesdays 10 AM to 8 PM May through September; 10 AM to 4:30 PM daily November through March. Adults $1, children (3 to 12) $.25, children under 3 free, senior citizens $.50*

On 5.5 acres, 450 animals of 100 species make their homes in a newly renovated naturalistic habitat which represents distinct climatic regions: the Tropic Zone, the Temperate Territory and the Polar Circle. On the Fifth Avenue side of the zoo is a severe massive building in gray stone and red brick, **The Arsenal** of the State of New York, built in the 1840s in Gothic Revival style. It is now the headquarters of the New York City Parks and Recreation Department. Changing exhibits are held on the third floor.

Continue a short distance to the northwest, to visit the Mall.

The Mall. – The Mall, the only formal area in the park, is a straight path lined with handsome elms and containing two rows of busts of famous writers. It leads to the bandshell where orchestras and popular musicians play *(most summer evenings during the week at 8:30 PM);* from the Mall, steps lead down to the Bethesda Fountain and the lake.

The Lake. – Steps, banks and irregular shores make the lake seem almost transplanted from some far-off mountains. A graceful iron bridge a short distance from Bethesda Fountain has been reproduced innumerable times in engravings and photographs.

Boats may be rented (must be over 16 years old) at the Loeb Boathouse (at the east end of the lake). Price: $6.00 per hour up to four people, and $20 refundable deposit.

To the west is **Strawberry Fields** and the International Garden of Peace honoring the late John Lennon. The 3-acre garden has 161 species of plants representing the 150 nations of the world.

(From photo Andreas Feininger, New York.)

Central Park. — The Lake.

This particularly serene setting is steps away from New York's first luxury apartment house, the **Dakota,** where Lennon lived and died.

Between the lake and Fifth Avenue, Conservatory Pond is given over to young mariners. To the north of the lake, **The Ramble** is a heavily wooded hill with a number of hidden paths which seem to wind aimlessly. At the top of the Ramble is Belvedere Castle.

Belvedere Castle. – This imitation medieval castle complete with merlons and crenels, serves as the Central Park Learning Center *(see above).* From its site atop Vista Rock the Castle overlooks the entire northern part of the park, affording good views of the park and neighboring parts of the city. Just to the north are Turtle Pond and Delacorte Theater, next to the **Shakespeare Garden,** originally planned to include every species of flower, herb, tree and shrub mentioned in the works of the bard. Beyond are the vast reaches of the Great Lawn which contains several playing fields; the Great Lawn was built on the site of the Receiving Reservoir, dug in 1862 to supply the city water system.

From Belvedere Castle walk northeast toward the Metropolitan Museum, its massive outline appearing through the trees. Just before the MMA, you will pass **"Cleopatra's Needle,"** a pink granite Egyptian obelisk from Heliopolis, given to the City of New York in 1880 by the Khedive Ismaël Pasha. It is 77ft high and bears its 3 000 years lightly.

Distance: 1 mile – Time: 4 hours

From the Museum of the City of New York to the Cooper-Hewitt Museum, Fifth Avenue is lined with fine town houses, modern structures and museums.

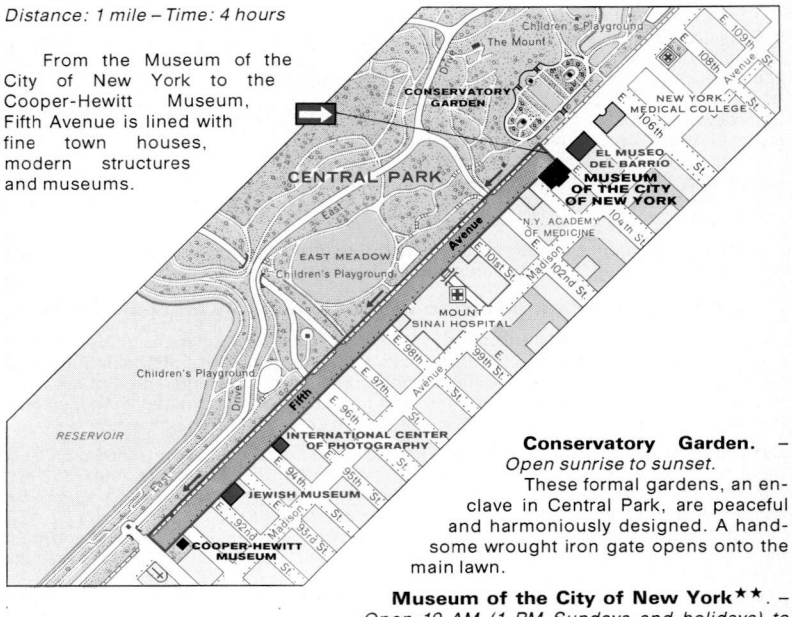

Conservatory Garden. – *Open sunrise to sunset.*

These formal gardens, an enclave in Central Park, are peaceful and harmoniously designed. A handsome wrought iron gate opens onto the main lawn.

Museum of the City of New York ★★. – *Open 10 AM (1 PM Sundays and holidays) to 5 PM; closed January 1, Thanksgiving Day and December 25. $3.00.*
The museum recreates in a most effective way the history of New York from its discovery by Verrazano to our time. It is housed in a Georgian Revival building completed in 1932.

Basement. – A gallery is devoted to fire fighting in New York.

First Floor. – Maps, models (the *Half Moon,* the *Dauphine*) and dioramas illustrate the history and growth of the city from its earliest beginnings through Dutch, English and Revolutionary times. In the Dutch Gallery you will find a scale model of Nieuw Amsterdam in 1660, and a model of Fort Amsterdam in the center of a circular panorama which depicts the city during the same period.

In the Big Apple Gallery, where a history of New York is presented in sight and sound, are fragments of the first boat built in New York, the *Tiger,* a horse drawn omnibus and the only remaining box from the old Metropolitan Opera House.

Second Floor. – The museum's fine collection of old New York silver is installed on this floor together with the J. Clarence Davies Gallery of New York prints and paintings. One section, devoted to the port of New York, exhibits models of ships from the 17C to our day. Here, note the ship's figurehead of Andrew Jackson carved for the *U.S.S. Constitution.* Lastly, the interior decoration of Old New York homes and the costumes worn by early New Yorkers are shown in life-size dioramas depicting a Dutch living room, a colonial home of the 18C (bedroom and living room) and parlors dating from 1830, 1850 and 1906.

Third Floor. – This floor houses the toy gallery, along with a sampling of the museum's furniture and portrait collection.

The toy gallery contains a collection of 18, 19 and 20C dolls' houses which reflect the varied architecture and lifestyles of these periods. In the **Stettheimer** dollhouse (1925) look, in the ballroom, for the miniature works of Marcel Duchamp *(Nude Descending a Staircase),* and Gaston Lachaise (nudes); note also on the terrace William Zorach's *Mother and Child.*

Fifth Floor. – You will be impressed by John D. Rockefeller, Sr.'s luxurious Second Empire bedroom and American Renaissance-style dressing room. The rooms came from Rockefeller's house at 4 West 54th Street. The house was demolished in 1938.

Cooper-Hewitt Museum, The Smithsonian Institution's National Museum of Design ★. – *2 East 91st Street. Open 10 AM (noon Sundays) to 5 PM (9 PM Tuesdays); closed Mondays and January 1, July 4, Thanksgiving Day and December 25; $3.00.*
In 1897, New York socialites Sarah and Eleanor Hewitt decided to start a museum of the decorative arts. The collection that resulted from their eclectic tastes and unorthodox acquisition methods was displayed at the Cooper Union of New York, the college of art, architecture and engineering founded by their grandfather Peter Cooper. Housed since 1967 in the Andrew Carnegie mansion, the museum is now a reference center as well as a display collection, dedicated to the study and preservation of design trends.

Exhibitions change regularly, each focusing on some aspect of design or some type of decorative or functional object. The permanent collection includes original 15 to 20C drawings and prints, including works by Frederic Church and Winslow Homer; textiles dating from 3 000 years ago; decorative arts including silver, bronze and wrought iron metalwork; examples of jewelry and goldsmith's work; wallpaper and rare bandboxes; porcelain, glass and earthenware; furniture, woodwork (18C paneling) and hardware (18 and 19C birdcages and splendid clocks).

The museum library includes a picture reference section and archives of color, pattern, textiles, symbols and interior design.

Distance: about 1 1/2 miles – Time: about 2 hours.

Manhattan's Lower East Side is most famous historically as the overcrowded tenement slum area where so many immigrants began their lives in the United States. Although no longer awash with immigrants, it remains run down and today is interesting mainly for its shopping possibilities. It is something of a bazaar, especially on Sundays when stores in other areas are closed, and there is nothing of the genteel or elegant about it. The streets are full of merchandise and crowds hunting for bargains.

The Governor's Farm. – Peter Stuyvesant (1592-1672) was the last Dutch governor of Nieuw Amsterdam from 1647 to 1664. He was stern, even forbidding, and always wore black – his peg-leg replaced the leg he had lost when attacking St Martin's Island in the Caribbean.

A colonizer to the core, he established a farm (*bouwerie* in Dutch) on the land of Indians he had helped to drive out, between Broadway and the East River and the present 5th and 17th Streets.

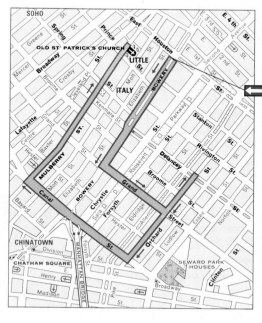

To reach his farm, Stuyvesant laid out a broad straight road which is now the Bowery. His own home was near a small chapel, rebuilt in 1799 by one of his descendants – the present Episcopal Church of St Mark's-in-the-Bouwerie *(p 132).*

Neighborhood of Beginnings and Dreams. – The mid-19C saw millions of refugees from Europe arriving in the United States *(p 26)* seeking relief from famine, war, economic and political repression, etc. They came in great waves enduring incredible hardships on the long voyage. They were desperately poor, living in ghettos in the cities as the assimilation process took place.

One of the largest groups were the Jews of Eastern Europe who arrived in ever-increasing numbers after 1870 as they fled the pogroms and economic restrictions placed on them in Poland, Hungary, Bohemia, Russia and the Balkans. It was to the Lower East Side that they came, to overcrowded and hastily constructed tenements, and the sweatshops of the needle trade. The flood of immigration was halted in the 20s with the passage of restrictive legislation, and most of the people moved away as they prospered. But the Lower East Side is still a Jewish area, although today visitors are as likely to hear Spanish, Chinese and Hindi as Yiddish.

VISIT

The Bowery. – Once a notorious entertainment center where vaudeville became fashionable and revues flourished, the Bowery later degenerated into an undesirable neighborhood frequented by homeless alcoholics and vagrants seeking handouts. In recent years the concentration of social problems along this street has diminished.

The stores on the Bowery specialize in electrical goods, especially lighting fixtures and accessories, restaurant equipment and furniture.

Grand Street. – In years past, the stores between the Bowery and Chrystie were known for their wedding gowns while those beyond Forsyth sold household linens. Today, fresh fish stalls, open-air vegetable markets and small restaurants support the Chinese community whose numbers continue to grow *(p 104).*

Orchard Street. – For blocks this street is a mecca for those seeking bargains in clothing. The tiny stores display their wares on stalls in the street, and there are great piles of dresses, coats and shoes. Delancey and Rivington Streets are similar.

Canal Street. – This street was long known for its jewelry and diamond merchants.

Mulberry Street★. – North of Canal Street, Mulberry, often called the Via San Gennaro, is the hub of **Little Italy**. Although few Italians live here today, they return for family festivities, marriages, funerals, festivals and saints' days. Cafés serve espresso and cappucino, and there are Italian grocery stores, restaurants and clam bars. During the feast of San Gennaro, the patron saint of Naples, in September *(see A New York City Calendar p 17)*, the street is a vast alfresco restaurant *(closed to traffic).*

At the corner of Prince Street, **Old St Patrick's Church,** the original Roman Catholic cathedral, was built in 1815 by Joseph Mangin *(p 107).* Only part of its Gothic facade escaped a fire in 1866. The present cathedral stands on Fifth Avenue *(p 46).*

Distance: about 1 mile – Time: 1 1/2 hours

Early in the 19C this part of New York was briefly a desirable residential quarter inhabited by the Astors, Vanderbilts and Delanos among others. The move to Greenwich Village and later north up Fifth Avenue left it stranded and gradually little remained from its fashionable era. It became industrial with light manufacturing and many warehouses as the century wore on. These loft buildings today are being reclaimed for housing and artists' studios. Cafés, ethnic restaurants, and shops have sprung up along St Marks Place and neighboring streets, and the area, with its growing number of off-Broadway theaters, is generally known as the **East Village.**

VISIT

From East 14th Street, walk south along Second Avenue to the little church standing among trees at the corner of 10th Street.

St Mark's-in-the-Bouwerie. – This fieldstone country church dating from 1799 stands on the site where a chapel was built on Peter Stuyvesant's farm *(p 131)*. Damaged by fire in 1978, the church was completely restored and officially rededicated in 1983. Note the bust of Stuyvesant to the right of the portico.

Take Stuyvesant Street past the **Renwick Triangle,** a series of 5-story town houses varying in width and depth designed by James Renwick in 1861.

Astor Place. – On either side of this place between Third and Fourth Avenues are the buildings of the Cooper Union for the Advancement of Science and Art. This college was founded in 1859 by **Peter Cooper** (1791-1883) to provide free education for all on a non-sectarian basis. Industrialist, inventor and philanthropist, Cooper manufactured *Tom Thumb*, the first steam engine to run in the United States; he also worked with Samuel Morse on the telegraph and with Cyrus Field on the trans-Atlantic cable.

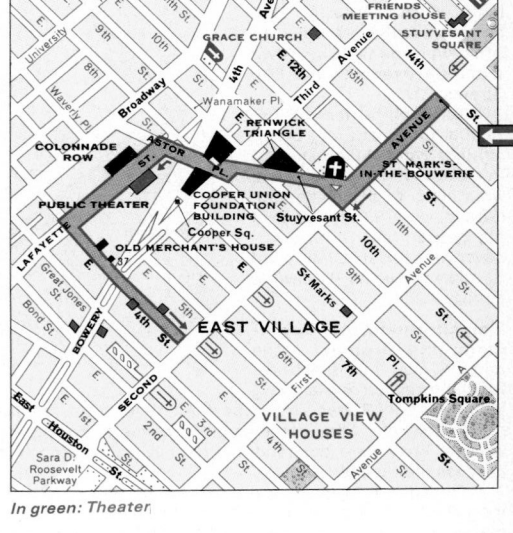

In green: Theater

The brownstone main building, **Cooper Union Foundation Building,** is the oldest extant structure in the United States supported by steel beams (also manufactured by Cooper). Many famous people have lectured in its Great Hall. Abraham Lincoln gave his "right makes might" speech on slavery here in 1860 which contributed to his presidential nomination. A statue of Cooper stands behind the building on Cooper Square.

Opposite the Cooper Union Building on the corner of Lafayette Street, once stood the majestic Astor Place Opera House. Opened in 1847, it was the scene, two years later, of a protest riot against the English actor William Macready, accused of stealing the limelight from local talent. Crying "Washington forever!", the mob tried to burn down the opera house where the unfortunate Englishman was playing but was dispersed by the Seventh Regiment, at a cost of 22 dead and 150 wounded.

Lafayette Street. – On the right stand a series of Corinthian columns of Westchester marble. With their air of faded aristocracy, they have obviously seen better days. **Colonnade Row** was originally known as La Grange Terrace, after the name of the Château de la Grange, near Paris, which belonged to the Marquis de Lafayette. When built in 1833, there were nine houses (only four remain) and they were one of the most sought after addresses in the city. John Jacob Astor, Cornelius Vanderbilt and Warren Delano (grandfather of Franklin Delano Roosevelt) all lived there for a time.

The monumental building across the street from Colonnade Row was the home of the Astor Library, opened in 1854 and later the nucleus of the present New York Public Library. About 100 000 volumes were available without charge, which was revolutionary at the time. In 1967, the building was converted into six theaters to house the **Public Theater,** home of the New York Shakespeare Festival. The Public presents a wide range of entertainment ranging from full scale productions of new plays to film classics.

Old Merchant's House*. – *Open Sundays 1 to 4 PM and weekdays for groups with reservations ☎ 777-1089; $2.00; closed August.*

This red brick town house (1832) with its Greek Revival doorway is a characteristic period piece. Bought in 1835 by Seabury Tredwell, a prosperous merchant, the house remained in his family for nearly a hundred years. It is the only 19C house in Manhattan to survive intact with its original furniture and family memorabilia.

Just up the street, no 37 built for Samuel Tredwell Skidmore, a cousin of Seabury Tredwell, is one other surviving house of the Greek Revival period.

MANHATTAN
Additional Sights

■ **HARLEM**

Harlem, one of the largest Black communities in the United States, although part of Manhattan, seems a world apart. More than 10 % of New York's 1.7 million Blacks live in Harlem, a "city within a city" of broad main streets, old tenements and brownstones, projects and low-rise commercial buildings. Other communities are on the West Side and in Brooklyn, which has 689 000 Black inhabitants.

The Dutch governor Peter Stuyvesant *(p 131)* founded the village of New Harlem; its church was located between the present 124th and 125th Streets, west of First Avenue.

Harlem was at that time completely rural, with farmhouses scattered among the green landscape. Later the area became more residential. During the second half of the 19C, elegant country homes could be reached by tree-lined streets, and by 1830 Harlem was a suburb connected to the city by boat and by the Harlem Railroad, whose terminus was on Fourth Avenue, between 26th and 27th Streets. Trotting races on Harlem Lane were the rage, giving way by 1900 to the bicycle craze.

During the early 20C, especially after World War I, a number of Blacks, who were attracted to the North by higher wages and a somewhat more tolerant atmosphere, started to rent in the area north of Central Park where speculators had overextended the building boom of the 1890s. Harlem became the Mecca of gaiety and pleasure celebrated by visitors during the 20s. Night-owls during the Prohibition Era finished their evenings at the Cotton Club and similar area establishments over bootleg liquor while listening to jazz stars such as Duke Ellington, Count Basie and Cab Calloway.

Today, Harlem extends approximately from 110th to 165th Streets, and from the Harlem River, west to the Hudson River. The area contains a few historic districts, including "Striver's Row," several blocks of distinguished turn-of-the century row houses at West 138th and 139th Streets, between Seventh and Eighth Avenues.

The eastern fringe, along Park Avenue is now carred "Spanish" Harlem and is largely inhabited by Puerto Ricans. Near East 116th Street, from Lexington Avenue to the East River, and in the vicinity of Amsterdam Avenue, is what remains of "Italian" Harlem, although many Puerto Ricans also inhabit this area. The liveliest areas in Harlem are along Martin Luther King, Jr. Boulevard (125th Street) between Fifth Avenue and Broadway and along 116th Street between Park and Lexington Avenues. It is advisable to travel through these areas during the day. Further north, Edgecombe Avenue, Hamilton Terrace and the surrounding area are inhabited by members of the Black middle class.

Harlem Spirituals, Inc. offers a daytime (Thursdays; time: 5 hours) tour of Harlem including soul food lunch; an evening tour (Thursdays, Fridays and Saturdays; time: 5 hours) including soul food and jazz; and a Sunday Gospel and Spiritual tour (time: 4 hours) featuring a service at a local church with Gospel singing. For reservations call 302-2594; tickets available at 1457 Broadway, Suite 1008.

The Schomburg Center for Research in Black Culture. – *515 Lenox Avenue. Open May through September Mondays and Wednesdays noon to 8 PM and Tuesdays, Thursdays and Fridays 10 AM to 6 PM, closed Saturdays, Sundays and holidays; the rest of the year Mondays through Wednesdays noon to 8 PM and Thursdays through Saturdays 10 AM to 6 PM, closed Sundays and holidays.*

Endowed with a reference and research library, this unique center is dedicated to the study of Black culture and is noted both for the quality of its works and wide variety of subjects covered. Changing exhibits of paintings and sculpture by Black artists, photographs and artifacts owned by the center are displayed in the gallery on the ground floor.

The Studio Museum in Harlem. – *144 West 125th Street. Open Wednesdays through Fridays 10 AM to 5 PM, Saturdays and Sundays 1 to 6 PM; closed Mondays and Tuesdays; $2.00.*

Established in the mid-1960s to serve as a working space for artists, the Studio Museum has expanded and grown into a major cultural center for the study of Black art. The museum mounts ten to twelve exhibitions each year, highlighting the work of prominent and emerging Black artists in all fields. Special programs include concerts, films, workshops and lectures.

The Abyssinian Baptist Church. – *132 West 138th Street.* The oldest Black church in the city, and one of the most famous in the nation, the Abyssinian Baptist Church became especially prominent under the leadership of Adam Clayton Powell, Jr., a former pastor of the church and congressman in the House of Representatives. The church is built of New York bluestone and has a Tudor-Gothic window in its facade. The focal point of the interior, which suggests an amphitheater, is the altar, set on a white marble dais. Artifacts in the memorial room trace the life of Adam Clayton Powell, Jr.

Hamilton Grange. – *287 Convent Avenue at 141st Street. Open Wednesdays through Sundays 9 AM to 4:30 PM; closed Mondays, Tuesdays and holidays.*

Built in 1801-2 by the architect John McComb *(p 107)*, this Federal style 2-story frame house was the country home of Alexander Hamilton. It was moved several hundred yards to this location in 1889.

Morris-Jumel Mansion★. – *Open 10 AM to 4 PM; closed Mondays and January 1, Thanksgiving Day and December 25; $2.00.* Located in a middle class Black section *(at 160th Street and Edgecombe Avenue)*, this handsome Georgian residence formerly "in the country" is one of the few surviving reminders of colonial New York. The house was built in 1765 for Colonel Roger Morris, a grandson of Sir Peter Jackson, and was first known as Mount Morris. Ten years later, in 1775, Colonel Morris left for England where his loyalist sentiments were more appreciated. During the Battle of Harlem Heights in the fall of 1776, the mansion served as General Washington's headquarters.

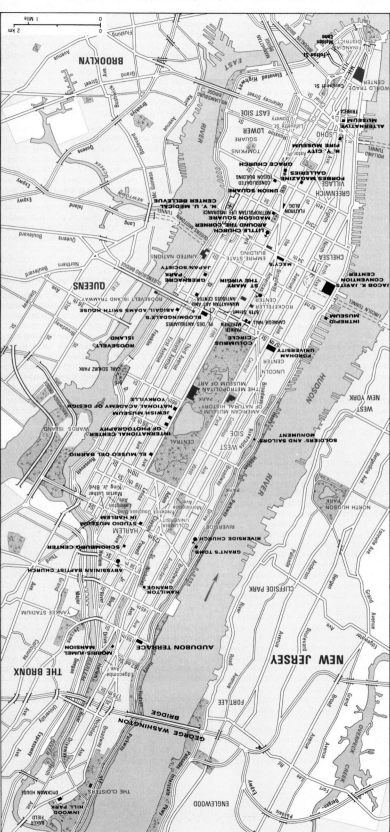

MANHATTAN - Additional Sights

In 1810 a wealthy wine merchant of French origin, **Stephen Jumel,** bought the estate for his wife Eliza and restored it to its original beauty. The Jumels made a number of trips to France during which they acquired some fine Empire furnishings and traveled in Napoleonic circles. In 1815 they offered the Emperor the use of their ship, *The Eliza,* to travel to America. He declined the invitation but legend has it that he gave his trunk and a carriage to the Jumels in gratitude. In 1820, Joseph Bonaparte, Napoleon's elder brother, may have visited the house. A year after Stephen Jumel's death, in 1832, Madame Jumel married Aaron Burr *(p 88),* third Vice President of the United States.

(From photo Washington Headquarters Association.)

Morris-Jumel Mansion.

Surrounded by a garden with a view overlooking the Harlem River, the Morris-Jumel Mansion is an almost bucolic enclave in Manhattan. The house is built of brick encased in wood. The wide boards and wooden corner quoins, and the 2-story colonnade and portico, although typical of the 19C, are part of the original structure and date back to 1765.

The interior of the house has been restored and furnished in excellent taste. The octagonal 18C drawing room on the 1st floor served as the Council Chamber for General Washington in the fall of 1776, and contains some handsome Chinese Chippendale pieces. The front parlor, where Aaron Burr and Madame Jumel were married, is decorated in 19C Empire Style, with twelve chairs, a sofa and a French chandelier that belonged to Madame Jumel. The dining room table is set with Madame Jumel's china and the grandfather clock that chimes in the hall told her the time.

On the 2nd floor, Madame Jumel's bedroom and dressing room contain furniture that once belonged to Napoleon and Queen Hortense of Holland, Empress Josephine's daughter. The 19C mahogany Empire daybed is especially impressive. Just outside Aaron Burr's bedroom is his office desk and trunk.

On the desk in the room used by Washington as a study, is a box that belonged to Silas Deane, the first United States Ambassador to France.

■ ROOSEVELT ISLAND

Roosevelt Island is located in the East River, 300yd off the shore of Manhattan. Formerly known as "Welfare Island" and the site of various institutions, it is now the home of a new residential "town-in-town" built by the New York State Urban Development Corporation in the 70s. The island, politically part of the borough of Manhattan, is 2 1/2 miles long, 800ft wide at its broadest point and 147 acres in size. It is linked to Manhattan by bridge and by an aerial tramway which provides a 3-minute ride across the East River with views in each direction.

The tram station is located on Second Avenue and 60th Street, and the fare each way is a New York City subway token ($1.00) which can be purchased at the station. The tram departs every 15 min on the quarter hour from 6 to 2 AM (3:30 AM Saturdays and Sundays). During rush hours (7 AM to 9:30 AM and 4:30 PM to 7:30 PM) the tram runs every 7 minutes. A minibus (free) operates from the tram station on the island to the heart of the community.

The island can also be reached by car from the borough of Queens across the bridge at 36th Avenue. Because automobile traffic is restricted on the island, all cars are required to park at the Motorgate Garage, just across the bridge on the island. From there take the minibus.

The buildings in the first phase of the Roosevelt Island Community were designed by the noted architectural firms Johanson and Bhavnani and Sert, Jackson and Associates, and based on a master plan by Philip Johnson and John Burgee. Manhattan Park, containing 1 108 units, was designed by Gruzen Sampton Steinglass. The community contains mixed-income housing, retail shops, schools, two city hospitals, parks and other recreational facilities. Three of the island's seven landmarks have been restored; they are: the **Chapel of the Good Shepherd,** built in 1889, the **Blackwell Farm House,** built shortly after the Revolutionary War and one of the oldest farm houses still standing in New York City, and the **Lighthouse,** built in 1872 with James Renwick as supervising architect. A waterfront promenade on both sides of the community affords good vantage points for viewing river traffic and the Manhattan skyline.

■ MONUMENTS, CHURCHES

Riverside Church★ and **Grant's Tomb★**. – Near the most picturesque part of Riverside Park, a pleasant strip of greenery overlooking the Hudson, Riverside Church and the tomb of President Grant are close neighbors.

Riverside Church★. – This church is an interdenominational, interracial and international Christian church, historically linked to the American Baptist Churches in the United States and the United Church of Christ. It is also a community cultural center which produces radio and TV programs, has its own sports center and clubs for persons of various ages, professions and interests, and offers language courses, a lecture series, concerts of religious music, and theater performances.

Built in the late 1920s in Gothic Revival style *(p 30),* the building was inspired in part by the Cathedral of Chartres. John D. Rockefeller, Jr. contributed to the cost of the 400ft tower (Chartres' *Clocher Neuf* measures about 330ft).

The carillon is composed of 74 bells. *(You may visit the tower and its carillon Mondays through Saturdays and holidays weather permitting 11 AM to 3 PM, Sundays 12:30 PM to 3 PM, $1.00; carillon recitals Sundays at 3 PM, Independence Day at 2 PM, Thanksgiving Day at noon.)* There is an interesting **view** of Manhattan.

The West Portal, facing Riverside Drive between 120th and 122nd Streets, is worth a pause to admire the large statues on the columns: prophets from the Old Testament to the left, and New Testament figures to the right; the tympanum bears a seated figure of Christ and the symbols of the Four Evangelists.

Pass through the West Portal and enter the portico. Notice the four stained glass windows depicting the Life of Christ, made in the 16C for Bruges Cathedral. From the portico you enter the nave which is 100ft high and 215ft long, with room for 2 500 worshippers. The nave clerestory windows are copies of those at Chartres. The inlaid "maze" design of the chancel floor is a reminder of medieval times when penitents followed the winding lines on their knees. The chancel screen is decorated with 80 figures of men and women whose lives illustrated Christian moral principles: Luther, Milton, Lincoln and Pasteur, among others.

A passage from the portico leads to Christ Chapel, in 11C Romanesque style. A stairway nearby leads down to the cloister.

Outside, in a courtyard on the east side of the church is a *Madonna and Child* by Sir Jacob Epstein, modeled after an Indian woman and her son. The statue was exhibited at the Museum of Modern Art *(p 39)* until 1959, when it was presented to Riverside Church.

Another work by Sir Jacob Epstein is mounted on the rear wall of the nave. It is entitled **Christ in Majesty**. The metal casting hangs in Llandaff Cathedral in Wales. The figure spans approximately 19 1/2ft by 6ft and is finished in gold leaf.

General Grant National Memorial★. – The memorial, popularly known as **Grant's Tomb,** is the final resting place of Ulysses Simpson Grant (1822-85), commander of the Union Army during the Civil War and President from 1868-76.

A granite-paved plaza leads to the monument on the west side of Riverside Drive. Once thronged with reverent crowds, it is now less frequented by visitors, but remains a memorable landmark perched high on a bluff overlooking the Hudson River. The building was started in 1891 and dedicated on April 27, 1897, the 75th anniversary of Grant's birth; 90 000 people contributed to the building fund of $600 000.

The white granite monument, 150ft high, somewhat resembles a Roman mausoleum, topped by a stepped pyramid. The south side bears two handsome Classic figures and an inscription of Grant's plea: "Let us have peace." A majestic stairway flanked by two eagles leads to the entrance portico.

(From photo Éd. Sun, Paris.)

Grant's Tomb

The interior *(open 9 AM to 5 PM; closed Mondays, Tuesdays and holidays),* with its white marble walls, is illuminated by golden stained glass windows whose half-light contributes to the solemnity of the monument.

In the center an open crypt, similar to Napoleon's Tomb at the Invalides in Paris, contains the sarcophagi of General Grant and his wife, Julia Dent Grant. In surrounding niches there are busts of Grant's comrades-in-arms: Sherman, Sheridan, Thomas, Ord and McPherson.

On the level above the crypt, two rooms contain displays related to Grant's life.

Soldiers' and Sailors' Monument. – *Riverside Drive at West 89th Street.* This white marble monument, with a peristyle of 12 Corinthian columns, was built in 1902 to commemorate those who lost their lives in the Civil War. From this point there is a good view overlooking the Hudson River.

Grace Church. – *802 Broadway at 10th Street.* This Episcopal church founded by Trinity Church *(p 86)* was built between 1843 and 1846 by James Renwick Jr., who later designed St Patrick's Cathedral and the Smithsonian Institution.

In 1863 **Barnum** arranged for the rector to marry two midgets from his circus, Charles S. Stratton, better known as Tom Thumb, and Lavinia Warren.

The church is an outstanding example of the Gothic Revival style; notice the elegant spire. To the left of the church the rectory (also by Renwick) is one of New York's earliest Gothic Revival residences.

The Little Church Around the Corner (Church of the Transfiguration). – On 29th Street, not far to the east of Fifth Avenue, the charming "Little Church Around the Corner" with its peaceful garden seems even smaller than it is, compared to the surrounding skyscrapers, especially the Empire State Building.

Built of red sandstone in the middle of the 19C, this Episcopal church earned its nickname in 1870. That year, the pastor of a nearby church refused to hold funeral services for an actor since that profession was then still looked upon as performed by Satan's henchmen. The cleric did, however, suggest that the actor's friends try "the little church around the corner" where a monument still commemorates its pastor's charitable decision. Since that time it has remained a favorite parish for theater people, and also one where many weddings are held.

The church is constructed in 14C Gothic style and is sometimes referred to as an example of "English Cottage Gothic."

The stained glass windows are dedicated to great New York actors: notice the one of Edwin Booth as Hamlet, designed by John La Farge and the one in the vestibule (leading to the south transept) which is studded with raw diamonds. It is dedicated to the memory of the Spanish actor José Maria Munoz. On the high altar reredos is the Transfiguration designed by Frederick Clark Withers.

Church of St Mary the Virgin. – Situated at 139 West 46th Street this Episcopal church with its neo-Gothic facade merits a stop. Note in the left side aisle the Madonna and Child, a porcelain bas-relief from a workshop in Florence. In the Lady Chapel the murals represent the Annunciation and the Epiphany. In the baptistry admire the wooden font cover which has 73 delicately carved figures. The Chapel of Our Lady of Mercy has a black marble altar and a 15C plaque showing the death of St Anthony.

■ HOSPITALS, BUILDINGS

New York University Medical Center - Bellevue★. – Along the East River, from 23rd to 34th Streets, is a modern hospital complex, including a Veterans Administration Hospital, Bellevue Hospital and the New York University Medical Center.

The **Medical Center,** part of New York University, consists of ten buildings completed between 1961 and 1986. They are the University Hospital, the Medical School, the Rusk Institute of Rehabilitation Medicine, the Medical Science Building, the Schwartz Lecture Hall, the Coles Medical Science Laboratories, the Schwartz Health Care Center, Alumni Hall, the Kips Bay Residence housing 110 students, and the Rubin Hall of Residence housing 304 students.

On the left is the hospital; the original building stood at 300 East 20th Street and dated back to 1882. Since its foundation, its medical and social role has been particularly significant: the first hospital infants' ward, the first therapeutic use of X-rays and the first research on blood transfusion were among its accomplishments. The new hospital, 18 stories in height and built at a cost of $25 000 000, has 726 beds and 17 operating rooms. Its dermatology and cancerology departments are especially well-known.

The Medical School, founded in 1841, then counted 239 students and 6 professors. Today about 670 students are instructed and administered by some 3 000 persons.

Thanks to one of its professors, Dr. Paine, the "Bone Bill" was voted in 1854 making dissection legal. More recently, it was here that Jonas Salk and Robert Sabin discovered the first polio vaccine. Enter the Medical School and Alumni Hall.

Bellevue Hospital, an even older institution, was established in 1736 and is the oldest public hospital in the United States. After an epidemic of yellow fever had caused the deaths of 700 New Yorkers during the summer of 1795 alone, the city then bought land at a spot named Bellevue, three miles north of town on the banks of the East River, and constructed a pavilion for contagious diseases. However, the hospital itself was not finished until 1826.

The annals of Bellevue are linked to those of American medical history: in 1808, first ligature of the femoral artery by Dr. Hosack; first ambulance service in 1863; first school of nursing in 1873; and first women medical students in New York in 1888. Dr. Jonas salk and Robert Sabin, discoverers of the polio vaccine are alumni of the School of Medicine. The concepts for open-heart surgery were developed at Bellevue and, more recently, Bellevue has been a leader in the field of reattachment of severed limbs, its micro-surgery team being one of the most active in the country.

A new modern 25-story Bellevue began accepting inpatients in 1975. Completely air-conditioned, it has transformed Bellevue into a modern setting. New York University Medical Center supplies the Medical House Staff for Bellevue as well as for University Hospital and the Veterans Administration Hospital.

Columbus Circle. – The focal point of this busy traffic circle is a statue of **Christopher Columbus,** erected on a high rostral column in 1894. Three bronze ships' prows adorn the column, representing the ships of his fleet: the *Niña,* the *Pinta,* and the *Santa María.* Just beyond, at the entrance to Central Park, is the **Maine Memorial** dedicated to the 260 men who lost their lives when the battleship *Maine* was destroyed in Havana harbor in 1898. A robed figure of Columbia triumphant graces the top of the monument.

The building on the south side of Columbus Circle, formerly the New York Cultural Center, now houses on its main floor the **New York Convention and Visitors Bureau** *(other location is 158 West 42nd Street in Times Square)* and the City of New York Department of Cultural Affairs.

To the north at One Gulf and Western Plaza stands the Gulf + Western Building.

Gulf + Western Building. – The world headquarters for Gulf + Western Industries, this gleaming 44-story rectangular tower of tinted glass, defends imposingly the entrance to Central Park West. The exterior of the first four floors of the building exhibit layers of white and black granite; the remaining 40 floors are sheathed in an outer skin of silver and black aluminum. Solar gray glass windows are spaced evenly over the entire structure. On the 43rd floor a bar and restaurant offer fine views over the city to the east and west.

Jacob K. Javits Convention Center★. – New York's Convention Center, a low-rise building stretching along the Hudson River from West 34th Street to West 39th Street, is named for Jacob K. Javits, the former U. S. senator from New York. Designed by I. M. Pei and Partners (1986) the center has 1.8 million sq ft of enclosed space, including two main exhibition halls, more than 100 meeting rooms, and restaurant and service areas.

Of special architectural interest is the enormous exposed-steel space frame which shapes the main exhibition hall. 76 000 tubes containing tension rods, and 19 000 nodes were used in constructing the space frame, giving it the appearance of an assemblage of gigantic tinker-toy components. Extremely flexible from a structural point of view, the frame serves as beams, walls and roof of the hall and is supported by columns which rise 90ft apart from the floor below.

The Convention Center has facilities to handle 85 000 persons daily.

Fordham University at Lincoln Center. – *60th Street and Columbus Avenue*. Fordham University, founded in 1841, has two major campuses. The original campus is at Rose Hill in the Bronx, while the new campus at Lincoln Center was founded in 1968 on a 7-acre site located beside the Lincoln Center for the Performing Arts. Among the several colleges, all of which are co-educational, housed in the campuses' two buildings are the graduate schools of Law, Social Service, Education and Business Administration. The undergraduate College at Lincoln Center, situated in the 14-story Leon Lowenstein Center, provides a liberal arts education for nearly 2 200 students.

■ MUSEUMS

National Academy of Design. – *1083 Fifth Avenue. Open noon to 5 PM (8 PM Tuesdays); closed Mondays and holidays; $2.50.*
    The National Academy, established in the early 19C to provide an art school and hold exhibitions of contemporary painting, sculpture, engraving and architecture, is one of New York's venerable cultural institutions.
    The practice of requiring a candidate for membership to present a portrait of himself and a representative example of his work, led to the growth of the Academy's rich holdings of 19 and 20C American art, and brought to the collection the works of such famous members as Winslow Homer, John Singer Sargent, Augustus Saint-Gaudens and Thomas Eakins. Temporary shows from the permanent collection, and traveling exhibits are held in the Academy's town house galleries.
    Through its School of Fine Arts, the National Academy offers programs in drawing, painting, sculpture and graphics.

El Museo del Barrio. – *1230 Fifth Avenue. Open 11 AM to 5 PM; closed Mondays, Tuesdays and major holidays; $2.00.*
    The museum is the leading cultural center for "El Barrio," the Hispanic – predominantly Puerto Rican – community of Spanish Harlem which extends north of the museum through East Harlem to about 120th Street.
    Changing displays of Caribbean artifacts and contemporary painting and sculpture in the galleries, as well as lunchtime concerts during the summer, a fall film series, chamber music recitals, lectures, and performances by a resident theater group, Teatro Cuatro, are among the museum's offerings. A permanent exhibit of 94 hand-carved Santos de Palo (saints) illustrates the traditional art of the saintmaker.

The International Center of Photography. – *1130 Fifth Avenue at 94th Street. Open Tuesdays to Fridays noon to 5 PM (8 PM Tuesdays), Saturdays and Sundays 11 AM to 6 PM; $3.50.*
    The center, located in an elegant early 20C town house, exhibits major works by 19 and 20C photographers and photojournalists and offers audiovisual presentations and educational programs. The center also operates a bookshop.

The Jewish Museum★. – *1109 Fifth Avenue. Open Mondays through Thursdays noon to 5 PM (8 PM Tuesdays), Sundays 11 AM to 6 PM; closed Fridays, Saturdays and holidays; $4.50. For information on current programs and events ☎ 860-1888.*
    The Jewish Museum occupies the former mansion of Felix and Frieda Warburg.
    The permanent collection of Jewish ceremonial objects includes the blue mosaic upper section of the Ark wall from a 16C Persian synagogue, a pair of ornate 17C silver Rimonim (used to decorate the Torah), and a wood carved Torah Ark from the 12C. The collection also contains contemporary art, textiles, archaeology from the Holy Land and Hebrew coins and medals.
    The museum houses the National Jewish Archive of Broadcasting and, in addition to its permanent collection, offers a program of rotating exhibits, special events, films and lectures.

■ AUDUBON TERRACE★★

    On Broadway, between 155th and 156th Streets, several museums and cultural institutions are grouped around a plaza where the naturalist Audubon *(p 96)* once had a country house named Minniesland. The present buildings were erected at the beginning of the 20C in Italian Renaissance style.

Museum of the American Indian★★. – *Open 10 AM – 5 PM; Sundays 1 to 5 PM; closed Mondays and major holidays; $3.00).* This unsurpassed collection of artifacts is related to the culture of the Indians of North, Central and South America: from the Eskimos of the Arctic, to the peoples of Tierra del Fuego; from the Paleo-Indian period to the present. The 1st floor features Indians of the Northeast Woodlands, the Plains, Great Lakes and Southeastern areas, displaying costumes, basketry, wood carving utensils, weapons and ritual objects. On the 2nd floor, exhibits are devoted to the Indians of the Northwest coast, the Southwest, Canadian tribes and Eskimo ethnology. In an adjoining hall is a display of North American archaeology. The 3rd floor houses a comprehensive presentation of pre-Columbian art and exhibits of South American ethnology.

Hispanic Society of America★. – *Open 10 AM to 4:30 PM, Sundays 1 to 4 PM; closed Mondays and holidays.* A library and a museum offer a panorama of Spanish civilization from pre-Roman times to the present century. Visitors should not miss the portraits by Goya, Renaissance tombs and collection of furniture in the interior court; and in the upper gallery, paintings by El Greco, Velázquez and Goya, and a large selection of earthenware.

American Numismatic Society★. – *Open 9 AM to 4:30 PM, Sundays 1 to 4 PM; closed Mondays and holidays.* The largest private museum of its kind, it includes two modern exhibition galleries. On the right medals of historic or artistic interest are displayed. The other gallery is devoted to topical exhibits.

American Academy and Institute of Arts and Letters. – This is the nation's highest honor society for the arts, with a membership of 250 of America's foremost artists, writers and composers. Recurrent art and manuscript exhibitions are held during the year *(exhibition hours are 1 to 4 PM; closed Mondays and holidays for exact dates and additional information ☏ 368-5900).*

Forbes Magazine Galleries ★ . – *62 Fifth Avenue. Open Tuesdays, Wednesdays, Fridays and Saturdays 10 AM to 4 PM; closed major holidays.*

The ground floor galleries of the Forbes Magazine Building, home of the well-known business bi-weekly, are given over to an eclectic group of collections gathered by the Forbes family. Best known for its beautiful series of Fabergé *objets de luxe*, the Galleries also feature toy boats which invite imaginary sea voyages, thousands of toy soldiers arranged in scenes dramatizing historic events; fine art, and American Presidential letters and manuscripts.

Among the many items on view created by Fabergé, the Imperial Easter Eggs, produced by Fabergé workshops for the Russian royal family between 1885 and 1916, are the most famous. Of 54 such eggs known to exist, the Forbes Galleries own 12. Gold, silver, precious stones and enameling decorate these exquisite fantasies and several offer hidden surprises: note the mechanical bird which emerges and sings when a certain orange is rotated (Orange Tree Egg); the replica of the royal coronation coach which in turn once held a diamond pendant (Coronation Egg); and the mechanical bird which appears on the hour crowing and flapping its wings (Cuckoo Egg).

(The FORBES Magazine Collection, New York.)

Fabergé Orange Tree Egg.

New York City Fire Museum. – *278 Spring Street. Open 10 AM to 4 PM; closed Sundays, Mondays and holidays. $3.00. ☏ 691-1303.*

Located in a 1904 firehouse, the museum displays artifacts from the collection of the New York Fire Department and the Home Insurance Company. Exhibits feature a variety of fire fighting memorabilia: hand drawn, horse drawn and motorized apparatus from 1765-1912; models, trumpets, helmets, badges, presentation shields and fire crafts and folk art from the 19C. The museum also has an extensive collection of firemarks.

Abigail Adams Smith House. – *421 East 61st Street. Guided tours (time: 40 min) Mondays through Fridays 10 AM to 4 PM; closed August and major holidays; $2.00.*

This Federal style stone building was completed in 1799, as the coach house and stable to a manor house on property previously owned by Colonel William Smith and his wife Abigail Adams, daughter of President John Adams. The manor house was destroyed by fire in 1826, while the stable was subsequently converted into an inn in 1826, then in 1833 a private residence, before being acquired by the Colonial Dames of America in 1924. The Colonial Dames restored the house and continue to maintain its nine period rooms and 18C garden.

The Alternative Museum. – *17 White Street. Open 11 AM to 6 PM; closed Sundays, Mondays and July through September.* This museum is located just south of SoHo *(p 105)* in **Tribeca** (- for the TRIangle BElow CAnal Street), a neighborhood of old factories and warehouses which emerged as an artists' community in the 1970s. The museum's commitment to a multimedia approach to the arts, is reflected in its diverse program of gallery shows, concerts, dance, readings, etc. featuring artists who have not yet received recognition.

The Intrepid Sea-Air-Space Museum. – *Pier 86 at West 46th Street and 12th Avenue. Open 10 AM to 5 PM; closed Mondays, Tuesdays and January 1 and December 25; $6.00, children $3.25.* Berthed at a pier in the Hudson River is the aircraft carrier *Intrepid*, a veteran of World War II, the Vietnam war, and recovery vessel on two occasions for Mercury and Gemini space missions. Decommissioned in the 1970s, the *Intrepid* now serves as a floating sea, air and space museum. On the hangar deck there are exhibits related to the Navy, aviation, the *Intrepid* and space technology, but visitors who have never before toured an aircraft carrier will most likely find the ship itself, with its maze of corridors, enormous decks, high island bridges, and slender bow flaring out above the waterline the most impressive attraction. On the flight deck aircraft appearing ready for flight on a moment's notice may be viewed closeup. Accompanying the exhibits are multimedia presentations including a film *(17 min)* on the day to day operations on board a carrier at sea, and a dramatic audiovisual recounting *(12 min)* of the events that occurred Thanksgiving Day 1944 when the ship was hit by two kamikaze attacks. Admission to the *Intrepid* includes a tour of the **USS Growler**, a 1958 guided missile submarine now decommissioned and open to the public *(last tour 5:30 PM)*. Also on view is the **USS Edson**, the 946th and last example of the United States Navy's all-gun destroyers.

Japan Society. – *333 East 47th Street. Open 11 AM to 5 PM; closed Mondays, between exhibitions (for program information ☏ 832-1155) and major holidays; $2.50.*

This low-rise building, a short walking distance from the United Nations, is the headquarters of the Japan Society, a cultural and educational organization. Designed in contemporary Japanese style, the interior has a bamboo pool, exhibition area, auditorium, library, conference rooms and garden, all of which blend together gracefully to create a simple and tranquil effect. Exhibitions of Japanese art, films, music and dance are presented on a regular basis.

■ DEPARTMENT STORES

Most of the large department stores are located on Fifth Avenue *(pp 43-48)* or on 34th Street between Lexington Avenue and the intersection of Avenue of the Americas and Broadway. The largest is Macy's at Herald Square.

Macy's. – *34th Street and Broadway.* Macy's Herald Square is the world's largest store, with 2 151 000sq ft of floor space and more than 300 selling departments. The main floor has been refurbished and restored to reveal the striking features of its original 1930s Art Deco style.

Macy's stocks over 500 000 different items including fashions for the family and complete furnishings for the home. The store also provides all sorts of services such as eyeglass prescriptions, watch and jewelry repair, interior decorating, fashion consulting, carpet cleaning, and custom drapery and upholstery.

To help foreign visitors there are bilingual employees who speak a total of over thirty languages.

Macy's promotional activities include their annual Flower Show Palm Sunday through the night before Easter, and the famous Thanksgiving Day Parade which is seen on television by more than 65 million people across the country.

Bloomingdale's. – Situated on Lexington Avenue between 59th and 60th Streets, Bloomingdale's is one of the most comprehensive fashion stores. Founded in 1872 the store was originally located at 938 Third Avenue, on the East Side, an unusual site at the time. The arrival of the Third Avenue Elevated ensured Bloomingdale's success and subsequent expansion necessitated a three block move to its present site.

Today, having passed its centennial, this vast store has a wide range of departments including many designer clothes boutiques for men, women and children, the famous food shop A Health Food Restaurant and, on the main floor, Cul-de-Sac, a shop with merchandise from all around the world.

A popular meeting place is near the eight digital Bulovas (clocks) which are recessed into a column, standing inside the Third Avenue entrance. One clock on each side shows New York time while the others give the hour in Paris, Rome, London, Tokyo and Rio de Janeiro.

■ WALKS

George Washington Bridge ★ ★. – The George Washington Bridge was for a number of years the longest bridge in the world; it links West 179th Street in Manhattan to Fort Lee, New Jersey.

Designed by **O.H. Ammann** (an American engineer of Swiss origin, also the designer of the Verrazano-Narrows Bridge) and the architect Cass Gilbert, the bridge was opened on October 25, 1931 and cost about $59 000 000 to build. In 1959, the growing volume of traffic required the construction of a lower level, opened in 1962. At the same time, an intricate system of interchanges was installed.

A tremendous feat of engineering, the George Washington Bridge spans the Hudson River in one pure line 3 500ft long. The towers are 604ft high and the supporting cables have a diameter of 36in. Eight lanes of traffic can cross the upper level, 205ft above the river; the lower level can take six lanes of traffic.

It is a toll bridge *(round trip toll: $3.00 per passenger car)* and the world's only 14-lane suspension bridge. In 1988 more than 100 million vehicles used the bridge.

The best view of the George Washington Bridge may be had from the sightseeing boats *(p 18)* which circle Manhattan, or from the Henry Hudson Parkway, along the river. Notice the Little Red Lighthouse on Jeffrey's Hook, a point of land on the Hudson near 178th Street; there is a little park here, and the lighthouse is a favorite with children.

Part of one of the bastions of Fort Washington can still be found near the bridge in Bennett Park, Fort Washington Avenue and 183rd Street.

Columbus Avenue. – Columbus Avenue, the northward extension of Ninth Avenue from 59th Street to 110th Street, has for the past decade been enjoying a renaissance as a lively new shopping and night spot. The tenements, apartment buildings and middle class houses on and near the avenue had slipped into a comfortable state of wear and neglect, and by the early 1970s the low priced rentals they offered were attracting young singles to the Upper West Side. The young clustered in the area from the Sixties just above Lincoln Center to the Eighties, and it was soon apparent that the character of Columbus Avenue was undergoing a change.

For many years a service street catering to the residents of Central Park West and nearby streets, Columbus Avenue became, overnight, the site of dozens of specialty shops, restaurants and glass-enclosed sidewalk cafes reflecting the tastes of the newcomers. Residential buildings were rehabilitated and apartments converted into co-ops and condominiums.

The avenue, with its low rise scale and warm neighborhood character, nevertheless remains a world apart from the glamour of the East Side. No doubt, for those who frequent the boutiques and eating places lining Columbus Avenue, this is its special charm.

Fulton Street. – Fulton Street which used to run from the Hudson to the East River, is now bounded to the west by the World Trade Center. Restaurants, snack bars and small shops line this narrow street.

Nassau Street which crosses Fulton Street, is closed to vehicular traffic from Maiden Lane to Spruce Street during the middle of the day, to accommodate thousands of shoppers; it has developed into a major shopping street in the area.

Fulton Street, along with Cortlandt Street, Wall Street and Beekman Street, was among the first to acquire gaslights (in 1830).

Schermerhorn Row at the foot of Fulton Street in South Street Seaport *(p 112)* illustrates the Georgian Federal style.

Cortlandt Street-Maiden Lane. – Cortlandt Street, running from the Hudson River dock to Broadway, was an area of sailors' dives and more or less reputable hotels during the 19C. Today it is a shopping area convenient for office workers, particularly animated at lunch time. Maiden Lane, the extension of Cortlandt Street to the east, still boasts several jewelers.

Since the building of the World Trade Center, many restaurants have opened on Greenwich Street.

The 57th Street Area. – Fifty-Seventh Street is one of the city's few wide cross streets that runs from the East River to the Hudson River, unbroken by parks or buildings. It is an elegant and animated thoroughfare still possessing a few of the aristocratic town houses which graced it early in the century. To the east of Fifth Avenue, 57th Street offers a succession of decorators and art galleries and some of New York's finest stores displaying home furnishings, tableware and decorative accessories. **Place des Antiquaires**, at 135 East 57th Street, is a showcase of antiques, art, paintings and decorative accessories offered by retailers from around the world.

Second and Third Avenues between 50th and 57th Streets harbor numerous antique shops and a few print sellers. On 56th Street at 1050 Second Avenue is the **Manhattan Art and Antiques Center** where art and antique dealers present attractive displays (porcelain, jewelry, furniture, etc.). West 57th Street is dense with art galleries, mostly between Fifth and Sixth Avenues.

At the corner of Seventh Avenue, **Carnegie Hall**, which miraculously escaped demolition in the 60s, is universally known in the world of music. It was built under the auspices of Andrew Carnegie, the steel magnate and philanthropist. Carnegie Hall opened in 1891 with a concert conducted by Tchaikovsky, who was followed in subsequent decades by illustrious maestros conducting the world's foremost orchestras. The concert hall, reconstructed as part of a major renovation program, seats 2 804 persons and continues to be highly reputed for its acoustics. The building also houses a recital hall, theater, studios and offices.

Rising nearby between 56th and 57th Streets is the luxurious 41-story French hotel, the **Parker Meridien**, one of New York's newest hotels.

■ PARKS

Inwood Hill Park. – At the northwestern tip of Manhattan, Inwood Hill Park is separated from Fort Tryon Park by a ravine dotted with a few apartment houses. Wooded and hilly, it seems to have changed very little since the Algonquins inhabited the spot, then known as Shora-Kapkok. You may still find caves used by them.

During the Revolution, British and Hessian troops were quartered there and it was the site of Cox Hill.

Weekdays the park is quite empty and it is unwise to walk there alone, but on Sundays New Yorkers will be seen picnicking here.

Not far from the park, to the northeast, along the Harlem River, is Baker Field, the playing field of Columbia University *(p 116)*.

To the east of Inwood Hill Park, between West 204th Street and West 207th Street, is **Dyckman House** *(open 11 AM to noon and 1 to 4 PM; closed Mondays and holidays; $1.00)*, the only 18C Dutch colonial farmhouse in modern Manhattan. Restored and furnished with period furniture, it evokes the atmosphere of the past, and a little garden adds to the pleasure of the visit.

Greenacre Park. – *51st Street between Second and Third Avenues.* One of the vest pocket parks, Greenacre is a haven of calm, away from the noise, dust and hustle and bustle of the New York streets.

Union Square. – Once the scene of large, sometimes unruly political gatherings, a New York equivalent of London's Hyde Park where political radicals and others indulged in soap box oratory, Union Square is now no more than a busy crossroads between Broadway and Park Avenue South and 14th and 17th Streets.

In 1836 the garden in the center of Union Square was enclosed by iron grillwork and locked at night. This was then the northern frontier of the city, but about 20 years later it became a fashionable address, rivaling Astor Place *(p 132)*. The park was then full of English nannies and French governesses supervising the offspring of New York's finest families.

As the city spread northward, wealthy residences gave way to theaters, the Academy of Music (an opera house), commercial establishments such as Tiffany's and Brentano's and restaurants like Delmonico's.

During the last years of the 19C and the early years of the 20C, Union Square witnessed mass demonstrations such as the one on August 22, 1927, when Sacco and Vanzetti were executed in Boston. A number of participants were wounded in the fray.

Today, the park harbors two interesting statues: Washington, on horseback, by Henry Kirke Brown, and Lafayette, on foot, by Bartholdi, better known as the sculptor of the Statue of Liberty *(p 90)*.

Walk a few steps to the east.

The **Consolidated Edison Building** *(4 Irving Place at 14th Street)* is the headquarters of the company which provides gas, electricity and steam for most of New York City.

Return to Park Avenue South, known for its second-hand and rare book stores; head south to Grace Church *(p 136)*.

Madison Square. – Like Union Square, Madison Square was first an almost rural promenade. It was here, in about 1845, the first baseball games of the city were played under the auspices of the Knickerbocker Club.

From 1853 to 1856 the Hippodrome, a kind of circus, drew as many as 10 000 spectators at a time to the square. Later, during the second half of the 19C, Madison Square became an elegant residential area with fashionable hotels, fine restaurants and expensive shops. The Hoffman House was celebrated for the mural (painted by the 19C French artist, Bouguereau) over its bar, and was patronized by the dandies of the day. In 1884, the arm of the Statue of Liberty, complete with torch, was exhibited in the center of the square.

Madison Square gave its name to the famous Madison Square Garden, now located on Eighth Avenue *(p 125)*.

At the end of the last century, an ornate sports arena with room for 8 000 spectators was built on the northwest corner of the square. It was designed by Stanford White, architect and man about town, who was shot on the garden roof by a jealous husband who resented White's attentions to his actress-wife Evelyn Nesbitt. Today Madison Square is a spot of greenery, still pleasant and at lunchtime frequented by office workers, but no longer at the height of its glory.

On the south side of the square is an unusual triangular Renaissance style building. One of the first New York skyscrapers, the **Flatiron Building** ★ adopted its nickname as its official title. Built in 1902 by the Chicago architect Daniel H. Burnham, the striking 21-story brick and limestone structure is 286ft high.

At the northeast corner of the square between East 26th and East 27th Streets, where the "Garden" once stood, is the New York Life Insurance Building designed in Louis XII style, complete with impressive gargoyles.

South of the New York Life Insurance Building, on the corner of East 25th Street, the elegant white marble building (1899) with Corinthian columns, is the Appellate Division of the Supreme Court of the State; the roof balustrade depicts symbolic figures and great teachers of law (Moses, Justinian, Confucius, etc.) of the past. Formerly on the far right, the Mohammed Statue has been removed at the request of the Moslems of New York, since their faith forbids the corporeal representation of the Prophet. The vestibule inside has a gilded ceiling, supported by yellow marble columns.

Completing the picture on the east side of the square (between East 24th and East 23rd Streets) is the **Metropolitan Life Insurance Company Tower** built in 1909. The design of the 700ft tower was inspired by the campanile of St Mark's in Venice; the minute hands of the clock each weigh 1 000 pounds and the hour hands 700 pounds.

NYC's SKYSCRAPERS

Flatiron Building	Daniel H. Burnham	1902	**21 stories**
Woolworth Building	Cass Gilbert	1913	**60 stories**
Empire State Building	Shreve, Lamb & Harmon	1931	**102 stories**
Seagram Building	Mies van der Rohe Philip Johnson	1958	**38 stories**
Chase Manhattan Bank Building	Skidmore, Owings & Merrill	1960	**60 stories**
Twin Towers (World Trade Center)	Minoru Yamasaki & Associates	1973	**110 stories**
Citicorp	Hugh Stubbins & Associates	1977	**59 stories**
Park Avenue Plaza	Skidmore, Owings & Merrill	1981	**44 stories**
AT & T Headquarters	Philip Johnson and John Burgee in association with Henry Simmons	1983	**40 stories**

THE BRONX

The only New York borough which is on the mainland, the Bronx has nearly 1 200 000 inhabitants. The number of residents, predominantly of central and Eastern European extraction, has steadily declined, while Black and Hispanic residents have increased in number. Its southern part is mainly inhabited by lower income groups, while more prosperous sections are found to the north. To the east is the largest park in New York, Pelham Bay Park (CXY), with its popular sandy beach, Orchard Beach. This borough was named after Johannes Bronck, a Danish emigré. The Bronx developed after the mid-1800s around the village of Morrisania (AZ), which now forms one section of the Bronx around Third Avenue and 161st Street. Two members of the Morris family, for whom Morrisania is named, were prominent during the Revolutionary period: Lewis Morris, a signer of the Declaration of Independence, and Gouverneur Morris, penman of the U.S. Constitution. The borough is linked to Manhattan by 12 bridges, and 6 subway tunnels. The Bronx was a part of Westchester County until 1898, when it was incorporated into New York City.

■ MAIN SIGHTS

The Bronx Zoo★★★. – *Open 10 AM to 5 PM (5:30 PM Sundays and holidays, 4:30 PM November through mid-March). Admission free Tuesdays, Wednesdays and Thursdays; $3.75, children $1.50 on the other days. Subway: East Tremont Ave station (2,5 lines) to reach the main entrance of the zoo (on the south).*

The Bronx Zoo is located in Bronx Park, laid out at the end of the 19C on the banks of the Bronx River where the windmills of "West Farms" turned. On 265 acres, over 4 000 animals of more than 700 species live in indoor and outdoor exhibit areas; the visitor can watch the animals cavort a few yards away, most often separated only by a moat.

Visit. – We recommend that you take the tractor train, Safari Tour *(10 AM to 4:30 PM; closed in winter; $1.00, children 75¢)* to ride around the zoo or the Skyfari aerial tramway *(same hours as Safari Tour; $1.25, children $1.00)* which offers fine views of the zoo. You can also walk leisurely throughout the zoo following the adjoining map. The Bengali Express monorail *($1.50, children $1.00; closed November through April)* passes through 38 acres

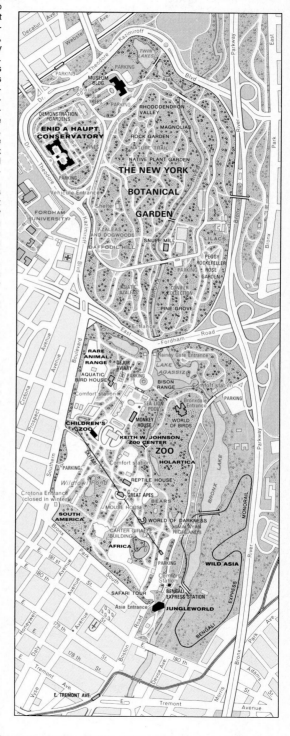

of hilly, wooded land on its journey into **Wild Asia** *(10 AM to 4:30 PM – 5 PM Sundays and holidays; closed November through April; $1.50, children $1.00).* Here, over 200 rare and endangered animals can be observed living in large, natural habitats. Among the animals not to be missed are the American bison (Bison Range), and on the **Rare Animals Range,** the Mongolian wild horses and the Pere David deer which have the feet of a cow, the neck of a camel, the tail of a donkey and deer antlers.

Jungleworld *(10 AM to 4:45 PM - 5 PM Sundays and holidays, 4:15 PM in winter; Fridays through Mondays 25¢, Tuesdays through Thursdays 50¢)* an indoor exhibit recreates a South Asian rain forest and other tropical environments.

Visit also **Africa** where wild animals roam at will; the Reptile House; the DeJur Aviary and the Aquatic Bird House; the World of Darkness *(night animals, Tuesdays through Thursdays 25¢, other times free)* and the World of Birds where hundreds of exotic birds can be observed in natural surroundings.

THE BRONX

0		2 km
0	1 Mile	

Allerton Ave.		BY
Bainbridge Ave.		BXY 2
Baychester Ave.		BCX
Boston Rd.		AZCX
Broadway		AX
Bronx and Pelham Pkwy		BCY
Bronxdale Ave.		BY 3
Bronx River Pkwy		BXZ
Bruckner Blvd		AZ
Bruckner Expwy		AZCY
Castle Hill Ave.		BYZ
City Island Ave.		CY
City Island Rd.		CY
Cross Bronx Expwy		AYCZ
Edw. L. Grant Hwy		AY 9
Eastchester Rd		BY 10
East Gun Hill Rd		BXY
E. Fordham Rd.		ABY
E. Tremont Ave.		BYCZ
E. 149 th St		AZ
E. 161 st St.		AZ
E. 163 rd St.		AZ
E. 204 th St.		BY 14
E. 233 rd St.		BCX
E. 241 st St.		BX
Goulden Ave.		AY
Grand Blvd and Concourse		ABYZ
Henry Hudson Pkwy.		AX
Hunts Point Ave.		BZ
Hutchinson River Pkwy		CXZ
Jerome Ave.		AZBX
Laconia Ave.		BX
Major Deegan Expwy		AZBX

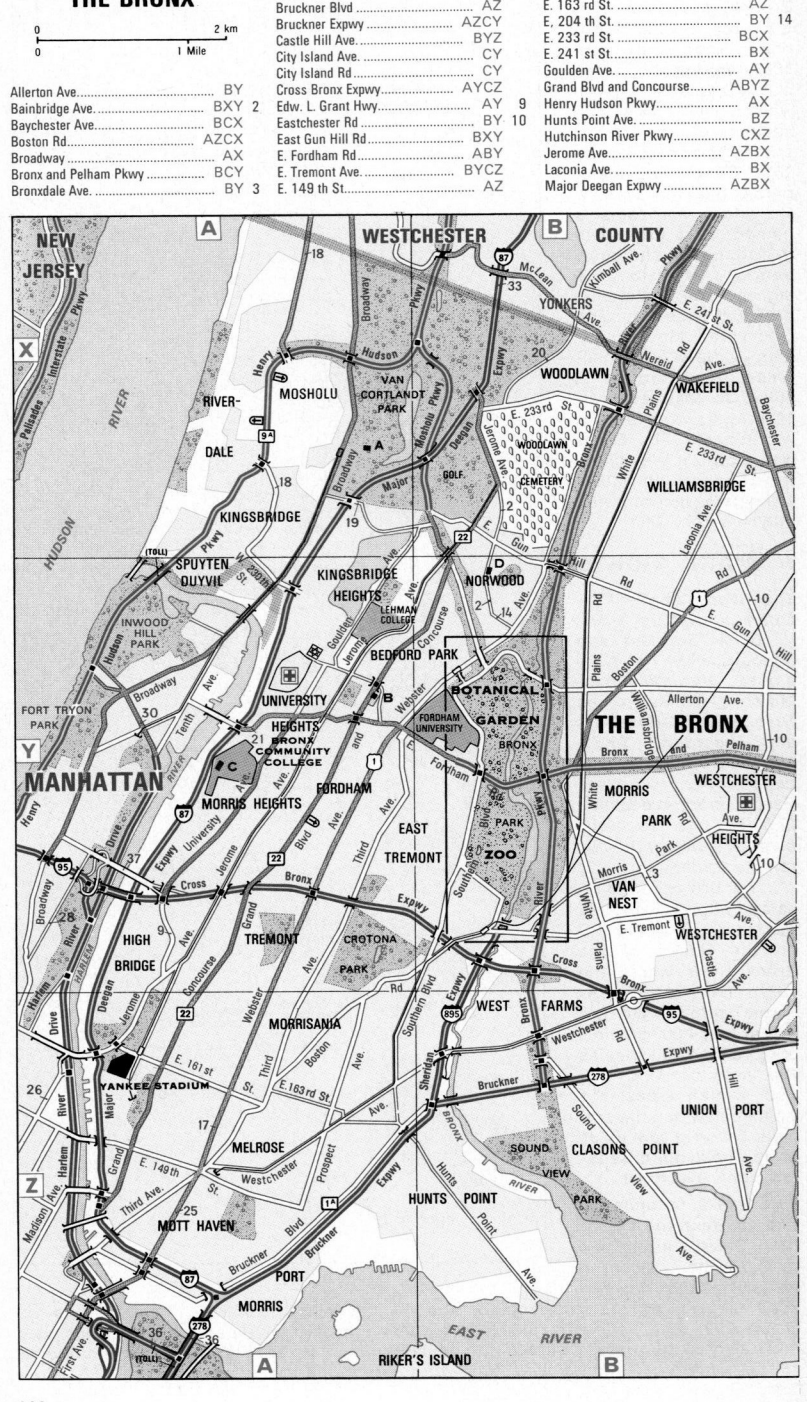

The **Children's Zoo** *(10 AM to 5 PM - 5:30 PM Sundays and holidays; closed November through March; $1.50, children $1.00)*, covering 3 acres of marsh and wooded land, has more than 100 animals shown in habitats similar to the areas where they would naturally live: marsh, forest, desert, woodland edge and domestic. Thematic exhibits encourage children to participate and learn about the homes, senses, defenses and locomotion of various animals.

In the Great Apes Building a full length mirror reminds the visitor of which animal is the most dangerous the world.

The New York Botanical Garden★★. – *The grounds are open 8 AM to 7 PM (6 PM November through March), closed January 1, Thanksgiving Day and December 25; vehicle entrance on Southern Boulevard: parking $4.00 per car. Subway: D train to Bedford Park Boulevard; 4 line to 200th Street and Jerome Avenue. Restaurant and gift shop.* The Botanical Garden, founded in 1891 and covering 250 acres, is about the same size as the zoo to the south. Many thousands of flowering trees, shrubs and plants are at their peak in spring and early summer.

Among the favorite attractions are the rose garden, the rhododendron valley, the demonstration gardens, the rock garden, the 40-acre virgin forest, the native plant garden and the Enid A. Haupt Conservatory.

The Museum Building *(open 10 AM to 5 PM, closed Mondays except Monday holidays)* houses the library *(open to the public)*, the herbarium with dried plant specimens and fossils, the auditorium and the gift shop.

A restaurant occupies the old Snuff Mill, an 18C stone building overlooking the Bronx River.

Enid A. Haupt Conservatory★★. – *Open 10 AM to 5 PM (last admission 4 PM); closed Mondays and January 1, Thanksgiving Day and December 25; $3.50, children $1.25.* The Conservatory, a glass pavilion built in 1901 and modeled after the crystal palaces of the 19C, was restored in 1978 and named for Enid A. Haupt whose gift to the garden made the restoration possible.

The entrance to the conservatory opens onto the Palm Court with its 90ft central dome and collection of lush, tropical plants. By exploring the 11 galleries visitors will pass through a variety of plant environments with flora from around the world: tropical container plants, a fern jungle, orangerie, deserts of the Old and New World displaying a variety of cacti and succulents and special collections that include carnivorous plants and rare orchids.

In House 1, planned especially for children, it is interesting to attempt to identify the vegetables, fruits and grains being raised, with the products on the "grocery store " shelves nearby.

Six seasonal floral displays are scheduled annually.

Yankee Stadium★ (AZ). – *Subway: 4, D, C lines to 161st St.* This famous baseball stadium, affectionately referred to by lovers of the sport as "the house that Babe Ruth built," is located at 161st Street and River Avenue. Built (1923) by brewery magnate Colonel Jacob Ruppert for the team he owned, the stadium underwent a massive remodeling program from 1974 to 1975. Major features of the 57 545 seat stadium include new sets of escalators serving the upper tiers of the grandstands, an unobstructed view of the playing field, a new electronically controlled scoreboard, etc.

Melrose Ave.	AZ 17
Morris Park Ave.	BY
Mosholu Pkwy	BX
Nereid Ave.	BX
New England Thruway..	CXY
Prospect Ave.	AZ
Pelham Bridge Rd	CY
Riverdale Ave.	AX 18
Sheridan Expwy	BZ
Sound View Ave.	BZ
Southern Blvd	BYZ
Third Ave.	AYZ
Throgs Neck Expwy	CZ
University Ave.	AY
Van Cortlandt Park South	AX 19
Van Cortlandt Park East..	BX 20
Webster Ave.	ABYZ
Westchester Ave.	AZCY
W. Fordham Rd	AY 21
W. 230 th St.	AY
White Plains Rd	BXZ
Williamsbridge Rd	BY
Willis Ave.	AZ 25

MANHATTAN

Adam Clayton Powell Jr. Blvd	AZ 26
Amsterdam Ave.	AY 28
Broadway	AY
Dyckman St.	AY 30
First Ave.	AZ
Harlem River Drive	AYZ
Henry Hudson Pkwy	AY
Madison Ave.	AZ
Tenth Ave.	AY

WESTCHESTER

Bronx River Pkwy	BX
Kimball Ave.	BX
McLean Ave.	BX
N.Y. State Thruway	BX 33
Pelham Rd	CX

BRIDGES

Bronx-Whitestone Bridge	CZ
Throgs Neck Bridge	CZ
Triborough Bridge	AZ 36
Washington Bridge	AY 37

145

THE BRONX

Yankees: Babe Ruth and Friends. – Yankee Stadium was built in 1923 for the baseball team of the same name. The stadium's first years were the heyday of Babe Ruth – "the Babe" – one of the outstanding athletes of all times. Babe Ruth hit 60 home runs in 1927, still the American record in the Major Leagues for a 154-game season, and when he died, in 1948, 100 000 fans paid their respects. A bronze plaque commemorates past Yankee greats: Babe Ruth, Lou Gehrig, Edward Grant Barrow, Joe Di Maggio and Mickey Mantle.

■ ADDITIONAL SIGHTS

Valentine-Varian House (BY D). – *3266 Bainbridge Avenue at East 208th Street. Guided tours (time: 1 hour) Saturdays 10 AM to 4 PM; Sundays 1 to 5 PM; Mondays through Fridays by 9 AM to 5 PM by appointment only ℡ 881-8900; closed January 1, Thanksgiving Day and December 25; $ 1.00. Subway: D line to 205th Street, 4 line to Mosholu Parkway.*

This fieldstone house originally stood on the opposite side of the street. The land was acquired in 1758 by Isaac Valentine and was the scene of many skirmishes during the Revolution. The ground was then bought in 1791 by Isaac Varian, a prosperous farmer whose son was to become the 63rd Mayor of New York.

The house, situated on its present site since 1965, now contains the **Museum of Bronx History** with a fine collection of prints, lithographs and photographs.

Poe Cottage (AY B). – *Open Wednesdays through Fridays 9 AM to 5 PM, Saturdays 10 AM to 4 PM; Sundays 1 to 5 PM; closed major holidays; $1.00; Subway: D or 4 line to Kingsbridge Road.*

In this little wooden house built in 1812, Edgar Allan Poe lived three years (1846-49) away from the noise and congestion of New York City, paying John Valentine an annual rental of $100. He was hoping to save his wife Virginia Clemm from tuberculosis. She died in 1847. Poe died three years later in Baltimore, while on a trip returning to the cottage from Virginia. Poe wrote *Annabel Lee* and *The Bells* as well as *Ulalume* and *Eureka* in this cottage. There are displays of memorabilia and manuscripts, and a 20 min audio-visual slide show.

Van Cortlandt House Museum★ (AX A). – *On Broadway behind Visitor's Center for Van Cortlandt Park. Open Fridays 1 to 3 PM, Sundays 2 to 5 PM. Call for information ℡ 543-3344; $2.00, children and senior citizens $1.00. Subway: 1 line to Van Cortlandt Park.*

This colonial manor built in 1748 is admirably preserved by the city and by the National Society of Colonial Dames in the State of New York. Washington is said to have used the house as headquarters before making his triumphant entry into New York in November, 1783.

The mansion reflects a refinement and style of living typical of the New York gentry. The furnishings in the colonial style have been carefully restored: in the nine rooms open to the public, notice the Dutch room, the kitchen, and, in the nursery, one of America's oldest doll houses.

Bronx Community College (AY). – *Subway: 4 line to Burnside Ave.*

Founded in 1891 as the Bronx campus of New York University *(p 120)* this group of eighteen buildings, now occupied by the Bronx Community College, stands on the calm banks of the Harlem River.

Hall of Fame for Great Americans ★ (C). – *Open daily 10 AM to 5 PM.*

The Hall of Fame reflects Stanford White's conception of an American pantheon in an outdoor colonnade, 630ft in length, surrounding three buildings in an imposing Beaux Arts style complex. This unique sculpture museum honors Americans outstanding in many fields. Candidates chosen at least 25 years after their death are selected by an electoral committee in each of the following categories: arts, sciences, humanities, government, and business and labor. Elections were temporarily suspended in 1979, but since that time the structure has undergone restoration and plans are underway to reinstate the election process.

Among those honored are: Harriet Beecher Stowe, George Washington Carver, Edgar Allan Poe *(see above)*, Walt Whitman, John James Audubon *(pp 96 and 138)*, Susan B. Anthony, the Wright Brothers, Henry Wadsworth Longfellow, Washington Irving *(p 160)*, Presidents Ulysses S. Grant, Thomas Jefferson and Abraham Lincoln.

Pelham Bay Park (CXCY). – The largest park in the city offers a variety of outdoor activities including golfing, hiking, cycling, tennis, horsebackriding, ball playing and fishing, but the most popular attraction is **Orchard Beach** where the mile-long sandy shore is a welcome refuge for swimmers on hot summer days.

Bartow-Pell Mansion★ (CY E). – *Open Wednesdays, Saturdays and Sundays noon to 4 PM. $1.00, accompanied children under 12 free.* The history of this site dates back to 1654 when Thomas Pell bought the land from the Siwanoy Indians. The neo-classic stone mansion overlooking Long Island Sound was built by Robert Bartow, a descendent of Pell's, between 1836 and 1842. The interior contains Greek Revival detailing including a freestanding elliptical staircase, and furnishings in the American Empire style.

Among the major medical units in New York are the New York University Medical Center (p 137); the New York Hospital, Cornell Medical Center and the nearby Rockefeller University of Medical Research (on the East River between 63rd and 71st Streets); the New York Hospital is the oldest in New York, chartered in 1771; Mount Sinai Hospital of Fifth Avenue at 100th Street (member institution of the Federation of Jewish Philanthropies); and the Columbia-Presbyterian Medical Center on 168th Street between Broadway and Fort Washington Avenue, the first hospital to assume direct responsibility for the basic health needs of the poor.

BROOKLYN

Situated southwest of Long Island *(p 163)*, Brooklyn (Kings County) extends over 70sq miles from the East River to Coney Island and from the Narrows to Jamaica Bay.

The population of Brooklyn is about 2 314 000 making it the most heavily populated borough of New York City.

A Long and Rich Past. – Brooklyn was founded in 1636 by Dutch settlers who called it Breukelen ("broken land") after a small town near Utrecht.

What is now the borough of Brooklyn was made up of six towns. One of the original settlements was located on Wallabout Bay, near the area where the Brooklyn Navy Yard was located until 1966.

Later, Brooklyn spread westward along the river, below the wooded bluffs of Clover Hill (Brooklyn Heights). By the 18C, regular ferry service to Manhattan was established, allowing Long Island farmers to cross the river and sell their produce in Lower Manhattan.

By the end of that century Brooklyn was a pleasant residential area where many prosperous New Yorkers had country places. At that time, most houses were still built of wood. A French émigré, Moreau de St-Méry, recounts that even then many financiers commuted to Wall Street in the summer.

In 1834, Brooklyn became an incorporated city with already about 30 000 inhabitants. It developed into an important industrial and trading center and was incorporated into New York City in 1898 after absorbing a number of villages the names of which still mark various sections of the borough.

By 1883, the Brooklyn Bridge formed the first direct link with Manhattan; the Williamsburg Bridge followed in 1903, and Manhattan Bridge in 1909. The first subway connection dates from 1905. More recently, the Brooklyn-Battery Tunnel, completed in 1950, and the Verrazano-Narrows Bridge, opened in 1965, have further facilitated travel to and from the other boroughs.

A Special World. – Although Brooklyn can hardly be considered isolated today, with the almost half a million Brooklynites who commute to Manhattan, the borough has retained its distinctive personality as vividly described by Betty Smith in her book *A Tree Grows in Brooklyn*. Furthermore, a number of writers have enjoyed living in Brooklyn, especially in the Brooklyn Heights area *(see below)*, from Walt Whitman who wrote for the now defunct *Brooklyn Daily Eagle* in 1846, to Norman Mailer in our time, as well as Herman Melville, John Dos Passos, Thomas Wolfe, Truman Capote, Arthur Miller and others.

A visitor passing through Brooklyn is first impressed by its huge size, and its labyrinth of streets and avenues lined with neat, straight rows of houses.

However, a closer look reveals a great variety of neighborhoods, such as Brooklyn Heights, a residential enclave that is still the refuge of a few "old families;" Williamsburg, containing both Hassidic Jewish and Puerto Rican communities; Flatbush, with fine private homes and lively commercial streets; Bensonhurst, a predominantly Italian section; and Bedford-Stuyvesant, an area where a substantial proportion of Brooklyn's Black families reside.

The borough's ethnic makeup includes Black, Italian (the tenor Mario Lanza was from Brooklyn), Jewish, Greek, Middle Eastern, Scandinavian, and Polish groups as well as a sizable Caribbean population.

■ BROOKLYN HEIGHTS★★ *visit: about 2 hours*

Heavily fortified during the Revolution, Brooklyn Heights was the site of General Washington's headquarters during the Battle of Long Island.

In the mid-19C this section of Brooklyn developed into a choice residential area, owing to its proximity to, as well as geographical isolation from, the city. The serenity of the Brooklyn Heights neighborhood has often been likened to the calm of a small countrified town. Its narrow tree-shaded streets are lined with brownstones and town houses that represent almost every style of 19C American architecture.

Tour. – Leaving the Clark Street subway station *(2, 3 lines)*, walk toward Monroe Place. You will pass in front of the Hotel St George once the largest hotel in New York City. The hotel was subdivided in the 1970s and for the most part converted into coops and luxury rental apartments; only one small section continues to operate as a hotel today. Turn onto **Monroe Place**. At **no 46**, a brick and brownstone Greek Revival dwelling, note the decorative wrought iron basket urns set on stone pedestals. The pineapple topping the baskets was a symbol of hospitality during the shipping era.

Arriving at Pierrepont Street, turn right and continue to the corner of Henry Street. **No 82 Pierrepont Street** is a splendid example of Romanesque Revival, with its bulky massing, rough unfinished masonry surfaces, rounded arches and low relief carving. Built in 1890 as a private residence, it was later enlarged and has recently been converted into apartments.

Turning into **Willow Street**, you will note **nos 155, 157 and 159**, three Federal style houses with handsomely detailed entranceways. A skylight in the pavement in front of no 157 allows daylight to filter down into a tunnel which connects no 159 to **no 151**, formerly a stable and now an attractive apartment. Further up the street, on the opposite side, **nos 108 to 112** are a picturesque example of the Queen Anne style, with their great variety of building materials, and blend of elements of the Romanesque, Gothic and Renaissance styles.

Continue on Clark Street, turn right on Orange Street and then left onto Hicks Street where at no 75 the entrance to **Plymouth Church of the Pilgrims** is located *(visit with reservations ☏ 624-4743)*. The first Congregational Church in Brooklyn, this simple brick meetinghouse which dates from 1846 served for forty years as the pulpit for Henry Ward Beecher who is well-remembered for his anti-slavery efforts and other progressive sentiments. President Lincoln worshipped here on two occasions in 1860, and many eminent authors and statesmen have spoken here over the years. In Hillis Hall, note the large stained glass windows by Tiffany.

Two blocks further down Hicks Street, turn left onto Middagh Street. Along this street are several Federal style clapboard houses which were built in the 1820s. Among the best preserved are the double frame house at **nos 31-33** and the charming dwelling at **no 24.**

Take Willow Street to Cranberry and continue toward the East River. You will reach the Brooklyn Heights Esplanade above the expressway and harbor. The esplanade offers a magnificent **view ★★★** of the Manhattan skyline; the view is especially impressive in the early evening when the lights begin to come on across the river. Behind the terrace is a series of houses with lovely private gardens.

Walk almost to the end of the esplanade, turn left onto Montague Street and left onto Pierrepont Place where you will see **nos 2 and 3 Pierrepont Place,** two of the most elegant brownstone mansions in New York. From Montague Terrace turn left onto Remsen Street, then follow Hicks Street to Joralemon Street; off to the left is **Grace Court Alley** a picturesque mews that was the stable alley for the fine homes on Remsen Street.

There are several pretty tree-lined streets off of Joralemon Street, such as **Garden Place** and **Sidney Place.** Just south of here at about Hicks and Joralemon Streets was the country home of Philip Livingston, a signer of the Declaration of Independence. It is reported that on August 29, 1776 General Washington met at Livingston's home with his chiefs of staff to plan the evacuation of his army *(see p 25).*

Next, take Joralemon Street to the Civic Center, a contrast to the residential section, with its massive public buildings, such as Borough Hall, the former Brooklyn City Hall and the massive Romanesque Revival Central Post Office.

Further down Fulton Street is Brooklyn's "downtown" including the famous department store Abraham & Strauss.

Turn left onto Court Street and left again on Montague Street with its unusual two story shops, reminiscent of old Boston. One block down, turn right on Clinton Street and continue to the next corner.

Brooklyn Historical Society. – The Society is the major source of material related to the history of Brooklyn and Long Island. It contains a large collection of books, documents and artifacts on Brooklyn, features special exhibitions, concerts and tours and houses the city's history museum.

Brooklyn's History Museum. – *Open noon to 5 PM Tuesdays through Sundays; closed Mondays and major holidays; $2.50 adults, $1.00 children under 12.*

Using five symbols of Brooklyn (the Brooklyn Bridge, The Brooklyn Navy Yard, the Brooklyn Dodgers, Brooklynites and Coney Island) the museum retraces the history of the borough and the diversity of its people.

If you are not pressed for time, we suggest a leisurely stroll on **Atlantic Avenue** at the foot of Brooklyn Heights.

Exotic restaurants, food stores and antique shops line the avenue, the commercial center for the neighboring Middle Eastern community.

■ PROSPECT PARK AND VICINITY

Prospect Park ★ . – *Subway: 2 or 3 lines to Grand Army Plaza. For recorded information on current events in the park ☏ (718) 788-0055.*

The main entrance of the park is at Grand Army Plaza, a majestic oval plaza with a monument to President Kennedy and a triumphal arch dedicated to the Civil War dead *(open Saturdays and Sundays in spring and fall only. 11 AM to 4:30 PM).*

The natural landscape of the park, 345 acres of meadows and wooded bluffs, streams, brooks and a lake, was left unspoiled when the park was designed in the 1860s by Frederick Olmsted and Calvert Vaux, and has been maintained in its original state.

A network of paths and roadways winds through the park linking its various sections. The city purchased the land in piecemeal fashion between 1859 and 1869 from the Litchfield family.

Boathouse Visitor Center. – *Open Wednesdays through Sundays 11 AM to 5 PM (mid-April through May and September through October, Saturdays and Sundays only); closed late November to late March and January 1 and December 25.* The former boathouse (1905), modeled after a 16C Venetian building, has been restored and serves as the park information center. The center is the departure point for tours conducted by the Urban Park Rangers.

Lefferts Homestead. – *Open 10 AM to 4 PM (5 PM Sunday), closed Mondays and Tuesdays; January through March open Saturdays, Sundays and Holidays only. Subway: Q, M, or D lines to Prospect Park.*

A graceful gambrel roof tops this 18C colonial farmhouse, which was moved to the park in 1918. The interior contains period furniture and handcarved paneling.

Brooklyn Botanic Garden★★. – *Open 8 AM (10 AM Saturdays, Sundays and holidays) to 6 PM (4:30 PM October through March); closed Mondays except Monday holidays. Subway: 2 or 3 lines to Eastern Parkway.*

Located to the east of Prospect Park, and to the south of the Brooklyn Museum, this outstanding botanical garden covering 50 acres has a great variety of vegetation.

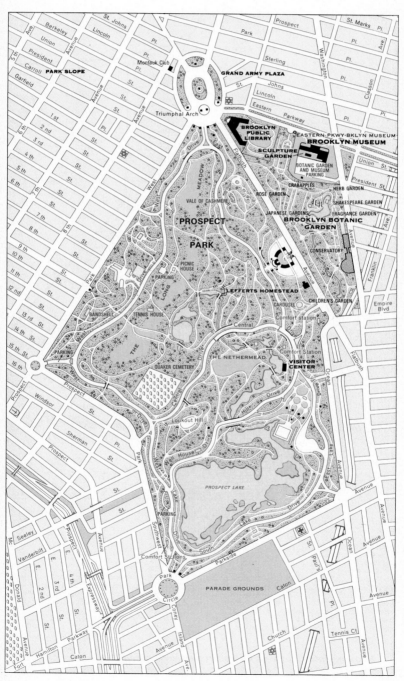

Two suggested programs for a short visit to New York City will be found on pp 18-21

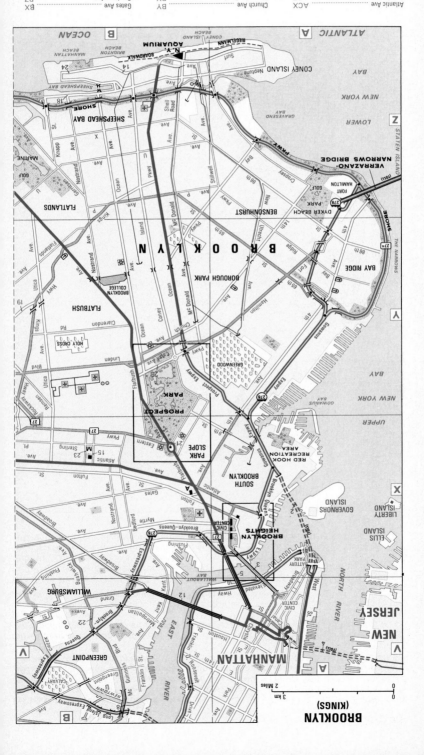

BROOKLYN
(KINGS)

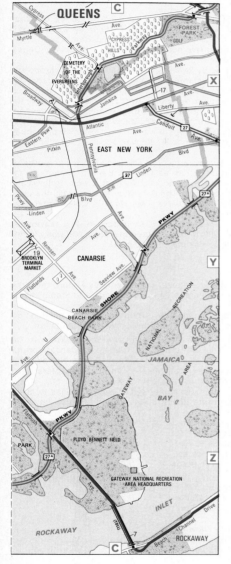

*For historical events related
to New York see pp 24-25*

BROOKLYN

The garden is a refreshing oasis that invites visitors to explore its Japanese gardens, a Shakespeare Garden, Children's Garden and Conservatory. The four-building **Conservatory** complex *(open 10 AM to 5 PM – 4 PM October through March – closed Mondays, $ 2.00)* houses numerous varieties of flora. We should also mention the rose garden, the rows of crabapple trees, the herb garden and the garden for the blind (Fragrance Garden).

Brooklyn Public Library. – *See plan p 149. Subway: 2 or 3 lines to Eastern Parkway.*

A monumental building occupying a triangular plot, the Public Library was completed in 1941. The main library contains about 1 600 000 volumes nearly all of which can be borrowed; there are also 58 branches in the borough.

Park Slope. – *See plan p 149.* Just west of Prospect Park, this is one of the most desirable residential areas in Brooklyn. Here wide tree-lined streets bordered with rows of handsome town houses, punctuated by church spires, preserve a picture of the borough as it existed in the 19 C. The architectural style is typical of the period between the Civil War and World War I.

Montauk Club. – Located on the northeast corner of Lincoln Place and 8th Ave, this clubhouse was constructed in 1891 in a style reminiscent of a Venetian palace. Of particular interest are the friezes which depict historic scenes associated with the Montauk Indians.

■ BROOKLYN MUSEUM★★

See plan p 149. Open 10 AM to 5 PM; closed Tuesdays, January 1, Thanksgiving Day and December 25; suggested contribution $3.00, under 12 free. Subway: 2 or 3 lines to Eastern Parkway.

A monumental building complete with peristyle and pediment, a typical design of McKim, Mead and White, the Brooklyn Museum displays on its five exhibit floors comprehensive and rich collections which are too often overlooked.

First Floor: Primitive Arts. – Galleries of art objects from Africa (handsome wooden statuettes, masks and totem poles, ceremonial shields witchdoctor's wands ...); Oceania, the Arctic, American Indian civilizations (golden pre-Columbian jewelry); Peru (zoomorphic pottery).

Second Floor: Middle and Far East. – China (bronzes, jades, porcelain, paintings); Korea and Japan (sculpture, ceramics, paintings, metalwork, prints); India, Nepal, Tibet and Southeast Asia (sculpture, paintings); Middle East (paintings, ceramics, metalwork, carpets, textiles).

Third Floor: Mediterranean, Near Eastern and Coptic Antiquity. – The outstanding Egyptian galleries trace the development of the Nile civilization: admire the sarcophagus in rose-colored granite from rose-colored granite from the Fourth Dynasty (2500 BC) and the limestone bust of Ptolemy II, as well as a curious sarcophagus for a sacred ibis in gilded wood and silver, and small precious objects in alabaster or stone. You will also notice a few exhibits from Greek and Roman antiquity (vases, mosaics, jewelry) and twelve bas-reliefs from Assurbanipal's Assyrian palace at Nimrud.

Fourth Floor: Furniture, Decorative Arts and Costumes. – The most interesting displays on this floor are an excellent series of American **interiors** from the 17C to the present: parlors, sitting rooms and dining rooms from both modest and wealthy homes, including an old Dutch home, the Jan Martense Schenck House (c 1625), moved from a street in what is today the Flatlands section of Brooklyn. The rest of this floor features furniture, glass, silver, pewter and ceramics.

The costumes galleries contain outstanding American and European fashions of the past and present.

Fifth Floor: Painting and Sculpture. – The early paintings include a series of Italian painters, Primitives and Renaissance: a splendid *St James Major* by Carlo Crivelli (Venice, 15C) and works by Sano di Pietro, Alvise Vivarini and Maso di Banco.

Among the more recent European painters notice the fine Impressionists: Degas, Monet, Berthe Morisot, Sisley and Pissarro.

The rotunda gallery displays sculpture by **Rodin,** portraits, partial figures, erotic and mythological subjects, and groups of works related to his best known commissions: *The Gates of Hell, The Burghers of Calais* and *Balzac.* The emotionally powerful figures of Eustache de St-Pierre, Pierre de Wiessant and Andrieu d'Andres represent three of the citizens of Calais who offered themselves in the 14C to the English king to save their city from starvation. Larger than life size, they are displayed to allow visitors to walk among them and view them from any angle. Equally powerful are two figures which present an interesting contrast: the virile *Age of Bronze* which Rodin was accused of casting from life, and the elderly *Helmet Maker's Wife.*

A series of eight galleries traces the development of **American painting** with portraits, genre and landscapes by such important artists as Copley, Eakins, Homer *(In the Mountains),* Sargent *(Paul Helleu Sketching, and his Wife),* Cassatt, Chase, Bellows and Rothko. In the section devoted to the Hudson River School note especially the large canvases by Bierstadt: *Storm in the Rocky Mountains – Mt. Rosalie,* Cole: *The Pic-Nic* and Durand: *First Harvest in the Wilderness.*

The first of its kind, the museum has gathered an important and fascinating collection of architectural ornaments salvaged from demolished buildings, in the **sculpture garden** *(behind the main building beside the parking area).*

■ AROUND BROOKLYN

Shore Parkway * (ACZ). – From Bay Ridge to Queens and Kennedy Airport, this drive follows the coast. There are successive views of the Verrazano Bridge and Staten Island, the Rockaways and Jamaica Bay.

A drive along Shore Parkway on a bright sunny day, when far-reaching horizons are visible across the glittering water, offers a complete change from citified Manhattan.

Verrazano-Narrows Bridge ** (AZ). – *Subway: R line to 95th St – Fourth Ave.* The spider web silhouette of the Verrazano-Narrows Bridge, the longest suspension bridge in the United States, links Brooklyn to Staten Island *(p 157)* above the Narrows, the entrance to New York Harbor. The bridge bears the name of the Italian explorer who, sailing for the French king Francis I, discovered the site of New York *(p 110).* At the Brooklyn entrance to the bridge is a monument composed in part of stones from the castle of Verrazano in Tuscany, and from the beach of Dieppe, the French port from which he sailed.

The Triborough Bridge and Tunnel Authority began construction of the bridge in January 1959. The project cost $305 000 000. On November 21, 1964, the opening took place; Governor Nelson Rockefeller and the bridge's engineer, O.H. Ammann, who also designed the George Washington Bridge *(p 140),* officiated.

A Few Figures. – Here are a few detailed figures:
Total length: 13 700ft – Main span: 4 260ft – Height of the towers above the high watermark: 690ft – Diameter of main cables: 3ft.

The bridge, which is high enough to allow the largest ocean liner to pass, has two levels of traffic (six lanes each) but no sidewalk for pedestrians. A toll bridge *($5.00 a car paid only on westbound crossing),* it shortens the trip from Staten Island to the other boroughs.

Coney Island (ABZ). – *Subway: B, N, F, Q, M, D lines.*

Despite its historical interest, Coney Island today is not longer the safe attraction of 1900's. To the south of Brooklyn and bathed by the Atlantic Ocean, the beach resort and amusement area at the height of its popularity attracted 1 000 000 people on a busy summer Sunday.

From Rabbits to Frock Coats to Bikinis. – In Dutch times there was nothing but a sandy island inhabited only by rabbits, who left their name *(Konijn Eiland –* Rabbit Island). This title was soon transformed into its rough English "sound-alike," Coney Island.

(From photo Nester's Map and Guide Corp., New York.)

Coney Island.
The former parachute jump.

In the 1830s the broad beaches on the island first began to be visited, principally by the well-to-do. Coney Island developed into a fashionable resort and became the site of elegant hotels, hippodromes and casinos.

Then, 50 years later, the resort became a popular amusement area and the clientele changed. The first roller coasters appeared in 1884, followed some years later by a huge Ferris wheel (George W.G. Ferris built the first one for the Chicago World's Fair in 1893) and a merry-go-round.

The Resort. – By 1900, a hot summer Sunday drew 100 000 people to the beach.

But the great attraction of Coney Island was its amusement parks, where scenic railways, loop-the-loops roller coasters and Ferris wheels competed with phantom trains, interplanetary rockets, merry-go-rounds and shooting galleries. For many years the star attraction was the **parachute jump,** still standing but out of action, erected during the World's Fair of 1939-40; the lover of thrills could drop in a chair attached to a parachute – but guided by cables.

Coney Island's heyday lasted into the 40s. Then, through the 50s, the crowds diminished and with a lack of prosperity, the area began to decline. Buildings grew shabby and were allowed to deteriorate and restaurants and other establishments were permanently closed. Today all but a small section of the once gigantic amusement area has fallen into disuse. For many New Yorkers and out-of-towners, however, a stroll on Coney Island's boardwalk, the 3 1/2 mile stretch of sandy beach and ocean water, the hotdog and cotton candy stands and handful of attractions still remain a pleasant diversion on a warm summer day. Every year some 14 000 000 people visit Coney Island.

The New York Aquarium★★ (BZ). – *Open 10 AM to 4:45 PM (5:45 PM weekends and holidays); $3.75, children $1.50. Subway: F or D lines to West 8th Street New York/Aquarium Station.*

The New York Aquarium has been located at the corner of the Boardwalk and West 8th Street since its move from the Battery *(p 110)* in 1957. In large outdoor pools, whales, seals, sea lions, dolphins and New York's only Pacific walrus go through their paces. There is also a penguin colony and a 90 000 gallon shark tank holding 5 types of free swimming and bottom-dwelling sharks. The stingrays are a type of bottom dwelling shark.

The indoor aquariums, some decorated with live corals, exhibit more than 200 different species including Pacific reef fishes, primitive fishes, pirahnas, chambered nautilus, clownfishes and anemones. The African Rift Lake and Red Sea exhibits are home to species found only in those two.

Discovery Cove, opened in 1989, features 65 exhibits including a 400-gallon wave tank showing subtidal, intertidal and upper tidal zones; an authentic reproduction of a living coral reef where jewel-like small fish dart among anemones and barnacles; and a New England lobster boat in its own salt water dock.

In summer and fall: dolphin and sea lion shows; in winter and spring beluga whales join the sea lions. Electric eel demonstrations daily.

Brooklyn Children's Museum (BX M). – *Open July, August and school vacations 10 AM to 5 PM, the rest of the year 2 PM (10 AM Saturdays, Sundays and holidays) to 5 PM; closed Tuesdays and January 1, Thanksgiving Day and December 25. $2.00. For additional information ☏ (718) 735-4432. Subway: 7th Avenue Express no 2 (New Lots Train) to Kingston Avenue; walk 1 block west to Brooklyn Avenue and 6 blocks north to St Mark's Avenue.*

Located at 145 Brooklyn Avenue in Brower Park on the same site where the original museum was launched in 1899, the museum contains "hands on " exhibits covering the areas of cultural and natural history, the sciences, the performing and creative arts. A museum geared to children, all its exhibits invite active participation.

Brooklyn Academy of Music (BX A). – *30 Lafayette Avenue.* Many famous people have been associated with the Brooklyn Academy of Music since it first opened in this imposing Renaissance building in 1908. It was here that Stanley recounted to the public the details of his meeting with Livingstone and that Enrico Caruso gave his last performance. Other well-known names are associated with the Academy, such as Arturo Toscanini, Isadora Duncan and Sarah Bernhardt. Acting as a cultural center, the BAM offers a varied program of dance, theater, music and lectures.

QUEENS

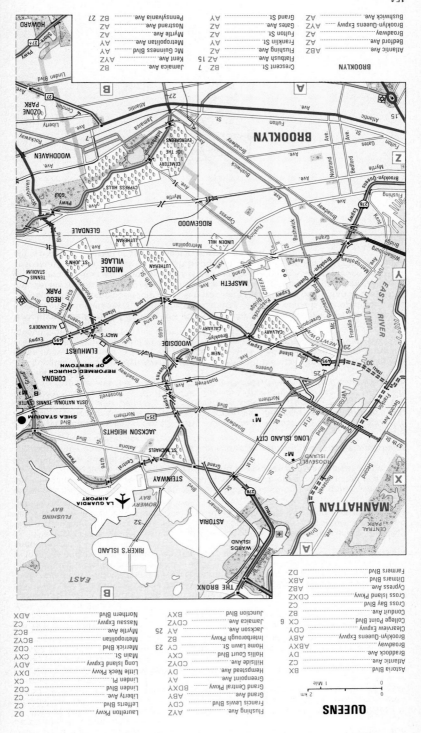

Named after Catherine of Braganza, the wife of Charles II, Queens, the largest borough of New York City, covers an area of 108sq miles. Situated on Long Island, and next door to Brooklyn, it extends from the East River in the north to Jamaica Bay in the south. It is in Queens that two Worlds Fairs took place and that the UN General Assembly met before completion of its permanent headquarters. A cluster of factories in the Long Island City area, where artists have renovated lofts into studio and living space, gives way to more residential sections to the southeast, such as Forest Hills and Jamaica. The borough also has two major airports (John F. Kennedy and La Guardia) and, for sports fans, Aqueduct Race Track (CZ), Shea Stadium (BX) and the U.S.T.A. National Tennis Center (BY).

QUEENS

Laurelton Pkwy	DZ
Lefferts Blvd	CZ
Liberty Ave	CZ
Linden Blvd	CDZ
Linden Pl	CX
Little Neck Pkwy	DXY
Long Island Expwy	ADY
Main St	CXY
Merrick Blvd	CDZ
Metropolitan	BCYZ
Myrtle Ave	BCZ
Nassau Expwy	CZ
Northern Blvd	ADX

Francis Lewis Blvd	CDY
Flushing Ave	AYZ
Grand Ave	ABY
Grand Central Pkwy	BDXY
Greenpoint Ave	AY
Hempstead Ave	DY
Hillside Ave	CDYZ
Hollis Court Blvd	CXY
Home Lawn St	CY 23
Interborough Pkwy	BZ
Jackson Ave	AY 25
Jamaica Ave	CDYZ
Junction Blvd	BXY

Astoria Blvd	BX
Atlantic Ave	CZ
Braddock Ave	DY
Broadway	ABXY
Brooklyn-Queens Expwy	ABY
Clearview Expwy	CDY
College Point Blvd	CX 6
Conduit Ave	BZ
Cross Bay Blvd	CZ
Cross Island Pkwy	CDXZ
Cypress Ave	ABZ
Ditmars Blvd	ABX
Farmers Blvd	DZ

BROOKLYN

Atlantic Ave	ABZ	Flatbush Ave	AZ 15	Crescent St	BZ 7
Bedford Ave	AYZ	Flushing Ave	AYZ	Jamaica Ave	BZ
Broadway	AYZ	Franklin Ave	AY	Kent Ave	AYZ
Brooklyn-Queens Expwy	AYZ	Fulton St	AZ	Mc Guinness Blvd	AY
Bushwick Ave	AZ	Gates Ave	AZ	Metropolitan Ave	AZ
		Grand St	AZ	Myrtle Ave	AZ
				Nostrand Ave	AZ
				Pennsylvania Ave	BZ 27

154

■ **SIGHTS** *Due to the distances between sights, the shortage of public transportation and the infrequency of taxis, it is advisable to visit Queens by car.*

Jamaica Bay Wildlife Refuge (CZ). – *Open 8:30 AM to 5 PM weekends until 6 PM; closed January 1 and December 25. Subway: A train to Broad Channel. From the station take Noel Street to cross Bay Boulevard, and turn right. 8 miles. Visitors Center on the left.*

Adjacent to JFK Airport is a peaceful wildlife refuge, a major migratory haven for birds where a wide variety of waterfowl, land and shore birds can be found. It is now part of Gateway National Recreation Area, one of the nation's largest urban parks.

A self-guided **nature trail★** through the marshes *(distance: 1 3/4 miles, time: 1 1/2 hours)* begins at the Visitor Center. *Permit is required (free at the Visitors Center).*

Parsons Blvd	CX	Whitestone Expwy	CX	
Queens Blvd	ACY	Willets Point Blvd	CX	
Rockaway Blvd	BDZ	Woodhaven Blvd	BCYZ	
Roosevelt Ave	ACY	14 th Ave	CX	
Shore Pkwy	BZ	21 st St	AX	
Southern Pkwy	CDZ	31 st St	AX	
Springfield Blvd	DYZ	46 th Ave	CX	
Sunrise Hway	DZ	63 rd Drive	BY	
Sutphin Blvd	CZ	69 th Rd	BY	
Union Turnpike	CDY	94 th St	BX	
Utopia Pkwy	CXY	161 st St	CZ	
Van Wyck Expwy	CYZ	164 th St	CY	
Vernon Blvd	AXY	212 th St	DY	

MANHATTAN

Franklin D. Roosevelt Drive	AXY
Second Ave	AXY
57 th St	AX

BRIDGES AND TUNNELS

Bronx-Whitestone Bridge	CX	2
Kosciuszko Bridge	AY	
Pulaski Bridge	AY	29
Queensboro Bridge	AXY	
Queens-Midtown Tunnel	AY	30
Rikers Island Bridge	BX	32
Throgs Neck Bridge	CX	33
Triborough Bridge	AX	
Williamsburg Bridge	AY	

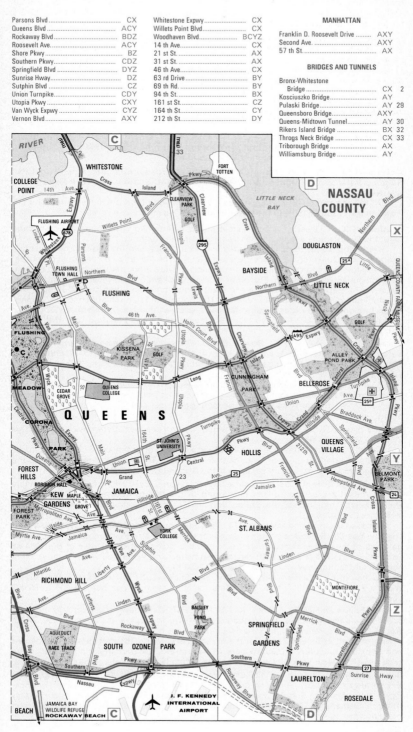

From the trail there are good views to the west of the Manhattan skyline.

Farther south on Cross Bay Boulevard, Beachfront communities dot the 5-mile length of **Rochaway Beach★**. *(Access from A, C and H lines at stations between 25th and 116th Streets)*. On sunny days the wide boardwalk is comfortably populated with strollers enjoying the fine breezes and ocean views.

American Museum of the Moving Image★ (AX M¹). – *35th Ave. and 36th Street in Astoria. Subway R or G lines to Steinway Street, Walk south on Steinway Street, turn right on 35th Ave. Open Tuesday. Friday 12 to 5 PM, Saturday and Sunday 11 AM to 6 PM; $5.00.*

Located on the former site of Astoria Film Studios, this unique museum is devoted to the history, technology and art of film media, encompassing motion pictures, television and video. The core collection ranges from works by video artists Nam June Paik and Red Grooms; costumes, props and memorabilia from the television and film industries; and clips from movies, videos and advertisements. Two theatres present selections from the film collection on a rotating basis.

Isamu Noguchi Garden Museum★ (AX M²). – *32-37 Vernon Blvd. Open Wednesday and Saturday 11 AM - 6 PM, April throug November.* Conflicting and harmonious relationships between nature and the man-made are a recurrent theme in the sculpture of Isamu Noguchi. The Japanese-American artist (1904-1988) whose works include public spaces (Detroit's Hart Plaza), playgrounds (Atlanta's Playscapes), gardens, fountains and theatre sets, designed and installed this museum in his former studio quarters. Several boulder pieces reside in the tranquil walled garden which is interspersed with Japanese black pine trees. A video presentation (50 min) on the artist's life is presented by request on the second floor.

Jamaica Arts Center (CZ E). – *Open 9 AM to 5 PM; closed Sundays, Mondays and major holidays. Subway: E or F train to Parsons Blvd then Q53 or Q54 bus to 161st St.* The center operates as a community cultural center.

Reformed Church of Newtown (BY). – *85-15 Broadway, Elmhurst. Open 1 to 5 PM, Sundays 9 AM to 8 PM; closed Mondays and holidays. Subway: R or G lines to Grand Ave-Newtown.*

In 1731 the church was organized as a congregation of the Dutch Reformed Church. It was entirely rebuilt (1831) in the Greek Revival period.

Flushing (CX). – As early as 1643, a small settlement named Vlissingen was established here; the Dutch name eventually was transformed into Flushing.

Beginning about 1655, local history was associated with the **Quakers,** or Society of Friends. The Quakers, believers in a simple way of life and of religious practices, complete tolerance towards others and pacificism, were often persecuted. John Bowne, an Englishman who settled in Flushing, allowed Quakers to hold meetings in his home. His arrest for permitting the Quakers to meet in his home, and ultimate acquittal helped to establish religious freedom in America. The Society of Friends flourished in Flushing, which has one of the oldest **Friends' Meeting Houses** in America *(on Northern Boulevard near Linden Place)*. At 137-15 Northern Boulevard, is the old Flushing **Town Hall,** a 1862 Romanesque building which has been restored.

Bowne House (CX A). – *37-01 Bowne Street. Guided tours (time: 45 min) Tuesdays, Saturdays, Sundays and holidays 2:30 to 4:30 PM, July/August also Wednesdays & Thursday 11 AM to 3 PM; closed mid-December to mid-January and Easter Sunday; $2.00. Subway: 7 line to Main Street.*

Built in 1661 this house, the oldest in Queens, was lived in by nine successive generations of the Bowne family including John Bowne *(see above)*. There is a collection of 17 and 18C furniture as well as pewter, paintings and documents, all of which belonged to the Bowne family.

Kingsland House (CX D). – *143-35 37th Avenue. Open Tuesdays, Saturdays and Sundays 2:30 to 4:30 PM; $1.00.*

This old, 3-story farmhouse built in 1774 is a mixture of Dutch and English traditions: notice its divided front door and central chimney. The house now serves as the headquarters and local history museum of the Queens Historical Society.

Flushing Meadow Park (BCY). – Once a swamp favored by ducks and then a sanitary landfill, this 1 275-acre park was developed in the 30s to accommodate New York's **World's Fairs.** From 1946-49 the United Nations General Assembly also met here in the New York City Building.

Meadow Lake, 3/4 mile long and 1/4 mile wide, was created for the 1939 World's Fair. The **New York City Building,** also constructed for the 1939 Fair, now contains the spacious galleries of the **Queens Museum** *(see below)* and a skating rink. Vestiges of the 1964-65 Fair include the **Hall of Science** (B) recently renovated and expanded, with its museum of science and technology and the **Unisphere** (C) 140ft high.

To the north of Flushing Meadow Park, **Shea Stadium** (BX) also dates from the 1964-65 World's Fair. Home of the New York Mets baseball team, it can hold 55 000 to 60 000 spectators.

Queens Museum (BY M³). – *Open 10 AM to 5 PM; Saturdays and Sundays noon to 5:30 PM; closed Mondays and January 1, Thanksgiving Day and December 25; $2.00. Subway: 7 line to Willets Point-Shea Stadium.*

Conceived as an arts center for the borough of Queens, the museum was renovated and its exhibition space expanded for temporary shows. On permanent display is a huge **scale model★** of New York City which presents a detailed panorama of the five boroughs.

Queens County Farm Museum – *73-50 Little Neck Parkway in Floral Park. Take Long Island Expressway to exit 32. South on Little Neck Parkway 10 blocks to museum entrance. Open Saturday and Sunday noon to 5 PM year round, Thursday noon to 5 PM May through September.* This 47-acre tract of nature-bound walkways, fields and farm buildings provides a refreshing change from the charms of the city.

The 18C Flemish-style farmhouse (currently under restoration) retains much of its original material and visits to the greenhouses, barns, sheds and petting zoo provides visitors, especially children, with an informative glimpse of Queens County's agrarian origins.

John F. Kennedy International Airport (CZ). – One of the busiest airports in the world, Kennedy International Airport covers 4 900 acres in the southeast corner of Queens, along Jamaica Bay, an area the size of Manhattan Island from Midtown to the Battery. Construction, begun in 1942, was placed under the jurisdiction of the Port Authority of New York and New Jersey in 1947. Opened as Idlewild Airport a year later, the airport was renamed in 1963 to honor the late President. The Kennedy air cargo center, the busiest in the world, handles approximately 40 % of all the nation's air imports and exports. *To visit JFK see To and From the Airports p 14.*

International Arrivals Building. – An arched pavilion forms the center of this 2 000ft long building, designed by Skidmore, Owings & Merrill, which houses the arrival hall and in its wings a number of airline terminals.

From the observation platform there is an overall **view** of the airport. Next to the building rises the 11-story control tower.

TWA International Terminal★. – Reminiscent of a huge bird with outspread wings, this contemporary structure is a masterpiece of the architect Eero Saarinen. The main building is composed of four vaults which intersect and rest only on four points.

La Guardia Airport (BX). – Close to Manhattan *(8 miles from 42nd Street)*, this major airport bordering on Flushing and Bowery Bays was established in 1939 and named after the city's mayor, **Fiorello H. La Guardia.** Mayor La Guardia, affectionately known as "The Little Flower" was himself a pilot and recognized the importance of air travel to New York. He served as mayor of the city from 1934-45.

Despite its relatively small size, which is 1/9 of Kennedy, La Guardia is capable of handling the bulk of the region's domestic flights.

STATEN ISLAND
(Richmond)

The fifth borough of New York City, Staten Island is still relatively rural with the exception of St George, the administrative and business center of the island. Its country air so close to Manhattan is often a surprise to visitors.

Most of the island is flat, although it boasts the highest point on the Atlantic coast south of Maine, Todt Hill (410ft above sea level). Formed by the terminal moraine of a Quaternary glacier, it is about 14 miles long and 8 miles wide. Large sandy beaches run along the southeastern shore. Still fairly uncrowded, the best known is South Beach; and the Gateway National Recreation Area includes Great Kills Park and Miller Field.

Named after the Dutch States General, Staten Island acquired its alternate name in honor of the Duke of Richmond, son of Charles II. The population is 374 600 and includes many Italians, as well as the descendants of some old families who have lived there since the 18C.

Visit. – Even if you do not have time to visit the island, you should take a trip on the Staten Island Ferry. For 50¢ round trip you will have a windy voyage, skirting the Statue of Liberty and enjoying magnificent **views**★★★ of Manhattan and the Bay. The ferry runs night and day (22.6 million passengers and 338 000 vehicles in 1988).

It is interesting to recall that this ferry was the start of "Commodore" Vanderbilt's fortune *(pp 82 and 87)*.

If you are traveling by car, we suggest that you drive out to Staten Island across the Verrazano-Narrows Bridge *(p 150)* and return to Manhattan by the ferry.

■ SIGHTS

To visit the sights described below, you may take buses m St George or, in some cases, the Staten Island Rapid Transit *(see map p 158)*.

St George (BY). – A small town facing Lower Manhattan across the bay, St George extends quite far inland, surrounded by attractive suburban homes and gardens. It was just off St George that quarantine was imposed on ships arriving from overseas in the 1850s. St George has been the administrative seat of the county and borough government since 1920.

Staten Island Institute of Arts and Sciences (BY M). – *Open 9 AM (1 PM Sundays) to 5 PM; closed Mondays, January 1, Memorial Day, July 4, Labor Day, Thanksgiving Day and December 25.*

Founded in 1881, the institute occupies a building at Stuyvesant Place and Wall Street. Interesting exhibits illustrating the history, geology, flora and fauna of the island as well as frequent shows of painting, sculpture, graphics, furniture and photography. The museum is scheduled to move to Snug Harbor *(see below)* in 1991.

Snug Harbor Cultural Center (BY B). – *1000 Richmond Terrace. Open daily dawn to dusk. For program information ℱ (718) 448-2500.*

Take the **Snug Harbor Trolley** from the St George Ferry *(departs every 1/2 hour from 1 PM, last trip at 5 PM; $1.00, children free with parent)* for a visit to the fast-growing cultural complex that was once a residence for aged seamen. Founded in 1833 as the first maritime hospital and retired sailors' home in the U.S., the 80-acre park and its 28 buildings are being restored and converted to a center for the visual and performing arts. Among the architectural treasures are a row of Greek Revival buildings overlooking the Kill van Kull. Concerts, art shows and special events are held year round at Snug Harbor which also is home to several arts organizations, the Staten Island Botanical Garden and the Staten Island Children's Museum.

Staten Island Children's Museum. – *Open during the school year from 1 PM to 5 PM, Wednesdays through Fridays, 11 AM to 5 PM Saturdays and Sundays and most school holidays; during the summer from 11 AM to 5 AM; Tuesdays through Sundays; closed Mondays; $2.00; ℱ (718) 273-2060.*

Interactive exhibits, performances, creative workshops and field trips encourage children to learn by doing. Most activities are designed for children between the ages of 5 and 12.

Staten Island Zoo (BY). – *Open 10 AM to 4:45 PM; closed January 1, Thanksgiving Day and December 25; $1.00.*

Located in Barrett Park, this small zoo is not lacking in interest. It was opened in 1936 and possesses a collection of snakes and reptiles which enjoys a fine reputation, rivaling that of the Bronx Zoo in this field. There is also a Children's Center.

Jacques Marchais Center of Tibetan Art★ (BZ E). – *338 Lighthouse Avenue. Open April through November, Wednesdays through Sundays 1 to 5 PM; December through March by appointment ℱ (718) 987-3500; $2.50.*

Laid out on Lighthouse Hill in enchanting terraced gardens, the center displays a collection of art covering the culture, religion and mythology of Tibet, China and India. A highlight of the museum is the large Tibetan thangka, or scroll painting, depicting the Green Tara, goddess of universal compassion. The thangka which was painted in the 17C has been painstakingly restored by Tibetan artist Pema Wangyal using only traditional techniques and materials.

High Rock Park Conservation Center (BY F). – *Open 9 AM to 5 PM; closed December 25. Guided Walks (time: 1 hour) Saturdays and Sundays 2 PM.*

This forest at the end of Nevada Avenue is being preserved in its natural state. A varied topography and wide range of flora and fauna make the place an attractive spot for hiking. The center provides a self-guided tour and conducts special environmental educational programs, workshops and holds a variety of cultural programs.

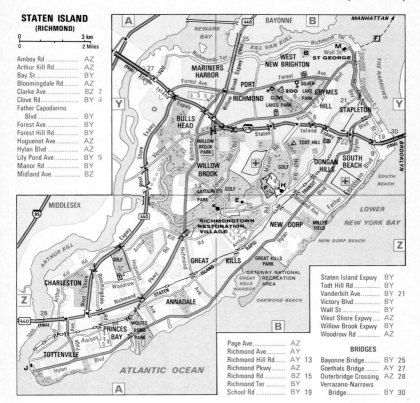

STATEN ISLAND
(RICHMOND)

0 _____ 3 km
0 _____ 2 Miles

Amboy Rd	AZ
Arthur Kill Rd	AZ
Bay St	BY
Bloomingdale Rd	AZ
Clarke Ave	BZ 2
Clove Rd	BY 6
Father Capodanno Blvd	BY
Forest Ave	BY
Forest Hill Rd	BY
Huguenot Ave	AZ
Hylan Blvd	AZ
Lily Pond Ave	BY 9
Manor Rd	BY
Midland Ave	BZ

Staten Island Expwy	BY	
Todt Hill Rd	BY	
Vanderbilt Ave	BY	21
Victory Blvd	BY	
Wall St	BY	
West Shore Expwy	AZ	
Willow Brook Expwy	BY	
Woodrow Rd	AZ	

Page Ave	AZ	
Richmond Ave	AY	
Richmond Hill Rd	AY	13
Richmond Pkwy	AZ	
Richmond Rd	BZ	15
Richmond Ter	BY	
School Rd	BY	19

BRIDGES

Bayonne Bridge	BY	25
Goethals Bridge	AY	27
Outerbridge Crossing	AZ	28
Verrazano-Narrows Bridge	BY	30

Richmondtown Restoration Village ★ (BZ). – _441 Clarke Avenue. From Richmond Road turn on St Patrick's Place, then right on Clarke Avenue. Open 10 AM (1 PM Saturdays, Sundays and Monday holidays) to 5 PM, closed January 1, Thanksgiving Day and December 25; $4.00, children $2.50. Tickets may be purchased at the Visitor Orientation Center in the Third County Court House._

Located in Richmondtown, one of the earliest settlements on Staten Island and the island's geographic center, the village traces the evolution of community life in Richmondtown from the 17 to 19C through the buildings, furniture, gardens and implements on display from different periods.

Of the 29 structures: private dwellings, craft shops, a schoolhouse and municipal buildings, have been restored and are open to the public. Staff members, dressed in costumes of the period reenact everyday chores and artisans demonstrate the crafts of yesteryear.

Visitor orientation Center. – The imposing Greek Revival structure which contains the center, was the **Third County Court House** (1837) to be built between the 18 and early 20C when Richmondtown was the seat of county government.

Staten Island Historical Society Museum. – Some parts of the attractive red brick building date back to the middle of the 19C when it served as the office of the county clerk and the Surrogates Court. Exhibits and documents relate the history of the island: costumes, ceramics, craftsmen's tools and a reconstructed old store.

Stephens-Black House. – Facing the Visitors Center, this building was the residence of the Stephen D. Stephens family who operated the adjoining general store until 1870. Today the house is decorated with furnishings of the mid-19C and the store is stocked with goods that would have been sold around the time of the War between the States.

The **Print Shop** and the **Tinsmith Shop** _(located on either side of the Stephens-Black House)_ are original structures that were moved to this site in the 1960s. They are furnished to represent shops of their trades and offer demonstrations of the crafts of printing and tinwork.

Bennett House. – The dolls, games and toys on exhibit on the upper floors of this residence are nostalgic reminders of the joys of childhood in days gone by. The cellar which once was a bakery now serves as the Restoration's snack bar.

Guyon-Lake-Tysen House. – The Dutch Colonial farmhouse across Richmond Road was built in the mid-18C and the interior furnishings are exemplary of the period. Domestic skills as spinning and weaving are demonstrated.

Treasure House. – A tannery was established here at the beginning of the 18C. A century later, a surprised new owner discovered $7 000 in gold hidden in a wall _(closed: restoration in progress)._

Voorlezer House. – Built at the end of the 17C, this building served a church and schoolhouse (the oldest known schoolhouse in America), as well as a residence for the church clerk _(voorlezer)._

STATEN ISLAND (Richmond)

Church of St Andrew. – Founded in 1713, this church was rebuilt twice: the present edifice is Romanesque Revival. Although not a part of the Restoration, the church is closely related to the latter by is history and proximity to the village.

Moravian Cemetery (BY H). – This peaceful, garden-like cemetery is affiliated with a Moravian church. The denomination, founded in the 15C as an evangelical communion in Bohemia (Moravia), accepted Protestantism in the 17C. Ascetic in the early years, their main precept was strict observance of the teachings of the Holy Bible.

The white church at the entrance, with its columned portico, was constructed in 1845 by the Vanderbilt family, one of whose ancestors belonged to the sect in the 17C. The original church, a Dutch colonial style structure erected in 1763, now serves as the cemetery office.

Conference House (AZ J). – *Guided tours (time: 1/2 hr) 1 to 4 PM; closed Mondays Tuesdays, Thanksgiving Day, December 15 through; $1.00.*

Situated at the southwestern tip of Staten Island, Conference House is named after the negotiations between the British and Americans, including John Adams and Benjamin Franklin, which took place here in September 1776 after the Battle of Long Island.

The 17C fieldstone manor house has been restored. The interior, furnished with 18C pieces, also displays remembrances of Benjamin Franklin.

From its beautiful waterfront vantage point, there are views across the river and the bay to New Jersey.

BEYOND THE CITY LIMITS

The fame of New York City has somewhat obscured the attractions of its outskirts. Nevertheless, not even the passing tourist should neglect the charms of the country air, hills and forests, islands and beaches, forts and historic mansions which abound in this region. New Yorkers are aware of these advantages, as may be seen from the estates as well as the more modest suburban homes on Long Island and in Westchester.

Suburban and even exurban, this area is also extremely well equipped for vacationers, with its extensive network of roads and parkways, and its hotels and motels complete with swimming pools and other recreational facilities which make it ideal for weekends or vacations; opportunities abound for tennis, golf, boating and sailing, horseback riding (from foxhunting to dude ranches), fishing, skiing and fresh- and salt-water swimming. About one-third of the people who work in Manhattan live in the suburbs.

Since this guide is devoted essentially to New York City, we shall describe only three basic excursion trips which provide a pleasant change from the hustle and bustle of Manhattan. There are many other possibilities for trips further afield: Niagara Falls, the Catskills or the Adirondacks, Albany and Saratoga in New York State; Tanglewood and Old Sturbridge Village in Massachusetts, or New Haven and Old Mystic Seaport in Connecticut among others (see the Michelin Green Guide to New England).

■ THE HUDSON RIVER VALLEY★★★

The majestic Hudson, which leads the way toward the Saint Lawrence and the Great Lakes, flows between rocky crags and wooded peaks, a romantic and even grandiose setting. The river has often been celebrated in literature and art, especially by the painters of the Hudson River School, whose best known representatives were Cole and Kensett.

Originating high in the Adirondacks, the Hudson flows 315 miles to the sea. Navigable as far as Albany, it is linked to the Great Lakes by the **Erie Canal**, once a busy waterway between Albany and Buffalo.

A THREE DAY EXCURSION

(175 miles round trip)

This trip covers only the southern part of the Hudson. It is at its best in the fall, when Indian summer gilds the forests along its banks. If you have only one day available, we recommend that you drive north on the east bank in the morning and return on the west bank in the afternoon, to avoid having the sun in your eyes.

Note: from Memorial Day to mid-September, you may take a boat trip up the Hudson from New York City, which is highly recommended. Call the Hudson River Day Line (Pier 81, West 41st Street) at 279-5151 for information.

Towns and Sights

Our description covers the main sights following the itinerary shown on the adjoining map. U.S. Route 9, going north, and U.S. Route 9W, for the return, afford frequent glimpses and occasionally sweeping views, of the river.

THE HUDSON RIVER VALLEY

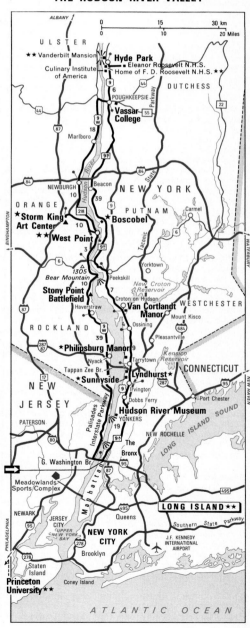

BEYOND THE CITY LIMITS

Leave Manhattan via the Henry Hudson Parkway, which leads into the Saw Mill River Parkway (local map p 23). Exit Executive Blvd., to its end at North Broadway; turn left, then right on Odell Avenue, then left on Warburton Avenue for 1.3 miles. After Yonkers, exit from the Saw Mill River Parkway at Ashford Ave – Dobbs Ferry. Follow Ashford Avenue west, then turn right on Broadway (Route 9). Beyond Irvington, a road to the left, West Sunnyside Lane, winds along a valley to Sunnyside, on the banks of the Hudson.

Hudson River Museum. – *511 Warburton Avenue, Yonkers. Open Wednesday, Friday, Saturday 10 AM to 5 PM; Thursday 10 AM to 9 PM; Sunday noon to 5 PM; $2.00, Planetarium $3.00.* This stone mansion on the banks of the Hudson was built for local financier John Trevor in 1876. Late Victorian in style, the house features Eastlake interiors and four rooms have been restored to depict the lifestyle of an upperclass 19C family.

A modern wing, added in 1969, presents changing exhibitions of art, architecture, and memorabilia of the Hudson River Valley. In the **Andrus Plantetarium,** star shows are presented using the museum's Zeiss M015 star machine.

Sunnyside★. – *Guided tours (time: 1 1/2 hours) 10 AM to 5 PM (4 PM last tour); closed weekdays January through March, January 1, Thanksgiving Day and December 25; $5.00, children $3.00. "Passport" for all sites entitles holder to 20% discount on admission fees to all sites.*

Sunnyside was the home of the author-humorist and scholar **Washington Irving** (1783-1859), who lived here for many of the last 25 years of his life. Irving transformed the original stone cottage which he had bought in 1835 into his "snuggery" with a mixture of architectural styles. Sunnyside lies along the east bank of the Hudson River and its 20 acres have been landscaped in the natural style, 19C. The museum includes furniture and memorabilia of the author of *Diedrich Knickerbocker's History of New York* and the chronicler of Rip van Winkle and Sleepy Hollow *(p 33).*

Lyndhurst★. – *Route 9 in Tarrytown, 1/2 mile north of Sunnyside. Open May through October and December, 10 AM to 5 PM (last tour 4:15 PM), closed Mondays (except Monday holidays); the rest of the year Saturdays and Sundays only; $5.00. Admission includes guided tour (time: 45 min) of the mansion.*

Perched on a wooded bluff above the Hudson River is the picturesque silhouette of Lyndhurst, resembling from the distance a baronial castle on the Rhine. Originally a 2-story villa designed in 1838 by Alexander Jackson Davis for William Paulding, a former mayor of New York City, the house was later (1864-65) enlarged by Davis for the subsequent owner, George Merritt.

In 1880 the 67-acre estate and its mansion were acquired by the financier and railroad tycoon, Jay Gould. Lyndhurst remained in the Gould family until the death of his daughter, the Duchess of Talleyrand-Périgord, in 1961.

The house is an outstanding expression of the Gothic Revival style applied to domestic architecture. A syncopated array of peaks, pinnacles, porches and turrets embellish the exterior, accenting its irregular shape. Inside, the Gothic mood dominates: ribbed and vaulted ceilings, pointed arches, stained glass windows, and heavy Gothic furnishings.

In the dining room, the simulated marble colonnettes and leather wall coverings are interesting examples of this craft which was popular in the 19C. Many other examples of marbleization and simulated masonry will be found throughout the house.

Philipsburg Manor★. – *On Route 9. Guided tours (time: 1 1/2 hours); same hours and admission as at Sunnyside.*

Philipsburg Manor appears as it did in the early 1700s when it was an important gristmill trading site along the Hudson River.

It now has an operational water-powered gristmill and its stone manor house, begun in the 1680s by Frederick Philipse I, is outfitted with period furnishings. Philipsburg also has a 200ft long oak dam and a large mid-18C barn.

Continue north on U.S. 9, passing through Ossining, site of the Ossining Correctional Facility formerly known as Sing Sing prison. Take the Croton Point Avenue exit. Turn right, then right again on South Riverside Avenue.

Van Cortlandt Manor. – *Guided tours (time: 1 1/2 hours); same hours and admission as at Sunnyside.*

The manor house was home to the Van Cortlandt family for 260 years and now appears as it did during the Revolutionary War period. Its owner then was Pierre van Cortlandt, patriot and the first lieutenant governor of New York State, who presided over 86 000 acres. Benjamin Franklin, the Marquis de Lafayette, Comte de Rochambeau and John Jay are all said to have visited the manor.

The house contains original family furniture, paintings and pewter. The Ferry House, Ferry House kitchen, fields and gardens recall 18C Hudson Valley life.

Continue on Route 9 North to Peekskill then bear left onto Route 6/202 West and at Bear Mountain Bridge follow Route 9D North. This drive offers beautiful views of the river and the New Jersey Palisades as the road descends into the valley and then rises.

Boscobel★. – *Route 9D, 4 miles north of the jct with Route 403. Guided tours (time: 50 min) 10 AM to 5 PM (4 PM November, December and March); closed Tuesdays and January, February, Thanksgiving Day and December 25. $5.00. Last tour 1/2 hour before closing.*

Set back from the road and overlooking the Hudson River is Boscobel, a handsome example of Federal domestic architecture begun by States Morris Dyckman (1755-1806) in 1804 and completed after his death by his wife, Elizabeth.

In the 1950s the property on which Boscobel originally stood was sold and the mansion was almost destroyed. Preservationists acquired the building and moved it piece by piece to Garrison. There, it was reconstructed on park-like grounds similar to its earlier setting, high above the Hudson and with sweeping views to the southwest. Rebuilt and refurbished, Boscobel opened to the public in 1961.

Outside and in, all is elegant and refined. The recessed central portion of the facade, with its slender columns and carved trim, adds a lightness to the solid-looking exterior.

Inside, there are graceful arches, fireplaces adorned with classical motifs, delicately carved woodwork, and a freestanding central staircase lit by a tall Palladian window. Furnishings are of the Federal period and include Dyckman family possessions; note the sideboards - a popular Federal piece - in the dining room.

Follow Route 9D North into Route 9 North.

We now reach Poughkeepsie, seat of Vassar College. From Route 9 head east on Route 44/55 then turn right onto Raymond Avenue (Route 376).

Vassar College. – Vassar is one of the best-known private liberal arts colleges in the United States. Founded as a women's college in 1861, it became coeducational in 1969 and now has 2 250 students of which 44 % are men. The buildings reflect American and European style traditions well over 100 years old, as well as modern trends in architecture: notice Marcel Breuer's Ferry House (1951), and Noyes House (1958) designed by Eero Saarinen, both dormitories. The library, expanded in 1976, houses 650 000 volumes.

6 miles north of Poughkeepsie, Hyde Park is also on Route 9. Before entering the village of Hyde Park note, on the left, the campus of **The Culinary Institute of America,** an educational institution which prepares men and women for careers in food service industries. It is possible to dine in the student staffed restaurants with reservations $\overline{f}^o$ (914) 471-6608.

Hyde Park. – Once a resort for wealthy New York families, and then for a time an occasional summer White House, Hyde Park has remained a rather quiet village.

Home of Franklin D. Roosevelt National Historic Site★★. – *Open 9 AM to 5 PM; closed Tuesdays and Wednesdays November through March, and January 1, Thanksgiving Day and December 25; $3.50 (combination ticket with the library and museum), children under 16 free.*

National Historic Site and last resting place of Franklin D. Roosevelt, the estate was acquired by the president's father in 1867; FDR. was born here in 1882. The house dates back to 1826 but was later remodeled and enlarged. Recently the house was extensively refurbished following severe fire damage in the early 1980s.

Memorabilia of the late president and his family will be found in the house, library and museum. Museum exhibits trace the life and career of Franklin Delano Roosevelt and his wife Eleanor, a prominent international figure in her own right.

In the rose garden is the simple slab of white Vermont marble which marks the final resting place of Franklin and Eleanor Roosevelt.

Eleanor Roosevelt National Historic Site. – *Rte 9G. Open 9 AM to 5 PM May through October; 10 AM to 4 PM weekends only in November, December, March and April. Closed January, February, Thanksgiving and December 25. A 20 min film on the life of Eleanor Roosevelt is shown in the playhouse where a guided tour of the grounds begins.*

This tranquil natural setting on the Fall Kill was a place the Roosevelts often came on family outings and picnics. A stone cottage was built on the property in 1925 and a year later a second structure, a factory workshop, was erected to house an experimental business operated by Eleanor Roosevelt (1884-1962) and her friends. It was this building which, after the business folded in the mid-1930s, was remodeled and eventually became Eleanor's beloved Val-Kill cottage, named for the stream which flowed close by.

Val-Kill was the only place the former First Lady ever considered truly to be her own home and after the president's death, it was there she chose to spend her remaining years working, entertaining her friends and receiving foreign dignitaries.

Vanderbilt Mansion★★. – *Guided tours April through October (time: 45 min) 9 AM to 6 PM, the rest of the year Thursdays through Mondays only 9 AM to 5 PM; closed January 1, Thanksgiving Day and December 25; $3.50.*

Just to the north of Hyde Park *(2 miles)*, McKim, Mead and White build this sumptuous Beaux-Arts style residence between 1896 and 1898 for Frederick W. Vanderbilt and his white, Louise. Now a National Historic Site, it bears witness to a bygone age of opulence. Before the Vanderbilts bought the property in the early 19C, it belonged to Dr. Hosack *(p 35)*. The interior contains a collection of furniture of 16-18C design and works of art.

There are walking trails along the river, below the mansion, which afford scenic **views** to the north and the south.

Return to Poughkeepsie and cross the Hudson, take 9W then Route 218 south.

Storm King Art Center★. – *Take Rte 9W to the Cornwall Hospital Exit, then bear left onto Rte 107; at the intersection turn right and follow Rte 32 North over the bridge, turning left immediately after the bridge onto Orr's Mill Road. Sculpture Park open April through November noon to 5:30 PM; indoor exhibits late May through October same hours, $3.00.*

This unique outdoor museum of contemporary sculpture covers 200 acres of meadow, hillsides, forest, lawns and terraces. Large-scale works by important artists: Alexander Calder *(The Arch)*, Mark di Suvero, Alexander Liberman *(Iliad)*, Henry Moore, Louise Nevelson, Isamu Noguchi *(Momo Taro)*, David Smith, are installed on the grounds, most in settings which have been specially landscaped for the sculpture. Changing exhibits of paintings, graphics and smaller sculptures from the center's collection are presented in the French Normandy-style museum building (1935), formerly a private residence on the property.

West Point★★. – Renowned as the site of the United States Military AcadLemy, West Point overlooks the Hudson River.

The Military Tradition. – Already serving as a military outpost dominating the Hudson in the 18C, West Point was used during the late 1700s as a training school for artillerists and engineers, under the tenure of General Henry Knox as Secretary of War.

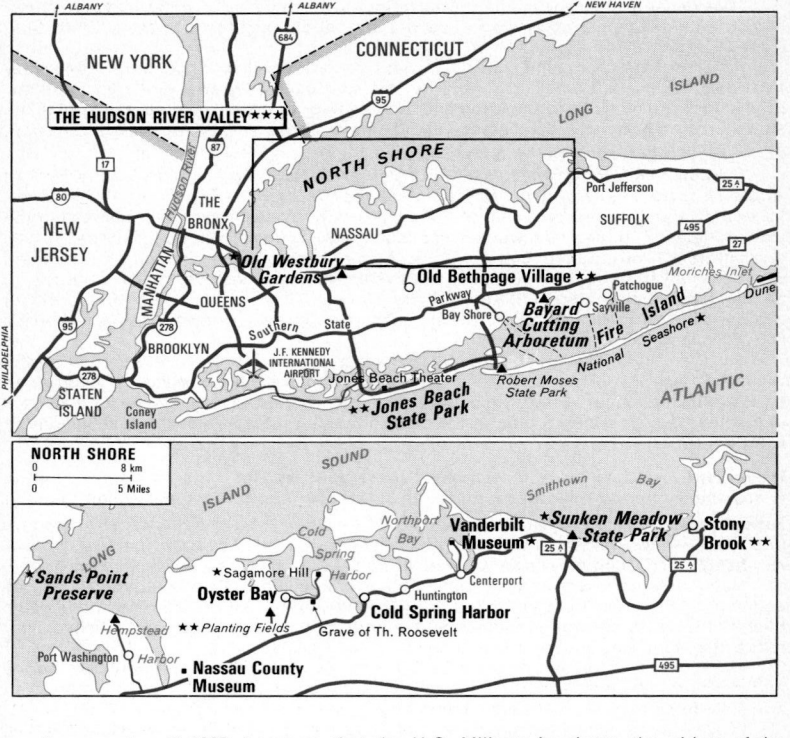

It was not until 1802, however, that the U.S. Military Academy, the oldest of the nation's service academies, was established by Congress, with West Point selected as its site.

In the Academy's first year 5 officers trained and instructed the 10 students; there are now more than 4 400 men and women cadets. Among its graduates are Generals MacArthur (1903), Patton (1909) and Eisenhower (1915) as well as astronauts Borman (1950), Aldrin (1951), Collins and White (1952) and Scott (1954).

Visitors Information Center. – *Open 9 AM to 4:45 PM; closed January 1, Thanksgiving Day and December 25. Guided tours Mondays through Saturdays 9:00 AM to 3:30 PM, Sundays 11:30 AM to 3:30 PM; tour leaves every 20 min, $3.00, children under 11, $2.00.*
Films and exhibits introduce visitors to the history and sights of West Point and the life of a cadet.

The Buildings. – The chapels, monuments and museum are open to the public . Of particular interest are the **museum** *(open 10:30 AM to 4:15 PM; closed January 1 and December 25)*, housed in a wing of the former indoor riding ring, Thayer Hall: among the exhibits are Napoleon's sword and Goering's marshal's jewel-encrusted baton, and a collection of arms which traces the development of automatic weapons from the Civil War to the present; the **Cadet Chapel** *(open 9 AM to 4 PM)*, an example of the "military Gothic" style, built in 1910; 18C **Fort Putnam** *(open 10:30 AM to 4 PM May through Octobrer, closed Tuesdays and Wednesdays)*, partially restored in 1907 with further restoration in 1976; the Battle Monument, in memory of the Civil War dead; and Trophy Point. Among the Revolutionary War relics at Trophy Point are links of the great chain, which was strung across the Hudson River to prevent British ships from navigating it.

The Parades. – From early September until November, and mid-March through May, the famous reviews are held; they are known for their precision of movement and the particular stance of the cadets. *For schedules ℡ (914) 938-2638 or 938-5261.*

Continuing south on Rte 9W, you will pass **Bear Mountain**, the highest point (1 305ft) in Palisades Interstate Park. There are many recreational facilities.

Stony Point Battlefield. – *Park Road, off of Route 9W. Open early May to late October 8:30 AM to 5 PM; closed Mondays Tuesdays.*

This marks the site of a former British fortified position, when they controlled Kings Ferry on the Hudson, vital in the American east-west line of communication. Stony Point was stormed by General Wayne's troops in July 1779. Signs indicate where the fiercest fighting – often hand to hand – took place. The battlefield area is now a state park with a **museum** *(open 9 AM to 4:30 PM closed Mondays and Tuesdays),* and picnic places and affords a view over the Hudson. A celebration of the battle is held in mid-July with simulations of 18C battle strategies.

Drive south on **Palisades Interstate Parkway,** high above the Hudson – superb **views**★★ of Yonkers, the Bronx and Manhattan – to the George Washington Bridge and Manhattan.

■ LONG ISLAND★★ *time: 2 days*

Long Island, covering an area of 1 723sq miles, has a population of approximately 6 878 300 and measures 125 miles long and 20 miles at its widest point. Although Long Island is often misleadingly said to include only Nassau and Suffolk counties, it actually comprises 4 counties, the other two being Queens (Queens County) and Brooklyn (Kings County), boroughs of New York City.

The western part of the island has developed into a suburban area due to its proximity to the city, whereas the eastern part is more rural. The North Shore because of its wealthy landowners from the city who built residences here attracted by the calm and natural beauty, became known as the "Gold Coast;" whereas the South Shore with its miles of white sandy beaches, developed into a vacation spot for New Yorkers. The attractions are considerable: small quiet lanes, a countryside flecked with golf courses and tennis courts, walks in one of the many wildlife refuges, a visit to a palatial "Gold Coast" mansion or the rustic charm of a small village.

The economy is quite diversified, encompassing light manufacturing, service industries and agriculture. Suffolk County is the largest producer of agricultural products in the state of New York, and a number of farms are engaged in truck farming (fruits and vegetables), and dairy and livestock farming. Ducklings and potatoes are noted area products. Wineries out east produce Long Island wines from grapes grown in vineyards covering hundreds of acres on the North and South Forks.

Seafood is particularly abundant on the eastern end of the Island: oysters, clams, scallops and lobsters have a well-deserved reputation. Commercial and chartered deep-sea fishing boats leave daily from South Shore communities and Montauk Point.

EXCURSIONS

North Shore

The North Shore faces Long Island Sound – there are rocky necks and beaches, thick woodlands, hilly coves, bays, inlets and steep bluffs; the northern peninsula extends 25 miles culminating at Orient Point.

Stony Brook★★. – A typical Federal style village of 18 and 19C America, Stony Brook shelters a number of reconstructed buildings in a charming rural setting. Situated within this idyllic hamlet since the 30s is **The Museums at Stony Brook,** a complex that now comprises a history museum, an art museum, a carriage museum and several period buildings (i.e. blacksmith shop, schoolhouse and barn) and a museum store.
Museums are open 10 AM (noon Sundays) to 5 PM; closed Mondays (except Monday holidays), Tuesdays and January 1, Thanksgiving Day and December 25; $4.00.

Carriage Museum★★. – This museum exhibits an exceptional collection of horse-drawn carriages presented in thematic displays which relate the impact of personal tranportation on American life. The collection includes sporting rigs, pleasure vehicles, farm and trade wagons, sleighs, children's vehicles, coaches, fire fighting equipment, an elaborately decorated omnibus and a Gypsy wagon.

Art Museum. – **The works**★ (paintings, drawings) of **William Sidney Mount** (1807-68) and other 19C artists, are presented in changing exhibits. Mount settled at Stony Brook where he painted anecdotal records of his rural surroundings. *Farmer Whetting his Scythe, Dancing on the Barn Floor,* and *The Banjo Players* are the best-known of these which are owned by the museum and may be on display.

History Museum. – Featured are permanent displays of antique decoys and **miniature period rooms,** and temporary exhibitions drawn from the museums collections.

Sunken Meadow State Park★. – Sunken Meadow is a large beach with fine sand, bordering a bay on Long Island Sound which is almost always calm. The park offers a wide range of recreational facilities.

Sands Point Preserve ★. – *95 Middleneck Road, Port Washington. Open mid-April to mid-November 10 AM to 5 PM; closed Thursdays, Fridays, Election Day and Veteran's Day; parking $2.00. Guided tours (time: 1 hour) of Falaise, $2.00; tickets may be purchased at the Visitor Center in Castlegould, the stone turreted building adjacent to the parking area.*

Set in this 226-acre park and preserve, one of the last remaining estates of the "Gold Coast," is **Falaise**★, the Normandy style manor house (1923), home of the late Captain Harry F. Guggenheim. A courtyard leads to the manor house with an arcaded loggia overlooking the Sound. Inside is a collection of 16 and 17C French and Spanish artifacts.

Vanderbilt Museum★. – *Little Neck Road, Centerport. Access to buildings by guided tours only (time: 1 hour) Purchase tickets in reception center down the hill from the parking lot. 10 AM to 4 PM; Sundays and holidays noon to 5 PM; closed Mondays (except Monday holidays); $4.00.*

This museum is the former country estate of William K. Vanderbilt Jr., great-grandson of "Commodore" Cornelius *(pp 82 and 87)*, and is set on a 43-acre site overlooking Northport Harbor.

The collections gathered by William during his travels include ship models, arms and weaponry, birds and artifacts, many of which are on display in the **marine museum.** The Vanderbilt Natural History Collections are on view in the house's Habitat wing. Also on the grounds is the **Vanderbilt Planetarium** which presents a variety of shows. *The Planetarium offers astronomy sky shows throughout the year. For programs and schedule ☎ (516) 262-7876; $4.00, children under 12, $2.00.*

Cold Spring Harbor. – From 1836-62 the Cold Spring Harbor whaling fleet of nine ships sailed to every ocean navigable in search of whale oil and bone. The masters of these vessels were from established whaling centers such as New Bedford and Sag Harbor.

The Whaling Museum★. – *Open 11 AM to 5 PM; closed Mondays September through May, and January 1, Thanksgiving Day and December 25; $2.00.*

The most outstanding exhibit is the fully equipped whaleboat, looking just as it did aboard the whaling brig *Daisy* on her 1912-13 voyage out of New Bedford; nearby is the diorama of Cold Spring Harbor – representing in detail: village houses, whaling company buildings, wharves – as it was in the 1840s, the zenith of the whaling period.

Dispersed throughout the museum are examples of whalecraft: harpoons, navigational instruments, whaleship models, old prints and maps. Note especially the extensive collection of scrimshaw demonstrating practically every form of the whaleman's folk art.

Nassau County Museum of Fine Art. – *In Roslyn Harbor. From Route 25A East, after crossing the Roslyn Viaduct turn left on Museum Drive. Open 11 AM to 5 PM, Tuesdays through Sundays; closed Mondays and holidays.*

The museum is headquartered on the grounds of a turn-of-the-century estate built for Lloyd Bryce, the Paymaster General of New York, and acquired in 1919 by Childs Frick, the son of Henry Clay Frick *(p 72)*. Changing art exhibitions covering all periods are held indoors in a brick neo-Georgian mansion, formerly the main house, which has been restored as gallery space. The attractively landscaped lawns, ponds and gardens are an ideal outdoor setting for the museum's sculpture shows.

Programs of dance, concerts, lectures, etc. are also offered.

Oyster Bay. – Vacation spot, port for pleasure craft and suburban residential town, Oyster Bay has nearly 7 000 inhabitants. In Young's Cemetery you will find the **grave of Theodore Roosevelt** *(p 118)*.

Planting Fields ★★. – *Planting Fields Road, Oyster Bay. Open 9 AM to 5 PM (greenhouses close at 4:30 PM); closed December 25; $3.00 per car (off-season no admission fee during the week). Guided tours (1 hour) of Coe Hall April through September 1:30 to 3:30 PM; $1.50.*

Formerly the private estate of William Robertson Coe, a financier, the Planting Fields Arboretum comprises 409 acres of planting fields. One hundred sixty acres have been developed as an arboretum and the remainder have been kept as a natural habitat.

The plant collections include over 600 rhododendrons and azalea species *(blooming period: mid-April through May)*, the camelia collection - the oldest and largest of its kind under glass *(blooming period: February, March)*, the Synoptic Garden, approximately 5 acres of selected ornamental shrubs for Long Island gardens; and greenhouses filled with orchids, hibiscus, begonias, cacti, etc. Amidst these landscaped gardens and spacious lawns stands Coe Hall, a fine example of Elizabethan architecture.

Sagamore Hill National Historic Site★. – *Cove Neck Road. Open 9:30 AM to 5 PM; closed January 1, Thanksgiving Day and December 25; $1.00.*

Located east of the village of Oyster Bay, the Theodore Roosevelt Home is maintained as it was during his presidency (1901-09). Exhibits depicting his public and private life are located in the **Old Orchard Museum,** where a biographical film is also shown.

Raynham Hall. – *20 West Main Street. Open 1 to 5 PM; closed Mondays and January 1, Thanksgiving Day and December 25; $2.00.*

This old farmhouse played an important role during the American Revolution. It was the home of Samuel Townsend whose son, Robert, was Washington's chief intelligence agent in New York City. The interior is complete with period furniture and memorabilia.

South Shore

The shoreline fronts the Atlantic Ocean and also faces the Great South Bay.

Jones Beach State Park★★. – A series of sandy beaches, 6 1/2 miles long, make up this bathing resort, with its double exposure (ocean and bay).

Extremely well equipped, Jones Beach includes the well-known **Jones Beach Theater,** a nautical stadium, heated pools, sports fields and play areas. The Water Tower, inspired by the Campanile of St Mark's Church in Venice, rises above a freshwater well.

Old Bethpage Restoration Village★★. – *Round Swamp Road. Open March through October 10 AM to 5 PM, closed Mondays; the rest of the year 10 AM to 4 PM, closed Mondays (and Saturdays in January and February); $4.00, children $2.00.*

Nestled in a 200-acre valley, Old Bethpage is an active farm community which recreates the lifestyle of a pre-Civil War American village. More than 25 historic buildings reflecting the architectural heritage of Long Island, have been moved to the site of the former Powell Farm. Strolling leisurely through the village you will see the blacksmith hammering at his anvil, the cobbler making shoes, the tailor sewing and the farmers working their fields. Depending on the time of the year, sheep shearing, candlemaking and other seasonal activities may also be observed.

The Hamptons★★. – A chain of seafaring towns dominating a 35-mile stretch of Long Island's South Shore, which have now become vacation colonies; starting at Westhampton Beach rimming Shinnecock Bay and subsiding at Amagansett.

Westhampton Beach. – Formerly a seafaring community, Westhampton is a lively resort where many New Yorkers among them musicians, writers, artists, etc., like to spend their weekends or take up summer residence. The annual Westhampton Beach Outdoor Art Show takes place in early August.

A drive along Dune Road on the narrow barrier beach passes by everything from the New England type home, brown shingled and trimmed with white, to the bungalow; there is a 15-mile long beach from Moriches Inlet to Shinnecock Inlet. *Sections of Dune Road are extremely narrow and may be impassable following a rain storm.*

Southampton. – This famous shore resort is the largest of the Hampton communities and the home of many fine estates.

In the village on Jobs Lane is the **Parrish Art Museum:** *open June 15 to September 15 10 AM (1 PM Sundays) to 5 PM, closed Wednesdays; the rest of the year 10 AM (1 PM Sundays) to 5 PM, closed Tuesdays and Wednesdays.* A large group of works by the 19C American painter William Merritt Chase is among the museum's permanent collection. Changing exhibits are presented regularly.

East Hampton. – The **Main Street** of this charming little town is lined on both sides by magnificent elm trees. Its village green with a central pond flanked by fine old houses gives it the appearance of an English country town. East Hampton's quaint charm has attracted writers and artists.

Old Westbury Gardens★. – *Old Westbury Road. Open May through October 10 AM to 5 PM; closed Mondays and Tuesdays; gardens $4.50, house an additional $3.00.*

Old Westbury Gardens is the former estate of the late John S. Phipps, sportsman and financier. The stately Georgian mansion is set in an 18C park; its interior is preserved as it was during the family's occupancy with antique furnishings, paintings by Thomas Gainsborough and John Singer Sargent, and is adorned with gilded mirrors and objets d'art.

The estate (100 acres) containing woods, meadows, lakes and formal gardens presents a continually changing picture with the seasons.

Bayard Cutting Arboretum. – *Route 27A. Open 10 AM to 5 PM (4 PM November through March); closed Mondays, Tuesdays and January 1 and December 25. $3.00 per car.*

Started in 1887 by William Cutting in accordance with plans by Olmsted, the Arboretum covers 690 acres of woodlands and planted areas. Many of the specimens in the Pinetum date back to the original planting of fir, spruce, pine and other evergreens. Rhododendrons and azaleas *(blooming period: May-June)* border the walks and drives; wild flowers are also featured.

Fire Island. – The island is 32 miles long and 1/2 mile to less than 200yd wide and has 1 400 acres of **National Seashore**★. A relaxed informality prevails in parts of the island which has no roads for automobile traffic.

Ferry service from Patchogue, Sayville and Bay Shore connects with the Fire Island communities and the main developed areas of the National Seashore: Watch Hill and Sailors Haven.

Ferry to Watch Hill from Patchogue: Davis Park Ferry Co. (516) 475-1665. Ferry to Sunken Forest-Sailors Haven from Sayville: Fire Island Seashore Ferry, Inc. (516) 589-8980.

For information on National Seashore programs, etc. ☎ *(516) 289-4810.*

National Seashore programs at Watch Hill and Sailors Haven feature interpretive walks and special events. Facilities at both areas include guarded swimming beach, snack bar and marina.

Robert Moses State Park. – The western part of Fire Island is named for Robert Moses, the former superintendent of Long Island parks. Its dunes are a refuge for waterfowl. The Atlantic coast is excellent for surf casting.

Montauk. – A 10-mile strip of natural woodlands, stark cliffs, dunes and white beaches jutting into the ocean, Montauk is a favorite center for sports fishermen (deep-sea fishing). Built in 1795, the Montauk Lighthouse, rising at the tip of the peninsula, is located in Montauk State Park.

Sag Harbor. – This sea town with its deepwater harbor, nestled in a sheltered cove, docks and **Custom House** (the first custom house established in New York State – *guided tours July to Labor Day 10 AM to 5 PM, closed Mondays; Memorial Day through June and Labor Day to Columbus Day 1 to 5 PM Saturdays and Sundays only; $1.50)* was named Port of Entry for the United States by George Washington.

With its fine colonial homes, Sag Harbor still preserves the salty flavor and nostalgia of yesteryear *(mid-June: Sag Harbor Cup Races).*

Stop at the **Sag Harbor Whaling Museum** *(open mid-May through September 10 AM – 1 PM Sundays – to 5 PM; $2.00),* a Greek Revival edifice containing exhibits of the whaling days, set in the atmosphere of a whaling captain's home.

■ PRINCETON UNIVERSITY★★ *time: 1 day*

Situated in the western part of New Jersey, Princeton University is the center of a residential town which remains a desirable place to live despite the widespread development of office and research complexes in the area.

Access. – *110 miles round trip. A bus line connects Princeton to New York: information at the Port Authority Bus Terminal.*

If you drive, leave Manhattan by the Lincoln Tunnel. Take the New Jersey Turnpike south to exit 9; turn right and cross the Lawrence River; take Route 1 toward Penns Neck; turn right at sign Princeton-Hightstown.

Princeton can also be reached by train (New Jersey Transit) from Penn Station.

A BIT OF HISTORY

It was in 1746 that a small group of Presbyterian ministers decided to found a college for the middle eastern colonies, and named it the College of New Jersey.

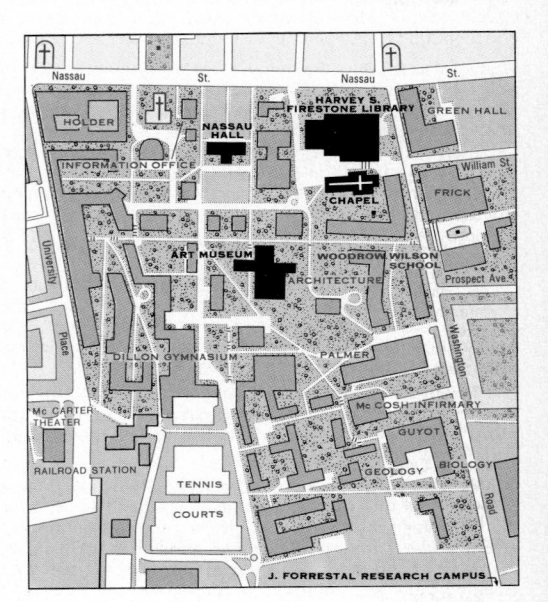

First established at Elizabeth, and then at Newark, it moved to the present site in 1756, after Nassau Hall was finished.

Nassau Hall was then the largest educational building in North America, and had room enough to house all of the college.

During the Revolution it served as barracks and hospitals, successively, for British and American troops. Its capture by Washington on January 3, 1777 marked the end of the Battle of Princeton and a victory for the colonists. The Continental Congress sat here for six months in 1783, and the final treaty of peace was signed here.

On its 150th anniversary, the College of New Jersey (already called Princeton College) became Princeton University.

Studies. – Princeton is one of the Ivy League colleges. Formerly all-male, it became coeducational in 1969. Women now make up over one-third of the undergraduate population.

Since the 18C, Princeton has been noted for its programs of scientific research and for its teaching of the arts of government; the first chair of chemistry in the United States was created here in 1795. Since Woodrow Wilson's presidency of the university, from 1902-10, Princeton has emphasized individual research and small seminars. An honor system prevails for examinations.

Princeton University has a full-time faculty of about 680 and about 6 000 students; 42 % of the undergraduates hold scholarships or receive special loans.

Visit. – *Free guide service is offered by the students year round; it is preferable to request a visit three days in advance. Information available at the Orange Key Guide Service, Maclean House ☎ (609) 258-3603.* The 222 buildings of the university are scattered over the 2 600 acre campus: we describe here only the most important ones.

Nassau Hall. – This majestic edifice is named for the Nassau dynasty of Orange which reigned in England at the time of the founding of the college. Around Nassau Hall stretches the shady green campus. Nassau Hall is now used as an administration building.

Harvey S. Firestone Library. – Containing approximately 4 000 000 volumes, it also provides 850 individual carrels for students and lecture rooms for 12 different disciplines.

Chapel. – A congregation of 2 000 can worship here. There is a 16C wooden pulpit from the north of France.

Art Museum. – *Open 10 AM to 4 PM; Sundays 1 to 5 PM (2 to 4 PM July and August); closed Mondays and major holidays.*

The museum is particularly strong in Medieval and Renaissance paintings and the Impressionists. The Prints and Drawings Gallery has a large collection of Italian drawings from the 16, 17 and 18C: works by Guerchin, Salvator Rosa and Tiepolo, among others. Selections of Ancient, Oriental and Classical art are presented on the lower level.

Woodrow Wilson School. – A noted school of public administration and international affairs.

James Forrestal Research Campus. – To the east of Princeton proper, beyond Lake Carnegie, this campus was opened in 1951 for research in applied mathematics, physics and chemistry. It houses the Plasma Physics Laboratory, the university's center for fusion research.

INDEX

(From photo Éd. Sun, Paris.)

Chinatown phone booth.

NOTES

1278